SECOND HISTORICAL SURVEY OF EDUCATIONAL DEVELOPMENT IN INDIA

Select Documents

1985-1990

CONCEPTS IN COMMUNICATION INFORMATICS & LIBRARIANSHIP (CICIL)

For list of books in this series, see pp 458-60 at the end of the book

Concepts in Communication
Informatics & Librarianship-15
General Editor: S.P. Agrawal

SECOND HISTORICAL SURVEY OF EDUCATIONAL DEVELOPMENT IN INDIA

SELECT DOCUMENTS 1985-1990

S.P. AGRAWAL
J.C. AGGARWAL

CONCEPT PUBLISHING COMPANY, NEW DELHI 110059

ISBN 81-7022-370-9

First Published 1991

S.P. **Agrawal** (*b*. 1929)
J.C. **Aggarwal** (*b*. 1928)

Published and Printed by
Ashok Kumar Mittal
Concept Publishing Company
A/15-16, Commercial Block, Mohan Garden
NEW DELHI 110059 (India)

Lasertypeset by
Microtech Advance Printing Systems (Pvt.) Ltd.
H-13, Bali Nagar
NEW DELHI 110015

GENERAL EDITOR'S INTRODUCTION

IN 1985 decision was taken by the Central Government to carve the Ministry of Human Resources Development with a massive budget of Rs. 16,000 crore.

An exercise to give a new orientation to education, as connoted by the new nomenclature, was then undertaken by the Ministry.

To give wide circulation to its line of thought and to benefit from critical appraisal and constructive suggestions, a number of meetings and seminars were organised throughout the country to look at the "Challenge".

It is, of course, futile to expect unanimity of opinion on the subject with all its ramifications, especially with the resource crunch we face and the 'Programme' and the 'National Policy' continue to be debated and occasionally attract flak.

It is not for authors to reason 'why' of the trends and directions, or the success or failures of various measures. That is a task best left to the analysts. What we have done is to facilitate their work and of those interested in education by bringing together basic documents and background information.

The publication in CICIL series covers the period 1985-1989 and is a sequel to earlier title *Development of Education in India: A Historical Survey of Educational Documents Before and After Independence.*

S.P. AGRAWAL

CONTENTS

PART II
Other Facets of Education

PART I

EDUCATIONAL PLANNING, POLICIES AND PROGRESS

1

EDUCATIONAL PLANNING : Seventh Five Year Plan (1985–90)[1]

Education, Culture and Sports

1. Human Resources development has necessarily to be assigned a key role in any development strategy, particularly in a country with a large population. Trained and educated on sound lines, a large population can itself become an asset in accelerating economic growth and in ensuring social change in desired directions. Education develops basic skills and abilities and fosters a value system conducive to, and in support of, national development goals, both long-term and immediate. In a world where knowledge is increasing at an exponential rate, the task of education in the diffusion of new knowledge and, at the same time, in the preservation and promotion of what is basic to India's culture and ethos, is both complex and challenging. It is, therefore, appropriate that the commencement of the Seventh Plan coincides with a comprehensive review of the education policy.
2. The resolution on the National Policy on Education adopted in 1968 pointed out that the great leaders of the Indian freedom movement realised the fundamental role of education and, throughout the nation's struggle for independence, stressed the unique significance of education for national development. The resolution further declared that the radical reconstruction of

---

1. Published by the Planning Commission, Government of India, New Delhi.

Note: Para numbers relate to the paras in Chapter 10 of the document.

education as envisaged involved (i) a transformation of the system to relate it more closely to the life of the people; (ii) a continuous effort to expand educational opportunity; (iii) a sustained and intensive effort to raise the quality of education at all stages; (iv) an emphasis on the development of science and technology; and (v) the cultivation of moral and social values. According to the resolution, the educational system must produce young men and women of character and ability, committed to national service and development.

3. There has been a great deal of accomplishment in the field of education since 1947. Any number which may be picked up as a parameter to define growth in education will show the magnitude of the massive quantitative expansion that has taken place. The number of recognised institutions has increased from 2,31,000 in 1951 to nearly 7,55,000 in 1984-85. The total enrolment over the same period in these institutions increased from 24 million to nearly 132 million. The national stock of educated manpower is estimated to have increased from less than 4 million to about 48 million the annual increment to the stock now being of the order of 35 million. It is significant to note that facilities have not only increased but also diversified at all levels and in different subjects. The enrolment for post-graduate studies, for instance has grown from a mere 20,000 in 1951 to over 3,00,000 by 1984-85 while that in science subjects is estimated to have increased from 4,400 to about 73,000. Extensive facilities are available for education in a variety of branches of engineering and technology. The output of this system has contributed significantly to our achievements in areas like atomic energy and satellite communication and provides the trained manpower for our economic development.
4. The expansion of educational facilities has also helped to some extent in the correction of regional and other imbalances and in achieving progress towards equality of educational opportunity and social justice. The annual non-Plan expenditure on education from the Central and State budgets has increased more than fifty times over the past 35 years, from Rs. 114 crores in 1950-51 to more than Rs. 6,000 crores in 1984-85.
5. Although the Indian education scene since independence has been characterised by massive quantitative expansion at all levels, it is still to undergo the kind of transformation envisaged in the

National Policy. It is faced with a staggering backlog; the level of illiteracy is as high as 63 per cent; to achieve universal elementary education, as enjoined by the Constitution. There will be need to enrol fifty million more children; vocationalisation of secondary education has yet to make headway; there is very significant pressure on the higher educational system and a decline in the standards of quality. There is an urgent need for a new design for education. The Approach to the Seventh Plan has emphasised that one of the primary tasks is the harnessing of the country's abundant human resources and improving their capability for development with equity. It is recognised that programmes for alleviation of poverty, reduction of social and economic inequalities and improving productivity can and should be integrated with educational development. Further, the strategies for educational programmes and training and their organisational designs should particularly focus on women, youth and economically weaker groups so that they can make increasing contribution to the socio-economic development of the country.

Sixth Plan Review

6. The Sixth Plan provided, *inter alia*, for mass education through programmes of elementary education (formal and non-formal streams) and adult education. The Plan also envisaged increased bias towards the practical secondary education, vocationalisation of higher secondary education and restructuring of undergraduate courses with a vocational bias. Forging beneficial linkages between education, employment and development was another objective in the field of higher education.
7. An enrolment target of 18 million additional children was set for the Sixth Plan period under the formal system of elementary education. According to the available reports, the additional enrolment is likely to be nearly 22 million. Although the target has thus been exceeded on an all-India basis, there have shortfalls in a few States, especially in regard to the enrolment of girls. Also, the enrolment ratio in 1984-85 was 92 per cent for primary and 53 per cent for middle stages of education. For girls it was only 69 per cent and 38 per cent respectively. Some of the notable measures taken for the promotion of elementary education were : 'earn while you learn' scheme, mid-day meals for children,

innovative curriculum renewal schemes, and special emphasis on appointment of women teachers. Funds available under the National Rural Employment Programme (NREP) and Rural Landless Employment Guarantee Programme (RLEGP) were also utilised for construction of school buildings.

8. Under the programme of non-formal education, although no specific targets were laid down, 8 million children were expected to be enrolled during the Sixth Plan. This was an experimental programme under which diverse models were to be worked out to suit the area-specific or beneficiary-group-specific requirements. It is estimated that over 3 million children would have been enrolled under this programme. Besides the non-formal education centres organised by the State Governments, innovative and experimental projects were taken up by a number of voluntary and academic institutions. Syllabus and instructional materials for use of learners enrolled in non-formal centres were developed following the integrated approach covering areas of health, hygiene, home science, agriculture, physics, chemistry, biology, history, geography and civics.
9. The position at the end of the Sixth Plan is that 80 per cent of the out-of-school children are in the nine States of Assam, Andhra Pradesh, Bihar, Jammu and Kashmir, Madhya Pradesh, Orissa, Rajasthan, Uttar Pradesh and West Bengal, but there is need in all States and Union Territories to improve the quality, relevance and effectiveness of the elementary education system, to improve enrolment and retention rates and to promote girls' education.
10. The Sixth Plan indicated the goal of reaching 100 per cent literacy in the age-group 15-35 years by 1990. While no definite physical target was laid down for the Sixth Plan, the adult education programme was to be developed on a large scale for the age-group 15-35 years to combat the problem of illiteracy among the productive segment of the population in general and, in particular, among the rural poor. The Central Government funded 386 rural functional literacy projects in the States besides giving assistance to 380 voluntary agencies and 49 universities for adult education programmes. In addition there were programmes of the State Governments. It is estimated that 20 million adult illiterates would have been covered by these programmes during the Sixth Plan. Fifteen States Resource Centres provided the resource support to adult education centres in terms of curriculum

formulation, preparation of teaching and learning material, development of methods and media, training of functionaries, monitoring and evaluation, and research and innovation. Development of learning materials for women and weaker sections was given special attention.

11. Enrolment in secondary and higher secondary levels has increased from about 10 million in 1979-80 to about 17 million in 1984-85. The 10 + 2 pattern of education has been adopted by 20 States and 9 Union Territories although it is yet to be fully implemented in some of these States. The National Council of Educational Research and Training, the State Councils of Educational Research and Training and the State Institutes of Education continued their efforts towards improvement in science and environmental education, value-orientation including national integration and curriculum reforms. Propagation of community singing in schools was launched as a national movement.
12. In the context of INSAT utilisation, State Institutes of Educational Technology (SIET) were set up in six States, namely, Andhra Pradesh, Bihar, Orissa, Gujarat, Maharashtra and Uttar Pradesh to produce educational television programmes. A Central Institute of Educational Technology (CIET) was set up for the production of programmes, training of personnel from the States as well as for providing guidance in the development of the programmes.
13. Vocationalisation of education at the higher secondary stage was one of the important reforms included in the Sixth Plan. This programme has made limited progress with an enrolment of about 55,000 students in vocational education, confined to nine States and three Union Territories where it has been introduced. Measures have been initiated to establish the necessary links combining vocationalisation, skill training, in-plant apprenticeship and placement in gainful employment as composite parts of an integrated effort to raise the level of utility of the programme, and its wider acceptance and success. The organisational requirements for the planning, implementation, supervision and evaluation of the integrated programme, along with the mechanism for effective coordination among the concerned agencies, are being assessed and defined.
14. Enrolment in higher education is estimated to have increased from 2.5 million in 1979-80 to 3.5 million in 1984-85. Efforts

were made for the consolidation of existing institutions and to equip universities and colleges with essential facilities within the limited resources available. Other important programmes taken up during the Sixth Plan included restructuring of under-graduate courses, improvement in standards of teaching of sciences and the humanities, strengthening of postgraduate education and promotion of research within the university system. A one-hour daily telecast on higher education was also initiated for the benefit of colleges. On the recommendation of the Science Advisory Committee to the Cabinet, a new scheme was introduced in 1983-84 for strengthening the infrastructure facilities for research and post-graduate education in science and technology within the university system.

15. During the Sixth Plan period, the major emphasis in technical education was on diversification and optimum utilisation of existing courses and institutional resources. Efforts were made to provide facilities in areas such as computer sciences, instrumentation, product development, maintenance engineering, bio-sciences and material sciences. Forty-six selected polytechnics were assisted and supported to develop them into a network of "community polytechnics" which would help transfer and apply available technology with the object of modernising rural structures. New manpower training programmes were undertaken for emerging areas in technology such as micro-processor application, remote sensing, laser technology, atmospheric sciences and energy sciences. Programmes of management education, particularly in the Institutes of Management, were reviewed by an Expert Committee and on its recommendation, the establishment of a new Institute at Lucknow was taken in hand.

16. The Resolution on National Sports Policy was laid before Parliament in 1984 to serve as a policy frame for the Central and State Governments and all organisations connected with sports. The policy gives a new thrust to sports activities towards achieving excellence in as many areas of sports and games as possible and at the same time making "sports for all" a reality. The Eastern Regional Centre, Calcutta, of Netaji National Institute of Sports, Patiala (NIS) started functioning from 1983 providing additional training courses for coaches. The national coaching scheme now has an authorised cadre strength of 800

coaches. Twenty five Regional sports coaching centres have been developed in State capitals and district headquarters. Besides its regular training programme, NIS implemented on behalf of the Central Government, programmes of National Sports Festival for Women, All India Rural Sports Tournament and Sports Talent Search Scholarship.

17. The Sports Authority of India was established in 1984 and undertook several sports activities in addition to maintaining and managing infrastructure and other facilities created for ASIAD 1982. Sports Councils with the assistance of Central and State Governments have jointly undertaken programmes for improving and developing facilities for the promotion of sports and games. Specifically, assistance was given for development of playfields, construction of stadia and swimming pools, construction of sports complexes, establishment and maintenance of rural sports centres, running annual coaching schemes and for purchase of sports equipment. The ceilings of financial assistance for these purposes were also enhanced. National Sports Federations were also assisted for organising coaching camps for preparing the Indian teams and competitors to participate in approved international competitions. Under the scheme of National Sports Organisation, financial assistance was provided for developing physical facilities for sports and games in colleges and universities, especially for developing playfields, and construction or gymnasia.

18. Youth programmes for student and non-student youth were continued and expanded during the Sixth Plan. A National Service Scheme originally launched in 1969-70 as a pilot scheme with 40,000 students, covered over six lakh students in the year 1984-85. The scheme enabled students to participate during their first degree studies in various programmes of social service and national development and provided them an opportunity to understand the conditions and problems of social environment. The activities undertaken by the students included environmental conservation, plantation of trees, cleaning of village ponds, construction of wells, health and family welfare programmes, family welfare education for rural women and sanitation drives in urban slums. They also undertook some production-oriented programmes. Nehru Yuvak Kendras set up to cater primarily to the needs of rural student and non-student youth, organised

several social service camps, slum clearance schemes and environmental awareness schemes as well programmes for training of youth leadership. In the year 1984-85, 120 youth leadership camps and 180 work camps were organised, involving 65,000 participants.

19. Programmes for preservation of monuments and sites of national importance were taken up on a priority basis. An expert group on archaeology carried out a professional study to prepare an overall plan of action. The number of archaeological circles which look after the preservation of monuments and sites of national importance was raised from 12 to 16. The number of excavation branches was also raised from three to five. Assistance was also provided to Indian National Trust for Art and Cultural Heritage (INTACH) for promoting the conservation and propagation of works of Indian art and culture. A large number of conservation programmes were taken up for repair and preservation of monuments and sites of national importance. The facilities at the National Museum, New Delhi, were further improved through taking up the first phase of its construction programme. The National Museum organised several aided tours and short-term in-service course. The Indian Museum, Calcutta, the Salar Jang Museum, Hyderabad, the National Gallery of Modern Art, New Delhi, the Nehru Memorial Museum and Library, the National Museum of Man and the National Archives were the other institutions whose programmes received support during the Sixth Plan. The National Council of Science Museums was also supported to undertake the task of popularising science and technology, among students in particular, through a wide range of programmes. The National Research Laboratory for Conservation of Cultural Property in Lucknow undertook a number of research programmes for technical studies with a view to improving conservation methods.

20. The Anthropological Survey of India was supported through funding of its several research projects on physical and cultural anthropology and allied disciplines. The Survey also undertook exploratory studies in the Himalayas, Narmada Valley and Costal Andhra Pradesh.

21. Library programmes were another area of importance during the Sixth Plan. The construction programme at National Library, Calcutta, was taken up. The Raja Ram Mohan Roy Library

Foundation which renders assistance to States and Union Territories for development of public libraries was further strengthened. Promotion and dissemination of culture was another major programme of the Department of Culture. The Sangeet Natak Akademi, the Sahitya Akademi and the Lalit Kala Akademi, besides the National School of Drama, undertook several programmes in this area. The Centre for Cultural Resources and Training, New Delhi, organised a number of in-service training programmes for the benefit of teachers drawn from primary and high or higher secondary schools in different parts of the country. Financial assistance was also provided to dance, drama and theatre ensembles and to selected cultural organisations.

Strategy and Thrust Areas in the Seventh Plan

22. The Seventh Plan provides for reorientation of the education system so as to prepare the country to meet the challenges of the next century. The main thrust areas in the Seventh Plan would be: (i) achievement of universal elementary education; (ii) eradication of illiteracy in the age-group 15-35 years; (iii) vocationalisation and skill-training programmes at different levels of education; (iv) upgradation of standards and modernisation at all stages of education with effective links with the world of work and with special emphasis on science and environment and on value orientation; (v) provision of facilities for education of high quality and excellence in every district of the country; and (vi) removal of obsolescence and modernisation of technical education.
23. The major strategies for achieving these objectives would include effective decentralised planning and organisational reforms, promotion of non-formal and open learning systems, adoption of low cost alternative and optimum use of resources, forging of beneficial linkages with industry and development agencies, and mobilisation of community resources and societal involvement.

Elementary Education

24. Overriding priority will be given to realising universalisation of elementary education for children in the age group 6-14 years by

1990; this will continue to be part of the Minimum Needs Programme. The emphasis will shift from mere enrolment to retention of pupils in schools and to the attainment by them of basic elements of learning. The objective is sought to be achieved through a combination of formal and non-formal methods, focusing sharply on the needs of girls and of children belonging to the economically and socially weaker sections.

25. The enrolment at the elementary stage is estimated to have reached nearly 112 million by the end of the Sixth Plan period. For achieving the goal of universalisation by the end of the Seventh Plan, over 50 million children will have to be additionally enrolled. A projection of enrolment in full-time elementary schools is given in Table 1.1. Increasing enrolment in full-time schools beyond this level of 137 million in classes I to VIII might not be feasible due to socio-economic reasons and other factors. Even to achieve this level effectively, sustained efforts will have to be made to reduce the number of drop-outs.

26. Non-formal education would be the other important programme for the achievement of universalisation of elementary education as this can be useful to those who are not able or willing to attend full-time schools. The number of children to be covered by the non-formal programme is reckoned to be of the order of 25 million. Non-formal education in the Seventh Plan will, therefore, have to be expanded at a fast pace and made acceptable with a variety of forms to suit the varying needs of the target groups. Non-formal system should be made flexible and appropriately linked to the formal system. Adequate textual material with area-specific background and supplementary reading material would be developed and made available to students. Adequate teacher-training arrangements will be made for teachers participating in the non-formal system. For optimum use of resources, the schools, the non-formal education centres and adult education centres should develop linkages and be educationally integrated with development programmes.

27. The enrolment projections in paras 24 and 25 above are indicative figures, worked out at the macro-level and disaggregated to the State level. Specific operational targets will require to be worked out by the State Governments concerned block-wise and village-wise through decentralised planning. Once such targets are worked out for the catchment area of each school or a cluster

of schools, it would be expected that the authorities responsible for the achievement of the target would adopt the most appropriate strategies of implementation and monitoring of progress.

TABLE 1.1: Expansion of Elementary Stage Education

(Enrolment figures in million)

Sl. No.	Classes/Age Group	Likely enrolment (1984-85)	Projected enrolment (1989-90)	Additional enrolment (1985-90)
1	2	3	4	5
I.	I-V (6-11)			
	Boys	51.20	55.00	3.80
		(117.48)	(110.00)	
	Girls	34.17	40.96	6.79
		(69.20)	(88.15)	
	TOTAL	*85.37*	*95.96*	*10.59*
		(91.84)	*(99.89)*	
II.	VI-VIII (11-14)			
	Boys	17.46	25.12	7.66
		(66.90)	(92.56)	
	Girls	9.27	16.55	7.28
		(38.19)	(65.44)	
	TOTAL	*26.73*	*41.67*	*14.94*
		(53.07)	*(79.46)*	
III.	I-VIII (6-14)			
	Boys	68.66	80.12	11.46
		(90.96)	(104.24)	
	Girls	43.44	57.51	14.07
		(64.02)	(80.28)	
	GRAND TOTAL	*112.10*	*137.63*	*25.53*
		(78.21)	*(92.60)*	

Note: Figures in parentheses indicate enrolment ratio relative to population in the corresponding age-group.

28. The role of the teacher is most crucial in achieving universal elementary education, especially in the motivation of children as well as their parents. They can play a leading role in improving the quality of primary education, bringing in environment and health education and value orientation. In-service training of

teachers thus becomes a programme of high priority. The training of teachers will include, apart from pedagogy, the use of mass media, science and technology, planning and curriculum design for local environment-based courses, mobilisation and use of community resources and other relevant subjects. There will also be special emphasis on teaching methods and other measures particularly required for first generation learners and for reducing the number of dropouts. Teacher training institutions will be developed and strengthened accordingly.

29. Facilities will have to be created for the training of additional teachers required during the Seventh Plan period. There is as yet no infrastructure in the country for training of teachers in non-formal and early childhood education. Training of such teachers would have to be organised by suitably strengthening the existing teacher training centres.

30. Considering the numbers involved (over 2.5 million teachers), institutionalised in-service education of teachers will be difficult to organise not only due to the huge costs involved but also due to lack of facilities for training. It is, therefore, necessary to think of a variety of training arrangements. Among others, these would include:

(a) In-service education by utilising the mass media, as was done during SITE;
(b) adoption of schools of lower levels of education by institutions of higher levels for upgrading of teacher competencies;
(c) dispatch of teacher guidance notes by training schools;
(d) publication of bulletins informing teachers of new developments; and
(e) use correspondence course materials supported by occasional contact.

31. Drop-outs and non-attendance of children at the primary stage of education are due to poor school facilities, unrelated curriculum, poor methods of teaching and poverty. The reorientation of teacher training referred to above will help to a large extent in tackling these factors. In addition, suitable supportive programmes for the provision of incentives, the improvement of facilities, increasing community awareness, curricular reforms,

adjusting of school timings, utilisation of local community resources and earn-while-you-learn scheme, etc., will be introduced or expanded selectively according to local requirements.

32. Enrolment of girls has been lagging behind despite special measures taken in the past. Towards the end of the Sixth Plan some steps were taken to promote enrolment of girls and for providing non-formal education to them wherever necessary. In the Seventh Plan, the focus of effort will be on promotion of girls' education through appointment of women teachers, attachment of pre-school centres, provision of free uniforms and other incentives.

33. Special emphasis will be given to the enhancement of quality and efficiency of elementary education. The Seventh Plan will seek to provide specific funds for those programmes which will enhance the efficiency of the system. There is need to have a fresh look at the design and construction of school buildings as well as at the text-books in use. Various projects like population education, environment and wild life education and curriculum renewal have helped in the preparation of suitable teaching-learning material and this material will be utilised.

34. Due to the difficult resource position and the magnitude of the task involved in the implementation of the programme of universalisation of elementary education, optimal use should be made of the available infrastructure and funds. The Plan and non-Plan budget provision for elementary education and the existing teacher resources should be reviewed and redeployed on the basis of actual requirements and attendance in classes. Part-time teachers or helper-teachers on fixed salary, selected from among locally available educated men and women will be utilised to augment teaching resources and also improve relevance and cost-effectiveness of elementary education. Community support and financial contributions will be mobilised especially for clearing the backlog of physical facilities and school buildings. The construction of school buildings will be taken up also under the National Rural Employment Programme (NREP) and similar programmes.

35. Early childhood education is important both from the point of view of the personality development of the child and for inculcating in the children a healthy attitude to school-going to

help increase their retention rate in schools. This programme will be dovetailed with nutrition, health care and social welfare as a package within the broad framework of the programme of Integrated Child Development Service (ICDS). Voluntary efforts to undertake innovative experiments in respect of early childhood education will be supported.

36. The National Policy Resolution on Education recommends the placement of disabled children in regular schools. The scheme of integrated education of disabled children was started by the Ministry of Social Welfare as a Centrally-sponsored scheme where handicapped children were sought to be integrated in the normal school system with a view to promoting their psychological acceptance. The scheme is now being implemented by the Ministry of Education. One of the difficulties facing this scheme is the lack of trained teachers in special education. As such, during the Seventh Plan, greater emphasis will be laid on teacher training.

Adult Education

37. Eradication of adult illiteracy and the development of a programme of continuing adult education is a major thrust area in the Seventh Plan. The task of covering all the illiterates in the age-group 15-35 years by 1990 is a formidable one. As motivation of the learner is crucial for success and as the number to be covered is about 90 million, the strategy to achieve the goal can only be through a mass movement involving social institutions, voluntary organisations, students, teachers, employers and the community. This programme will also have to be linked effectively with various development programmes especially the Integrated Rural Development Programme (IRDP). Active participation of village panchayats, mahila mandals, community centres, etc. is essential. Employers will be required to impart necessary functional education to all their illiterate employees. The programmes of Nehru Yuvak Kendras (NYK) and the National Service Scheme (NSS) will also focus on eradication of illiteracy. Programmes for motivating the learners by holding community meetings and through publicity through posters, films, broadcasting, etc., will be implemented on an adequate scale and with sufficient intensity to create a conducive

climate. A network of libraries and the development of literature for neo-literates will also be initiated as a follow-up programme to avoid lapse into illiteracy. Community participation in all literacy programmes will be an essential feature from village level upwards to give proper direction and orientation and lend effective support to this national programme.

38. Another aspect of education of adults relates to training in functional skills relevant to their respective economic activities. Programmes for this purpose will be strengthened and adequate resource support provided for organising technical and vocational skill-based courses for the benefit of adult learners through Shramik Vidyapeeths and other similar institutions. As a part of the post-literacy and follow-up services, short-duration condensed training courses will be organised for upgrading the skills of the neo-literates and for increasing their awareness of various social events. The existing programmes on rural functional literacy and State adult education programmes and various training programmes for adult learners will be consolidated and dovetailed in the new mass movement programmes of adult education. Citizenship education including adult education, will be a necessary part of the entire education system, and will be specially promoted.

Secondary Education

39. The demand for secondary education has been growing. The expansion and effectiveness of elementary education will provide a further impetus to this growth. The projected demand for additional facilities will, to some extent, be met by better utilisation of resources in the existing schools. Provision has been made for this purpose and for promoting distance learning techniques and open school systems. Unplanned growth of high/higher secondary schools will be checked. Norms for the establishments of secondary school will be evolved and strictly observed in order to avoid proliferation of economically non-viable and educationally inefficient institutions. In expanding the facilities, special attention will be given to the needs of backward area, of under-privileged sections of the population and of girls. Girls education will be free up to the higher secondary.

40. The teaching of science and mathematics at high/higher secondary stage of education will be strengthened and made universal. Efforts will be made to update and modernise science curricula, improve laboratories and libraries in schools and ensure the quality of science teachers through large-scale in-service training programmes. Environment education will form an important aspect of science education.
41. The socially useful productive work (work experience) programme component seeks to highlight the link between work and education and to develop positive work ethics and work habits. The programme would allow for better utilisation and integration of community expertise in the teaching-learning process and the use of facilities available with local industry and development institutions. Besides, the support system for development, training, management and supervision available for vocationalisation programmes, will also be utilised for the programme of socially useful productive work at the secondary stage. Some courses/activities of pre-vocational character will also be introduced for more effective implementation of this programme.
42. In view of the importance of linking education with productivity, a major impetus will be given in the Seventh Plan to vocationalisation of the higher secondary stage. Facilities for vocational education will be suitably diversified to cover a large number of fields in agriculture, industry, trade and commerce, and services. It will be ensured that there is no duplication of courses between technical and vocational institutions and the schools. The skills imparted, will be of adequate standard for securing gainful employment or self-employment. At the same time, opportunities for pursuing higher general and professional education would be provided.
43. Vocational/career courses in educational institutions will be introduced in a flexible manner linked to emerging work opportunities. The current intake will be considerably increased by introducing vocational courses in many more institutions.
44. Based on the evaluation of the on-going scheme of vocationalisation, States are taking steps to re-organise and improve the programme. An Expert Committee has been set up to suggest ways and means of implementing an expanded programme of vocationalisation fully coordinated with the

education system and manpower needs of economic development. The report of this Committee will provide guidelines for further development.

45. The present wide reach of the media will be used for improving education, especially at the secondary stage. Facilities for production of the requisite audio-visual material including educational software for broadcasting and telecasting will be augmented substantially in the Seventh Plan. During the Sixth Plan, a small beginning was made in providing computer literacy to students in selected secondary schools, based on this experience, steps will be taken to extend the programme to cover different aspects of computer appreciation and application.
46. One of the essential conditions for continuous improvement in the quality of secondary education is an effective system of in-service training of teachers. The existing facilities will be assessed, additional requirements identified and steps taken to meet them. The opportunity provided by the new communication technology will be explored for this purpose. Here again, special attention will be paid to the development of requisite software. Training of personnel required for effective use of modern communication technology and computers in education will be given very high priority. The NCERT which has already initiated programmes in this regard, will help the States build a network for this purpose.
47. Education has a crucial contribution to make towards promoting national integration, understanding and a sense of togetherness and harmony. There is, therefore, great need for an integrated and value-oriented education with a national perspective. This programme should be so designed that its various threads can be woven into the curricular and co-curricular activities. Suitable revision of text-books, strengthening of school libraries and training of teachers would be important from this point of view.

University Education

48. The main emphasis in higher education will be on consolidation, improvement in standards and reforms in the system to make higher education more relevant to national needs and to forge forward and backward linkages of higher education with employment and economic development. Expansion of general higher education facilities will be carefully planned so as to take

care of the need to provide larger access to weaker sections and first generation learners from backward areas. In doing so, emphasis will be laid on providing access to existing institutions through appropriate reservation, scholarships provision of hostel facilities. A network of facilities will be provided through open universities, correspondence courses and part-time education to meet social demand and the needs of continuing education.

49. The need and urgency for restructuring of undergraduate courses so as to bring in the necessary concern for relevance and use, application orientation, flexibility and diversification is well recognised. The guidelines for restructuring of courses of study indicated by the University Grants Commission (UGC) provide for addition of groups of courses that may be relevant and useful according to local or regional needs. Extension activities will be developed as components within each subject/discipline. Beneficial linkages will be developed between colleges and development institutions and programmes. Application oriented courses will be given due emphasis.

50. The Indira Gandhi National Open University, which is being established as a pace setting institution, will besides offering courses in higher education based on the principles of the open learning system, be also responsible for training of personnel, production of programmes and development of material for utilisation through the electronic media. The National Open University will function as a nodal resource centre for coordination of programmes and development of models for distance education, documentation and dissemination of information and organisation of appropriate support programmes. Besides this, six centres of educational technology being developed by UGC would serve as regional centres for the production of software for educational technology and training of personnel engaged in the programme of distance education and correspondence courses for higher education.

51. In the area of post-graduate education and research, emphasis will be placed on promoting quality programmes, inter-disciplinary studies and on new emerging frontiers. Research within the university system will get due emphasis and be coordinated with national research efforts under the Science and Technology programme. The programme of strengthening infrastructure facilities for research in science and technology and of

postgraduate education within the university system which was started on the recommendation of the Science Advisory Committee to the Cabinet, will be further developed.

52. Training of teachers in higher education is another area which needs special attention in the Seventh Plan. The faculty improvement programmes will be designed to impart knowledge of new methods and techniques of teaching, learning and evaluation, to develop a national value system, and to prepare the teachers for the task of restructuring undergraduate courses.
53. Many of the reforms initiated earlier, such as autonomous colleges and examination reform, seem to have faced obstacles and delays in the process of implementation. The Seventh Plan will give high priority to the speedy implementation of various reforms already initiated and to the modernisation of university administration.
54. Besides concerted efforts to increase the enrolment of Scheduled Castes/Scheduled Tribes students, the most significant programmes for these students will consist of remedial teaching, preparatory training and special coaching. These programmes will be implemented on a large scale by institutions with sizeable student population drawn from the Scheduled Castes and Scheduled Tribes and other weaker sections. These institutions will be strengthened to impart a better quality of education. The scope of these programmes will also be enlarged to include training for employment, coaching for competitive examinations for recruitment to various services and adult and continuing education programmes.

Technical Education

55. In the context of the rapid modernisation of the economy envisaged in the near future and given the Seventh Plan objective of improvement in productivity, technical education has to play a leading role. The main emphasis in the field of technical education during the Seventh Plan period will be on the following:

(i) Consolidation of infrastructure and facilities already created;

(ii) Optimum utilisation of the existing facilities with attention to cost effectiveness;

(iii) Identification of critical areas with a view to strengthening the facilities in the fields where weaknesses exist in the system at present;
(iv) Creation of infrastructure in new areas of emerging technology vital for the development of the country and provision of necessary facilities for education, training and research in those fields;
(v) Improvement of quality and standards of technical education;
(vi) Removal of obsolescence;
(vii) Modernisation of engineering laboratories and workshops in the technical education institutions;
(viii) Effective management of the overall system of technical education for an optimum return on investments made;
(ix) Innovative measures to improve existing facilities to provide low-cost alternatives to achieve various goals and objectives laid down in the Plan; and
(x) Institutional linkages between technical education on the one hand, and rural development and other development sectors, on the other.

56. To achieve these objectives there would be a balanced development of institutions of technical education at all levels. The Indian Institutes of Technology which have been set up as pace-setting institutions, would be further developed as advanced centres of excellence. The institutes have already initiated research work in a number of new areas. An expert committee has been set up to look into the requirements of these Institutes in the context of the challenges ahead. The regional and other engineering colleges would also be developed further, particularly with a view to their modernisation and to making their courses relevant to the emerging requirements. The upgradation of standards and modernisation of polytechnics will also be accorded a high priority. A major task in the Seventh Plan will be the removal of obsolescence in equipment and revision of courses in all technical education institutions, many of which were drawn up more than two decades ago. The All India Council for Technical Education has recommended that it is necessary also to restructure polytechnic education with a view to:

(a) improving the standard and contents of technical courses;

(b) providing a lateral entry to the vocational stream from 10 + 2 stage;
(c) restoring the balance in the employment pattern of engineering graduates and diploma holders; and
(d) providing multi-point entry to the various courses.

Besides the improvement on these lines, polytechnic education for women will be given greater attention to meet their special requirements. Further, as a result of reorganisation of school education in the 10 + 2 system and with vocationalisation becoming the major thrust in it, the polytechnics will play a significant role in the promotion and development of vocational education, particularly in engineering and allied trades. Besides modernisation polytechnics and removing obsolescence in courses and equipment, special attention will be paid to emerging technologies and computerisation. Development of interaction between the technical institutions and industry will be taken up. Removal of regional imbalances would be another major objective in the development of technical education at all levels. The faculty in the technical institutions have to keep themselves, abreast of the latest knowledge and advances taking place elsewhere in the world and also have to be in constant touch with industry. A number of schemes have already been instituted under the quality improvement programme including M. Tech., and Ph.D. courses, short-term and mid-term courses and industrial training for engineering college and polytechnic teachers. However, these arrangements need considerable strengthening. Special attention will be paid to the problems of staff training and retraining and to continuing education for staff, including those of the polytechnics, to facilitate academic and professional advancement.

57. A reliable manpower information system is a prerequisite to planning in the field of technical education. A national manpower information system is being developed for storage, updating, retrieval and analysis of manpower information to assist in technical education planning. It has at present 17 nodal centres and is coordinated by the Technical Education Division of the Department of Education with the assistance of the lead centre located at the Institute of Applied Manpower Research. The manpower information system will be considerably strengthened

and integrated with the planning of technical education.

58. Besides general improvements, polytechnics will be assisted to undertake extension services for the benefit of the community. The programme of community polytechnics, already initiated in the earlier Plans, will be expanded in the Seventh Plan to cover as many polytechnics as possible.

59. Curriculum changes need to be introduced periodically in the light of emerging trends in technology. This will require more effective collaborative linkages with industry and research and development establishments and agencies. The allocations provided from budgetary funds for technical education have to be supplemented by contributions from user industries and organisations, which will be facilitated when closer collaborative arrangements are established.

S and T Component

60. Considerable emphasis will be laid on the improvement of the quality of teaching science and technology at all levels of education. At school level NCERT at the centre and SCERTs/SIEs in States will provide training to teachers on all aspects of science and technology including design, development and production of science kits and strengthen science laboratories of secondary schools. A National Science Centre will be established for displaying experimental models and projects.

61. The quality of higher science and technology education has to match the best in the world. In this connection, university departments and colleges will be selected for providing special assistance to bring about improvements in science education.

62. Modernisation of laboratories in Indian Institutes of Technology, Regional Engineering Colleges and other institutions of technical education will be accorded priority for providing research in technology. An International Centre for Science and Technology Education will be established. This will operate through a net work of existing institutions and serve as a resource centre for cooperative research, and will also disseminate ideas, methods and materials to bring about basic improvement and modernisation is Science and Technology education. The total estimated outlay for S & T component in the education sector will be of the order of Rs. 180 crores, including Rs. 35 crores for the

programmes recommended by the Science Advisory Committee to the Cabinet.

Examination Reforms

63. The present examination-oriented system has distorted the very character of education and has converted it into a mere system of certification to regulate the flow of manpower to the labour market. The dominance of the examination system over the educational process has led not only to the wrong type of learning, but has also led to many attendant malpractices. Examination reforms to remedy the present malaise would be given the utmost priority. At the same time, the employing sector should be helped to devise its own selection procedures, lay down academic qualifications, prepare assessment tests and evaluation systems in keeping with job content and the ability and skill for performance of the tasks attached to a job.

Other Programmes

64. The Seventh Plan provides for the continuation and limited expansion of on-going programmes relating to scholarships, development of languages, book promotion, educational planning and administration as well to effective monitoring, particularly of elementary (including non-formal) and adult education.
65. The existing schemes of scholarships will be reviewed and, if necessary, re-oriented to help talented students to develop their full potential. The Central Government schemes of national scholarships including that for talented children from rural areas will continue in the Seventh Plan. Financial assistance by itself is not adequate for the development of talented children, especially from the poorer sections of society and from backward areas. Their access to, and placement in, good academic institutions is equality necessary. Placements in residential schools will be particularly helpful and a scheme for this purpose is already in operation.
66. To provide good quality modern education with Indian values to talented children, particularly from the rural areas, it is proposed to set up 432 model secondary schools, one in each district, during the Seventh Five Year Plan. These schools will offer a

common core curriculum, ensuring comparability in standards and promoting National Integration and National Values. They will bring together students from different parts of the country, providing opportunities to talented children to fully develop their potential. Admission to these schools will be through a test conducted at tahsil/block level, in which the best performers from every primary school in the district will be eligible to appear. The test would be designed by the NCERT, and it will be associated in conducting and evaluating the test. Residential facilities will be provided in these schools. An autonomous organisation, registered under the Registration of Societies Act, will be set up for establishing and running these schools.

Development of Languages

67. The development of languages is of basic importance for all educational development programmes. The activities and programmes undertaken in the field of languages comprise : (i) promotion of Hindi (as envisaged under Article 351 of the Constitution); (ii) promotion of modern Indian languages (as provided in National Policy of Education); (iii) promotion of English and other foreign languages; and (iv) promotion of Sanskrit and other classical languages such as Arabic and Persian. Other languages for which the Centre has special responsibility, like Urdu and Sindhi, have also received attention. These activities will be further developed in the Seventh Plan, with special attention being paid for raising the standards of language competency, spoken as well as written.
68. The capabilities of existing institutions will be strengthened, particularly, with a view to enabling them to undertake a much larger programme of in-service training, publication of textual and other materials. Production of software for transmission through radio and television and to work at the grass-roots level. A selective approach will be adopted in respect of publications, so as to ensure that materials of good quality become available and are widely disseminated. Instead of entrusting publication of dictionaries, terminologies, text-books etc., exclusively to governmental agencies, it is proposed to involve creative scholars, university departments and literary organisations with publication activities. Voluntary organisations working for the

development and promotion of various languages will be supported, particularly, for undertaking innovative and experimental projects the experience from which will assist in more effective teaching and learning of languages, whether by formal or informal methods.

69. In Sanskrit, emphasis will be given to activities which will ensure preservation of Shastric and Vedic traditions in oral and written forms, preservation, editing and cataloguing of rare manuscripts, publications of rare and out-of-print books, and training of teachers. It is proposed to assist selected institutions for audio and video taping of recitations of various *sakhas* which for want of continuing training of scholars in the oral tradition, are becoming extinct. Support will be provided for inter-disciplinary research, particularly with a view of identifying the scientific and technical advancement that had taken place in the past and has been recorded in various Sanskrit texts.

70. The programmes being undertaken for the development of modern Indian languages, including Urdu and Sindhi and also classical languages like Arabic and Persian will be continued and additional support provided to increase their coverage.

Art and Culture

71. In Art and Culture the main thrust in the Seventh Five Year Plan would be on the development of culture in all aspects, with emphasis on dissemination, and on the promotion and development of regional cultures and building up of a sense of the oneness and underlying unity and cohesiveness of India. This would require the involvement of the masses in cultural activities. In order to achieve these objectives, the programmes of the Seventh Plan would include:

(i) Zonal Cultural Centres being set up in different regions of the country. The essential thrust of the creative development efforts of these zonal centres would be to bring about awareness and participation at the grass-root level, cutting across-territorial/linguistic boundaries.

(ii) The existing activities of various cultural organisations for dissemination of culture would be stepped up on a wide scale with adequate financial inputs.

(iii) Introduction of a cultural component into the educational system at different levels. The Departments of Education and Cultural Affairs would work together in close coordination for inter-linking education and culture through appropriate programmes.

(iv) Cultural inputs would be integrated in youth activities, rural development activities, domestic tourism etc.

(v) For the dissemination of culture to the masses, the mass media would be utilised.

(vi) Besides the national cultural organisations, the State agencies would also strengthen their programmes. The Central and State Agencies would work with greater coordination towards this objective.

72. It is proposed to set up seven zonal cultural centres which while developing the unique cultural identities of various areas in the States would also stress and explore their cultural kinship in relation to the totality of India's composite culture, highlighting the essential unity in diversity of the Indian cultural heritage. The Centres would provide facilities for creative development of arts; with special emphasis on folk arts as also the revival of vanishing arts.

73. The traditional fairs and festivals which provide the continuing link with the rich traditions of the past would be supported through the State agencies and Zonal Cultural Centres. Appropriate programmes would be taken up to provide exposure to youth to the cultural diversity of the country to raise their awareness of the rich heritage that exists in the country.

74. Preservation, documentation and conservation of our rich and varied cultural heritage would continue to receive priority in the Seventh Plan. This would mean greater attention to the development of archaeology museums, archives, manuscript libraries, Buddhist Tibetan studies, and to folk-lore and oral traditions. It is recognised that strands of cultural heritage run through a wide range of development sectors and programmes. These need to be identified and demonstrated as diverse aspects of our rich traditions. Art forms and cultural institutions provide a powerful medium to foster national integration as well as national development. Necessary co-ordination links will be established and co-operative programmes will be undertaken for this purpose.

75. Greater emphasis will be laid on strengthening of arts through institutions, such as the Akademies. Assistance would continue to be provided to voluntary organisations engaged in the promotion of art and culture. Library systems would be strengthened throughout the country with special attention to improving the facilities in the National level institutions.
76. Some of the rich art forms existing are in the realm of tribal and folk art. The development of folk and tribal arts, especially those which are facing extinction such as the folk art of the Himalayan regions, threatened ecologically as also culturally, would be supported through assistance to voluntary organisations engaged in these fields and areas.
77. In the field of anthropology, new projects have been identified to study the people of India and promote dissemination of culture. The Rashtriya Manav Sangrahalaya which is expected to be completed in the Seventh Plan, would recreate the history of human evolution, the evolution of culture and the range of living cultures in India.
78. The Indira Gandhi National Centre for Art will be set up at New Delhi as a resource centre and data base for the arts. It will also develop a major informatics library of cultural materials. The National Theatre will also be established on the same premises to support and project activities particularly in the field of visual arts, including folk and tribal arts.

Youth and Sports

79. According to the 1981 Census, 220 million or about 30 per cent of our population is in the age-group of 15-34 years, with 73% living in the rural areas. The majority of them do not have the benefit of formal education. The problems of youth, therefore have to be identified, with existing programmes being strengthened and new programmes devised to involve their participation and development. The two existing programmes of National Service Scheme (NSS) and Nehru Yuvak Kendras (NYKs) have proved useful in promoting the involvement of youth, both student and non-student, and urban and rural, and in creating awareness among them of nationally accepted objectives and motivating them to work towards their fulfilment. Both these programmes will be further developed and expanded in the

Seventh Plan. The strength of the NSS will be raised from six hundred and ten thousand at the end of the Sixth Plan to one million at the end of the Seventh Plan. Activities of Nehru Yuvak Kendras will be expanded to cover all the districts in the country and will also be diversified. The organisational structure of the Yuvak Kendras will also be revamped to impart greater flexibility in the development of programmes for youth, their speedier execution and closer monitoring. The aim will be to make the Kendras effective by ensuring coordinating links between youth and the various agencies of Government and public sector in the national development effort. Programmes of scouting and guiding, mountaineering and adventure, Commonwealth youth programmes and International Youth Exchange Delegations, and National Service Volunteer Schemes will be continued.

80. A major step will be taken during the Seventh Plan to translate into action the newly adopted Resolution on National Sports Policy, by giving high priority to the development of infrastructure and facilities for sports and games at grass-root levels and developing the potential of our human resources both in the rural and urban areas. Efforts will be made to raise national standards in games and sports. Programmes for spotting and nurturing potential sports talent through coaching, training and nutrition required for helping the talented to realise their highest level would be continued. Present schemes like Rural Sports Tournaments, Women's Sports Festivals, National Talent Search Scholarships, grants to National Federations and State Sports Councils etc., will be expanded. The activities of the Netaji Subhash National Institute of Sports, Patiala will be intensified and its coverage enlarged. The Sports Authority of India will be assisted to pursue its main objective of promotion and broad-basing of sports in the country and creation of health consciousness among citizens through appropriate and meaningful schemes.

Outlays

81. The Seventh Plan outlay for education is of the order of Rs. 6383 crores of which the States sector outlay is Rs. 3994 crores.

82. The provision for education is mainly in the States' sector. The Centre will play a coordinating role and provide leadership and

guidance for new and innovative programmes. Out of the total non-plan budget estimates of education in 1983-84, amounting to Rs. 5229 crores, nearly 91 per cent was in the States' Sector. Nearly 87 per cent of the total national expenditure on education is incurred on non-plan side. In view of the constraints on resources for education, the structure and pattern of utilisation of Plan and non-Plan funds needs to be reviewed, to ensure the optimal use of funds in relation to the goals of the Seventh Plan. It is proposed to adopt low cost designs and devices for effecting economy and for reducing unit costs. Besides, non-budgetary resources have to be tapped and substantial resources mobilised from the community especially for replenishing and augmenting physical facilities in educational institutions.

83. It is also necessary to emphasise the non-monetary inputs in educational development, i.e., better planning, advanced technologies and practices, careful block level and institutional planning, and school mapping; better systems of supervision and administration; monitoring and evaluation; a good information system; dedicated efforts by teachers, students and educational administrators; intensive utilisation of existing resources and facilities; and , above all, commitment and active involvement of the local community. Educational research and training, and planning and administration of education needs to be streamlined. The State level capabilities particularly require to be built up under the leadership of the National Council of Educational Research and Training and National Institute of Educational Planning and Administration.

2

EDUCATIONAL POLICIES AND REFORMS

2.1 CHALLENGE OF EDUCATION (1985)[1]

Introduction

Immediately after the announcement of the Prime Minister on January 5, 1985, the Ministry of Education prepared a 'Status Report' entitled Challenge of Education – A Policy Perspective and presented it to the Prime Minister. Thare was a nation-wide debate on this report and it became the background paper for the formulation of the National Policy on Education.

Appraisal of the Existing System of Education

The document "Challenge of Education" provided a critical appraisal of the educational system in the following areas :

1. Elementary Education
2. Adult Education and Functional Literacy
3. Secondary Education
4. Vocationalisation of Education
5. Higher Education
6. Technical Education
7. Management Education
8. Teachers and Teacher Education
9. General Appraisal of Educational Issues.

---

1. Published by the Ministry of Human Resource Development, Government of India, New Delhi, 1985.

Appraisal of Elementary Education

1. By and large methods of teaching are quite out-moded.
2. New methods of teaching are being ignored in many States.
3. Most of the schools do not have even the relatively inexpensive teaching hits developed by NCERT.
4. The programme of Work Experience or Socially useful Work productive Work on which Gandhiji's Basic system of Education paid stress has not been implemented in most of the schools.
5. Overall enrolment position is unsatisfactory.
6. What is more disturbing is the alarming rate of drop-outs.
7. The total expenditure per student per year by the Centre and States has declined in real terms.
8. There is total dependence on Government in running the schools.
9. There is hardly any effort on the part of a village or the Community leadership or at the level of block or district, to set up or even to help the proper running of schools.
10. No systematic study of the effectiveness of Non-Formal education is available.

Appraisal of Adult Education and Functional Literacy

Following deficiencies have been pointed out:

1(i) One direct result of the failure on front of Universalisation of Elementary Education has been the large number of illiterate in the country.

(ii) Want of sufficient motivation prevents illiterates from continuous participation in adult education programmes.

(iii) There is no support to the programme from developmental agencies and the involvement of grassroot voluntary agencies and educational institutions has remained marginal.

(iv) Literacy has not been used and propagated as an instrument of development because the positive nexus between poverty and illiteracy has not been recognised.

(v) The potential of the educated population, especially college and university students has not been exploited in eradication of illiteracy.

(vi) The talk of assigning a greater role to NSS and making a minimal performance for removal of illiteracy, a pre-condition of or the award of first degree has not received serious consideration.

Appraisal of Secondary Education

Following limitations have been observed:

(a) Only 22 per cent of the students in the age-group corresponding to classes IX and X are in school and this ratio is nowhere near that of developed countries.
(b) A discriminatory situation is being created for the scientific and technological professions in favour of the urban and more affluent sections of society.
(c) The variability in the standard of education available in different schools is a cause of concern.
(d) Some States have not introduced the 10+2+3 pattern.
(e) The wastage involved in the present pass percentage of 30 to 40 is high.
(f) Pupil-teacher ratio is very high.
(g) Out-dated methods of teaching are adopted.
(h) There are poor laboratory facilities.
(i) Curriculum is uninspiring.
(j) Management system discourages innovation.
(k) Many Boards of Secondary Education are perpetually the subject of acrimonious controversy for leakage of papers, mass-copying, tampering with results and other unethical practices.
(l) The quality and orientation of teaching in the 'general stream' is so unsatisfactory even in the best schools that almost all entrants to the Medical or Engineering streams have to arrange for extra-coaching.

Appraisal of Vocationalisation

Following observations have been made:

(i) Attempts have not borne fruits and enrolment in this stream has remained marginal and confined to a few States.
(ii) Courses have been started with little imagination.
(iii) The work-experience component of secondary education has remained weak.
(iv) There has been a poor linkage between the vocational courses and

industry or opportunities for self-employment.

(v) vocationalisation within the secondary school system has been a casualty at the hands of educational planners.

Appraisal of Higher Education

Following aspects deserve attention:

1. Developments in this field have been extremely uneven.
2. Rural areas have been touched only marginally.
3. Facilities in the colleges are far below the level of qualitative ability.
4. Neither the colleges nor even the universities have been started after due consideration of academic need.
5. Universities and colleges are becoming notorious for rampant casteism, regionalism and inbreeding.
6. Universities and colleges, barring a few honourable exceptions have become virtual battle-fields in which political staff, often fight pitched battles for power and supremacy.
7. Some Vice-Chancellors spend their entire term of office behind barricades, operating as well as they can, from their houses.
8. The achievement of a university is judged not on the basis of the quality of its research or the competence of its students but by its adherence to the schedules of examinations and the prevention of forced closures.
9. The number of effective working days in a year is far below desired levels.
10. There is a colossal wastage of resources on account of large number of dropouts and failures.
11. Teaching often degenerates into dictation of unrevised notes prepared years ago.
12. Examination system has lost its credibility.
13. There is very little quality research work.
14. No institutional arrangements to evaluate, renew, pretest and monitor curricular for the universities and colleges exist.
15. Adequate arrangements in the laboratories in the form of kits, apparatus and instruments to relate theory with practical utility do not exist.
16. Facilities for corporate life, cultural activities and sports are either non-existent or remain grossly under-utilised for want of

rapport and informal contact between teachers and students.

17. Teaching and studying in colleges and universities is no more than a part-time occupation aimed essentially at the award of degrees, which have generally lost credibility and value.
18. There is a wide-spread feeling that the present state of higher education is largely the result of the overt and covert interference by external agencies.
19. As with other sectors, resources available for higher education have been extremely inadequate.

Appraisal of Technical Education

Following limitation have been noted:

1. There is the issue of obsolescence of machinery and equipment.
2. There is the problem of non-availability of the where withal to deal with the training and research requirements in respect of new technologies.
3. The industrial sector is coming under increasing pressure of international competition.
4. The orientation and quality of polytechnic education remains a major concern.
5. The inability of the institutions of technical education to attract good teachers has remained a major problem.
6. The work-ethos in many technical institutions leaves much to be desired.
7. The interaction between industry and technical institutions, which is so crucial for ensuring relevant quality and cost effectiveness, remains weak, despite exhortations for closer cooperation.
8. Industrial investment in research undertaken by technical institutions continues to be negligible.
9. There is hardly any exchange of personnel or involvement in common projects.
10. There is a wide-spread feeling that the products of IITs are geared more to the requirements of international technology market rather than to India's own needs for development.
11. In a fashion, therefore, the culture and the very excellence of IITs is a contributive factor to the phenomenon of brain-drain.
12. The linkage of technical education with manpower planning has remained weak.

Appraisal of Management Education

(a) In the rush to meet the heavy pressure on demand many institutions have come up without adequate human and financial resources.
(b) Linkage between the institutes of management, university departments of business administration and public sector and private institutions are practically non-existent.

Appraisal of Teachers and Teacher Education

1. The process of up-dating the curricula of teacher education has been very slow.
2. Much of teacher education is irrelevant.
3. The selection procedures and recruitment systems for teachers have not kept pace with the needs in terms of either number or of quality.
4. Teaching has become the last choice in the job market.
5. Adequate attention has not been made to develop communication skills which are crucial to the functioning of teachers.
6. The training programme does not make use of audio-visual equipment.
7. Teachers in the Training Colleges are not exposed to the ideas of national integration, cultural cohesion and development of humanitarian values.
8. Many teachers do not get any opportunity to keep themselves abreast with technical aids for more effective teaching.
9. There is a good deal of politicization in teacher's organisations.

General Appraisal of Various Educational Issues

Following conclusions have been drawn:

1. Even though the rural areas account for three-fourths of the population they are getting much less by way of resources for education than the urban areas.
2. The quality and maintenance of school and college buildings in urban areas is very much better than in rural areas.
3. The dropout rates among urban children is lower than in the rural areas.
4. Privately managed "quality" institutions are generally located in urban areas.

5. Despite considerable acceleration in recent years girls education is still far behind the boys.
6. Fewer girls seek admission to professional courses, other than pertaining to medicine, teacher training and nursing.
7. The spread of education among the girls students of scheduled castes and scheduled tribes has not been as much as among the male members of the group.
8. For about 90 per cent of the labour force educational activities have not been organised keeping in view their role and responsibilities.
9. Three major expert bodies at the national level namely National Council of Educational Research and Training (NCERT), the National Institute of Education Planning and Administration (NIEPA) and the University Grants Commission (UGC) have not met with the expected response.
10. It appears that things have gone away due to progressive centralisation and bureaucratisation and non-enforcement of discipline standards and performance norms.
11. Very meagre funds have been provided for the development of education.
12. The share of elementary education in fund allocation has gone down considerably. From 56 per cent in the First Plan it has gone down to 36 per cent in the Sixth Plan whereas the share of University education went up from 9 to 16 per cent.
13. In the total expenditure on education, private donations and endowments accounted for nearly 29 per cent at the beginning of this century but declined to the level of 3 per cent in 1980-81.
14. Education has till now been essentially the responsibility of the States. This means the availability of educational facilities has been dependent not upon the commitment of the nation as a whole, but upon the vicissitudes of the resources allocated by States.

2.2 NATIONAL POLICY ON EDUCATION (1986)[2]

Introduction

Rajiv Gandhi, the then Prime Minister of India in his address to the

2. *Note*: *see* also Appendices I and II.

nation on January 5, 1985 declared that he has asked a new education policy to be drafted". He said, "Education must promote national cohesion and the work ethic. The grandeur of our freedom struggle and its significance for national integration have to be brought home to every student. Our schools and colleges should acquaint the young generations with ancient heritage and culture, the curricula and textbooks should curb parochial and communal interpretations of our composite culture.

We are formulating programmes to use on a large scale the new communication technology in our school system. Delinking the degrees from jobs under government is under active consideration. Steps are being taken to open an Open University to bring higher education within easy reach of all. The Central Schools Organization will be expanded. These schools will function as centres of excellence in every district of our country."

Further in his address to the Conference of Education Ministers of States and Union Territories, held on August 29-30, 1985, the Prime Minister put forward his views on education in greater detail under the title "Revamping the Education System". The views of the Prime Minister served as important guidelines for the framers of the National Policy on Education (1986).

Immediately after the Prime Minister broadcast of January 5, 1985, the Ministry of Education now known as the Ministry of Human Resource Development (MHRD) started work on the formulation of the new policy on education.

Challenge of Education

A status report entitled 'Challenge of Education – A Policy Perspective', was presented to the Prime Minister on 20th August, 1985, by K.C. Pant, the then Education Minister. The document was presented to Parliament the same day. This document contained an overview of the state of education in the country and gave pointers to the direction of future initiatives. It also pointed out the inadequacies of the present system of education to provide a background for realistic policy-making so that the limitations and constraints were appreciated while defining the tasks and formulating the measures for their implementation.

The document 'The Challenge of Education' and the inaugural speech of the Prime Minister under the title 'Revamping the

Educational System' formed the basis of discussion at the Conference of State Education Ministers, held on August 29-30, 1985. The document was translated into practically all the regional languages. 5,80,000 copies of this document in English, 2,40,000 in Hindi and 4,000 in Urdu were distributed by the Ministry, inviting suggestions and comments from all sections of the people. As a part of the nation-wide debate on the new education policy, 12 national seminars and 17 sponsored seminars were organised by the Ministry of Education and its national organisations. All State Governments and Union Territories also organised numerous seminars, workshops and symposia. A detailed analysis was made of all the communications and recommendations received in the Ministry. Thereafter in April 1986, the Ministry of Human Resource Development brought out a revised document, 'National Policy on Education, 1986 – A Presentation'. This paper was discussed at the meetings of the State Minister of Education, the National Development Council and the Central Advisory Board of Education. It was revised in the light of these discussions and the 'Draft National Policy on Education, 1986'[3] given below, was finally laid on the table of Parliament in the first week of May 1986. The draft was debated and adopted by the Lok Sabha on May 8, 1986 and the Rajya Sabha on May 12, 1986. Thus the 'National Policy on Education' emerged as a national commitment.

Draft National Policy on Education, 1986[3]

PART I

Introductory

1.1 Education has continued to evolve, diversify and extend its reach and coverage since the dawn of human history. Every country develops its system of education to express and promote its unique socio-cultural identity and also to meet the challenges of the times. There are moments in history when a new direction has to be given to an age-old process. That moment is today.

1.2 The country has reached a stage in its economic and technical development when a major effort must be made to derive the

3. Published by the Ministry of Human Resource Development, Government of India, New Delhi, 1988.

maximum benefit from the assets already created and to ensure that the fruits of change reach all sections. Education is the highway to that goal.

1.3 With this aim in view, the Government of India announced in January 1985 that a new Education Policy would be formulated for the country. A comprehensive appraisal of the existing educational scene was made, followed by a countrywide debate. The views and suggestions received from different quarters were carefully studied.

The 1968 Education Policy and After

1.4 The National Policy of 1968 marked a significant step in the history of education in post-Independence India. It aimed to promote national progress, a sense of common citizenship and culture, and to strengthen national integration. It laid stress on the need for a radical reconstruction of the education system, to improve its quality at all stages, and gave much greater attention to science and technology, the cultivation of moral values and a closer relation between education and the life of the people.

1.5 Since the adoption of the 1968 Policy, there has been considerable expansion in educational facilities all over the country at all levels. More than 90 per cent of the country's rural habitations now have schooling facilities within a radius of one kilometre. There has been sizeable augmentation of facilities at other stages also.

1.6 Perhaps the most notable development has been the acceptance of a common structure of education throughout the country and the introduction of the 10+2+3 system by most States. In the school curricula, in addition to laying down a common scheme of studies for boys and girls, science and mathematics were incorporated as compulsory subjects and work experience assigned a place of importance.

1.7 A beginning was also made in restructuring of courses at the undergraduate level. Centres of Advanced Studies were set up for post-graduate education and research. And we have been able to meet our requirements of educated manpower.

1.8 While these achievements are impressive by themselves, the general formulations incorporated in the 1968 Policy did not, however, get translated into a detailed strategy of implementation, accompanied by the assignment of specific responsibilities and financial and organisational support. As a result, problems of access, quality, quantity, utility and financial outlay, accumulated over the years, have now assumed such massive proportions that they must be tackled with the utmost urgency.

1.9 Education in India stands at the cross-roads today. Neither normal linear expansion nor the existing pace and nature of improvement can meet the needs of the situation.

1.10 In the Indian way of thinking, a human being is a positive asset and a precious national resource which needs to be cherished, nurtured and developed with tenderness and care, coupled with dynamism. Each individual's growth presents a different range of problems and requirements, at every stage - from the womb to the tomb. The catalytic action of Education in this complex and dynamic growth process needs to be planned meticulously and executed with great sensitivity.

1.11 India's political and social life is passing through a phase which poses the danger of erosion to long-accepted values. The goals of secularism, socialism, democracy and professional ethics are coming under increasing strain.

1.12 The rural areas, with poor infrastructure and social services, will not get the benefit of trained and educated youth, unless rural-urban disparities are reduced and determined measures are taken to promote diversification and dispersal of employment opportunities.

1.13 The growth of our population needs to be brought down significantly over the coming decades. The largest single factor that could help achieve this is the spread of literacy and education among women.

1.14 Life in the coming decades is likely to bring new tensions together with unprecedented opportunities. To enable the people to benefit in the new environment will require new designs of human resource development. The coming generations should have the ability to internalise new ideas constantly and creatively. They have to be imbued with a strong commitment to humane values and to social justice. All this implies better education.

1.15 Besides, a variety of new challenges and social needs make it imperative for the Government to formulate and implement a new Education Policy for the country. Nothing short of this will meet the situation.

PART II

The Essence and Role of Education

2.1 In our national perception education is essentially for all. This is fundamental to our all-round development, material and spiritual.

2.2 Education has an acculturating role. It refines sensitivities and perceptions that contribute to national cohesion, a scientific temper and independence of mind and spirit–thus furthering the goals of socialism, secularism and democracy enshrined in our Constitution.

2.3 Education develops manpower for different levels of the economy. It is also the substrate on which research and development flourish, being the ultimate guarantee of national self-reliance.

2.4 In sum, Education is a unique investment in the present and the future. This cardinal principle is the key to the National Policy on Education.

PART III

National System of Education

3.1 The Constitution embodies the principles on which the National System of Education is conceived of.

3.2 The concept of a National System of Education implies that, up to a given level, all students, irrespective of caste, creed, location or sex, have access to education of a comparable quality. To achieve this, the Government will initiate appropriately funded programmes. Effective measures will be taken in the direction of the Common School System recommended in the 1968 Policy.

3.3 The National System of Education envisages a common educational structure. The 10+2+3 structure has now been accepted in all parts of the country. Regarding the further break-up of the first 10 years efforts will be made to move towards an elementary system comprising 5 years of primary education and 3 years of upper primary, followed by 2 years of High School.

3.4 The National System of Education will be based on a national curricular framework which contains a common core along with other components that are flexible. The common core will include the history of India's freedom movement, the constitutional obligations and other content essential to nurture national identity. These elements will cut across subject areas and will be designed to promote values such as India's common cultural heritage, egalitarianism, democracy and secularism, equality of the sexes, protection of the environment, removal of social barriers, observance of the small family norm and inculcation of the scientific temper. All educational programmes will be carried on in strict conformity with secular values.

3.5 India has always worked for peace and understanding between nations, treating the whole world as one family. True to this hoary tradition, Education has to strengthen this world view and motivate the younger generations for international cooperation and peaceful co-existence. This aspect cannot be neglected.

3.6 To promote equality, it will be necessary to provide for equal opportunity to all not only in access, but also in the conditions for success. Besides, awareness of the inherent equality of all will be created through the core curriculum. The purpose is to remove prejudices and complexes transmitted through the social environment and the accident of birth.

3.7 Minimum levels of learning will be laid down for each stage of education. Steps will also be taken to foster among students an understanding of the diverse cultural and social systems of the people living in different parts of the country. Besides the promotion of the link language, programmes will also be launched to increase substantially the translation of books from one language to another and to publish multi-lingual dictionaries and glossaries. The young will be encouraged to undertake the rediscovery of India, each in his own image and perception.

3.8 In higher education in general, and technical education in particular, steps will be taken to facilitate inter-regional mobility by providing equal access to every Indian of requisite merit, regardless of his origins. The universal character of universities and other institutions of higher education is to be underscored.

3.9 In the areas of research and development, and education in science and technology, special measures will be taken to establish network arrangements between different institutions in the country to pool their resources and participate in projects of national importance.

3.10 The Nation as a whole will assume the responsibility of providing resource support for implementing programmes of educational transformation, reducing disparities, universalisation of elementary education, adult literacy, scientific and technological research, etc.

3.11 Life-long education is a cherished goal of the educational process. This presupposes universal literacy. Opportunities will be provided to the youth, housewives, agricultural and industrial workers and professionals to continue the education of their choice, at the pace suited to them. The future thrust will be in the direction of open and distance learning.

3.12 The institutions which will be strengthened to play an important role in giving shape to the National System of Education are the University Grants Commission, the All India Council of Technical Education, the Indian Council of Agricultural Research and the Indian Medical Council. Integrated planning will be instituted among all these bodies so as to establish functional linkages and reinforce programmes of research and postgraduate education. These, together with the National Council of Educational Research and Training, the National Institute of Educational Planning and Administration and the International Institute of Science and Technology Education will be involved in implementing the Education Policy.

A Meaningful Partnership

3.13 The Constitutional Amendment of 1976, which includes Education in the Concurrent List, was a far-reaching step whose implications – substantive, financial and administrative – require a new sharing of responsibility between the Union Government and the States in respect of this vital area of national life. While the role and responsibility of the States in regard to education will remain essentially unchanged, the Union Government would accept a larger responsibility to reinforce the national and integrative character of education, to maintain quality and standards (including those of the teaching profession at all levels), to study and monitor the educational requirements of the country as a whole in regard to manpower for development, to cater to the needs of research and advanced study, to look after the international aspects of education, culture and Human Resource Development and, in general, to promote excellence at all levels of the educational pyramid throughout the country. Concurrency signifies a partnership which is at once meaningful and challenging; the National Policy will be oriented towards giving effect to it in letter and spirit.

PART IV

EDUCATION FOR EQUALITY

Disparities

4.1. The new policy will lay special emphasis on the removal of disparities and to equalise educational opportunity by attending to the specific needs of those who have been denied equality so far.

Education for Women's Equality

4.2 Education will be used as an agent of basic change in the status of woman. In order to neutralise the accumulated distortions of the past, there will be well-conceived edge in favour of women. The National Education System will play a positive, interventionist role in the empowerment of women. It will foster the development of new values through redesigned curricula, textbooks, the training and orientation of teachers, decision-makers and administrators, and the active involvement of educational institutions. This will be an act of faith and social engineering. Women's studies will be promoted as a part of various courses and educational institutions encouraged to take up active programmes to further women's development.

4.3 The removal of women's illiteracy and obstacles inhibiting their access to, and retention in, elementary education will receive overriding priority, through provision of special support services, setting of time targets, and effective monitoring. Major emphasis will be laid on women's participation in vocational, technical and professional education at different levels. The policy of non-discrimination will be pursued vigorously to eliminate sex stereo-typing in vocational and professional courses and to promote women's participation in non-traditional occupations, as well as in existing and emergent technologies.

The Education of Scheduled Castes

4.4 The central focus in the SCs' education development is their equalisation with the non-SC population at all stages and levels of education, in all areas and in all the four dimensions – rural male, rural female, urban male and urban female.

4.5 The measures contemplated for this purpose include:

(i) Incentives to indigent families to send their children to school regularly till they reach the age of 14;
(ii) Pre-matric Scholarship scheme for children of families engaged in occupations such as scavenging, flaying and tanning to be made applicable from Class I onwards. All children of such families, regardless of incomes, will be covered by this scheme and time-bound programmes targetted on them will be undertaken;
(iii) Constant micro-planning and verification to ensure that the enrolment, retention and successful completion of courses by SC students do not fall at any stage, and provision of remedial courses to improve their prospects for further education and employment.
(iv) Recruitment of teachers from Scheduled Castes;
(v) Provision of facilities for SC students in students' hostels at district headquarters, according to a phased programme;
(vi) Location of school buildings, Balwadis and Adult Education Centres in such a way as to facilitate full participation of the Scheduled Castes;
(vii) The utilization of N.R.E.P. and R.L.E.G.P. resources so as to make substantial educational facilities available to the Scheduled Castes; and
(viii) Constant innovation in finding new methods to increase the participation of the Scheduled Castes in the educational process.

The Education of Scheduled Tribes

4.6 The following measures will be taken urgently to bring the Scheduled Tribes on par with others :–

(i) Priority will be accorded to opening primary schools in tribal areas. The construction of school buildings will be undertaken in these areas on a priority basis under the normal funds for education, as well as under the N.R.E.P., R.L.E.G.P, Tribal Welfare Schemes, etc.
(ii) The socio-cultural milieu of the STs has its distinctive characteristics including, in many cases, their own spoken

languages. This underlines the need to develop the curricula and devise instructional materials in tribal languages at the initial stages, with arrangements for switching over to the regional language.

(iii) Educated and promising Scheduled Tribe youths will be encouraged and trained to take up teaching in tribal areas.

(iv) Residential schools, including Ashram Schools, will be established on a large scale.

(v) Incentive schemes will be formulated for the Scheduled Tribes, keeping in view their special needs and life styles. Scholarships for higher education will emphasise technical, professional and para-professional courses. Special remedial courses and other programmes to remove psycho-social impediments will be provided to improve their performance in various courses.

(vi) Anganwadis, Non-formal and Adult Education Centres will be opened on a priority basis in areas predominantly inhabited by the Scheduled Tribes.

(vii) The curriculum at all stages of education will be designed to create an awareness of the rich cultural identity of the tribal people as also of their enormous creative talent.

Other Educationally Backward Sections and Areas

4.7 Suitable incentives will be provided to all educationally backward sections of society, particularly in the rural areas. Hill and desert districts, remote and inaccessible areas and islands will be provided adequate institutional infrastructure.

Minorities

4.8 Some minority groups are educationally deprived or backward. Greater attention will be paid to the education of these groups in the interests of equality and social justice. This will naturally include the Constitutional guarantees given to them to establish and administer their own educational institutions, and protection to their languages and culture. Simultaneously, objectivity will be reflected in the preparation of textbooks and in all school activities, and all possible measures will be taken to promote an integration based on appreciation of common national goals and ideals, in conformity with the core curriculum.

The Handicapped

4.9 The objective should be to integrate the physically and mentally handicapped with the general community as equal partners, to prepare them for normal growth and to enable them to face life with courage and confidence. The following measures will be taken in this regard :–

(i) Wherever it is feasible, the education of children with motor handicaps and other mild handicaps will be common with that of others.

(ii) Special schools with hostels will be provided, as far as possible at district headquarters, for the severely handicapped children.

(iii) Adequate arrangements will be made to give vocational training to the disabled.

(iv) Teachers' training programmes will be reoriented, in particular for teachers of primary classes, to deal with the special difficulties of the handicapped children; and

(v) Voluntary effort for the education of the disabled, will be encouraged in every possible manner.

Adult Education

4.10 Our ancient scriptures define education as that which liberates i.e. provides the instruments for liberation from ignorance and oppression. In the modern world, it would naturally include the ability to read and write, since that is the main instrument of learning. Hence the crucial importance of adult education, including adult literacy.

4.11 The critical development issue today is the continuous upgradation of skills so as to produce manpower resources of the kind and the number required by the society. Since participation by beneficiaries in the developmental programmes is of crucial importance, systematic programmes of adult education linked with national goals such a alleviation of poverty, national integration, environmental conservation, energisation of the cultural creativity of the people, observance of small family norm, promotion of women's equality, etc. will be organised and the existing programmes reviewed and strengthened.

4.12 The whole nation must pledge itself to the eradication of illiteracy, particularly in the 15-35 age group. The Central and State Governments, political parties and their mass organisations, the mass media and educational institutions must commit themselves to mass literacy programmes of diverse nature. It will also have to involve on a large scale teachers, students, youth, voluntary agencies, employers, etc. Concerted efforts will be made to harness various research agencies to improve the pedagogical aspects of adult literacy. The mass literacy programme would include, in addition to literacy, functional knowledge and skills, and also awareness among learners about the socio-economic reality and the possibility to change it.

4.13 A vast programme of adult and continuing education will be implemented through various ways and channels, including–

(a) establishment of centres in rural areas for continuing education;
(b) workers' education through the employers, trade unions and concerned agencies of government;
(c) post-secondary education institutions;
(d) wider promotion of books, libraries and reading rooms;
(e) use of radio, TV and films, as mass and group learning media;
(f) creation of learners' groups and organisation;
(g) programmes of distance learning;
(h) organizing assistance in self-learning; and
(i) organising need and interest based vocational training programmes.

PART V

REORGANISATION OF EDUCATION AT DIFFERENT STAGES

Early Childhood Care and Education

5.1 The national policy on Children specially emphasises investment in the development of the young child, particularly children from sections of the population in which first generation learners predominate.

5.2 Recognising the holistic nature of child development, viz., nutrition, health and social, mental, physical, moral and emotional development, Early Childhood Care and Education (ECCE) will receive high priority and be suitably integrated with the integrated Child Development Services programme, wherever possible. Day-care centres will be provided as a support service for universalisation of primary education, to enable girls engaged in taking care of siblings to attend school and as a support service for working women belonging to poorer sections.

5.3 Programmes of ECCE will be child-oriented, focused around play and the individuality of the child. Formal methods and introduction of the 3 R's will be discouraged at this stage. The local community will be fully involved in these programmes.

5.4 A full integration of child care and pre-primary education will be brought about, both as a feeder and a strengthening factor for primary education and for human resource development in general. In continuation of this stage, the School Health Programme will be strengthened.

Elementary Education

5.5 The new thrust in elementary education will emphasise two aspects : (i) universal enrolment and universal retention of children up to 14 years of age, and (ii) a substantial improvement in the quality of education.

Child-Centred Approach

5.6 A warm, welcoming and encouraging approach, in which all concerned share a solicitude for the needs of the child, is the best motivation for the child to attend school and learn. A child-centred and activity-based process of learning should be adopted at the primary stage. First generation learners should be allowed to set their own pace and be given supplementary remedial instruction. As the child grows, the component of cognitive learning will be increased and skills organised through practice. The policy of non-detention at the primary stage will be retained, making evaluation as disaggregated as feasible. Corporal punishment will be firmly excluded from the educational system and school timings as well as vacations adjusted to the convenience of children.

School Facilities

5.7 Provision will be made of essential facilities in primary schools, including at least two reasonably large rooms that are usable in all weather, and the necessary toys, blackboards, maps, charts, and other learning material. At least two teachers, one of whom a woman, should work in every school, the number increasing as early as possible to one teacher per class. A phased drive, symbolically called OPERATION BLACKBOARD will be undertaken with immediate effect to improve Primary Schools all over the country. Government, local bodies, voluntary agencies and individuals will be fully involved. Construction of school buildings will be the first charge on NREP and RLEGP funds.

Non-Formal Education

5.8 A large and systematic programme of non-formal education will be launched for school drop-outs, for children from habitations without schools, working children and girls who cannot attend whole-day schools.

5.9 Modern technological aids will be used to improve the learning environment of NFE centres. Talented and dedicated young men and women from the local community will be chosen to serve as instructors, and particular attention paid to their training. Steps will be taken to facilitate their entry into the formal system in deserving cases. All necessary measures will be taken to ensure that the quality of non-formal education is comparable with formal education.

5.10. Effective steps will be taken to provide a framework for the curriculum on the lines of the national core curriculum, but based on the needs of the learners and related to the local environment. Learning material of high quality will be developed and provided free of charge to all pupils. NFE programmes will provide participatory learning environment, and activities such as games and sports, cultural programmes, excursions, etc.

5.11 Much of the work of running NFE centres will be done through voluntary agencies and panchayati raj institutions. The provision of funds to these agencies will be adequate and timely. The Government will take over-all responsibility for this vital sector.

A Resolve

5.12 The New Education Policy will give the highest priority to solving the problem of children dropping out of school and will adopt an array of meticulously formulated strategies based on micro-planning, and applied at the grass-roots level all over the country, to ensure children's retention at school. This effort will be fully coordinated with the network of non-formal education. It shall be ensured that all children who attain the age of about 11 years by 1990 will have had five years of schooling, or its equivalent through the non-formal stream. Likewise, by 1995 all children will be provided free and compulsory education upto 14 years of age.

Secondary Education

5.13 Secondary education begins to expose students to the differentiated roles of science, the humanities and social sciences. This is also an appropriate stage to provide children with a sense of history and national perspective and give them opportunities to understand their constitutional duties and rights as citizens. Conscious internalisation of a healthy work ethos and of the values of a humane and composite culture will be brought about through appropriately formulated curricula. Vocationalisation through specialised institutions or through the refashioning of secondary education can, at this stage, provide valuable manpower for economic growth. Access to secondary education will be widened to cover areas unserved by it at present. In other areas, the main emphasis will be on consolidation.

Pace-Setting Schools

5.14 It is universally accepted that children with special talent or aptitude should be provided opportunities to proceed at a faster pace, by making good quality education available to them, irrespective of their capacity to pay for it.

5.15 Pace-setting schools intended to serve this purpose will be established in various parts of the country on a given pattern, but with full scope for innovation and experimentation. Their broad aims will be to serve the objective of excellence, coupled with equity and social justice (with reservation for SCs and STs), to promote national integration by providing opportunities to talented children largely rural, from different parts of the country to live and learn together, to develop their full potential, and, most importantly, to become catalysts of a nation-wide programme of school improvement. The schools will be residential and free of charge.

Vocationalisation

5.16 The introduction of systematic, well-planned and rigorously implemented programmes of vocational education is crucial in the proposed educational reorganisation. These elements are meant to enhance individual employability, to reduce the mis-match between the demand and supply of skilled manpower, and to provide an alternative for those pursuing higher education without particular interest or purpose.

5.17 Vocational education will be a distinct stream, intended to prepare students for identified occupations spanning several areas of activity. These courses will ordinarily be provided after the secondary stage, but keeping the scheme flexible, they may also be made available after Class VIII. In the interests of integrating vocational education better with their facilities the Industrial Training Institutes will also conform to the larger vocational pattern.

5.18 Health planning and health service management should optimally interlock with the education and training of appropriate categories of health manpower through health-related vocational courses. Health education at the primary and middle levels will ensure the commitment of the individual to family and community health, and lead to health-related vocational courses at the +2 stage of higher secondary education. Efforts will be made to devise similar vocational courses based on Agriculture, Marketing, Social Services, etc. An emphasis in vocational education will also be on development of attitudes, knowledge, and skills for entrepreneurship and self-employment.

5.19 The establishment of vocational courses or institutions will be the responsibility of the Government as well as employers in the public and private sectors; the Government will, however, take special steps to cater to the needs of women, rural and tribal students and the deprived sections of society. Appropriate programmes will also be started for the handicapped.

5.20 Graduates of vocational courses will be given opportunities, under predetermined conditions, for professional growth, career improvement and lateral entry into courses of general, technical and professional education through appropriate bridge courses.

5.21. Non-formal, flexible and need-based vocational programmes will also be made available to neoliterates, youth who have completed primary education, school drop-outs, persons engaged in work and unemployed or partially employed persons. Special attention in this regard will be given to women.

5.22 Tertiary level courses will be organised for the young who graduate from the higher secondary courses of the academic stream and may also require vocational courses.

5.23 It is proposed that vocational courses cover 10 per cent of higher secondary students by 1990 and 25 per cent by 1995. Steps will be taken to see that a substantial majority of the products of vocational courses are employed or become self-employed. Review of the courses offered would be regularly undertaken. Government will also review its recruitment policy to encourage diversification at the secondary level.

Higher Education

5.24 Higher education provides people with an opportunity to reflect on the critical social, economic, cultural, moral and spiritual issues facing humanity. It contributes to national development through dissemination of specialised knowledge and skills. It is therefore a crucial factor for survival. Being at the apex of the educational pyramid, it has also a key role in producing teachers for the education system.

5.25 In the context of the unprecedented explosion of knowledge, higher education has to become dynamic as never before, constantly entering uncharted areas.

5.26 There are around 150 universities and about 5,000 colleges in India today. In view of the need to effect an all round improvement in these institutions, it is proposed that, in the near future, the main emphasis will be on the consolidation of, and expansion of facilities in, the existing institutions.

5.27 Urgent steps will be taken to protect the system from degradation.

5.28 In view of mixed experiences with the system of affiliation, autonomous colleges will be helped to develop in large numbers until the affiliating system is replaced by a freer and more creative association of universities with colleges. Similarly, the creation of autonomous departments within universities on a selective basis will be encouraged. Autonomy and freedom will be accompanied by accountability.

5.29 Courses and programmes will be redesigned to meet the demands of specialisation better. Special emphasis will be laid on linguistic competence. There will be increasing flexibility in the combination of courses.

5.30 State level planning and coordination of higher education will be done through Councils of Higher Education. The UGC and these Councils will develop coordinative methods to keep a watch on standards.

5.31 Provision will be made for minimum facilities and admission will be regulated according to capacity. A major effort will be directed towards the transformation of teaching methods. Audio-visual aids and electronic equipment will be introduced; development of science and technology curricula and material, research, and teacher orientation will receive attention. This will require preparation of teachers at the beginning of the service as well as continuing education thereafter. Teachers' performance will be systematically assessed. All posts will be filled on the basis of merit.

5.32 Research in the universities will be provided enhanced support and steps will be taken to ensure its high quality. Suitable mechanisms will be set up by the UGC for coordinating research in the universities, particularly in thrust areas of science and technology, with research undertaken by other agencies. An effort will be made to encourage the setting up of national research facilities within the university system, with proper forms of autonomous management.

5.33 Research in Indology, the humanities and social sciences will receive adequate support. To fulfil the need for the synthesis of knowledge, inter-disciplinary research will be encouraged. Efforts will be made to delve into India's ancient fund of knowledge and to relate it to contemporary reality. This effort will imply the development of facilities for the intensive study of Sanskrit and other Classical languages.

5.34 In the interest of greater coordination and consistency in policy, sharing of facilities and developing inter-disciplinary research, a national body covering higher education in general, agricultural, medical, technical, legal and other professional fields will be set up.

Open University and Distance Learning

5.35 The Open University system has been initiated in order to augment opportunities for higher education and as an instrument of democratising education.

5.36 The Indira Gandhi National Open University, established in 1985 in fulfilment of these objectives, will be strengthened.

5.37 This powerful instrument will have to be developed with care and extended with caution.

Delinking Degrees from Jobs

5.38 A beginning will be made in de-linking degrees from jobs in selected areas.

5.39 The proposal cannot be applied to occupation-specific courses like Engineering, Medicine, Law, Teaching, etc. Similarly, the services of specialists with academic qualifications in the humanities, social sciences, sciences, etc. will continue to be required in various job positions.

5.40 De-linking will be applied in services for which a university degree need not be a necessary qualification. Its implementation will lead to a re-fashioning of job-specific courses and afford greater justice to those candidates who, despite being equipped for a given job, are unable to get it because of an unnecessary preference for graduate candidates.

5.41 Concomitant with de-linking, an appropriate machinery, such as a National Testing Service, will be established, in appropriate phases, to conduct tests on a voluntary basis to determine the suitability of candidates for specified jobs and to pave the way for the emergence of norms of comparable competence across the nation.

Rural University

5.42 The new pattern of the Rural University will be consolidated and developed on the lines of Mahatma Gandhi's revolutionary ideas on education so as to take up the challenges of micro-planning at grassroot levels for the transformation of rural areas. Institutions and programmes of Gandhian basic education will be supported.

PART VI

Technical and Management Education

6.1 Although the two streams of technical and management

education are functioning separately, it is essential to look at them together, in view of their close relationship and complementary concerns. The reorganisation of Technical and Management Education should take into account the anticipated scenario by the turn of the century, with specific reference to the likely changes in the economy, social environment, production and management processes, the rapid expansion of knowledge and the great advances in science and technology.

6.2 The infrastructure and services sectors as well as the unorganised rural sector also need a greater induction of improved technologies and a supply of technical and managerial manpower. This will be attended to by the Government.

6.3 In order to improve the situation regarding manpower information, the recently set up Technical Manpower Information System will be further developed and strengthened.

6.4 Continuing education, covering established as well as emerging technologies, will be promoted.

6.5 As computers have become important and ubiquitous tools, a minimal exposure to computers and a training in their use will form part of professional education. Programmes of computer literacy will be organised on wide scale from the school stage.

6.6 In view of the present rigid entry requirements to formal courses restricting the access of a large segment of people to technical and managerial education, programmes through a distance-learning process, including use of the mass media, will be offered. Technical and management education programmes, including education in polytechnics, will also be on a flexible modular pattern based on credits, with provision for multi-point entry. A strong guidance and counselling service will be provided.

6.7 In order to increase the relevance of management education, particularly in the non-corporate and under-managed sectors, the management education system will study and document the Indian experience and create a body of knowledge and specific educational programmes suited to these sectors.

6.8 Appropriate formal and non-formal programmes of technical education will be devised for the benefit of women, the economically and socially weaker sections, and the physically handicapped.

6.9 The emphasis on vocational education and its expansion will need a large number of teachers and professionals in vocational education, educational technology, curriculum development, etc.

Programmes will be started to meet this demand.

6.10 To encourage students to consider "self-employment" as a career option, training in entrepreneurship will be provided through modular or optional courses, in degree or diploma programmes.

6.11 In order to meet the continuing needs of updating curriculum, renewal should systematically phase out obsolescence and introduce new technologies or disciplines.

Institutional Thrusts

6.12 Some polytechnics in the rural areas have started training weaker groups in those areas for productive occupations through a system of community polytechnics. The community polytechnic system will be appraised and appropriately strengthened to increase its quality and coverage.

Innovation, Research and Development

6.13 Research as a means of renovation and renewal of educational processes will be undertaken by all higher technical institutions. It will primarily aim at producing quality manpower capable of taking up R&D functions. Research for development will focus on improving present technologies, developing new indigenous ones and enhancing production and productivity. A suitable system for watching and forecasting technology will be set up.

6.14 The scope for cooperation, collaboration and networking relationships between institutions at various levels and with the user systems will be utilised. Proper maintenance, and an attitude of innovation and improvement will be promoted systematically.

Promoting Efficiency and Effectiveness at All Levels

6.15 As technical and management education is expensive, the following major steps will be taken for cost-effectiveness and to promote excellence:

(i) High priority will be given to modernisation and removal of obsolescence. However, modernisation will be undertaken to enhance functional efficiency and not for its own sake or as a status symbol;

(ii) Institutions will be encouraged to generate resources using their capacities to provide services to the community and industry. They will be equipped with up to date learning resources, library and computer facilities;

(iii) Adequate hostel accommodation will be provided, specially for girls. Facilities for sports, creative work and cultural activities will be expanded;

(iv) More effective procedures will be adopted in the recruitment of staff. Career opportunities, service conditions, consultancy norms and other perquisites will be improved;

(v) Teachers will have multiple roles to perform: teaching, research, development of learning resource material, extension, and managing the institution. Initial and in-service training will be made mandatory for faculty members and adequate training reserves will be provided. Staff Development Programmes will be integrated at the State, and coordinated at Regional and National levels;

(vi) The curricula of technical and management programmes will be targeted on current as well as the projected needs of industry or user systems. Active interaction between technical or management institutions and industry will be promoted in programme planning and implementation, exchange of personnel, training facilities and resources, research and consultancy and other areas of mutual interest;

(vii) Excellence in performance of institutions and individuals will be recognised and rewarded. The emergence of substandard and institutions will be checked. A climate conducive to excellence and innovation will be promoted with full involvement of the faculty;

(viii) Select institutions will be awarded academic, administrative and financial autonomy of varying degrees, building in safeguards with respect to accountability;

(ix) Networking systems will have to be established between technical education and industry, R&D organisations, programmes of rural and community development, and with other sectors of education with complementary characteristics.

Management Functions and Change

6.16 In view of the likely emergence of changes in management systems and the need to equip students with the ability to cope with them, effective mechanisms will be devised to understand the nature and direction of change *per se* and to develop the important skill of managing change.

6.17 In view of the integrated nature of the task, the Ministry of Human Resource Development will coordinate the balanced development of engineering, vocational and management education as well as the education of technicians and craftsmen.

6.18 Professional societies will be encouraged and enabled to perform their due role in the advancement of technical and management education.

6.19 The All India Council for Technical Education will be vested with statutory authority for planning, formulation and the maintenance of norms and standards, accreditation, funding of priority areas, monitoring and evaluation, maintaining parity of certification and awards and ensuring the coordinated and integrated development of technical and management education. Mandatory periodic evaluation will be carried out by a duly constituted Accreditation Board.

6.20 In the interests of maintaining standards and for several other valid reasons, the commercialisation of technical and professional education will be curbed. An alternative system will be devised to involve private and voluntary effort in this sector of education, in conformity with accepted norms and goals.

PART VII

Making the System Work

7.1 It is obvious that these and many other new tasks of education cannot be performed in a state of disorder. Education needs to be managed in an atmosphere of utmost intellectual rigour, seriousness of purpose and, at the same time, of freedom essential for innovation and creativity. While far-reaching changes will have to be incorporated in the quality and range of education, the process of introducing discipline into the system will have to be started, here and now, in what exists.

7.2 The country has placed boundless trust in the educational system. The people have a right to expect concrete results. The first task is to make it work. All teachers should teach and all students study.

7.3 The strategy in this behalf will consist of –

(a) a better deal to teachers with greater accountability;
(b) provision of improved students' services and insistence on observance of acceptable norms of behaviour;
(c) provision of better facilities to institutions; and
(d) creation of a system of performance appraisals of institutions according to standards and norms set at the National or State levels.

PART VIII

REORIENTING THE CONTENT AND PROCESS OF EDUCATION

The Cultural Perspective

8.1 The existing schism between the formal system of education and the country's rich and varied cultural traditions needs to be bridged. The preoccupation with modern technologies cannot be allowed to sever our new generations from the roots in India's history and culture. De-culturisation, de-humanisation and alienation must be avoided at all costs. Education can and must bring about the fine synthesis between change-oriented technologies and the country's continuity of cultural tradition.

8.2 The curricula and processes of education will be enriched by cultural content in as many manifestations as possible. Children will be enabled to develop sensitivity to beauty, harmony and refinement. Resource persons in the community, irrespective of their formal educational qualifications, will be invited to contribute to the cultural enrichment of education, employing both the literate and oral traditions of communication. To sustain and carry forward the cultural tradition, the role of old masters, who train pupils through traditional modes will be supported and recognised.

8.3 Linkages will be established between the university system and institutions of higher learning in art, archaeology, oriental studies etc. Due attention will also be paid to the specialised disciplines of Fine

Arts, Museology, Folklore etc. Teaching, training and research in these disciplines will be strengthened so as to replenish specialised manpower in them.

Value Education

8.4 The growing concern over the erosion of essential values and an increasing cynicism in society has brought to focus the need for readjustments in the curriculum in order to make education a forceful tool for the cultivation of social and moral values.

8.5 In our culturally plural society, education should foster universal and eternal values, oriented towards the unity and integration of our people. Such value education should help eliminate obscurantism, religious fanaticism, violence, superstition and fatalism.

8.6 Apart from this combative role, value education has a profound positive content, based on our heritage, national goals universal perceptions. It should lay primary emphasis on this aspect.

Languages

8.7 The Education Policy of 1968 had examined the question of the development of languages in great detail; its essential provisions can hardly be improved upon and are as relevant today as before. The implementation of this part of the 1968 Policy has, however, been uneven. The Policy will be implemented more energetically and purposefully.

Books and Libraries

8.8 The availability of books at low prices is indispensable for people's education. Effort will be made to secure easy accessibility to books for all segments of the population. Measures will be taken to improve the quality of books, promote the reading habit and encourage creative writing. Authors' interests will be protected. Good translations of foreign books into Indian languages will be supported. Special attention will be paid to the production of quality books for children, including text-books and work books.

8.9 Together with the development of books, a nation-wide movement for the improvement of existing libraries and the establishment of new ones will be taken up. Provision will be made in all educational institutions for library facilities and the status of librarians improved.

Media and Educational Technology

8.10 Modern communication technologies have the potential to bypass several stages and sequences in the process of development encountered in earlier decades. Both the constraints of time and distance at once become manageable. In order to avoid structural dualism, modern educational technology must reach our to the most distant areas and the most deprived sections of beneficiaries simultaneously with the areas of comparative affluence and ready availability.

8.11 Educational technology will be employed in the spread of useful information, the training and re-training of teachers, to improve quality, sharpen awareness of art and culture, inculcate abiding values, etc., both in the formal and non-formal sectors. Maximum use will be made of the available infrastructure. In villages without electricity, batteries or solar packs will be used to run the programme.

8.12 The generation of relevant and culturally compatible educational programmes will form an important component of educational technology, and all available resources in the country will be utilised for this purpose.

8.13 The media have a profound influence on the minds of children as well as adults; some of them tend to encourage consumerism, violence etc. and have a deleterious effect. Radio and TV programmes which clearly militate against proper educational objectives will be prevented. Steps will be taken to discourage such trends in films and other media also. An active movement will be started to promote the production of children's films of high quality and usefulness.

Work Experience

8.14 Work experience, viewed as purposive and meaningful manual work, organised as an integral part of the learning process and resulting in either goods or services useful to the community, is considered as an essential component at all stages of education, to be provided through well-structured and graded programmes. It would comprise activities in accord with the interests, abilities and needs of students, the level of skills and knowledge to be upgraded with the stages of education. This experience would be helpful on his entry into the workforce. Prevocational programmes provided at the lower secondary stage will also facilitate the choice of the vocational courses at the higher secondary stage.

Education and Environment

8.15 There is a paramount need to create a consciousness of the environment. It must permeate all ages and all sections of society, beginning with the child. Environmental consciousness should inform teaching in schools and colleges. This aspect will be integrated in the entire educational process.

Mathematics Teaching

8.16 Mathematics should be visualised as the vehicle to train a child to think, reason, analyse and to articulate logically. Apart from being a specific subject, it should be treated as a concomitant to any subject involving analysis and reasoning.

8.17 With the recent introduction of computers in schools, educational computing and the emergence of learning through the understanding of cause-effect relationships and the interplay of variables, the teaching of mathematics will be suitably redesigned to bring it in line with modern technological devices.

Science Education

8.18 Science education will be strengthened so as to develop in the child well defined abilities and values such as the spirit of inquiry, creativity, objectivity, the courage to question, and an aesthetic sensibility.

8.19 Science education programmes will be designed to enable the learner to acquire problem solving and decision making skills and to discover the relationship of science with health, agriculture, industry and other aspects of daily life. Every effort will be made to extend science education to the vast numbers who have remained outside the pale of formal education.

Sports and Physical Education

8.20 Sports and physical education are an integral part of the learning process, and will be included in the evaluation of performance. A nation-wide infrastructure for physical education, sports and games will be built into the educational edifice.

8.21 The infrastructure will consist of playfields, equipment, coaches and teachers of physical education as part of the School Improvement Programme. Available open spaces in urban areas will be reserved for playgrounds, if necessary by legislation. Efforts will be made to establish sports institutions and hostels where specialised attention will be given to sports activities and sports-related studies, along with normal education. Appropriate encouragement will be given to those talented in sports and games. Due stress will be laid on indigenous traditional games. As a system which promotes an integrated development of body and mind, Yoga will receive special attention. Efforts will be made to introduce Yoga in all schools; to this end, it will be introduced in teacher training courses.

The Role of Youth

8.22 Opportunities will be provided for the youth to involve themselves in national and social development through educational institutions and outside them. Students will be required to participate in one or the other of existing schemes, namely, the National Service Scheme, National Cadet Corps, etc. Outside the institutions, the youth will be encouraged to take up programmes of development, reform and extension. The National Service Volunteer Scheme will be strengthened.

The Evaluation Process and Examination Reform

8.23 Assessment of performance is an integral part of any process of learning and teaching. As part of sound educational strategy, examinations should be employed to bring about qualitative improvements in education.

8.24 The objective will be to re-cast the examination system so as to ensure a method of assessment that is a valid and reliable measure of student development and a powerful instrument for improving teaching and learning. In functional terms, this would mean:

(i) The elimination of excessive element of chance and subjectivity;

(ii) The de-emphasis of memorisation;

(iii) Continuous and comprehensive evaluation that incorporates both scholastic and non-scholastic aspects of education, spread over the total span of instructional time;

(iv) Effective use of the evaluation process by teachers, students and parents:

(v) Improvement in the conduct of examinations;

(vi) The introduction of concomitant changes in instructional materials and methodology;

(vii) Introduction of the semester system from the secondary stage in a phased manner; and

(viii) The use of grades in place of marks.

8.25 The above goals are relevant both for external examinations and evaluation within educational institutions. Evaluation at the institutional level will be streamlined and the predominance of external examinations reduced.

PART IX

THE TEACHER

9.1 The status of the teacher reflects the socio-cultural ethos of a society; it is said that no people can rise above the level of its teachers. The Government and the community should endeavour to create conditions which will help motivate and inspire teachers on constructive and creative lines. Teachers should have the freedom to innovate, to devise appropriate methods of communication and activities relevant to the needs and capabilities of and the concerns of the community.

9.2 The methods of recruiting teachers will be reorganised to ensure merit, objectivity and conformity with spatial and functional requirements. The pay and service conditions of teachers have to be commensurate with their social and professional responsibilities and with the need to attract talent to the profession. Efforts will be made to reach the desirable objective of uniform emoluments, service conditions and grievance-removal mechanisms for teachers throughout the country. Guidelines will be formulated to ensure objectivity in the postings and transfers of teachers. A system of teacher evaluation – open, participative and data-based – will be created and reasonable opportunities of promotion to higher grades provided. Norms of accountability will be laid down with incentives for good performance and disincentives for non-performance. Teachers will continue to play a crucial role in the formulation and implementation of educational programmes.

9.3 Teachers' associations must play a significant role in upholding professional integrity, enhancing the dignity of the teacher and in curbing professional misconduct. National level associations of teachers, could prepare a Code of Professional Ethics for Teachers and see to its observance.

Teacher Education

9.4. Teacher education is a continuous process, and its pre-service and in-service components are inseparable. As the first step, the system of teacher education will be overhauled.

9.5. The new programmes of teacher-education will emphasise continuing education and the need for teachers to meet the thrusts envisaged in this Policy.

9.6. District Institutes of Education and Training (DIET) will be established with the capability to organise pre-service and in-service courses for elementary school teachers and for the personnel working in non-formal and adult education. As DIETs get established, sub-standard institutions will be phased out. Selected Secondary Teacher Training Colleges will be upgraded to complement the work of State Councils of Educational Research and Training. The National Council of Teacher Education will be provided the necessary resources and capability to accredit institutions of teacher-education and provide guidance regarding curricula and methods. Networking arrangements will be created between institutions of teacher education and university departments of education.

PART X

THE MANAGEMENT OF EDUCATION

10.1 An overhaul of the system of planning and the management of education will receive high priority. The guiding considerations will be: –

(a) Evolving a long-term planning and management perspective of education and its integration with the country's developmental and manpower needs;
(b) Decentralisation and the creation of a spirit of autonomy for educational institutions;
(c) Giving pre-eminence to people's involvement, including association of non-governmental agencies and voluntary effort;
(d) Inducting more women in the planning and management of education;
(e) Establishing the principle of accountability in relation to given objectives and norms.

National Level

10.2 The Advisory Board of Education will play a pivotal role in reviewing educational development, determining the changes required to improve the system and monitoring implementation. It will function through appropriate Committees and other mechanisms created to ensure contact with, and coordination among, the various areas of Human Resource Development. The Departments of Education at the Centre and in the States will be strengthened through the involvement of professionals.

Indian Education Service

10.3 A proper management structure in education will entail the establishment of the Indian Education Service as an All-India Service. It will bring a national perspective to this vital sector. The basic principles, functions and procedures of recruitment to this service will be decided in consultation with the State Governments.

State Level

10.4 State Governments may establish State Advisory Boards of Education on the lines of CAHE. Effective measures should be taken to integrate mechanisms in the various State departments concerned with Human Resource Development.

10.5 Special attention will be paid to the training of educational planners, administrators and heads of institutions. Institutional arrangements for this purpose should be set up in stages.

District and Local Level

10.6 District Boards of Education will be created to manage education up to the higher secondary level. State Governments will attend to this aspect with all possible expedition. Within a multi-level framework of educational development, Central, State, District and Local level agencies will participate in planning, coordination, monitoring and evaluation.

10.7 A very important role must be assigned to the head of an educational institution. Heads will be specially selected and trained. School complexes will be promoted on a flexible pattern so as to serve as networks of institutions and to enable the sharing of experiences and facilities. It is expected that a developed system of school complexes will take over much of the inspection functions in due course.

10.8 Local communities, through appropriate bodies, will be assigned a major role in programmes of school improvement.

Voluntary Agencies and Aided Institutions

10.9 Non-government and voluntary effort including social activist groups will be encouraged, subject to proper management, and financial assistance provided. At the same time, steps will be taken to prevent the establishment of institutions set up to commercialise education.

PART XI

Resources and Review

11.1 The Education Commission of 1964-66, the National Education Policy of 1968 and practically all others concerned with education have stressed that the egalitarian goals and the practical, development-oriented objectives of Indian society can be realised only by making investments in education of an order commensurate with the nature and dimensions of the task.

11.2 Resources, to the extent possible, will be raised by mobilising donations, asking the beneficiary communities to maintain school buildings and supplies of some consumables, raising fees at the higher levels of education and effecting some savings by the efficient use of facilities. Institutions involved with research and the development of technical and scientific manpower should also mobilise some funds by levying a cess or charge on the user agencies, including Government departments, and entrepreneurs. All these measures will be taken not only to reduce the burden on State resources but also for creating a greater sense of responsibility within the educational system. However, such measures will contribute only marginally to the total funding. The Government and the community in general will find funds for such programmes as : the universalisation of elementary education; liquidating illiteracy; equality of access to educational opportunities to all sections throughout the country; enhancing the social relevance, quality and functional effectiveness of educational programmes; generating knowledge and developing technologies in scientific fields crucial to self-sustaining economic development; and creating a critical consciousness of the values and imperatives of national survival.

11.3 The deleterious consequences of non-investment or inadequate investment in education are indeed very serious. Similarly, the cost of neglecting vocational and technical education and of research is also unacceptable. Sub-optimal performance in these fields could cause irreparable damage to the Indian economy. The network of institutions set up from time to time since Independence to facilitate the application of science and technology would need to be substantially and expeditiously updated, since they are fast becoming obsolete.

11.4 In view of these imperatives, education will be treated as a crucial area of investment for national development and survival. The National Policy on Education, 1968, had laid down that the investment on education be gradually increased to reach a level of expenditure of 6 percent of the national income as early as possible. Since the actual level of investment has remained far short of that target, it is important that greater determination be shown now to find the funds for the programmes laid down in this Policy. While the actual requirements will be computed from time to time on the basis of monitoring and review, the outlay on education will be shaped up to the extent essential for policy implementation in the Seventh Plan. It will be ensured that from the Eighth Five Year Plan onwards it will uniformly exceed to 6 per cent of the National Income.

Review

11.5 The implementation of the various parameters of the New

Policy must be reviewed every five years. Appraisals at short intervals will also be made to ascertain the progress of implementation and the trends emerging from time to time.

PART XII

The Future

12.1 The future shape of education in India is too complex to envision with precision. Yet, given our tradition which has almost always put a high premium on intellectual and spiritual attainment, we are bound to succeed in achieving our objectives.

12.2 The main task is to strengthen the base of the pyramid, which might come close to a billion people at the turn of the century. Equally, it is important to ensure that those at the top of the pyramid are among the best in the world. Our cultural well-springs had taken good care of both ends in the past; the skew set in with foreign domination and influence. It should now be possible to further intensify the nation-wide effort in Human Resource Development, with Education playing its multifaceted role.

2.3 PROGRAMME OF ACTION (1986)[4]

Introduction

At the time of the adoption of the 'National Policy on Education, 1986', it was promised by the Ministry of Human Resource Development that he would present in the Monsoon Session a Programme of Action for the implementation of the policy. Accordingly, the Ministry undertook an intensive exercise to prepare the promised Programme of Action. Twenty-three Task Forces were constituted and each was assigned a specific topic covered by the National Policy on Education, 1986 (NPE). Eminent educationists, experts, senior bureaucrats and representatives of Central and State Governments were associated with these Task Forces.

The Task Forces examined the situation in respect of the subjects assigned to them and elaborated upon the implications of the specific

4. Published by Ministry of Human Resource Development Government of India, New Delhi.

statements contained in the NPE. The Task Forces also projected the necessary action and indicated the broad targets. They submitted their reports in July 1986. These reports were discussed in a series of meetings taken by the Minister of Human Resource Development. A conference of Education Secretaries of the State Governments and Union Territories also considered these reports on July 20, 1986. Further, the document on the Programme of Action was discussed in the meeting of the Central advisory Board of Education held at New Delhi on the 1st and 2nd of August, 1986. All the suggestions emerging at the meeting at the meeting were taken into account, and the final Programme of Action was presented to Parliament on August 8, 1986. The Lok Sabha and the Rajya Sabha discussed and approved the Programme of Action August 22 and 23 respectively.

The Programme of Action covers the following subjects under 511 paragraphs:

Sl. No.	Subject	No. of Paragraphs
1.	Early Childhood Care and Education	13
2.	Elementary Education, Non-Formal Education and Operation Blackboard	33
3.	Secondary Education and Navodaya Vidyalayas	5
4.	Vocationalisation of Education	59
5.	Higher Education	30
6.	Open University and Distant Education	2
7.	Rural Universities and Institutes	5
8.	Technical and Management Education	102
9.	Making the System Work	10
10.	Delinking of Degrees from Jobs and Manpower Planning	11
11.	Research and Development	22
12.	Education for Women's Equality	20
13.	Education of Scheduled Castes, Scheduled Tribes and Others	8
14.	Minorities Education	3
15.	Education of the Handicapped	33
16.	Adult Education	20
17.	Content and Process of School Education	6
18.	Evaluation Process and Examination Reforms	3
19.	Youth and Sports	10
20.	Language Development	10
21.	The Cultural Perspective	22
22.	Media and Educational Technology (Including use of Computers in Education)	9
23.	Teachers and their Training	29
24.	Management of Education	46

2.4 SEMINARS ON MONITORING AND IMPLEMENTATION OF NATIONAL POLICY ON EDUCATION (1988)[5]

Introduction

In order to carry out all the programmes and schemes as envisaged in the National Policy on Education and Programme of Action, it was considered necessary to monitor the progress effectively. Accordingly on the invitation by the Ministry of Human Resource Development, Government of India, the Association of Indian Universities (AIU) organised four seminars in various regions of India during April-July 1988 to access the status of implementation and to identify constraints, if any, as well as to consider the development of formats and tools for continuous monitoring of NPE and POA at the tertiary level.

Main Objectives of the Seminars

1. to record the prèsent status of implementation in these four clusters of topics,
2. to identify impediments and constraints in implementation undertaken so far,
3. to devise methodologies for monitoring and continuously evaluating the progress and, if possible, develop formats to assess the progress of implementation,
4. to consider possible alternative strategies of implementation, particularly in the context of problems faced and to make practical suggestions.

Scheme of Seminars

The AIU decided to organise the four seminars in four different regions drawing participation from all over India, maintaining a high proportion of participation from universities in and around that area. It was further decided to invite around 50 participants to each seminar, two delegates from each participating university, a Dean, Principal or Professor involved in the actual implementation of the programmes, besides the Vice-Chancellor.

Four universities in the four regions were selected to act at host

5. Published by the Association of Indian Universities, New Delhi, 1988.

universities for the four seminars. They were:

1. Seminar I, April 14-16, 1988, IIT, New Delhi.
2. Seminar II, May 19-21, 1988, Manipur University, Imphal;
3. Seminar III, June 27-29, 1988 University of Poona, and
4. Seminar IV, July 25-27, 1988, Madurai Kamaraj University.

Major Recommendations

I. Consolidation and Expansion of Institutions

1. The University Grants Commission (UGC) should issue guidelines and norms to the universities to enable them to formulate their requirements in respect of courses, intake and equipments, etc.
2. The UGC should appoint a task force to establish institutions within the university system, which will develop and maintain close ties with National laboratories.
3. No government grants should be available to newly established institutions unless their plans have been approved by the UGC and State governments.
4. Guidelines relating to a pattern of a common entrance examination may be developed.

II. Academic Staff Colleges

1. The Academic Staff College (ASC) scheme should be modified in order to enable it to contribute to the change of environment in the colleges/universities. The current orientation course should be followed by refresher courses for senior faculty.
2. The UGC should provide financial support to ASC's.
3. A comprehensive list of resource persons in different subjects and specialisations should be prepared.
4. A central advisory committee be framed for monitoring and coordinating the activities of all ASC's.

III. Distance Teaching/Learning

1. Correspondence courses should be helped with training for preparation of resource materials, well equipped study centres,

and overall improvement of study materials.

2. The state open universities should use the courses and materials developed by the Indira Gandhi National Open University (IGNOU).
3. Norms and standards should be laid down for Distance Education.

IV. Youth Services, Sports and Physical Fitness Programmes

1. The Universities should pay more attention to programmes relating to youth.
2. The AIU should continue and expand its programmes of inter-varsity tournaments, athletic and sports meets and presenting consciousness of sports in colleges and universities.

V. Improvement in Efficiency

1. Educational institutions should have adequate infrastructural facilities such as class-rooms, library, laboratories, hostels, sports complexes, health centres etc. Libraries should have sufficient number of text books, reference books, reprographic and bibliographic services. Laboratories should have adequate modern equipments and consumables.
2. Each university should be equipped with a suitable computer for research and administrative purposes. Selected institutions from all parts of the country should be linked with a network (with terminals for each) for academic and research purpose. This network should supply information about availability of text books, reference books and laboratory equipments, etc.
3. Teachers with consistently good academic record preferably with M.Phil/Ph.D qualifications, should be recruited. Their salary scales should be attractive. They should be encouraged to involve themselves in quality research. They should be compulsorily provided with initial and in-service training through Academic Staff Colleges. Individuals and institutions with outstanding performance should be recognised and rewarded. Autonomous institutions should be set up on the basis of proper and judicious selection.

VI. Technical Education

Each State should have a technical university. The All India

Council for Technical Education (AICTE) norms about physical and academic facilities should be enforced. Uniform pattern of technical education and examination system should be followed.

Academic autonomy, to be followed by financial and administrative autonomy, should be granted to institutions which have attained a minimum standard of excellence.

VII. Teachers

Initial and in-service training facilities should be mandatory. Institutional and individual consultancy facilities should be liberalised. Interaction between institutions and industry should be promoted through exchange of personnel.

VIII. Students

Stipendiery practical training for the students, for a period of at least ninety days in the pre-final/final year should be organised.

IX. Mobility of Teachers and Students

1. Indian Educational Service should be set up with a cadre of 4000 officers to be built up over a period of 10 years. The IES should have parity of status and grades with the I.A.S.
2. Universities may be linked with each other on regional basis in order to facilitate exchange of teachers. Facilities like residential accommodation, migration of their wards to academic institutions, etc. should be provided.
3. Each university must have a research cell headed by a social scientist of professor cadre for collecting, processing and analysing data regarding education, teachers, students and manpower requirements in the region and the state.

Student Mobility

The State governments/universities should select 5 to 10 per cent students from each batch and send them to other universities/institutions for pursuing specific courses through sufficient financial grants and hostel facilities. Students may also be allowed to go to other universities/institutions for completing specialised courses with adequate financial support. Liberal equivalence of courses/ units in universities should be established and strengthened. Youth festivals, interuniversity sports and other youth programmes should be promoted.

XI. Making the System Work

A. *University Functionaries*

1. In order to make the system work efficiently, it is necessary that responsibilities of various functionaries of the university and norms of their performance should be fixed. These functionaries include the Vice-Chancellor, the Registrar, Principals of colleges, Finance Officers, and Controller of Examinations etc. The seminar made suggestions about the specific responsibilities of the various functionaries. These responsibilities include the academic, administrative, legal and financial powers of the various functionaries.

B. *Teachers*

1. It was emphasised that the teachers should participate in the curricular and co-curricular activities. They should devote themselves full time to their academic and non-academic duties and should not engage themselves in private tuitions and/or part time jobs.

C. *Students*

1. Students should involve themselves whole heartedly in the curricular and co-curricular activities. They should maintain discipline and help in maintaining an orderly academic environment.

D. *Educational Institutions*

1. Educational institutions should have adequate finances and, at least, minimum physical and academic facilities. They should provide security and promote healthy community life on their campuses.

E. *Other Recommendations*

1. The procedure of appointing Vice-Chancellors should be strengthened with a view to ensuring the personal, moral and academic integrity of the incumbent. The judicial functions of the Chancellor should be entrusted to a Tribunal or a bench of the Central Educational Tribunal as recommended by the Law Commission.
2. A Council of Higher Education should be set up in each State to coordinate and monitor the implementation of New Education Policy and to look after the finance, evaluation, exchange programmes and identification of study areas for the universities in the State. The council will recommend the provision of adequate finances by the UGC/Central/State Governments to the universities.
3. The seminar also made recommendations about penalties or sanctions to be imposed against the defaulting functionaries at various levels in the universities. It also made suggestions about enforcing the teaching schedule in educational institutions. Recommendations were also made about teacher evaluation, minimum student facilities, students participation in making the system work, grievance redressal machinery for teachers and administrative staff, etc.

XII. *Language Development and Cultural Perspective*

1. All universities and colleges should impart instruction in regional languages. Regional languages should also be encouraged in research at the doctoral level. For this purpose, adequate funds should be provided.
2. The three language formula should be implemented in all States. Teacher training programmes should be organised to orient teachers to teach in modern Indian languages.
3. All efforts should be made to improve the language competencies of students in terms of both expression and comprehension.
4. In every State, Institutes of Indian Languages should be set up for teaching and learning of Indian languages.
5. Suggestions were also made for promoting Hindi as the Link Language of the Union of India in terms of Article 351 of the Indian Constitution. It was also suggested that an International

Hindi University should be set up.

6. Cultural content in education should be concretised with a view to reflect the composite culture of India and Indian value system. Sanskrit should be given a special status and classical languages such as Pali, Prakrit, Old Tamil, Old Kannada, Old Telugu, Apabhramsa, Persian and Arabic should be promoted. The teaching of foreign languages should also be encouraged. The distinct cultural identity of tribals should be safeguarded. An all India survey of folk literature should be organised. Universities should set up departments of Mass Communication for developing regional languages and promotion of their culture.
7. A performing arts institute should also be set up in each State.

XIII Education for Women, Scheduled Castes and Scheduled Tribes, Backward Minorities and Handicapped

A. *Women*

1. Every university should set up a Women's Cell for implementation of programmes for women's education.
2. Courses should be devised with emphasis an women's equality. These courses should be common for all students.
3. Women's education should be free at all levels. As a part of adult literacy, development linked education should be preferred.
4. Women's polytechnics should be established in large numbers.
5. Awareness of women's equality should be created through all possible media.

B. *Scheduled Castes and Scheduled Tribes*

1. To promote educational interests of SC & ST, there should be coordination between Centre, States, universities and voluntary agencies.
2. Adequate reservation should be given to SC & ST in educationalSinstitutions for admission up to secondary level.
3. Remedial courses and special classes for training for public services examinations should be organised.
4. Funds and Staff should be available from UGC for State governments for implementation of SC/ST Welfare programmes. Sufficient funds should be provided for research on problems

relating to SC & ST.

C. *Minority Education*

1. The definition of 'minority' should be more specific and be defined by law. National integration, secularism and egalitarianism should be consciously promoted through education.

D. *Handicapped*

1. Special institutions should be established for the handicapped; special research programmes should be taken up to study the problems of education of the handicapped.

XIV. *Research and Extension*

1. Inter-disciplinary research in Extension should be promoted at the Ph.D. level. Universities must provide adequate facilities for research. A research committee should be set up for guiding research scholars. women, SC & ST should be provided adequate opportunities for research.
2. Extension work should be encouraged. The concept of community colleges should be fully explored to encourage extension.

XV. *Teachers and Their Training*

1. There should be close collaboration between university departments of education and college of education with state level agencies of teachers training including DIETS.
2. Research in educational training with dynamic linkage between research and training process should be promoted.
3. Correspondence courses in education should be discouraged.
4. The UGC should formulate and enforce objective criteria for the establishment of advanced centres of studies in education. Adequate funds should be provided for teacher-orientation programmes.
5. Language teachers should be given adequate training in teaching of the third language under the three language formula.

XVI. In-service Education of Teachers

1. In-service refresher programmes should be organised for school teachers by B.Ed. colleges & university departments of education.
2. The AIU should prepare a draft of educational planning management and implementation in the light of the development of the Indian Universities and higher education in general; AIU should forward the model act to the UGC for onward transmission to the state authorities for adoption.

XVII. Living and Working Conditions of Teachers

1. The principals of B.Ed. colleges should be given salary scales at par with those of the general education colleges.
2. Adequate liberal housing loans should be made available to teachers. Leave Travel Concession facilities should also be extended to them.
3. Teachers moving from one university to the other should be allowed to carry service benefits from previous employment.

XIX. Grievance Removal

1. Central Educational Tribunal, as recommended by the Law Commission should be set up. Orientation of Principals/Deans/V.C's in the procedures of the Tribunal must be undertaken.

XX. Restructuring of Courses

1. A uniform model of restructured courses should be implemented at the regional and national level. Scheme of restructuring of undergraduate courses may also include vocational courses and personality development courses. The weightage scheme of the UGC should be modified.
2. The contract hours per week for the arts stream should be increased to 25.
3. The existing Boards of Studies should be reconstituted to cater to the needs of restructured courses.
4. Special funds should be made available to universities for reorganisation of courses under the NPE & POA.

XXI. Autonomous Colleges

1. The universities should set up committees for implementing programmes of NPE & POA. Seminars should be organised to create awareness among the teachers and the management about the programmes.
2. The UGC should monitor the progress of the NPE programmes.
3. The UGC may grant financial assistance to colleges, which show outstanding performance for various quality improvement programmes. It should maintain a balanced approach in assisting universities and colleges for implementing NPE & POA programmes.
4. 500 colleges should be given autonomous status by the end of the seventh plan; each university should confer autonomous status on 10 percent of its colleges. All-out efforts should be made to remove misconceptions in the minds of teachers towards autonomy.
5. Colleges should be financially helped to get permanent affiliation status.
6. (a) The State governments should provide timely and adequate assistance to colleges and universities for implementing NPE programmes.
   (b) The States should amend university acts enabling the universities to grant autonomy to colleges.

7. The autonomous colleges may be encouraged to:

   (a) Change their internal management structure.
   (b) Provide incentives to teachers by upgrading their posts.
   (c) to attain the status of "deemed to be university" in course of time.
8. The maintenance expenditure on autonomous colleges should be met by the UGC on a permanent basis.

XXII. Education in Human Values

Value Orientation for Teachers

1. Preservice and periodic training in value-oriented education should be given to teachers. This programme should be

emphasised in the Academic Staff Colleges.

Co-curricular and Extra-curricular Activities for Value Orientation

1. Programmes like NCC and NSS, sports and games as well as cultural programmes should be encouraged and their coverage increased.

XXIII. Evaluation Process and Examination Reforms

1. Hundred per cent internal evaluation at post-graduate level in unitary universities and autonomous colleges should be introduced in 1990-91 and extended to undergraduate level by 1993-94.
2. Students' performance in terms of letter grades and overall performance on the basis of cumulative grade point average should be made and recorded.
3. Examination process in the case of non-autonomous affiliated colleges should be decentralised.

XXIV. Conduct of Examinations

1. Central and State legislation should be introduced to make malpractices in examinations as cognizable and non-bailable offences.

XXV. Interacting the Process of Evaluation with Teaching and Training

1. Affiliating universities should evolve alternative systems for the conduct of examinations; they should decentralise the process of course designing.
2. Cells for continuous research and development in evaluation procedures may be set up at the UGC as also at the institutional level.

XXVI. General Recommendation

There is need for introducing innovative practices in evaluation like Question Banks, open book examination system, clearing examinations in parts in accordance with the pattern of courses.

National Testing Service

1. National Testing Service should be established and developed to evolve norms and for quality control.
2. The AIU should analyse the system of evaluation of M.Phil. and Ph.D. Programmes and evolve a more suitable system.
3. Teachers should be provided orientation and refresher courses in various evaluation procedures.

Evaluation and Accreditation

1. Accreditation should be a compulsory follow-up to the evaluation system for all higher education institutions. It should have built in benefits to the accredited institutions in terms of funds, priority clearance of projects, etc.
2. Institutional evaluation should have a three-tier structure: Self-evaluation, outside evaluation and coordination of expert panel reports by State level assessment council.
3. The national level apex body should issue suitable guidelines for evaluation. The evaluation body should consist of experts from within the educational system and outside the system.

XXVII. State Council of Higher Education

1. The State Council of Higher Education should be a statutory body to be set up for improving academic standards, further development of university system and co-ordination of students, teaching, research and examinations, etc.
2. The council should consist of a full time Chairman, Vice-Chancellors, teachers and distinguished educationists and industrialists besides nominees of the Government. The term of the Chairman and members should be limited to one term of three years. It will have a Secretary and other supporting staff.
3. The Council will be the main coordinating body in the field of higher education and will take up the following functions:

   (a) Planning and coordination
   (b) Academic

(c) Advisory and
(d) Administrative

4. The State Council for Higher Education will work-out the quantum of block maintenance grants for higher education. It will also prepare a comprehensive perspective plan for the development of higher education. It will scrutinise and process the development plans of universities/colleges in that perspective and prepare five years plans regarding higher education. The council shall follow the guidelines issued by other funding bodies like UGC, ICAR, AICTE, etc.
5. A State Research and Development Board should be set up under the council to establish linkages and coordination between the research in educational institutions and other research agencies and identify priority areas of research.
6. The Council should have the function of accreditation of institutions through an accreditation board at the State level in cooperation with the national accreditation council.

2.5 EDUCATION FOR ALL BY 2000: INDIAN PERSPECTIVE (1990)[6]

Introduction

The publication of this document coincided with the World Conference on Education for All by 2000, held in March 1990. It reiterates the country's renewed commitment for universalisation on elementary education and eradication of adult illiteracy. It attempts to indicate possible directions in which the country should move to achieve this goal. It provides an analytical study of various aspects of education in the context of the Indian situation.

Extracts relating to Goals, Targets and Human Resources are given below for having an overview of the document.

6. Published by the National Institute of Educational Planning and Administration, New Delhi, 1990.

3. GOALS AND TARGETS

Targets at National Level

The mechanism of micro-level planning will result in separate targets for each planning unit – State, district, block, and village. In a truly decentralised approach of planning, realistic targets fixed by all the villages of the block should lead to the target of the block, the targets of all the blocks in a district should lead to the target of the district and so on. However, such a process will not only be time-consuming, it would also lack a national goal reference. By expecting certain national level targets on the basis of disaggregation, we are also hoping to oblige the national and state level planners to pay higher attention to areas and groups and within them to girls/women, receiving special attention.

A. *Access*

1. By the year 1995, primary schools or their alternatives will be provided to every child in rural area within a distance of 1 km.
2. By the year 2000, upper primary schools or their alternatives will be provided to every child in rural area within a distance of 3 km.

Accordance to the All India Educational Survey (1986), conducted by the NCERT, 94 per cent of the rural population is being served by a primary school within 1 km. and 85.39 per cent of the rural population is being served by an upper primary school within a distance of 3 km. In view of this, it should not be difficult to provide a school or an alternative education centre in the next 5 years to the remaining 6 per cent of the rural population for primary education, and the remaining 14.61 per cent for upper primary education in the next 10 years. In this we are assuming a growth rate of slightly above 1 per cent, which is not very high.

B. *Participation*

3. Primary education through schools or alternatives will be provided to:

(a) Eighty per cent of all childern up to the age of 11 years by

1995, which will necessarily include at least 70 per cent belong to every identified disadvantaged group; and

(b) Ninety-five per cent of all children upto the age of girls 11 years by the year 2000, which will necessarily include 85 per cent belonging to every identified disadvantaged group.

Taking into account the current lower participation rate of the children of disadvantaged groups as compared to the total participation of children, different levels of participation are proposed for children of disadvantaged groups and for the overall participation.

4. Upper primary education through schools or alternatives will be provided to:

(a) sixty per cent of all children upto the age of 14 years by 1995, which will necessarily include at least 50 per cent girls belonging to every identified disadvantaged group; and
(b) seventy-five per cent of all children upto the age of 14 years by 1995, which will necessarily include at least 65 per cent girls belonging to every identified disadvantaged group.

The dropout rate is extremely high in the early stages of primary education and is considerably less between the conclusion of primary and the start of the upper primary education. Of those who complete primary education roughly 75 per cent continue studies for upper primary education. Most of the children who continue studies for upper primary education usually complete that stage. Keeping this in view, the targets for participation in upper primary education have been kept at approximately 75 per cent of those for primary education. An assumption implicit is that if the existing transfer rate from primary to upper primary is 75 per cent, it is likely to go up and similarly the the dropout rate at the upper primary stage would also be reduced. The effect of the level achieved in 1995 at the end of the upper primary stage will usually be seen at the end of the primary stage after three years. However, in view of the improved environment for education, it has been visualised that improved transfer to and retention in upper primary education will not be sequential but partly contemporaneous with improvement in primary education.

C. *Achievement*

(a) seventy per cent of children, including at least 60 per cent girls of every disadvantaged group, pursuing elementary education, will achieve the minimum levels of learning by the year 1995; and
(b) Eighty per cent of children, including at least 70 per cent girls of every disadvantaged group, pursuing elementary education, will achieve the minimum levels of learning by the year 2000.

These targets highlight the new approach and thrust in the plan for education for All by the year 2000. Minimum levels of learning will be clearly defined and laid down for the end of primary education and upper primary education. To enable the monitoring of progress of children towards these levels, the teachers will be suitably oriented to appreciate the concept of minimum levels of learning, to work towards their achievements, to design and administer tests, and to ensure progress, as has been spelt out elsewhere.

Adult Education

In the age group 15-35, 80 per cent of the persons of each gender of every identified disadvantaged group will be enable to become functionally literate by the year 1995, and the remaining by the year 2000.

The present number of illiterate persons in this age group is estimated to be about 110 million. With the emphasis on prevention of illiterate persons entering this age group through higher participation in primary education, it would be reasonable to work on the basis of a target of 100 million. Thus, the target, laid down in the National Literacy Mission, of 80 million by 1995 can remain, unathered, leaving the 20-30 million left out for coverage between 1995 and 2000.

For the general population and disadvantaged categories, as well as women, disaggregated targets have been suggested to ensure focusing attention on the latter. This will mean enhanced effort and much greater attention to cover such a high percentage of women and disadvantaged groups.

Continuing Education

All persons who are functionally literate and all those who have received primary or upper primary education through formal or non-formal channels will be provided opportunities to at least maintain, and if possible upgrade, their education through the public education system including *Jana Shikshan Nilayams*, public libraries, media, and other channels of distance education.

This target relating to continuing education is very critical. An elaborate public education system will have to be built. In addition to the existing *Jana Shikshan Nilayams*, public libraries, and reading rooms, an attempt will be made to run continuing education programmes with the help of all possible agencies/institutions. These would include secondary/senior secondary schools, farmers' training centres, *Krishi vigyan kendras*, etc. Programmes for development of skills among rural people, such as TRYSEM and SCYTE, will be utilised for skill development. A detailed survey for identifying needs and interests of people of different age groups will be undertaken, along with a massive programme for preparation and production of books. Radio and television programmes will also be steered to meet these needs and interests.

Future Requirements

Elementary Education

According to population projections, the target population for elementary education, i.e., of the age group 6-14, will be 163 million in A.D. 2000; 102 million of the age group 6-11, and 61 million of the age group 11-14. How much would it cost to provide primary education to 95 per cent of children of the age group 6-11, and upper primary education to 80 per cent of children of the 11-14 age groups, as pragmatically suggested in this document? It is proposed that 70 per cent of the children will be provided formal education and the remaining 30 per cent will have to be covered by non-formal education. Further, it is felt that the number of over and underage children in elementary education would come down gradually to levels of 25 per cent in primary education and 15 per cent in upper primary education.

In the absence of recent estimates on expenditure per student, we shall consider here the salary of teachers in estimating the requirement of resources. After all, teachers' salaries constitute about 95 per cent of the total recurring expenditure. The average salary of teachers in primary schools is found to be Rs.24000 per annum and in the upper primary schools Rs.36000 per annum. Assuming teacher-pupil ratios of 40 and 35 in primary and upper primary schools respectively, the total number of teachers required in A.D.2000 is estimated at 2.1 million in primary and 1.1 million in upper primary schools. Accordingly the teacher costs worked out to Rs.91.2 thousand million, Rs. 50.9 thousand million in primary schools and Rs.40.3 thousand million in upper primary schools. To this, we add 5 per cent non-teaching recurring cost, i.e., Rs.0.46 thousand million. Thus the total recurring cost amounts to Rs. 91.7 thousand million.

Now, this is only recurring expenditure, and it does not cover expenditure on capital items; it also does not make any allowance for improvement in the quality of education. This is the level of resources required for elementary education by A.D. 2000.

One may briefly note that the additional resources required, in the context of several measures of improvement in quality as suggested in the present document, would be quite substantial. The working Group on Resources for Education for the Eight Five Year Plan (1990-95) has estimated the requirements for a few such items. The Group estimated the indirect expenditure on administration and supervision, quality improvement, stipends, scholarships and other incentives, at Rs.2067 million, the cost of construction of classrooms for additional children at Rs. 11095 million, and the cost of construction of the backlog of schools, based on the Fifth All India Educational Survey, at Rs.38561 million. In addition, for Operation Blackboard, an additional amount of Rs. 15139 million was estimated as the requirement, and in all Rs. 88 thousand million. It is assumed that during 1995-2000 an additional amount of Rs.23 thousand million would be required. Thus on an average, Rs. 11.2 thousand million would be required for formal elementary education as non-recurring expenditure every year during 1991-2000. These estimates excluded normal recurring expenditure in the form of teacher cost etc., that we have estimated separately.

Thus in all, putting recurring and non-recurring expenditures together, elementary education requires about Rs.800 thousand million during the next ten years; in other words the total expenditure should gradually increase to Rs. 103 thousand million in A.D. 2000 at 1989-90 prices.

Non-formal Education

It is being planned that 30 per cent of the children of the age group

6-14 would be provided education through the non-formal channel.

We believe that the non-formal system of education should be comparable with formal. system as far as the quality and content are concerned. Then only vertical mobility of the students into the formal system of education would be possible. This obviously requires more resources.

At present it is estimated by the Ministry of Human Resource Development (Department of Education), that a centre for non-formal education costs about Rs.12000 per year and it provides education to 20 students. Within two years of non-formal education, one is expected to have acquired an education equivalent to compulsory elementary education. The unit costs of no-formal education for two years per student works out to Rs.1200 (at current 1989-90 prices). Accordingly it is estimated that non-formal education will require Rs.52.6 thousand million in A.D.2000 at 1989-90 prices. It amounts to about Rs.500 thousand million for the 10 years until A.D.2000.

In all, the requirements of elementary education, including non-formal education in A.D.2000 would be of the order of Rs.156 thousand million at 1989-90 prices. Given the earlier trends, it seems to be a gigantic task. Between 1960-61 and 1970-71, the real expenditure on elementary education was nearly doubled; and between 1970-71 and 1980-81 it increased by about 40 per cent. The present estimates suggest that these trends would be substantially reversed: the total expenditure should be doubled by the turn of the century.

Adult Education

The 15-35 age group constitutes the most productive work force. Constained by resources made available to the education sector, adult education programmes have been confined to this age group only. On the basis of the projections of population, we had in 1986, 259 million adults (15-35 age group) among whom 151 million were literates, and 108 million illiterates. By 2000 the total population in this age group to likely to increase to 364 million. They need to be made literate through adult education programmes.

In the absence of reliable estimates of costs per head, it is assumed, as suggested by the Ministry of Human Resource Development (Department of Education), that an amount of Rs.200 will have to be invested per head to make one person functionally literate, which means that on average, each year, we would require Rs.4200 million at

1989-90 prices to provide literacy to about 21 million persons each year.

It might be necessary to provide organised post-literacy education to the newly turned literates, lest they replace into illiteracy. However, this is not not being explicitly planned here, except marginally through the *Jana Shikshan Nilayams*, discussed below. Thus our estimates on literacy programmes form a bare minimum level of resources required.

Continuing Education

It is proposed in this document that all literates should be provided with opportunities to improve their skills. *Jana Shikshan Nilayams*, and public libraries, along with extensive use of the media are proposed in this context. It is felt that every 50 villages should have a *Juna Shikshan Nilayam*, and that at least every block should have a good public library that will provide learning materials to the people. This means that during the next ten years 10,000 *Jana Shikshan Nilayams* and 5,000 public libraries have to be created. According to the estimates of the Ministry of Human Resource Development (Department of Education), a *Jana Shikshan Nilayam* would cost Rs. 7,000 per year as recurring expenditure, besides Rs. 7,000 as non-recurring expenditure. Similarly, a public library would cost Rs.50,000 as non-recurring expenditure, and Rs.25,000 every year as recurring expenditure. Accordingly the total resources required are estimated at about Rs.1.4 thousand million.

Thus the requirements of resources for a few major programmes is estimated here. It should also be noted that the estimates are based on some crude and quick calculations. More importantly, these estimates allow for mere enrolment in the system by A.D.2000. Hence they should be viewed as the minimum level of resources required.

It is clear that, the estimates made here do not cover several programmes and policies suggested in this document, such as training, of teachers, administrators, voluntary agencies, mothers, community leaders, public provision of incentives to school children, particularly, of the weaker sections, establishment of special organisations like National Testing Services at Central, State, and district levels, district boards of education, village education committees, school complexes, and mechanisms of monitoring, etc. These are only illustrative. If one were to cost each item, assuming that reliable estimates of unit costs of the items are available, it is likely that the actual level of requirement of resources would be of a very high order.

While every effort should be made to generate additional resources for education, it is also required that non-conventional strategies need to be devised in mobilising and effectively utilising monitoring, physical, and human resources. As an example, a few strategies relating to human resources are outlined below. However, it may be noted that these strategies do not necessarily mean that the level of resources required for education could be substantially lowered.

Human Resources

The stupendous task of Education for All will require massive human resources. For this, we will have to diversify the sources.

The local community is a tremendous fund of human resources, if imaginatively used. Our present approach of looking towards outside sources will have to change to enable us to properly identify and utilise the local human resources. The teachers and instructors for NFE and adult education can be drawn from the community. They will have a greater motivation and involvement. Volunteers from the community can be identified and their assistance obtained. Persons in the community with special skills and expertise can be identified and used as resource persons for development of those specified skills.

3

EDUCATIONAL SURVEY AND INNOVATIONS

3.1. INNOVATIONS IN EDUCATION[1]

The Post-Independence era has seen rapid expansion of education in India. As against 1,50,000 elementary schools, 4,000 secondary schools and 214 intermediate/junior colleges in the country in the year 1947, the total number of institutions has increased respectively to 6,35,000, 55,000 and 4,000 in 1983-84. The enrolment also increased nine times at elementary, 25 times at secondary and 20 times at intermediate levels during the same period. The Education Departments of Centre and States spent Rs. 5517 crores in 1983-84 as against total expenditure of 55 crores in 1947. Despite significant expansion in physical facilities and increase in expenditure, the education sector faces many challenges. The literacy rate in the country is barely 36 per cent, and about 50 million children remain to be enrolled in elementary education by the end of Seventh Five Year Plan. Improvement in the quality of education is an area of immediate concern. In the context of resource constraints for education, which has been a limiting factor, and adverse socio-economic conditions especially of the first generation learners introduction of new and innovative practices of learning to optimise the results, should call for special emphasis.

Several States/organisations have experimented with innovative methods to make education cost-effective, purposeful and suiting to the

---

1. Published by the Ministry of Human Resource Development, Department of Education, Government of India, New Delhi, 1986.

convenience of learners. An attempt has been made to present some innovative methods practised in the field of school education and adult education.

SCHOOL EDUCATION

Innovative Project/Practices Mainly Related to Elementary Education

1. Pilot Project Schools (Meghalaya)
2. Innovations in the Teaching of Mathematics in Primary Schools (Nagaland)
3. Schools Adoption by Training Institutes (Punjab)
4. Integrated Education of the Disabled (Rajasthan)
5. Correspondence-cum-Contact Course for Higher Grade Teachers (Tamil Nadu)
6. Chief Minister's Nutritious Meal Programme (Tamil Nadu)
7. Problem of Wastage and Stagnation and its Eradication (Uttar Pradesh)
8. Using the Environment and Local Resources for Science Education at the Primary Stage (NCERT, New Delhi)
9. Training of In-Service Teacher Education Personnel in Environmental Studies for Primary Schools (NCERT, New Delhi)
10. Guidance at the Elementary School Stage (NCERT, New Delhi)
11. Radio Pilot Project (NCERT, New Delhi)
12. Nutrition, Health, Education and Environmental Sanitation (NHEES) UNICEF Assisted Project, (NCERT, New Delhi)
13. Primary Education Curriculum renewal (PECR) a UNICEF Assisted Project (NCERT, New Delhi)
14. Early Childhood Education Project (ECE) and Children's Media Laboratory (CML) a UNICEF Assisted Project (NCERT, New Delhi)
15. Education of Special Groups

Innovative Projects/Practices Mainly Related to Secondary Education

1. Vocationalisation of Education at Secondary School Level (Andhra Pradesh)
2. Raising the Standard of Performance at Matriculation Level in Pulwama District (J&K)

3. Rapport-Based Programme of School Improvement (Maharashtra)
4. Science Forum (Maharashtra)
5. A Study of Utilisation of proxy periods with a view to suggesting some useful and definite activities to be conducted during such periods (Maharashtra)
6. Construction of Diagnostic Tests in Algebra for Standard IX (Maharashtra)
7. Open School (Tamil Nadu)
8. Vocationalisation of Education in Higher Secondary Stage (Tamil Nadu)
9. Incentive Cash Awards (Dadra & Nagar Haveli)
10. Educational and Vocational Guidance in Secondary Schools (Mizoram)
11. National Level Science Centre (NCERT, New Delhi)
12. Computer Literacy and Studies in Schools (NCERT, New Delhi)
13. Individually Guided System of Instruction (IGSI) (NCERT, New Delhi)
14. Development of New Series – Let's Enrich Our English (NCERT) New Delhi
15. Graphic Communications (Regional College of Education, Ajmer) (NCERT, New Delhi).

Innovative Projects/Practices Related to both Elementary and Secondary Education

1. A Critical Study of the Stress and Strain of the Curriculum on the Students (Maharashtra)
2. Continuing Education Programme (CEP) (Manipur)
3. Orientation Programme on Teaching of English (OPTE) (Manipur)
4. Educational Dissemination Programme Through Bulletins and Annuals (EDPBA) (Manipur)
5. Hardyal-Kishanpuri Teaching Aid (HKTA) (Punjab)
6. Chief Minister's Scheme of Life Oriented Education (Tamil Nadu)
7. Reading to Learn (NCERT, New Delhi)
8. Moral Education and Yoga (NCERT, New Delhi)
9. Behaviour Modification Workshop (NCERT, New Delhi)

10. Identifying and Nurturing Creative Potential of School Children (NCERT, New Delhi)
11. INSAT for Education (NCERT, New Delhi)
12. National Population Education (NPE) (NCERT, New Delhi)

Innovative Projects/Practices Related to Non-formal Education

1. Earn While You Learn Scheme (Madhya Pradesh)
2. Action Research Project on Universal Primary Education (Maharashtra)
3. Investigation into Reasons for the Low Progress in Mathematics of the Night School Students (Maharashtra)
4. Calcutta Pavement Schools (Janshiksha Prachar, W.B.)
5. Development of Relevance Based Curriculum and Teaching-Learning Materials for Non-Formal Education Programme (NCERT, New Delhi)
6. Developmental Activities in Community Education and Participation (DACEP) UNICEF Assisted Project (NCERT, New Delhi)
7. Comprehensive Access to Primary Education (CAPE) UNICEF Assisted Project (NCERT, New Delhi)
8. The Pauta Experiment (Bihar)

ADULT EDUCATION

Innovative Projects/Practices Related to Adult Education

1. Chalk Making through Adult Education (Haryana)
2. Developing functional skill: Knitting (Haryana)
3. Adult Education Centre for Lepers (Himachal Pradesh)
4. Adult Education through Integrated Child Development Scheme (Jammu & Kashmir)
5. Involvement of Mass Media (Jammu & Kashmir)
6. Income Generating Activities at Adult Education Centres (Jammu & Kashmir)
7. Promotion of Adult Education through 1. Prodh Sangam 2. Kala Pathak 3. Rural Libraries and Reading Rooms and 4. Mobile Cinema Vans (Madhya Pradesh)
8. Savitribai Phule Shield (Maharashtra)
9. Vocational Adult Education for Urban Areas (Tamil Nadu)

10. Industries Non-Formal Education Scheme (Tamil Nadu)
11. Mathura Pilot Project – An Experiment in Inter-Departmental Coordination (Uttar Pradesh)
12. Small Saving through Adult Education (West Bengal)
13. Development Oriented Activities in Adult Education (Andaman & Nicobar Islands)

3.2 FIFTH ALL INDIA EDUCATIONAL SURVEY (1989)[2]

Introduction

In order to meet the need for proper planning of school facilities at the grassroot level and for ensuring a balanced growth in all areas, rural and urban, All India Educational Surveys have been conducted by the Ministry of Education in 1957 and after that the Second, Third, Forth and Fifth Surveys by NCERT in 1965, 1973, 1978 and 1986 respectively.

The Fifth All India Education Survey provides data as on September 30, 1986.

Main Findings

1. *Demographic Information*

The total estimated population of the country was 784069 thousand including 593520 thousand (75.70%) in the rural areas. The percentage increase for the period 1981–86 worked out to be 17.86 per cent. The population in the rural areas was estimated at the habitation level and then aggregated to get rural population of the blocks, districts and States. The population in urban areas was estimated on the basis of the latest estimates available and using the population growth rate of the state for the decade 1971–81. There were 578682 inhabited villages having 979065 habitations. On an average there were 1.69 habitations per inhabited village.

2. *Schools*

2.1 The number of recognised educational institutions (up to the

2. Published by the National Council of Educational Research and Training, New Delhi, 1989.

higher secondary stage) in the country was 735785 including 634719 (86.26%) in the rural areas as against 634144 in 1978. There has been an increase of 16.03 per cent in institutions over the period 1978–86. The corresponding increase in the rural areas has been 13.98%. Of the 735785 institutions, 631394 (85.81%) had primary stage classes, 187026 (25.42%) upper primary stage classes, 66952 (9.10%) secondary stage classes and 15498 (2.11%) had the higher secondary stage classes.

2.2 Among the total 735785 schools, there were 529392 (71.95%) primary schools, 138687 (18.85%) upper primary schools, 52208 (7.09%) secondary schools and 15498 (2.11%) higher secondary schools. Of these, 475938 (89.90%) primary schools, 112836 (81.36%) upper primary schools, 38720 (74.16%) secondary schools and 7225 (46.62%) higher secondary schools were located in rural areas.

2.3 Of the 529392 primary schools, 219837 (41.53%) were government schools, 251699 (47.54%) local body schools, 44701 (8.44%) private aided schools and 13155 (2.49%) private unaided schools. In most of the States the majority of the primary schools were government or local body schools. However, 52.70% primary schools in Andhra Pradesh and 58.84% in Kerala were private aided schools. Of the 138687 upper primary schools 59650 (43.01%) 42568 (30.69%), 24827 (17.90%) and 11642 (8.40%) schools were government, local body, private aided and private unaided schools respectively. As in the case of primary schools, majority (73.70%) of the upper primary schools were either run by the government or by the local bodies. However, more than 50% upper primary schools in the states of Kerala (65.77%), Meghalaya (85.56%), Mizoram (72.14%), Orissa (90.13%) and in West Bengal (99.74%) were private aided schools. Only 6158 (35.52%) upper primary schools in Uttar Pradesh were private unaided. Of the 52208 secondary schools, 19452 (37.26%) were government schools, 3248 (6.22%) local body schools, 22901 (43.86%) private aided and 6607 (12.66%) private unaided schools. More than 50 per cent secondary schools in the States of Goa (84.51%), Gujarat (91.85%), Kerala (57.09%), Maharashtra (60.15%), Meghalaya (89.58%), Mizoram (81.88%), Orissa (60.23%), Uttar Pradesh (65.07%) and West Bengal (97.95%) were private aided schools. In most of the remaining States and Union Territories the schools run by the government out-numbered the number of schools run by other managements.

Of the 15498 higher secondary schools 6001 (38.72%) schools

were government schools, 460 (2.97%) local body schools, 8114 (52.35%) private aided and 923 (5.96%) private unaided schools. Further, 16 (69.57%) in Goa, 1096 (88.24%) schools in Gujarat, 1146 (82.92%) in Maharashtra, 2 (100.0%) in Meghalaya, 2770 (82.12%) in Uttar Pradesh and 1088 (93.63%) in West Bengal were private aided schools. In most of the other States and Union Territories, the schools run by the government were 50 per cent or more.

2.4 The number of primary schools increased by 11.54 per cent, upper primary schools by 23.38 per cent, secondary schools by 42.35 per cent and higher secondary schools by 48.60 per cent over the period 1978–86. The increase for the total number of schools was 16.03 per cent during the foresaid period.

2.5 Of the 15498 higher secondary schools, 13245 (85.46%) offered Arts, 10608 (68.45%) offered Science, 5585 (36.04%) offered Commerce, 1003 (6.47%) offered Agriculture, 990 (6.39%) offered Technical Courses and 1667 (10.76%) offered Home Science. Ninety-four schools had computer science.

2.6 1706 (11.0%) higher secondary schools offered vocational courses at +2 stage and the enrolment in these courses was 126571.

2.7 As regards facilities for teaching physical education/Yoga, 13513 (2.55%) primary schools, 16869 (12.16%) upper primary schools, 36312 (69.55%) secondary schools and 12503 (80.67%) higher secondary schools had teachers exclusively for physical education/Yoga.

3. *Educational Facilities*

3.1 *Primary Stage*: Out of total habitations, 502806 (51.36%) habitations covering 80.34 per cent rural population had primary schools/sections. The corresponding percentage at the time of the Fourth Survey (1978) were 46.80 and 78.53 respectively. 94.60 per cent rural population was served by primary sections located either within the habitation or up to a walking distance of one km as against 92.82 per cent population in 1978. The States of Andhra Pradesh, Gujarat, Haryana, Nagaland, Punjab and Union Territories of Chandigarh, Delhi, Lakshadweep and Pondicherry have attained almost universal provision of educational facilities for primary stage. The percentage of rural population served by primary schools/sections was less than 90 per cent in respect of the States of Arunachal Pradesh (73.35%), Himachal Pradesh (76.64%), Meghalaya (89.22%), Sikkim

(83.10%), Tripura (84.11%), Uttar Pradesh (88.56%) and Union Territories of A & N Islands (83.02%) and Dadra & Nagar Haveli (85.19%).

The country had 530176 (54.15%) habitations with population 300 or more. Of these, 76.98 per cent had the facility for primary stage within the habitation of residence and 94.01 per cent had the facility either within the habitation of residence or within a walking distance of one km.

3.2 *Upper Primary Stage*: Only 129710 (13.25%) habitations covering 36.98 per cent rural population had upper primary schools/sections within the habitation of residence. The corresponding percentages for the Forth Survey (1978) were 10.74 per cent and 33.47 per cent respectively. 85.39 per cent rural population had the facility for upper primary stage either within the habitation of residence or within a walking distance of 3 km as against 78.83 per cent population in 1978.

Among States, Andhra Pradesh (97.28%), Goa (91.79%), Gujarat (94.43%), Haryana (93.12%), Kerala (96.22%) and Punjab (92.49%) had more than 90 per cent rural population served within three km. The Union Territories of Chandigarh (100.0%), Daman & Diu (99.44%), Delhi (98.60%), Lakshadweep (99.16%) and Pondicherry (96.48%) belonged to this category. Among the States Arunachal Pradesh (42.19%), Himachal Pradesh (76.04%), Madhya Pradesh (69.58%), Meghalaya (64.99%), Nagaland (66.41%), Rajasthan (77.00%) and Sikkim (76.20%) had less than 80 per cent population served within three km. Among Union Territories, A & N Islands (73.57%) and Dadra & Nagar Haveli (65.33%) belonged to this category.

There were 358996 (36.67%) habitations with population 500 or more. Of these, 29.93 per cent were served by schools/sections for Upper Primary stage within the habitation of residence and 84.45 per cent habitations had the facility either within the habitation or within a walking distance of three km.

4. *Enrolment*

4.1 The enrolment in classes I-V was 86683289 including 6679707 (77.06%) enrolment in rural areas. Enrolment of girls in classes I-V was 35676643 (41.16%). The percentage increase in enrolment over the period 1978-86 was 26.36 per cent.

Enrolment in classes VI-VIII was 27200656 including 9642537

(35.45%) girls. The corresponding enrolment for the rural areas was 17795293 (65.42%). The percentage increase in enrolment over the period 1978–86 was 51.46 per cent.

The total enrolment and enrolment in rural areas for classes IX-X were 11474962 and 6488568 (56.55%) respectively. There were 3642267 (31.74%) girls in these classes. The percentage increase in enrolment over the period 1978–86 was 63.03 per cent

The total enrolment in classes XI-XII was 3440863 including 1056592 (30.71%) girls. The corresponding enrolment in rural areas was 1345589 (39.11%). The percentage increase in enrolment over the period 1978–86 was 87.66 per cent.

4.2 Enrolment of Scheduled Castes was 15039683 in classes I-V, 4064405 in classes VI-VIII, 1539301 in classes IX-X and 394023 in classes XI-XII. The S.C. enrolment in classes I-V, VI-VIII, IX-X and XI-XII was 17.35 per cent, 14.94 per cent, 13.41 per cent, and 11.45 per cent of the corresponding total enrolments. The enrolment of Scheduled Tribes was 6995848 in classes I-V, 1377992 in classes VI-VIII, 492708 in classes IX-X and 92533 in classes XI-XII. These enrolments were 8.07 per cent, 5.07 per cent, 4.29 per cent and 2.69 per cent of the corresponding total enrolments.

4.3 Gross Enrolment Ratio for classes I-V (6-11 years) was 93.63 as against 81.65 in 1978. These ratios for boys and girls were 106.42 and 79.89 respectively. The Gross Enrolment Ratio for classes VI-VIII (11-14 years) was 48.51 as against 37.94 in 1978. These ratios for boys and girls were 60.61 and 35.57 respectively.

4.4. Enrolment in class VIII as percentage of enrolment in class I at the national level was 31.11. These percentages for States and Union Territories ranged from 82.08 for Goa to 15.88 for Andhra Pradesh.

5. *Teachers*

5.1 There were 3692751 teachers in schools as against 2940337 in 1978. There has been an increase in number of teachers to the tune of 25.58 per cent.

Of the 3692751 teachers, 1530145 (41.44%) were in primary schools, 1011049 (27.38%) in upper primary schools, 725935 (19.66%) in secondary schools and 425622 (11.52%) in higher secondary schools. 28.76 per cent teachers in primary schools, 33.27 per cent in upper primary schools, 31.65 per cent in secondary schools and 27.65 per cent in higher secondary schools were women teachers.

The corresponding percentages for S.C. teachers were 11.22, 8.60, 5.84 and 4.82 respectively and for S.T. teachers were 5.99, 4.61 2.51 and 1.32 respectively.

5.2 Of the 3692751 teachers in schools, 1865503 (50.52%) were working at the primary stage, 921612 (24.96%) at the upper primary stage, 682204 (18.47%) at the secondary stage and 223432 (6.05%) at the higher secondary stage. Women teachers constituted 30.56 per cent, 32.18 per cent, 28.12 per cent and 29.33 per cent of teachers working at primary, upper primary, secondary and higher secondary stages respectively. 86.66 per cent teachers at the primary stage, 87.33 per cent at the upper primary stage, 90.23 per cent at the secondary stage and 88.55 per cent at the higher secondary stage were trained.

5.3 The pupil-teacher ratio for the primary stage at the national level was 44. Among the States and Union Territories it ranged from as low as 15 in Sikkim to as high as 61 in Gujarat. The pupil-teacher ratios for the upper primary stage, the secondary stage and the higher secondary stage were 29, 21 and 15 respectively.

5.4 Among the primary schools, 148033 (27.96%) were single-teacher schools and 171389 (32.38%) were two-teacher schools. In the States of Arunachal Pradesh (55.25%). Jammu & Kashmir (58.67%), Karnataka (62.33%), Meghalaya (53.33%), Rajasthan (54.63%) and in Union Territory of Dadra & Nagar Haveli (66.94%), the single teacher schools constituted more than 50 per cent of the primary schools.

6. *Facilities*

6.1 Among the primary schools, 71495 (13.50%) were without building, that is, they were run in thatched huts, tents or in open space. Of the rest, 385120 (72.75%) primary schools had pucca or partly pucca buildings. Among upper primary schools 121707 (87.76%) had pucca or partly pucca buildings and 11280 (8.13%) schools had kachcha buildings.

6.2 Further among the primary schools, 40732 (7.69%), 200077 (37.79%), and 134551 (25.42%) had zero instructional room, one instructional room and two instructional rooms respectively. In case of upper primary schools, 3192 schools had no instructional room and 24909 had one or two instructional rooms.

4

EDUCATIONAL STATISTICS AND OVERVIEW 1950-51 TO 1986-87, 1987-88 AND 1988-89

TABLE 4.1: Number of Educational Institutions 1950-51 to 1986-87

	1950-51	1960-61	1970-71	1980-81	1986-87
Number of Primary schools (000's)	210	330	408	494	537
Number of Middle Schools (000's)	14	50	91	119	137
Number of Secondary/Higher Secondary Schools (000's)	7	17	37	51	69
Numbers of Colleges for General Education (Degree & above level)	542	1082	2285	3421	4151
Colleges for Professional Education (Degree & above level)	182	810	992	1156	1280

TABLE 4.2: Enrolment (1950-51 to 1986-87)

Number of pupils in Classes (Lakh)	1950-51	1960-61	1970-71	1980-81	1986-87
I-V	192	350	570	738	900
	(43.1)	(62.4)	(72.6)	(80.5)	(96.0)
VI-VIII	31	67	133	208	288
	(12.9)	(22.5)	(34.2)	(41.9)	(53.14)
IX-XI/XII	14	33	76	119	176
Number of puplis studying in degree level & above courses (Lakh)	2	6	25	30	34

Note: Figure in parentheses indicate percentage of enrolment to total population in the age groups of 6-10 and 11-14 years.

TABLE 4.3: Enrolment of Girls

(in Lakhs)

Stage		1950-51	1960-61	1970-71	1980-81	1986-87
Primary	(I-V)	54 (28.1)	114 (32.6)	213 (37.4)	285 (8.6)	361 (40.1)
Middle	(VI-VIII)	5	16	39	88	102
Secondary/Hr. Secondary/ 10+2/Intermediate		2	6	19	35	54
Higher Education (Degree & above level)		.20 (10.0)	1 (16.7)	4 (20.0)	8 (26.7)	10 * (29.4)

Note: Figures in parentheses indicate percentage to total entolment (Boys & Girls).
* Relates to 1982-82.

TABLE 4.4: Number of Teachers

(In Thousands)

	1950-51	1960-61	1970-71	1980-81	1986-87
Primary Schools	535	742	1060	1363	1522
Middle Schools	85	345	638	852	979
Secondary/Hr. Secondary Schools	127	296	629	912	1199

TABLE 4.5: Increase in Enrolment and Number of Teachers

(Figs. in Percentage)

Increase in Enrolments	In all areas	In rural areas	Amongst S.Cs.	Amongst S.Ts.
1	2	3	4	5
Primary Stage	26	28.6	49	62
Upper Primary Stage	51	62.3	102	12.6
Secondary Stage	63	80.8	121	124
Higher Secondary Stage	88	127.5	132	185
Increase in the Number of Teachers				
Primary Stage	17			
Upper Primary Stage	24			
Secondary Stage	49			
Higher Secondary Stage	62			

Note: Situation at the time of Fifth All India Educational Survey (1986) *vis-a-vis* Fourth All India Educational Survey (1978).

1987-88

TABLE 4.6: Number of Educational Institutions (1987-88)

Sl. No.	Institution	No. of institutions
1.	Pre-primary/Pre-Basic Schools	14765
2.	Primary/Junior Basic Schools	543677
3.	Middle/Senior Basic Schools	141014
4.	High/Post-Basic Schools	54845
5.	Higher Secondary (Old Pattern)	897
6.	Higher Secondary (10+2 New Pattern)	11115
7.	Intermediate/Junior Colleges	4448
8.	Teacher Training Colleges	485
9.	Medical Colleges (M.B.B.S.)	129
10.	Engineering and Technology Colleges	262
11.	Arts, Science and Commerce Colleges	4329
12.	Research Institutions	49
13.	Board of Intermediate/Secondary Education	34
14.	Institutions of National Importance	10
15.	Institutions deemed as Universities	24
16.	Universities	142
17.	Teacher Training Schools	990
18.	Polytechnic Institutes	782
19.	Technical Industrial Arts & Crafts Schools	3720

TABLE 4.7: Enrolment (1987-88)

Sl. No.	Institution	Boys	Girls	Total
1	2	3	4	5
1.	Pre-Primary/Pre-Basic stage	773613	647096	1420709
2.	Primary stage (classes I-V)	55168885	37774671	92943556
3.	Middle/Senior Basic stage (classes VI-VIII)	19208445	10706054	29914499
4.	High/Post Basic (classes IX-X)	8539698	3912585	12452283
5.	Hr. Secondary (Old Pattern)	107109	23255	130364
6.	Hr. Secondary (New Pattern) (classes XI-XII)	1918382	996849	2915231
7.	Pre-University (One year course)	8091	3164	11255
8.	Pre-Degree/Pre-University (Two years course)	227032	166243	393275
9.	Intermediate/Junior Colleges	1477513	479126	1956639
10.	M.B.B.S	54845	26522	81367

1	2	3	4	5
11.	B. Ed./B.T.	53567	39253	92820
12.	B.E./B.Sc (Engg.)/B. Arch.	175618	15161	190779
13.	B. Com./B. Com. (Hons.)	588703	169675	758378
14.	B. Sc./B.Sc (Hons.)	454616	199474	654090
15.	B.A./B.A. (Hons.)	798314	522272	1320586
16.	M. Com.	54673	10354	65027
17.	M. Sc.	48684	23459	72143
18.	M.A.	122699	75113	197812
19.	Ph. D./D. Sc./D.Phill	20591	10396	30987
20.	Teacher Training School	47244	44861	92105
21.	Polytechnic Institutes	207216	36173	243389
22.	Technical, Industrial, Art and Craft School	240617	73487	314104

TABLE 4.8: Number of Teachers and Percentage of Trained Teachers (1987-88)

Sl. No.		Men	Women	Total	% age
1.	Primary/Junior Basic Schools	1191146	425539	1616685	88.41
2.	Middle/Senior Basic Schools	687051	327111	1014162	90.10
3.	High/Post-Basic Schools	503437	252082	755519	86.49
4.	Higher Secondary School (Old Pattern) (IX-XI)	20910	6034	26944	96.75
5.	Higher Secondary School (New Pattern) (10+2)	330111	130249	460360	92.00

Source: *Selected Educational Statistics 1987-88*, Ministry of Human Resource Development, Department of Education, Government of India, New Delhi, 1989.

1988-89

TABLE 4.9: Number of Universities and Institutions Deemed to be Universities in India *(as on 31-3-1989)*

Sl. No.	Name of University/Institutions	Year of establishment
1	2	3
1.	Calcutta	1857
2.	Bombay	1857
3.	Madras	1857
4.	Allahabad	1887
5.	Banaras Hindu	1916
6.	Mysore	1916

1	2	3
7.	Patna	1917
8.	Osmania	1918
9.	Aligarh Muslim	1921
10.	Lucknow	1921
11.	Delhi	1922
12.	Nagpur	1923
13.	Andhra	1926
14.	Agra	1927
15.	Annamalai	1929
16.	Kerala	1937
17.	Utkal	1943
18.	Dr. Hari Singh Gaur	1946
19.	Rajasthan	1947
20.	Punjab	1947
21.	Gauhati	1948
22.	Kashmir	1949
23.	Roorkee	1949
24.	Poona	1949
25.	M.S. University of Baroda	1949
26.	Karnataka	1949
27.	Gujarat	1950
28.	S.N.D.T. Women's	1951
29.	Vishwa Bharati	1951
30.	Bihar	1952
31.	Sri Venkateshwara	1954
32.	Sardar Patel	1955
33.	Jadavpur	1955
34.	Kurukshetra	1956
35.	Indira Kala Sangeet	1956
36.	Vikram	1957
37.	Gorakhpur	1957
38.	Rani Durgavati	1957
39.	Sampurnanand Sanskrit	1958
40.	Marathwada	1958
41.	G.B. Pant University of Agriculture and Technology	1960
42.	Burdwan	1960
43.	Kalyani	1960
44.	Bhagalpur	1960
45.	Ranchi	1960
46.	K.S. Darbhanga Sanskrit	1961
47.	Punjab Agricultural	1962
48.	Punjabi	1962
49.	Orissa University of Agriculture & Technology	1962
50.	North Bengal	1962
51.	Rabindra Bharati	1962
52.	Magadh	1962

1	2	3
53.	Jodhpur	1962
54.	Sukhadia	1962
55.	Shivaji	1962
56.	Devi Ahilya	1964
57.	Jiwaji	1964
58.	Ravi Shankar	1964
59.	University of Agricultural Sciences	1964
60.	Andhra Pradesh Agriculture	1964
61.	Bangalore	1964
62.	Jawaharlal Nehru Krishi	1964
63.	Dibrugarh	1965
64.	Kanpur	1965
65.	Meerut	1965
66.	Madhurai Kamraj	1965
67.	Saurashtra	1965
68.	South Gujarat	1965
69.	Berhampur	1967
70.	Sambalpur	1967
71.	Gujarat Ayurveda	1968
72.	Jawaharlal Nehru	1968
73.	Mahatma Phule Krishi	1968
74.	Calicut	1968
75.	Awadesh Pratap Singh	1968
76.	Assam Agricultural	1968
77.	Guru Nanak Dev	1969
78.	Jammu	1969
79.	Punjabrao Krishi	1969
80.	Haryana Agriculture	1970
81.	Himachal Pradesh	1970
82.	Barkatullah	1970
83.	Rajendra Agricultural	1970
84.	Tamilnadu Agricultural	1971
85.	Cochin	1971
86.	Kerala Agricultural	1972
87.	Gujarat Agricultural	1972
88.	Konkan Krishi	1972
89.	L.N. Mithila	1972
90.	Marathwada Krishi	1972
91.	Jawaharlal Nehru Technological	1972
92.	North Eastern Hill	1973
93.	Kumaun	1973
94.	Hemvati Nandan Bahuguna	1973
95.	Kashi Vidyapith	1974
96.	Bidhan Chandra Krishi	1974
97.	Hyderabad	1974
98.	N.D. University of Agriculture & Technology	1974

1	2	3
99.	C.S. Azad University of Agriculture & Technology	1974
100.	Avadh	1975
101.	Bundelkhand	1975
102.	Rohilkhand	1975
103.	Maharishi Dayanand	1976
104.	Kakatiya	1976
105.	Nagarjuna	1976
106.	Bhavnagar	1978
107.	Anna	1978
108.	Himachal Pradesh Krishi	1978
109.	Manipur	1980
110.	Gulbarga	1980
111.	Mangalore	1980
112.	Birsa Agricultural	1980
113.	Vidyasagar	1981
114.	Sri Jagannath Sanskrit	1981
115.	Sri Krishnadevaraya	1981
116.	Tamil	1981
117.	Bharathiar	1982
118.	Bharathidasan	1982
119.	Sher-e-Kashmir University of Agricultural Science & Technology	1982
120.	Andhra Pradesh Open	1982
121.	Sri Padmavati Mahila	1983
122.	Amravati	1983
123.	Guru Ghasi Das	1983
124.	Mahatama Gandhi	1983
125.	Mother Teressa	1984
126.	Alagappa	1985
127.	Arunachal	1985
128.	Pondicherry	1985
129.	Goa	1985
130.	Indira Gandhi National Open	1985
131.	Telugu	1985
132.	Dr. Yashwant Singh Parmar	1986
133.	Andhra Pradesh University of Health Sciences	1986
134.	University of Agricultural Sciences, Dharwad	1986
135.	North Gujarat	1986
136.	Indira Gandhi Krishi	1987
137.	Kota Open	1987
138.	Ajmer	1987
139.	Tripura	1987
140.	Kuvempu	1987
141.	Rajasthan Agricultural	1987
142.	Purvanchal	1987
143.	Jamia Millia Islamic	1988
144.	Dr. M.G.R. Medical	1989

1	2	3
	INSTITUTE ESTABLISHED UNDER STATE LEGISLATURE ACT	
145.	Sanjay Gandhi Postgraduate Institute of Medical Scienecs, Lucknow	1983
	INSTITUTION DEEMED TO BE UNIVERSITIES	
1.	Indian Institute of Science, Bangalore	1958
2.	Indian Agriculture Research Institute	1958
3.	Gurukul Kangri Vishwavidyala, Haridwar	1962
4.	Gujarat Vidyapith, Ahmedabad	1963
5.	Tata Institute of Social Sciences, Bombay	1964
6.	Birla Institute of Technology and Science, Pillani	1964
7.	Indian School of Mines, Dhanbad	1967
8.	Central Institute of English and Foreign Languages, Hyderabad	1973
9.	Gandhigram Rural Institute, Gandhigram	1976
10.	School of Planning and Architecture, New Delhi	1979
11.	Dayalbagh Educational Institute, Agra	1981
12.	Sri Sathya Sai Institute of Higher Learning, Prassanthinilyam	1981
13.	Banasthali Vidyapati, Rajasthan	1983
14.	Indian 'Veterinary' Research Institute, Izatnagar	1983
15.	International Institute for Population Sciences, Bombay	1985
16.	Thapar Institute of Engineering & Technology, Patiala	1985
17.	Birla Institute of Technology, Mesra	1986
18.	Rajasthan Vidyapith	1987
19.	Rashtriya Sanskrit Vidyapith, Tirupati	1987
20.	Sri Lal Bahadur Shastri Sanskrit Vidyapith, New Delhi	1987
21.	Tilak Maharashtra Vidyapith, Pune	1987
22.	Sri Avinash Lingam Institute for Home Sciences & Higher Education for Women	1988
23.	Central Institute of Higher Tibatan Studies	1989
24.	National Dairy Reserch Institute	1989
25.	Central Institute of Fisheries Education	1989
26.	Jamia Hamdard	1989
27.	National Museum Institute of History of Arts Conservation & Muscology	1989

TABLE 4.10: Number of Universities, Colleges and Students (1979-80 to 1988-89)

Year	Number of Universities	Number of Colleges	Number of Students
1	2	3	4
1979-80	108+11 institutions deemed to be universities	4,558	26,48,579
1980-81	112+11 institutions deemed to be universities	4,722	27,52,437
1981-82	118+13 institutions deemed to be universities	4,886	29,52,066
1982-83	120+13 institutions deemed to be universities	5,039	31,33,093
1983-84	124+15 institutions deemed to be universities	5,246	33,22,939
1984-85	125+15 institutions deemed to be universities	5,590	34,04,096
1985-86	132+17 institutions deemed to be universities	5,816	35,70,897*
1986-87	136+19 institutions deemed to be universities	6,512	36,81,870*
1987-88	142+22 institutions deemed to be universities	6,647**	38,14,417*
1988-89	144+25 institutions deemed to be universities	6,912**	39,47,922*

Note: The number of colleges given above excludes junior colleges and those offering diploma/certificate courses.

* Estimated

** Provisional

Source: *Annual Report for the Year 1988-89*, University Grants Commission, New Delhi, 1990.

TABLE 4.11:: Growth of Students Enrolment (1969-70 to 1988-89)

Year	Total enrolment	Increase over the preceding year	Percentage Increase
1969-70	17,92,780	2,26,677	14.5
1970-71	19,53,700	1,60,920	9.0
1971-72	20,65,041	1,11,341	5.7
1972-73	21,68,107	1,03,066	5.9
1973-74	22,34,385	66,278	3.1
1974-75	23,66,541	1,32,156	5.9
1975-76	24,26,109	59,568	2.5
1976-77	24,31,563	5,454	0.2
1977-78	25,64,972	1,33,409	5.5
1978-79	26,18,228	53,256	2.1
1979-80	26,48,579	30,351	1.2
1980-81	27,52,437	1,03,858	3.9
1981-82	29,52,066	1,99,629	7.3
1982-83	31,33,093	1,81,027	6.1
1983-84	33,07,649	1,74,556	5.6
1984-85	34,04,096	96,447	2.9
1985-86*	35,70,897	1,66,801	4.9
1986-87*	36,81,870	1,10,973	3.1
1987-88*	38,14,417	1,32,547	3.6
1988-89*	39,47,922	1,33,505	3.5

TABLE 4.12: Sex-wise Distribution of Enrolments: Stage-wise (1980-81 to 1988-89)

Year	Graduate			Postgraduate			Reasearch			Diploma/Certificate			Total		
	T	W	%	T	W	%	T	W	%	T	W	%	T	W	%
1980-81	24,01,485	6,52,808	27.2	2,73,337	77,001	28.2	32,171	8,780	27.3	45,444	9,936	21.9	27,52,437	7,48,525	27.2
1981-82	25,88,759	7,16,249	27.7	2,85,892	81,645	28.6	34,588	9,581	27.7	42,827	9,229	21.5	29,52,006	8,16,704	27.7
1982-83	27,57,893	7,73,342	28.0	2,96,103	86,380	29.2	36,731	10,673	29.1	42,366	9,811	23.2	31,33,093	8,80,156	28.1
1983-84	29,12,487	8,25,409	28.3	3,13,110	93,728	29.9	36,249	10,615	29.3	45,803	10,501	22.9	33,07,619	9,40,253	28.4
1984-85	29,99,621	8,71,571	29.1	3,22,541	98,415	30.5	38,160	11,332	29.7	43,774	10,821	24.7	34,04,096	9,92,139	29.1
1985-86*	31,42,389	9,29,461	29.6	3,39,235	1,04,803	30.9	39,200	12,703	32.3	49,993	11,645	23.3	35,70,897	10,58,612	29.6
1986-87*	32,40,046	9,88,017	30.5	3,49,778	1,11,405	31.5	40,500	13,504	33.3	51,546	12,378	24.0	36,81,870	11,25,304	30.6
1987-88*	33,56,687	10,49,274	31.3	3,62,370	1,18,312	32.7	41,958	14,341	34.2	53,402	13,146	24.6	38,14,417	11,95,073	31.3
1988-89*	34,74,171	10,98,809	31.6	3,75,053	1,23,898	33.0	43,427	15,018	34.6	55,271	13,766	24.9	39,47,922	12,51,491	31.7

* Estimated   T = Total enrolment   W = Women enrolment   N.A. = Not available

TABLE 4.13: Distribution of Student Enrolment : Sex-wise and Faculty-wise (1980-81 to 1988-89)

Year	Arts			Science			Commerce		
	T	W	%	T	W	%	T	W	%
1980-81	11,14,417	4,20,276	37.7	5,33,859	1,53,868	28.8	5,54,253	88,067	15.9
1981-82	11,90,177	4,54,990	38.2	5,78,766	1,65,666	28.6	6,28,031	1,04,964	16.7
1982-83	12,59,587	4,87,620	38.7	6,23,545	1,79,650	28.8	6,69,813	1,16,837	17.4
1983-84	13,38,106	5,17,017	38.6	6,53,092	1,89,685	29.0	7,03,638	1,31,379	18.7
1984-85	13,72,227	5,40,686	39.4	6,69,563	2,00,632	30.0	7,38,506	1,42,222	19.3
1985-86*	14,39,071	5,81,813	40.4	7,03,467	2,14,581	30.5	7,67,743	1,46,724	19.1
1986-87*	14,83,794	6,18,467	41.6	7,25,328	2,28,099	31.4	7,91,602	1,55,967	19.7
1987-88*	15,37,210	6,56,812	42.7	7,51,440	2,42,241	32.2	8,20,100	1,65,637	20.2
1988-89*	15,91,012	6,87,069	43.2	7,77,740	2,53,427	32.6	8,48,804	1,73,957	20.5

(Contd.)

TABLE 4.13 (*Contd.*)

	Education			Engg/Tech.			Medicine		
	T	W	%	T	W	%	T	W	%
1980-81	71,204	33,708	47.3	1,28,937	4,949	3.8	1,10,020	26,797	24.4
1981-82	71,168	34,383	48.3	1,30,189	5,866	4.5	1,13,794	29,792	26.2
1982-83	74,167	34,893	47.0	1,42,440	7,173	5.0	1,13,902	31,648	27.8
1983-84	74,679	35,337	47.3	1,53,131	8,469	5.5	1,18,989	33,676	28.3
1984-85	76,522	36,555	47.8	1,59,046	10,052	6.3	1,18,890	35,190	29.6
1985-86*	82,131	40,227	49.0	1,64,261	9,634	5.9	1,28,552	37,898	29.5
1986-87*	84,683	42,762	50.5	1,69,366	10,240	6.0	1,32,547	40,286	30.4
1987-88*	87,732	45,413	51.8	1,75,463	10,874	6.2	1,37,319	42,784	31.1
1988-89*	90,803	47,557	52.4	1,81,604	11,263	6.2	1,42,125	45,054	31.7

* Estimated

TABLE 4.14: Distribution of Student Enrolment : Sex-wise and Faculty-wise (1980-81 to 1988-89)

Year	Agriculture			Vet. Science			Law			Diploma/Certificate			Total		
	T	W	%	T	W	%	T	W	%	T	W	%	T	W	%
1980-81	39,231	1,311	3.3	7,648	249	3.3	1,74,374	11,948	6.9	18,494	7,352	39.8	27,52,437	7,48,525	27.2
1981-82	39,318	1,390	3.5	8,173	352	4.3	1,74,445	12,309	7.1	18,005	6,992	38.8	29,52,066	8,16,704	27.7
1982-83	39,425 **	1,595	4.0	8,797	424	4.8	1,83,153	13,576	7.4	18,264	6,740	36.9	31,33,093	8,80,156	28.1
1983-84	41,588	1,719	4.1	9,268	470	5.1	1,94,555	15,156	7.8	20,603	7,345	35.7	33,07,649	9,40,253	28.4
1984-85	41,741	2,045	4.9	9,413	50	5.4	1,95,708	15,745	8.0	22,430	8,506	37.9	34,04,096	9,92,139	29.1
1985-86*	46,422	2,011	4.3	10,713	529	4.9	2,07,112	16,726	8.1	21,425	8,469	39.5	35,70,897	10,58,612	29.6
1986-87*	47,864	2,138	4.5.	11,046	563	5.1	2,13,549	17,780	8.3	22,091	9,002	40.7	36,81,870	11,25,304	30.6
1987-88*	49,587	2,271	4.6	11,443	599	5.2	2,21,236	18,882	8.5	22,887	9,560	41.8	38,14,417	11,95,073	31.3
1988-89*	51,323	2,503	4.9	11,844	625	5.3	2,28,979	20,024	8.7	23,668	10,012	42.3	39,47,922	12,51,491	31.7

* Estimated

TABLE 4.15: Women Higher Education: Women's Colleges (1979-80 to 1988-89)

Year	Number of Colleges	Number of Colleges for women only
1979-80	4,558	577
1980-81	4,722	609
1981-82	4,886	624
1982-83	5,039	647
1983-84	5,246	676
1984-85	5,590	712
1985-86	5,816	741*
1986-87	6,512	771*
1987-88	6,647 **	802*
1988-89	6,912 **	824*

* Estimated

** Provisional

Source: *Annual Report for the Year 1988-89*, University Grants Commission, New Delhi, 1990.

TABLE 4.16: Women Higher Education: Number of Women for Hundred Men (1950-51 to 1988-89)

Year	Total Women Enrolment (In Thousands)	Number of Women Per Hundred Men
1950-51	40	14
1955-56	84	17
1960-61	150	23
1965-66	271	24
1975-76	595	33
1981-82	817	38
1982-82	880	39
1983-84	940	40
1984-85	992	41
1985-86*	1059	42
1986-87*	1125	44
1987-88*	1195	46
1988-89*	1251	46

* Estimated

Source: *Annual Report for the Year 1988-89*, University Grants Commission, New Delhi, 1990.

TABLE 4.17: Correspondence Courses

Enrolment in Correspondence Courses offered by University during 1988-89

State/University	Title of the Correspondence Course	Enrolment		
		Men	Women	Total
1	2	3	4	5
ANDHRA PRADESH				
Andhra	1. B.Ed.	327	185	512
	2. B.A.	14035	7603	21638
	3. B.Com.	3208	758	3966
	4. M.A.	1484	852	2336
	5. M.Com.	726	280	1006
	6. B.Sc.	252	24	276
	7. P.G. Diploma in Cooperation and Rural Studies	84	5	89
	8. M.Ed.	80	20	100
	9. Introductory Courses@	561	199	760
Andhra Pradesh Open	1. B.A./B.Sc./B.Com. (Ist Year)	11506	5341	16847
	2. B.Sc. (II & III year)	NA	NA	1402
	3. B.Com. (II & III year)	NA	NA	2044
	4. B.A. (II & III year)	NA	NA	12684
	5. Bachelor of Library and Information Science*	40	205	245
	6. P.G. Diploma in Public Accounts*	2147	267	2414
	7. P.G. Diploma in Public Relation*	623	100	723
	8. C.P.F.N. (Cert. Programme in Food and Nutrition)	642	434	1076
J.N. Technological	1. B.Tech*	439	21	460
Osmania	1. B.A.	337	599	936
	2. B.Com.	658	641	1299
	3. B.Ed.	373	128	501
	4. M.Ed.	78	24	102
	5. M.A.	110	150	260
	6. M.Com.	703	543	1246
	7. P.G. Diploma in Mathematics	83	26	109
Sri Venkateswara	1. B.A.	28	21	49
	2. B.Com.	9	12	21
	3. M.A.	130	61	191
	4. M.Sc.	326	56	382
	5. M.Com.	246	57	303

1	2	3	4	5
	6. B.Ed.	268	137	405
	7. Junior Diploma in Linguitics*	5	9	14
	8. Diploma in Public Administration*	55	8	63
	9. Cert. in Library Sc.	494	109	603
	10. Senior Dip. in Linguistics*	12	5	17
Central Instt. of English & Foreign Languages**	1. M.A.	12	9	21
	2. P.G. Certificate in the Teaching of English	412	359	771
	3. P.G. Diploma in the Teaching English	115	89	204
BIHAR				
Patna	1. Inter Arts	499	325	824
	2. Inter Com.	251	11	262
	3. B.A.	979	385	1364
	4. B.Com.	381	5	386
	5. B.A.(Hons.)	276	87	363
	6. B.Com.(Hons.)	58	5	63
Ranchi	Information not available			
GUJARAT				
Gujarat Vidyapeeth** (1987-88 Information)	1. M.A. in Gandhian Thought*	41	4	45
	2. M.Ed.	86	21	107
HARYANA				
Kurukshetra	1. B.A.	1130	76	1206
	2. M.Com.	259	115	374
	3. P.G. Diploma in Tourism and Hotel Management	345	30	375
	4. One Year pre-degree course	555	449	1004
Maharshi Dayanand	Information not available			
HIMACHAL PRADESH				
Himachal Pradesh	1. B.A.	283	605	888
	2. M.A.	6601	2054	8655
	3. M.Com.	3071	833	3904
	4. M.Ed.	4253	1322	5575
	5. XI class	118	13	131
	6. XII class	98	6	104

1	2	3	4	5
JAMMU & KASHMIR				
Jammu	1. B.A.	25	15	40
	2. B.Com.	12	1	13
	3. M.Com.	72	99	171
	4. LL.B.	295	32	327
	5. B.Ed.	324	157	481
	6. Certificate Course in Urdu	7	2	9
	7. Certificate Course in English Improvement	15	7	22
Kashmir	1. B.A.	19	3	22
	2. B.Com.			
	3. B.Ed.	248	115	363
	4. LL.B.+	181	22	203
	5. Certificate Course in Hindi	10	14	24
	+ Excluding IV semester enrolment which is not available			
	6. Certificate Course in Urdu	78	11	89
	7. Certificate Course in Library and Information Science	14	22	36
	8. M.A.	69	34	103
	9. M.Com.	33	3	36
KARNATAKA				
Bangalore	1. B.A.	214	198	412
Mysore	1. B.A.	761	680	1441
	2. B.Com.	540	212	752
	3. M.A.	4741	1673	6414
	4. Certificate Course in Kannada for Non-Kannada speakers, through English, Urdu & Hindi Media	32	26	58
	5. Post Pre-University Diploma Course in Kannada	82	36	118
	6. P.G. Diploma Course in English	159	94	253
	7. P.G. Diploma Course in Journalism	237	44	281
	Open University System			
	1. B.A.*	1776	1274	3050
	2. B.Com.*	289	60	349
	3. M.A.*	3182	1305	4487

1	2	3	4	5
KERALA				
Calicut	1. Pre-Degree	70	24	94
	2. B.A.	326	76	402
	3. B.Com.	63	37	100
	4. M.A.	165	49	214
	5. B.A. Under open university system	2503	625	3128
	6. B.Com. Under open university system	1495	374	1869
Kerala	1. Pre-degree	324	72	396
	2. B.A.	722	504	1226
	3. B.Com.	349	166	515
	4. M.A.	1074	605	1679
	5. M.Com.	456	115	571
MADHYA PRADESH				
Bhopal	1. B.A.	154	84	238
	2. B.Com.	58	7	65
MAHARASHTRA				
Bombay	1. B.A.	1906	1808	3714
	2. B.Com.	2089	1152	3241
	3. Diploma in Financial Management	424	106	530
	4. Diploma in Operation Research for Management	95	12	107
Poona	1. B.A.	323	160	483
	2. B.Com.	352	108	460
Shivaji	B.Ed.	55	21	76
S.N.D.T. Women's	1. B.A.	—	7785	7785
	2. B.Com.	—	295	295
	3. Improve Your English	—	25	25
	4. Cert. in Family Saving & Investment	—	23	23
Tilak Maharashtra Vidyapeeth**	1. B.A. (Visharad)	2854	830	3684
ORISSA				
Utkal (1987-88 Information)	1. B.A.	1670	1051	2721
	2. B.Com.	179	8	187
	3. B.Ed.	589	411	1000
Berhampur	B.Ed.	302	113	415

1	2	3	4	5
PUNJAB				
Punjab (1987-88 Information)	1. B.A.	4027	609	4636
	2. B.Com.	639	77	716
	3. M.A.	1608	1523	3131
	4. Diploma in office organisation and procedures	89	21	110
	5. Dip. in Statistics	126	51	177
	6. Dip. in Population Education	40	30	70
Punjabi	1. Punjabi Praveshika	4	5	9
	2. Gyani	117	114	231
	3. B.Com.	153	16	169
	4. B.A.	1037	200	1237
	5. M.A.	2155	1495	3650
	6. M.B.A.*	134	—	134
	7. M.Phil	28	45	73
	8. M.Ed.	167	133	300
	9. Dip. Course in Library	188	320	508
	10. P.G. Dip. Course in mngt. of Public Enterprises	190	22	212
	11. P.G.Dip. Course in Public Relations and Advertising	167	13	180
	12. Dip. Course in Personnel Mngt. and Industrial Relations*	167	4	171
	13. Dip. in International Marketing*	19	1	20
	14. Dip. in Marketing Management*	114	—	114
	15. Dip. in Material Management*	177	—	177
	16. Dip. in Project Management*	36	—	36
	17. Dip. in Production Management*	65	—	65
	18. Dip. in Banking*	21	—	21
	19. Dip. in Divinity	130	26	·156
RAJASTHAN				
Kota Open (1987-88 Information)	1. B.A.	NA	NA	45
	2. B.Com.	NA	NA	30
	3. M.A.	NA	NA	2,435
	4. M.Com.	NA	NA	1,695
	5. LL.B. Open University System	NA	NA	14
	6. Dip. in Labour Law, Labour Welfare and personnel Management	NA	NA	NA
	7. P.G. Dip. in Journalism	NA	NA	NA
	8. Certificate in Library Sc.	NA	NA	NA
	9. B.A.	NA	NA	2131
	10. B.Com.	NA	NA	370

1	2	3	4	5
	11. B.Ed.	NA	NA	9000
	12. B.J.M.C.	NA	NA	997
	13. Dip. in Library Sc.	NA	NA	3829
	14. Dip. in Hotal Management and Tourism	NA	NA	1000
	15. Dip. in Mngt. (Module 1) (IGNOU)	NA	NA	1000
TAMIL NADU				
Alagappa	1. Dip. in Computer and Software Application	277	45	322
Annamalai	1. Foundation Course	457	232	689
	2. B.A.	1275	1325	2600
	3. B.Litt.	835	771	1606
	4. B.Sc.(Maths)	445	284	729
	5. (I) Bachalor of Academic Laws	445	22	467
	(II) B.G.L.	347	12	359
	6. B.Com.	1558	779	2337
	7. M.A.	3077	2448	5525
	8. M.Sc.	3187	1311	4498
	9. M.Com.	1843	476	2319
	10. B.Ed.	6839	6639	13478
	11. M.Ed.	3196	2395	5591
	12. P.G. Dip. in Business Administration	735	5	740
	13. P.G. Dip. in Marketing Management	774	23	797
	14. P.G. Dip. in Production Management	1238	77	1315
	15. P.G. Dip. in Personnel Management	1345	75	1420
	16. P.G. Dip. in Material Management	483	17	500
	17. P.G. Dip in Financial Management	285	16	301
	18. Dip. in Company Law with Banking Law and Practice	64	2	66
	19. Dip. in Labour Law	681	16	697
	20. Dip. in Management Law	33	2	35
	21. Dip. in Taxation Law	89	9	98
	22. Dip. in Criminology, Admn., Criminal Justice	53	4	57
	23. Dip. in Insurance Law	4	40	44

1	2	3	4	5
	Job Oriented Courses			
	1. Dip. in Chemical Process Instrumentation and Control	1557	23	1580
	2. Dip. in Concrete Tech. and Design of Concrete Structure	599	6	605
	3. Dip. in Maintenance Mngt.	171	4	175
	4. Cert. in Automobile Technology	306	—	306
Madras	1. B.A. (Including B.Litt.)	9968	8656	18624
	2. B.A. (Including B.Litt.) (Open University System)	17285	8226	25511
	3. B.Com.	9422	5627	15049
	4. B.Com. (Open Univ. System)	6001	1231	7232
	5. B.Ed.	2055	2447	4502
	6. B.Sc. (Maths.)	3010	1519	4529
	7. B.Sc. (Maths.) (Open University)	1239	333	1572
	8. M.A.	10851	6825	17676
	9. M.Com	4010	1990	6000
	10. M.Ed.	600	437	1037
	11. M.Lab. & Information Sc.	240	113	353
	12. Certificate Course in lab. & Information Sc.	507	104	611
	13. Dip. in Geography	43	37	80
	14. B.Lib. & Information Sc.	295	227	522
	15. Dip. in Labour Law	551	40	591
	16. Dip. in Taxation	268	25	293
	17. Dip. in Insurance Law	44	10	54
	18. Dip. in Mercantile Law	36	7	43
	19. Dip. in Indian Constitution Law	29	2	31
	20. Dip. in Criminal Law	54	6	60
Madurai Kamraj	1. B.A.	8833	6643	15476
	2. B.Sc. (Maths.)	971	546	1517
	3. B.Com.	4028	2573	6601
	4. B.B.G.L.	1284	161	1445
	5. M.A.	5306	2754	8060
	6. M.Com.	2418	984	3402
	7. B.Ed.	671	696	1367
	8. M.Ed.	555	567	1122
	9. Cert. in Journalism & Mass Communication	338	101	439

1	2	3	4	5
	Open University Course			
	i. Introductory Course	555	212	767
	ii. Pre-Foundation Course	1043	350	1393
	iii. Foundation Course	1642	1164	2806
	iv. Cert. in Child Health & Family Welfare	24	46	70
	v. Pre-University	118	75	193
UTTAR PRADESH				
Allahabad	1. B.A.	1981	551	2532
	2. B.Com.	394	13	407
Meerut	1. B.A.	145	98	243
	2. B.Com.	27	19	46
	3. M.A.	927	614	1541
DELHI				
Delhi	1. B.A.(Pass)	9871	11147	21018
	2. B.Com.(Pass)	7203	2283	9486
	3. B.Com.(Hons)	952	268	1220
	4. M.A.	330	851	1181
	5. M.Com.	301	439	740
	6. Special Courses in (Hindi, Pol.Sc.)*	22	15	37
	7. B.A.(Hons) English	74	134	208
Indira Gandhi National Open University	1. B.A.	6843	2103	8946
	2. B.Com.	3157	420	3577
	3. Dip. in Distance Education	792	301	1093
	4. Dip. in Management	5045	180	5225
	5. Dip. in Creative Writing	221	89	310
	6. Cert. in Rural Development	NA	NA	287
	7. Cert. Prog. in Food & Nutrition	945	1603	2548

Note: 1. * 1987-88 data.
2. ** Instituion deemed to be University.
3. NA Not Available.

@ Introductary course to prepare the candidates for entrance examination for liberali[illegible] admission into B.A./B.Com courses without any formal academic qualifications.

4.18 OVERVIEW: NATIONAL POLICY ON EDUCATION (1986) AND AFTER

The most significant achievement has been the adoption by the Parliament of the National Policy on Education (NPE) in May 1986, after a nation-wide debate. This was followed up by the formulation of a comprehensive Programme of Action (POA), based on examination of every aspect of the Policy by 23 Task Forces. The Programme of Action was adopted by the Parliament in August, 1986.

The National Policy on Education, 1986 was different from the earlier Policy of 1968 in the following respects:

- Adoption of a comprehensive Programme of Action as mentioned above.
- Stipulation of specific targets like for Universalisation of Elementary Education, Adult Education, Vocationalisation, etc.
- Prescription of Non-formal Education as a system.
- Overt call for employment orientation of Education, as distinct from employability of students adverted to by the earlier Policy.
- Presentation of Education in the Perspective of Human Resource Development.
- Prescription of concrete steps in respect of education for women's equality.
- Offer of special programmes for SCs/STs, minorities, handicapped and educationally backward classes.
- Offer of a programme for management of education.
- Delineation of programmes for the rural population.
- Stipulation of a National System of Education based on national curricular framework.
- Call for delinking of jobs from degrees.

NPE Review Committee, 1990

In pursuance of its Election Manifesto to review NPE, the National Front Government, announced on 7th May, 1990, the constitution of a Review Committee of 17 members, under the Chairmanship of Acharya Ramamurti. The NPE Review Committee issued a Perspective Paper on Education entitled, *Towards an Enlightened and Humane Society* that contains ideas and thoughts that the Committee could bring to bear on the problems of education as perceived by it.

The reasons that influenced the decision of the Government to appoint the Committee as given in its resolution are given below:

one, the Right to Work which is proposed to be enshrined in the Constitution:

two, the unity and integrity of the nation that are seriously threatened;
three, the improvement of the inner man in India.

The Committee in its 409 page report presented to the Parliament in January 1991 has envisaged the following modalities of educational reforms:

- Opening up and Non-formalising the School System.
- Common School System.
- Empowering People for Work.
- Examination Reform.
- Fresh Language Survey.
- Removal of Regional Disparities.
- Decentralised School Management.
- A Significant Increase in Public Expenditure – At least 6 per cent of GNP.

PART II

OTHER FACETS OF EDUCATION

5

COLLEGE/UNIVERSITY BUILDINGS
UGC Recommendations for Different Types of Buildings, (1986)[1]

5.1 GUIDELINES FOR APPROVAL OF VARIOUS BUILDING PROJECTS

I. Building Committee – Its Composition and Functions

1. Each University/deemed to be University should be a Building Committee consisting of Vice-Chancellor or his nominee not below the rank of a Professor, representative of the CPWD/PWD of the level of the Superintending Engineer, a representative of the Planning Board Finance Officer, University Engineer, University Architect/Government Architect and Registrar as member Secretary. In the case of Colleges the Building Committee should have a representative each of the Management and the local P.W.D. not below the rank of Assistant Engineer, Government Architect if available in the city and the Principal.
2. The composition of the Building Committee should be intimated to the University Grants Commission immediately after it is constituted.
3. The Building Committee should be responsible for finalising the plans and estimates of the various building projects approved by the Commission and for ensuring completion of the buildings in accordance with the accepted plans and estimates and proper

1. Published by University Grants Commission, New Delhi, 1986.

utilisation of the grants received from the University Grants Commission and the State Government/University/College.

II. Procedure for Preparation of Plans and Estimates

1. The plans and estimates of the building projects approved by the Commission should conform to the norms laid-down by the Commission for each type of buildings. Provision for ramps and toilets on the ground floor may be made in the buildings, where necessary, to enable use of buildings for physically handicapped persons.
2. Provision for services, (internal water supply and sanitary installation, internal electrification and external services), contingency, Architect fees etc. may be made in the estimates as per norms laid down by the Commission for various buildings.
3. While sending a proposal for the building project the institution should indicate the code number of the building and give a certificate that the plans and estimates are in conformity with the norms as suggested by the Commission for this particular type of the building (code number). Justification of variation, if any, may be given by the Institution.
4. In such cases where the building is proposed to be constructed on an existing building a certificate from the Building Committee that the structure on which the construction is proposed to be done is under undisputed ownership and under the possession of the University/College and structurally sound to bear the load of another building is required.
5. The University/Institution may adopt one of the following alternatives in order to priority for completing the building projects approved by the Commission including their planning, architectural design, structural design, preparation of estimates and construction work, but it may be ensured that not more than two agencies are involved in the planning and execution of work:

   (i) The work relating to planning, architectural design, structural design, preparation of estimates and execution of construction work may be assigned to the CPWD or the State PWD as the case may be in toto as deposit work.

   (ii) The architects may prepare the architectural design and the rest of the job, viz., structural design, preparation of estimates and execution of work may be entrusted to the CPWD/State P.W.D./University/College.

(iii) The work relating to planning, architectural design, structural design and preparation of estimates may be entrusted to a firm of architects and other government and semi-government agencies and the executing of work may be entrusted to the University/College.

The services of a firm of architects and other government and Semi-government agencies may be utilised for planning architectural design, structural design, preparation of estimates and supervision of the construction work.

6. It may be noted that Architect engaged by the University/College should be registered with the Council of Architecture.
7. The Architect/Engineer while preparing the estimates should see that these are based on the specifications and schedule of the rates of the C.P.W.D./P.W.D. Estimates should indicate the relevant item number in the C.P.W.D./P.W.D. schedule on the basis of which estimates have been prepared and the registered Architect/Engineer who prepared the estimates should certify that they are in accordance with the schedule of rates of the C.P.W.D/P.W.D. concerned.
8. The plans and estimates prepared by the Architect/Engineer according to the norms suggested by the University Grants Commission for a particular type of the building should be got scrutinised by the University/College from the C.P.W.D./ P.W.D. as the case may be.
9. After this scrutiny has been done and necessary modifications made, the plans and estimates for a building construction project should be approved by the Building Committee of the educational institution and in the meeting concerned the C.P.W.D./P.W.D. Engineer member should invariably be present. An appropriate certificate from the Head of the institution (Registrar or Principal) to the effect that preliminary plans and estimates have been scrutinised by the C.P.W.D./P.W.D., and these have been approved by the Building Committee at a meeting in which the representative of the C.P.W.D./P.W.D. was present and that these are in accordance with the norms laid down by the University Grants Commission, should be sent to the UGC alongwith the proposal.

10. On the basis of the above certificate, the University Grants Commission will process the proposal and convey its approval "in principle" or otherwise to the Institution. In case the proposal is approved by the Commission, the scrutiny, charges paid by the institution to the C.P.W.D./P.W.D. will be borne by the University Grants Commission on the usual percentage approved by the C.P.W.D./P.W.D.
11. On receipt of the approval "in principle" from the University Grants Commission, the University/College may then proceed with the preparation of the detailed estimates, and invite tenders on item-rate basis. The tender information should contain the following:

    (a) Value of the estimates put to tender
    (b) Number of tenders received
    (c) Value of the lowest tender
    (d) Value of the tender accepted and
    (e) Specific reasons if the lowest tender has not been accepted

    This information is not required in case the construction work is undertaken by the C.P.W.D./P.W.D. as deposit work. The detailed estimates, and the acceptance of tender may be finalised with the approval of the building Committee in the meeting where the representative of the C.P.W.D./P.W.D. should invariably be present. This should also be certified by the Head of the Institution concerned.
12. On receipt of tender information and also a certificate from the Registered Architect/Engineer responsible for the execution of the work duly countersigned by the Registrar/Principal to the effect that the University/College agrees to abide by the terms and conditions laid down by the Commission and also that they are in a position to undertake the construction work, the University Grants Commission may convey the final approval, approved cost and the University Grants Commission share and also release 25 per cent of the approved grant as University Grants Commission share as the first instalment of the grant. In case where the building is being constructed by the C.P.W.D./ P.W.D. concerned as deposit work, adequate instalment of grant will be released. Subsequent instalments of grants will be released on receipt of progress report of work and expenditure in the prescribed proforma (Annexure).

13. The final instalment of approved grants as University Grants Commission share will be released after the building has been completed in all respects and on receipt of an exact statement of final cost and a completion certificate in the following form duly signed by the agency who prepared the plans and estimates and supervised the construction work or the C.P.W.D./P.W.D. as the case may be and duly countersigned by the Registrar/Principal.

    "Certified that the building approved by the commission has been constructed in accordance with the design, specification and estimates accepted by the University Grants Commission on the recommendation of the Building Committee of the University/College and found complete. This site has also been properly cleared."

    The above certificate should also indicate the total completion cost of the building. This would be subject to adjustment if any on receipt of statement of accounts duly audited indicating details of expenditure on each item viz. civil cost, services, architect fees etc. along with utilisation certificate for the total expenditure from the statutory auditors of the University/Chartered Accountant/Government Auditor of the college in the prescribed form.
14. While calculating the total approved expenditure of a building project, the actual expenditure on various items such as civil cost, electrification, sanitation etc. as certified by the auditors or the amount approved by the commission as per norms for that item whichever is less will be admissible.
15. The University/College will have to complete the approved building in accordance with the plans accepted by Building Committee and the Commission and within the period stipulated in the estimates. In case the expenditure on completion of building exceeds the amount approved by the Commission, the excess expenditure will have to be met by the University/College from their own resources.

ANNEXURE

Progress Report for the Release of Fund

.... University/College

1. Name of the Scheme
2. No. and date of the Sanction letter of UGC approving the scheme
3. Total Cost approved

   (a) Share of UGC
   (b) Share of University/College/State Government

4. Total tendered cost accepted
5. Total amount received

   (a) From UGC and
   (b) From University/College/State Government against 3 above

6. Total expenditure actually incurred i.e. Bills paid for work done or supplies received

   (a) Against UGC share
   (b) Against University/College/State Government Share

7. Balance, if any, in hand from amount received

   (a) from UGC share
   (b) from University/College/State Govt. Share

8. Amount required to be released to meet expenditure likely to be incurred in the next three/six months
9. In the case of a project involving construction work, a brief description of the construction so far accomplished may be given, and it may be certified that the construction is being carried on in accordance with the plan accepted by the Commission
10. Deviation, if any, should be clearly indicated. Its impact on the cost of construction should be specified.

Certified that the grant has been utilised for the purpose for which it was sanctioned and in accordance with the terms and conditions attached to the grant

If as a result of check or audit objections some irregularity is noticed at a later stage, action will be taken to refund, adjust or regularise the objected amount

Engineer/Architect Registrar (University)

Principal (College)

NB. This may not include any amount relating to orders placed or likely to be placed, commitments entered into or amount earmarked for specific items likely to be obtained in future.

Consultation Fees for Project

1. Projects coming under this purview are basically buildings allied services and development works in University/College Camps. Therefore, the basis for the preparation of preliminary estimates, detailed estimates, tender documents etc. shall be as per the practice adopted in C.P.W.D. or local P.W.D. The provisions for sanitary installations, water supply, electrical installation, furniture etc. shall be as prescribed in Annexure II. In the estimates a provision of 3 per cent on the cost of buildings & services shall be made as Contingencies. In revised estimates on provision shall be made for Contingencies since the revised estimates will be on the basis of actual cost which will include the cost of plant/machinery, equipment and materials for all services. The cost shall not include salaries of Site Staff. Cost of land, payment to Local authorities and Telephone equipments etc. No changes involving financial considerations shall be made without authorisation from the client.
2. The University or College authorities normally go in for consultancy for their Projects either (a) for Total Services to be provided by the Consultant or (b) for Total Services to be provided by one or more Consultants/Construction agencies. The selection of such Consultants shall be on the basis of merit and not on the basis of quotation as it will affect quality adversely. No security deposit is required from the consultants.

   The Fees for these Works shall be as fallows:

a. *Total Services*

Total services include preparations of preliminary/conceptual drawings, preparation of preliminary estimates/feasibility reports/submission to the local bodies, preparation of detailed Architectural Drawings, structural designs, services planning, detailed estimates and tenders, specification and local periodical visits to the 100 Universities by the Consultants to the Site. The total fees payable for all the above work shall be five per cent of the executed cost of the Project.

b. *Partial Services*

In certain cases the University/College Authorities may have their own "In-House" facilities or like to engage Consultants to provide partial services as follows:

(i) *Architectural Planning*

Preparation of preliminary/conceptual drawings, layout plan preliminary estimates, brief specifications, submission to the local bodies preparation of detailed. Architectural working drawings, large details and detailed specifications for execution. Fees payable for these works shall be 2.5 per cent of the cost of the Project.

(ii) *Architectural Supervision*

Periodical Site Visits and coordination with other Consultants/Agencies – Fees payable is 1 per cent.

(iii) *Structural Planning*

The consultant shall provide the structural including calculations and drawings for the execution and the Fees payable for this service is 1 per cent of the executed cost 1.0 per cent.

(iv) *Services Planning*

This includes sanitary installations, water supply

electrical installations, Air-Conditioning and preparation of necessary drawings for all these services.

Fees payable for these services shall be 2.5% of the cost of each service to a ceiling of 0.75% of the total executed cost including the planning of all the services if done by once Agency. 0.75%

(v) *Detailed Estimates*

Detailed estimates including Tender documents and processing of Tenders. Fees payable shall be 0.75% of the cost of the project. 0.75%

(vi) *Project Management*

In case the responsibility for execution and Project management of the scheme is estimated to the Consultant, the additional fees payable shall be 2.5% of the executed cost for all Project original or repetitive and also for total or partial works, irrespective of the nature and cost of the project, the daily construction supervision will include one qualified part-time graduate at site, part-time secretarial services for laboratory tests, maintenance of Stores and Accounts progress report; and project management and Monitoring. 2.7%

c. *Repetitive Project*

The term Repetitive Projects refers to any construction where more than one building or one block is constructed based on the same design and drawings. The fee payable in this case shall be:–

(1) For the first building or multi-storeyed block (Residential or Non-residential), Full Fees are mentioned in above (a) or (b) depending on the extent of services provided by the Consultant.
(2) For subsequent buildings or Multistoreyed block repeated; the fees payable shall be 50% of what is mentioned in above (a) or (b) depending on the services provided by the Consultant except that 100% fee is payable for the Project Management and Supervision of construction work, if entrusted to them. When a type

design is repeated beyond 250 Dwelling Units without the involvement of the original consultant a royalty of 0.5% per D.U. shall be paid.

Mode of Payment

The payment in instalments will be made to the Architect, based on the total Architectural Fees due, calculated on the latest cost of construction at that stage. The percentage of Fees are mentioned separately for total and partial services:

	Based on latest cost		*Percentage of fee for*	
			Total Services	*Partial Services*
1			2	3
Preliminary Stage				
1. Feasibility Report and conceptual design	Preliminary		10	15
2. Final approved design, brief specification and preliminary estimates	"		15	20
3. Submission to local bodies for approval	"		5	5
		Total:	30	40
Detailed Stage				
4. Architectural working drawings and essential details	Detailed estimates		10	20
5. Structural & Services designs Preliminary & Detailed	"		15	25
6. Detailed estimates, specifications and Tender documents	"		10	15
		Total:	65	100
Construction Stage				
7. Tenders, Call, Analysis and recommendations. Award of works and issue of Set of construction drawings	Awarded Cost		10	
8. Construction progress: Payment related to contractors Bill	"		20	
9. Completion of Project	"		5	
10. Submission of 'As Built'	Executed Cost		Balance	
		Total:	100	

Out of Pocket Expenses

These should be reimbursed to the Consultant for:

a. Extra copies of drawings (beyond normal 8 copies), soil and water investigation, land surveys and levels, Models, perspectives and presentation drawings.
b. *For Outstation works over 100 km*
   Travel expenses: Air or Rail (A.C.) fare, Hotel Charges, Local conveyance, Daily Allowance subject to a maximum of .5% of the total cost of the project.
c. The Consultant is entitled to be compensated over and above the recommended fees in case there is a delay of more than One Year over the stipulated period of completion of the Project.

Recommended Norms

Hostels (Up to four storeys)

1. *Orientation*

The blocks should be so oriented that the living rooms get sufficient day light, natural ventilation and better comfort conditions. In this reference, a reference be made to IS-76626 (Part-I)-1974, IS-2440-75 and IS-3362-77.
The following climatological factors may also be taken into account for better orientation and internal environment:

- Solar radiation and temperature
- Rainfall
- Wind direction
- Humidity

2. *Living Room*

The optimum space requirements for a living room in a hostel for graduate level will have the following parameters:

Single seated accommodation 8-9 sq. mt.
Double seated accommodation 7.5 to 8 sq. mt.

Triple seated accommodation 7-7.5 sq. mt.
The area of room for post graduate level will not exceed 10 sq. mt.

3. *Kitchen & Dining*

The dining area shall be determined at the rate of 1 sq. ft. per diner. The space shall be provided for 50% of the strength of the Hostel subject to a minimum of 40m² The kitchen area shall be provided at the rate of 5.5 sq. ft. (0.5m²) per diner subject to a minimum of 60m². The kitchen area shall be provided with the facilities of water taps and locker, cooking arrangements can also be provided within the norms at the choice of his University/College. Fuel yard shall be provided near the kitchen.

The dining and kitchen space shall be provided with the following:
Toilet facilities for diners:

Less than 100 Diners

Urinals	3
Wash Basin	5
W.C.	1

More than 100 Diners

Urinals	6
Wash Basin	8
W.C.	1

The floors of the dining and kitchen space shall be finished with terrazo and dedo upto cill level. All doors and windows will be provided with fly mesh shutters.

4. *Common Room*

The common room space shall be provided for 25% of hostel strength at the rate of 2m² per user up to a minimum of 60m². The common room accommodation shall be provided preferably on the ground floor and as far as possible near the dining space so that these facilities could be combined when required. There is no need of providing a separate lavatory in case common room is near to dining space.

5. *Toilet Facilities*

The toilet unit will have the following facilities:

– W.C.	1 for every 10 students
	1 for every 8 women/Girl Students
– Urinal	1 for 20-25 students
– Wash hand basin	1 for 8-10 students
– Shower	1 for 8-10 students

Based on above norms provisions an area of 0.7m^2 per student is adequate for toilet units. W.C. should normally be of Indian type but one toilet of European type may be provided in special circumstances. A small storage space for brooms, floor brushes etc. shall be provided within the toilet block. The location of the block shall be so marked that the bad smell is not carried to living accommodation through the prevailing breeze. Provision of Exhaust Fan may also be provided in each Toilet Block, Provision may be made for Hot water supply in regions where necessary.

6. *Area of Openings*

The area of openings excluding doors and ventilators shall lie between 12 to 15% of the floor area.

7. *Total Floor Area*

An overall area of 17 sq. mt. per hostler including circulation will be adequate. This includes living rooms Circulation Space. Wall area, Service area and Common room but it does not include Dining and Kitchen area.

8. *Provision of Services*

The following provision shall be made for internal water supply, sanitation while determining the cost of the hostel.

Internal water supply and Sanitation	7-.5% of total cost of Civil Works

Internal Electrification	10% of total cost of Civil works without fans, 12-.5% of total cost of Civil works with fans

9. *Furniture*

The following furniture shall be provided in each room of the hostel per student

Cot	1 No.
Reading table	1 No.
Chair	1 No.
Tea Table	1 No.

10. *Warden's Office*

80 to 90 sq. ft. (7.5 to 8.4m²) of office accommodation shall be provided for the office of the Warden.

11. *Furniture Store*

Furniture Store 160 to 180 sq. ft. (15 to 17 m²) shall be provided for extra/Repairable furnitures.

12. *Parking Space*

A separate covered space at a convenient location shall be provided for cycle and scooter parking at the rate of 1.8 m per cycle/scooter for 35% of the strength of the hostlers.

13. *Drinking Water*

Adequate space for water coolers at convenient locations shall be planned for installation of water coolers in future when funds are available.

14. *Circulation Space*

Attempts should be made to keep the circulation area to the

minimum. It should be around 25% of the total plinth area excluding the area for stair case. Hostels are planned either with central corridor or passage on one side. Though the Central corridor system is economical but it is often not feasible because of inadequate natural lighting, cross ventilation and noise level. The width of Central corridor should not be less than 5′-0" (1.5 m). However, for singly loaded corridor it could be 4′-2" (1.2 m) only. The location of stair cases, toilet blocks shall be such that the walking distance from the farthest room is within 100 ft. (30 m), the width of the stair case flight should be 4′ (120 cm) clear.

Note:
1. The Planning efficiency shall be achieved to the maximum by functionally grouping together various activity spaces. Preferably the total built up area should be 2.3 to 2.5 times the total living unit area.
2. A room with an area of 22.5 sq. mt. may be provided for the guests and relatives of the students coming from out stations, the space shall be provided to accommodate at least three guests at a time.

TEACHERS HOSTELS (Up to 4 storeyed)

(1) *Space requirements*

(a) For single occupancy 40 sq. mt.
(b) For married couples 60 sq. mt.

(2) In addition circulation and common facilities may be provided @ 20 sq. mt. per unit.

GENERAL

Requirements for fitments for drainage and sanitation may be added (See NBC 1983 Part IX Sec.[2] or IS 1172/-1983 code of Basic requirements for water supply Drainage and Sanitation (Third Revision).

Accommodation for Staff Quarters

Staff Quarters

		Accommodation	Plinth Area
1. (a)	Type I:	Professor/Readers House Flats	Basic Structure 150 sq. metres
	Note:	Houses/Flats may be built with servants and quarter garage	
(b)	Type II:	Lecturer's Quarters 100 sq. metres	
	Note:	House/Flats may be built with scooter shed	4 sq. metres

Note: Where only one watercloset is provided, the bath and watercloset shall be separately accommodated. Water closet unless indicated otherwise shall be of Indian Standard (squating type).

STANDARDS FOR LIBRARY BUILDINGS AND DESIGN

Based on IS 1553–1976-Indian Standard Recommendation relating to Primary Elements in the Design of Library Buildings. (First Revision)

1. *Location*

The library should be centrally located with reference to buildings of faculties and departments, laboratories and hostels.

2. Rooms to be provided are as follows:

Sl. No.	Rooms Normally Separate	Academic library*	
		UCL*	UDL**
1	2	3	4
(i)	Stack Room	R	—
(ii)	Catalogue Room	R	—
(iii)	General Reading Room	R	R
(iv)	Periodical Reading Room	R	—
(v)	Special Reading Room	R	—
(vi)	Research Cubicles	R	—
(vii)	Group Study Room	R	—
(viii)	Seminar Room	R	—

* Each unit rack 2 m long may be assumed to house 700 to 750 volumes and 1 m^2 of stack room area may be assumed to house 150 volumes.

		*	**
(ix)	Conference Room	R	—
(x)	Exhibition Room	—	—
(xi)	Librarian's Room	R	—
(xii)	Deputy Librarian's Room	R	—
(xiii)	Technical Staff Room	R	—
(xiv)	Administrative Staff Room	R	—
(xv)	Committee Room	R	—
(xvi)	Display Room	R	—
(xvii)	Night Watchmen's Room	R	—
(xviii)	Microfilm Reading Room	R	—
(xix)	Document Reproduction Room	R	—
(xx)	Audio Visual Room	—	—
(xxi)	Store Room	R	R

* University Central Library

** University/College Departmental Library

Note: 1. The centre to centre distance between consecutive racks is 1.80 m. (on the basis of 0.45 m of rack depth plus 1.35 m of cross gangway width).

2. The distance from an end wall of the stack room to the centre of the nearest row of rack is 1.55 m (on the basis of 1.325 m of the end cross gangway plus 0.225 m of half rack depth).

3.0 *Stack Room*

3.1 Dimension of stack Room should be as follows:

(a) *Clear Length* in metres–1.80 *n*+3.10 where *n* is the number of rows of book racks*

(b) *Clear Width*

(1) 3 m (on the basis of one rack 2 m long plus one longitudinal gangway of m) close to a longitudinal wall.

(2) 5 m (on the basis of 2 racks each 2 m long plus one longitudinal gangway of 1 m) close to a longitudinal wall.

(3) 8 m (on the basis of 3 racks each 2 m long plus two longitudinal gangways of 1 m each) close to each of the longitudinal wall, and

(4) 10 m (on the basis of 4 racks each 2 m long plus two longitudinal gangways of 1 m each) close to each of the longitudinal walls.

Note: Three metres and five metres widths are generally only in case of stack spaces, as the stack room and the reading room may be combined into a single room, in such cases.

(c) *Clear Height*–Floor to ceiling, 2.40 m.

Note: 1. The height of the rack is 2.20 m and allovance for bay guids is 0.20 m.
2. The stackroom should be combined with necessary devices for effective ventilation.

3.2 Stackroom should be so oriented as to avoid direct sun.

4.0 *Windows*

4.1 Stackroom-Windows in the side walls of the stackroom should be opposite each cross gangway.

4.2 Each window should be provided with glass shutters and protected with wire fabric having its aperture sufficiently small to prevent squirrels, rats, etc., from getting in. In its fully open position the glass shutter should not project into the gangway.

4.3 Other Rooms – All windows and ventilators in the rooms accessible from outside should be provided with wire fabric to prevent books, pamphlets, etc. being passed out through them.

5.0 *Sizes of rooms*

5.1 Reading Rooms – The average area per reader in the reading room should be 2.33 m^2, minimum.
Note – The size of the reading table is 2.4×0.6 m the centre to centre distance between two consecutive rows of reading room tables is 1.8 m with seating arrangement on one side of the table only.

5.2 Sizes of other rooms shall normally be as follows:

For use of	Area m^2
(a) Librarian and deputy librarian	30
(b) Classifier, Cataloguer, accession librarian and maintenance librarian	9 per person
(c) Secretary to the librarian	19
(d) Visitor's room	15
(e) Administrative and professional staff not at service points and other than those mentioned in (b)	5 per person
(f) Group discussion room	2 per person
(g) Conference room	2 per person
(h) Seminar room	2 per person
(i) Committee room	2 per person
(j) Cubicles	7 per person

6.0 Libraries of all types are expanding at an enormous rate. Increase in demand for documents, official policy and increase in literacy make this process inevitable. Since the development of new libraries takes several years the stock to be accommodated on the opening day, therefore, will be larger than was estimated when planning started. Therefore, it is absolutely essential to estimate the areas of the library at a given future date and relate the requirements to that date.

7.0 *Circulation*

7.1 Each floor of the library building will be at one single level to facilitate the movement of book trolley from one part to another. Thresholds shall not be provided anywhere inside the building.

7.1.1 The movement of the book trolley from one tier to another, where there are three or more tiers in the stackroom, should be thorough electric lifts provided within the stackroom with landing at every tier of the stackroom and at other connected adjacent rooms. In large libraries where quick mechanical carriage of books and related materials are required, special arrangements, such as pneumatic tubes and belt conveyers may become necessary. This may require to be considered at the initial stages of design of the library and its building.

7.1.2 The rooms shall be arranged in such a way that the staff other than those servicing the reading room shall not have to pass through the reading room disturbing the readers.

8.0 *Relative Positions of Rooms*

8.1 The stack room should be so placed that it is easily accessible from and proximate to every part of the library.

8.2 The catalogue room should be like an ante-room to the stack room on the way from the general reading room to the stack room.

8.3 The general reading room should be close to the entrance.

8.4 Periodicals rooms may be further removed from the general reading room. But independent access to it shall be possible when the other rooms in the library are closed.

8.5 Special reading rooms may be still further removed from the general reading room.

8.6 The librarian or the deputy librarian should have his room in close proximity to the general reading room.

8.7 The rooms of the technical and administrative staff should be placed in close proximity to the rooms of the librarian and the deputy librarian.

8.8 The technical staff shall have independent access to the stack and catalogue areas.

8.9 The cubicles, the room for group study, the çommittee room, etc. may be in a separate wing or a separate floor.

8.10 The exhibition room may be combined with the entrance lobby or placed as close to it as possible.

9.0 The furniture and fittings for library shall be as per IS: 1829 (part I and II) and IS: Library furniture and fittings: Part I Timber (First Revision) and Part II steel and IS: 3663-1981 dimensions for rigid couplings. Tables and Chairs for general office purpose.

10.0 Requirements for fitment for drainage and sanitation for library building shall be as per the table enclosed.

Libraries-Based on IS: 1972—1983 Indian Standard Code of Basic requirements for water supply, Drainage and Sanitation (Third Revision)

ART GALLERIES, LIBRARIES AND MUSEUMS

Sl. No.	Fitments	For male public	For female public	For male staff	For female staff
1	2	3	4	5	6
(i)	Waterclosets	1 per 200 persons up to 400 persons; and for over 400 persons, add at the rate of ❣ per 250 persons or part thereof	1 per 100 persons up to 200 persons; and for over 200 persons, add at the rate of 1 per 150 persons or part thereof	1 for 1 to 15 persons 2 for 16 to 35 persons	1 for 1 to 12 persons 2 for 13 to 25 persons
(ii)	Ablution taps	1 in each water-closet	1 in each water-closet	1 in each water-closet	1 in each water-closet
			1 water tap with drainage arrangements shall be provided for every 50 persons or part thereof in the vicinity of water-closets and urinals		

1	2	3	4	5	6
(iii)	Urinals	1 per 50 persons		Nil up to 6 persons 1 for 7 to 20 persons 2 for 21 to 45 persons	
(iv)	Wash Basins	1 for every 200 persons or part thereof; and for over 400 persons add at the rate of 1 per 250 persons or part thereof	1 for every 200 persons or part thereof; and for over 200 persons add at the rate of 1 per 150 persons or part thereof	1 for 1 to 15 persons 2 for 15 to 35 persons	1 for 1 to 12 persons 2 for 13 to 25 persons
(v)	Cleaner's Sinks	———	1 per floor, Min	———	
(vi)	Drinking water + fountain	———	1 per 100 persons or part thereof	———	

NORMS AND STANDARDS FOR CONSTRUCTION OF GUEST HOUSE

	Guest House	
(i)	Single rooms (with attached bath rooms)	8
(ii)	Double rooms	4
(iii)	VIP Suit	1
(iv)	Lounge (with attached toilet)	1
(v)	Dining room, kitchen, pantry etc.	1 each
(vi)	Small office cum reception	1

The areas of the above purpose may be as follows:

	Living area plus accommodation for bath room, w.c., entrance lobby, dressing	*Total*	
(i)	Single room 12.00 sq.m.	8 sq.mt	200 sq.ft
(ii)	Double room 20.00 sq.m.	10 sq.mt.	300 sq.ft
(iii)	VIP Suit 28.00 sq.m. (This will consist of one bed room plus one sitting room)	12 sq.mt.	400 sq.ft
(iv)	Lounge with attached toilet	800 sq.ft.	(600+200 sq.ft.)
(v)	Indoor games and Reading room		600 sq.ft
(vi)	Dining room (with facilities for 25 persons dining at a time)		300 sq.ft.
(vii)	Kitchen, Pantry etc.		250 sq.ft.
(viii)	Small office cum reception		150 sq.ft
(ix)	Store & Linen room		150 sq.ft.

SPACE NORMS FOR HEALTH CENTRE

Sl. No.	*Name of facility*	*For 6 Beds*		
		No. of Rooms	*Size*	*Area in m²*
Out Patient				
	(a) Consultation & Examination	2	4—3.5 m	14 sq.m
	(b) Dispensary	1	3.5—2.5 m	8.75 sq.m
	(c) Dressing	1	4—3.5 m	14 sq.m
In Patient				
	(a) Ward area/2 bed ward	—	3.5—3.5 m	12.25 sq.m
	Ward area/4 bed ward	—	6.0—3.5 m	21.00 sq.m
	(b) Attendants room	3—2.5 m	7.5 sq.m	7.5 sq.m
Common & Ancillary				
	(a) Laboratory	1 2.5—3.5 m		
	(b) X-Ray with Dark room & Store	1	7.0X3.5 m	24.5 sq.m
	(c) Operation room with sterilisation abd scrubup	1	5.0X3.5 m	17.5 sq.m
	(d) Preparation room	1	3X3.5 m	10.5 sq.m
	(e) Labour room/delivery	1	4X3.5 m	14.00 sq.m
	(f) Office room with storage	1	4X3.5 m	14.00 sq. m
	(g) *Store*			
	(i) Medicine	1	4X3.5 m	14 sq.m
	(ii) Linen & Equipment	1		
	(iii) General	1	3X2.5 m	7.5 sq.m
	(h) Garrage for Ambulance	1	5.5X3.5 m	19.25 sq.m
MCH & FP				
	(i) MCH room with exam toilet and urine testing shelf	1	5.5X3.0 m	16.5 sq.m
	(ii) Multipurpose Cum F.P.		3.5X7.5	26.25 sq.m
Waiting				
	(a) Consultation & examination	10 persons		
	(b) Dispensary & Dressing	10 persons		
	(c) Operation & Labour	4 persons	50 sq.m	
	(d) MCH	5 persons		

Toilets	*W.C.*	*Urinal*	*Washbasin*
Public			
Male	1	2	1
Female	1	—	1
Wards			
Male	1	1	1
Female	1	—	1
Staff			
Male	1	1	1
Female	1	—	1

(The sizes shall be in accordance with the norm recommended by ISI/National Building Code)

Note
1. To start with provision of only 6 beds may be made. The facility for provision of more beds will depend upon the size of the University and other local needs.
2. The overall plinth area of the Health Centre including the area for circulation, services and wall area may not exceed 600 sq.m

6

CURRICULUM

6.1 NCERT WORKING GROUP ON CURRICULUM LOAD (1983-85)[1]

Introduction

The problem of curriculum load was felt in India for the first time in 1975 soon after the introduction of new curriculum under the 10+2 pattern of education. The Ishwar Bhai Patel Committee (1977), suggested deletion of a few topics from the syllabus of different subjects. The problem was discussed time and again in various forums even after the implementation of the recommendations of the Patel Committee. NCERT set up a Working Group in 1983 to make a quick appraisal of the curriculum load. The Director of NCERT was the Chairman of this Working Group. The Working Group submitted the report titled 'Curriculum Load at the School Level: A Quick Appraisal'.

Recommendations

A detailed report based on the results of the work done by the Working Group was presented before a National Seminar which was attended by eminent educationists and high level educational functionaries of various States and Union territories. The Seminar deliberated upon various aspects of school curriculum and made a number of suggestions to tackle the problem of curriculum load. Keeping in view

1. Published by National Council of Educational Research and Training (NCERT), New Delhi, 1985).

the deliberations of the seminar and also those of the earlier workshops, the Working Group recommends that the following measures should be undertaken to improve the overall curriculum scenario at the school level in the country:

1. In order to develop national cohesion, integration, value orientation as reflected in our rich traditions and composite cultural heritage; in order to synthesize the above with modernisation in terms of Science and Technology and to promote a genuine Indian ethos, there is an urgent need to formulate a national core curriculum applicable to all the schools in the country. NCERT should undertake the responsibility of developing the national core curriculum.
2. The national core curriculum, applicable to all the schools in the country should be supplemented by specific curricula to meet the local ecological, sociological, cultural, economic and developmental requirements relevant to states, districts and geographical typologies. It is recommended that national core curriculum should constitute two thirds of the total curriculum. However, the proportion may differ in respect of different subjects and different stages of education.
3. School curriculum should present a happy blend of physical culture, culture and knowledge. The knowledge component should further comprise humanities, science and technology. The relative proportion of each component should vary at different stages of school education.
4. Curriculum should be developed keeping in view the majority of students, teachers and physical facilities available in majority of schools. There is need to check unnecessary disparities and elitism arising from the curriculum.
5. Information load, specially at the earlier stages, should be kept at a minimum. At the higher level also, practice of competitive overloading of information in the textbooks should be avoided. It is recommended that there should not be more than two textbooks of Classes I and II.
6. At least 33 per cent of the instructional time should be allocated for the teaching of mother tongue/regional language at the primary stage because proficiency in language skills will equip the child to learn the content of other subjects with ease. At the primary stage, mother tongue should be the medium of instruction.

7. Teaching of formal skills of reading and writing should not be attempted before the age of five. But informal, joyful pre-primary schooling may be introduced. Particularly for the first generation learners.
8. The language and the writing style followed in the textbooks should be easily intelligible to students. Books written in simple language help the pupils to learn things better and in less time. The non-language books should reinforce the linguistic abilities of pupils and should in no case pose additional problems of comprehension for them. When books prepared first in one language, are got translated into another language, artificial and mechanical translation should be avoided. Where translation needs to be done, the help of practising teachers should be obtained.
9. Quality of education should not be equated with quantum of curriculum content. For the development of creative thinking, it is better to cover a few topics more intensively rather than providing superficial knowledge of too many things.
10. There is a definite place for research in curriculum development particularly to ensure that the concepts introduced are compatible with the mental development of the child.
11. As the syllabi and textbooks are the concrete manifestations of curriculum, these should be of high quality. There should be a mechanism for determining the suitability of textbooks.
12. Since curriculum development is a continuous process, it should be evaluated periodically and recast in its totality. NCERT should provide academic guidance to the State Education Departments for the evaluation of their curricula, particularly from the point of view of load.
13. Keeping in view the present time allocation of 6 or 7 periods per week, the existing curriculum in social science at the secondary stage in Delhi proves to be lengthy. Besides there are some overlappings in the curriculum of middle and secondary stages. Therefore, the whole course of social science from Class VI-X should be reorganised so as to remove the overlappings between the curriculum of middle and secondary stages. At the middle/upper primary stage integrated approach should be adopted.
14. The present curriculum in science for Classes VI-X in Delhi has been found to be lengthy. Besides a few topics included in the

syllabuses of different classes, as mentioned on page 13 of this report, have been found to be difficult for students. At the secondary stage, Course A in general proves to be difficult for students. The topics found to be difficult should be considered for simplification and deletion from the course. At the middle stage integrated science rather than physics, chemistry and biology as such should form a part of school curriculum.

15. Two types of courses (A and B) in science and mathematics (as in the case of CBSE) at the secondary stage gives the indication that one type of course is of a higher level while the other is of low level. Most of the students, particularly in urban areas, are attracted towards the higher level course but subsequently find it difficult to cope with the curriculum. For example, Science Course 'A' is found to be heavy for pupils. This type of differentiation should be done away with as it is against the concept of general education.

Facilities

16. Minimum facilities for teaching learning such as Chalk, blackboard, books, source books, maps, charts, models etc. should be provided in every school. Absence of these facilities increases the load of curriculum for pupils and teachers.
17. Overcrowding in classes increases the work load of teachers which affects adversely the quality of curriculum transaction. This may give rise to the problem of curriculum load. The optimum number of pupils in a class should be around 35.

Curriculum Transaction

18. Directorates of Education should ensure 220 working days out of which there should be at least 190 instructional days. Duration of a school day should be at least six hours, out of which five hours should be available for the transaction of curriculum.
19. lack of order and system in any aspect of human life makes things heavier and more difficult than they are. This is also true in the case of home work and periodical tests. It should be made obligatory on the part of school to prepare and display in each class an agreed time table for home work assignment and for the conduct of periodical/unit tests. It is further recommended that no

formal home work should be assigned at the primary stage.

20. Since the teacher is the major single factor in fostering teaching and learning, it is desirable that he should be suitably trained to discharge his duties effectively. Therefore, curriculum for pre-service training, both for elementary stage and secondary stage, should be simultaneously updated and intensified. Training strategies should be designed in such a way that the trainees are adequately prepare to handle the revised school curriculum. Mushroom growth of substandard teacher training colleges should be checked.
21. In-service training programmes should be organised on a continuing basis to help the teachers update their knowledge in content as well as in pedagogy. However, it may take a very long time to provide in-service training to teachers through regular contact programmes. Teachers Guides or curriculum supplements should be made available to all the teachers. Proper use of mass media should be made in a big way for the continuing education of teachers.

Examinations/Tests

22. There should be no public examination till Class VII. Internal formative and summative evaluation should be carried continuously with a view to diagnose pupil's weaknesses in learning. Subsequently remedial teaching for those pupils who lag behind in some aspect of learning should be arranged. Time spent by teachers on remedial teaching should be considered as part of their regular workload.

6.2 NATIONAL CURRICULUM FOR ELEMENTARY AND SECONDARY EDUCATION : A FRAMEWORK, (1988)[2]

Introduction

With a view to implementing the directions contained in the National Policy on Education, 1986 regarding 'Reorienting the Content and Process of Education', the NCERT revised the earlier curriculum. The revised curriculum is the outcome of the deliberations of a large

2. Published by NCERT, New Delhi, 1988.

number of seminars attended by eminent educationists, curriculum specialists, subject experts principals of schools, teacher educators, legislators, Members of Parliament, journalists and representatives of teachers organisations.

Main Features of the Curriculum

Framework

The national curricular framework for elementary and secondary education is envisaged in the context of the National System of Education as elaborated earlier. The basic features and the main thrusts of the curricular framework are as follows:

(i) Emphasis on the development of human resources for the realisation of the national goals of development.
(ii) Broad-based general education to all learners at the elementary (primary and upper primary) secondary stages.
(iii) A common scheme of studies for elementary and secondary stages.
(iv) The common core components comprising the following:

- The history of India's freedom movement;
- The constitutional obligations;
- Content essential to nature national identity;
- India's common cultural heritage;
- Egalitarianism, democracy and secularism;
- Equality of the sexes;
- Protection of the environment;
- Removal of social barriers;
- Observance of the small family norm; and
- Inculcation of the scientific temper.

(v) Emphasis on defining Minimum Learning Outcomes (MLOs) for each area of learning at all stages of education.
(vi) Provision for flexibility in terms of selection of content/components and learning experiences which would facilitate the attainment of minimum learning outcomes laid down for each stage of school education.
(vii) Emphasis on child-centred and activity-based processes rather than the teacher-centred approach during the transaction of curriculum.

(viii) Recasting of the examination system and introduction of continuous and comprehensive evaluation that incorporates both scholastic and specific objectives for each stage of education, to precisely stated specific objectives of each subject area in the form of expected learning outcomes indicating what exact behaviour would a learner be able to demonstrate after the curriculum transaction. Thus, the curriculum organisers are required at the outset to indicate overall objectives of curriculum which would coincide with the overall aim of school education. It is necessary to further formulate carefully the stage-wise objectives keeping in view the developmental characteristics and level associated with different stages of education. Each subjected area would have its own specific objectives clearly defined in terms of behavioural outcomes. Put differently, efforts should be directed at the achievement of a particular set of objectives for which specific learning experiences are provided under a particular subject area. However, it should not be forgotten that human learning makes one unified whole and that separate subject area have been created only for the sake of convenience.

For education to help our country to express and promote its unique socio-cultural identity, to meet the challenges of the times and to develop appropriately its human resources, the objectives will have to be formulated with utmost care keeping in view the national priorities and values enshrined in our constitution, socio-economic and cultural considerations, position of physical resources, global inter-relationships, pedagogical concerns and nature and level of learners. Needless to mention objectives related to Common Core Components should be given a central place.

General Objectives of Education

School curriculum, on the whole, should aim at enabling the learners to acquire knowledge, develop concepts, and inculcate skills, attitudes, values and habits conducive to the all-round development of their personality and commensurate with the social, cultural, economic and environmental realities at national and international levels.

Schools curriculum should, therefore, help to promote development in the learner of:

- Language abilities and communication skills needed for social living and further learning;
- Competencies that facilitate mathematical operations and their applications in day-to-day life and learning;
- Knowledge, attitudes and habits necessary for keeping physically fit and strong in conformity with normal developmental pattern;
- A proper understanding about the role and importance of sex in human life, and healthy attitude towards sex and members of opposite sex;
- Qualities that make a man socially effective and happy in various social settings such as friendliness, cooperativeness, comparison, self-discipline, self-criticism, self-control, humour, courage, love for social justice, self-control, etc.;
- Moral and character values such as honesty, truthfulness, dependability, courtesy, fearlessness, comparison, etc.
- Pre-vocational/vocational skills, willingness to work hard, entrepreneurship and dignity of manual work necessary for increased productivity and job satisfaction;
- Ability to appreciate and discover beauty in various life situations and integrate it into one's own personality;
- Understanding of the environmental and its limited resources and the need for conservation of natural resources and energy;
- Appreciation of various consequences of large families and over population and need of checking population growth;
- Understanding of the diverse cultural and social systems of people living in different parts of the country and the country's composite cultural heritage;
- Appreciation for the need of a balanced synthesis between the change-oriented technologies and the continuity of country's cultural heritage;
- Knowledge of national symbols and desire and determination to uphold the ideas of national identity and unity;
- Capability of appreciating and tolerating differences and diversities of various sorts and the capacity to choose between alternative value systems;
- An awareness of the inherent equality of all and need of global fraternity with a strong commitment to humane values and to social justice;
- Scientific temper characterised by spirit of inquiry, courage to

question and objectivity leading to elimination of obscurantism superstitionand fatalism;

- Knowledge of scientific methods of inquiry and its use in solving problems;
- Appreciation of sacrifices and contribution made by the freedom-fighters and social workers in the country's freedom struggle and social regenerations and readiness to follow their ideals;
- Appreciation of and readiness to practice in life the national goals of socialism, secularism, democracy and non-violence;
- Divergent and independent thinking and ability to discover new relationships and combinations;
- Qualities and characteristics necessary for self-learning and for life-long learning leading to creation of a learning society.

Objectives at Various Levels of Education

The emphasis on the 'child-centered approach' to education necessarily implies that objectives of education to be achieved at a particular stage/class level should be determined carefully, keeping in view the norms of development–physical, mental, social, emotional and moral of children of relevant age groups. Exact expected learning outcomes related to each objective for a particular class should be precisely worked out.

Most of the objectives indicated above will continue through various classes. However, the level of achievement with regard to a particular objective will be rising from one class to another class in a spiral fashion. Thus there will be sort of learning continuum so far as targets of achievement with regard to a particular objectives are concerned and it will reach its terminal point at a particular class level depending on the nature of the concerned objectives.

Subjects at Various Stages and Time Allocation

	Elementary Allocation (8 Years)	*Time Allocation*
Primary Stage (5 Years)		
(a)	One language — the Mother Tongue/Regional Language	30%
(b)	Mathematics	15%
(c)	Environmental Studies I & II	15%

(d)	Work Experience	20%
(e)	Art Education	10%
(f)	Health and Physical Education	10%
		100%

Upper Primary Stage (3 Years)

(a)	Three Languages	32%
(b)	Mathematics	12%
(c)	Science	12%
(d)	Social Science	12%
(e)	Work Experience	12%
(f)	Art Education	10%
(g)	Health and Physical Education	10%
		100%

Secondary Stage (2 Years)

(a)	Three Languages	30%
(b)	Mathematics	13%
(c)	Science	13%
(d)	Social Sciences	13%
(e)	Work Experience	13%
(f)	Art Education	9%
(g)	Health and Physical Education	9%
		100%

7

ENVIRONMENT EDUCATION

7.1 NPE ON ENVIRONMENT EDUCATION

There is a paramount need to create a consciousness of the environment. It must permeate all ages and all sections of society, beginning with the child. Environmental consciousness should inform teaching in schools and colleges. This aspect will be integrated in the entire educational process (Chapter 8, Para 15).

Centrally-sponsored Scheme

A Centrally-Sponsored Scheme of Environmental Orientation to School Education was started during 1988 under which 100 per cent financial assistance is provided to States/UTs and voluntary organizations working in the field of environmental education. It is envisaged to organise various programmes aiming at creating environmental consciousness among the students and the community.

The project activities would include review of curriculum, preparation of revised textbooks, curricular and extra-curricular materials, preparation of general informative books/brochures/posters/ audio visual materials, adoption of monuments by schools for study and upkeep, study of ecological problems in the neighbourhood, participation in conservation projects, etc. Setting up of the school nurseries will be taken as one of the preferred activities with the help of State Departments of Environment and forest and National Wastelands Development Board. The scheme also provides for involvement of voluntary organisations in innovative projects relating to environment education.

Following proposals were sanctioned during 1988-89:

- Uttrakhand Seva Nidhi, Almora for environmental orientation to elementary education in Kumaon and Garhwal regions of Uttar Pradesh.
- Sanchal Foundation, New Delhi for a project on social imperatives of development which seeks to establish a linkage between the natural disasters and environmental degradation.
- Centre of Environment Education (CEE), Ahmedabad to act as a nodal agency for involving NGOs working in the area of environment education to take up locale-specific activities in a cluster of schools around them.

Multi-media Package

The Central Institute of Technology (CIET) of the NCERT has produced a multi-media package on environment education. The package is in the form of video tapes, tape-slides and posters that deal with such issues as air pollution, water shortage and pollution destruction of forests, soil erosion, etc.

A 21-minute film on the 'Doon Valley' depicts how the Himalayas are dying with blasts of dynamite and being scarred by the remains of what were once lush green forests. The valley which once had the best water distribution system provided by nature itself was to-day devoid of water due to man's carelessness, callousness and greed.

The film 'the Great Thrust' reveals that the present drought was not due to the failure of rain alone. The non-availability of groundwater has particularly worsened the situation. The film shows that productive soil is disappearing due to erosion by wind and rain. Soil erosion has increased 400 times to large scale deforestation.

The film titled 'Castles in the Air' conveys the message that there is a risk of the Bhopal gas tragedy being repeated in Delhi if proper measures are not taken against the emission of over 400 tonnes of pollutants by the over 10 lakh vehicles plying daily in the city. The film shows how over-population, poverty, factories, power houses, surface and air transport have increased anaemia and cancer-producing gases in the environment.

The nine-minute film 'Portrait of a City' underscores the message of atmospheric pollution caused by industries and power-houses set up around cities. Although these are essential for a growing society, few have installed the vitally important pollution control system.

Source: *NCERT Newsletter*, 1988.

8

HIGHER EDUCATION

8.1 UGC REVIEW COMMITTEE ON UNIVERSITY SYSTEM AND EXTENSION AS THE THIRD DIMENSION (1985)[1]

Introduction

The University Grants Commission's support to the Universities and Colleges for undertaking programmes of eradication of illiteracy has run into two phases. The first phase was from October 1983 up to 31-3-1985 and the second phase was from 1-4-1985 to 31-3-1990. This was envisaged by the Commission on the recommendations made in the report of the Working Group that was constituted under the Chairpersonship of Dr. (Mrs.) Madhuri R. Shah, the then Chairperson of the University Grants Commission.

For increasing the involvement of the Universities in the programmes of Adult Education as well as making the current programmes more effective during the Seventh Five Year Plan period, it was considered necessary to review the implementation of the programmes of the first phase, i.e., up to 31-3-1985.

Composition

With this in view, the Commission appointed a Committee consisting of the following persons:–

1. Published by the University Grants Commission, New Delhi, 1985.

Chairperson

Prof. Ramlal Parikh
Vice-Chancellor
Gujarat Vidyapith
Ahmedabad

Members

Prof. M. Aram
Vice-Chancellor
Gandhigram Rural Institute
Gandhigram

Prof. Ram Takwale
Professor of Physics
University of Poona
Poona

Smt. Kamalini H. Bansali
Registrar
SNDT Women's University
Bombay

Member-Secretary

Dr. M.L. Mehta
Joint Secretary
University Grants Commission
New Delhi

Terms of Reference

The terms of reference of the Committee are:

- Review of the current programmes of Adult Education undertaken by the Universities and Colleges with a view to identify their shortfalls, problems, achievements and so no.
- To make recommendations for greater and more effective involvement of Universities/Colleges in the programmes of Adult Education so as to fulfil aims and goals of the Government of India.

The Committee has to review all the programmes included within the broader umbrella of Adult and Continuing Education and Extension, i.e., (1) eradication of illiteracy; (2) programmes of continuing education; (3) population education activities; (4) planning forums; and (5) rural development, etc.

Meetings

At Bombay, Patna and Poona, the Committee held discussions with the Directors/Assistant Directors/Co-Ordinators of the programmes of Adult and Continuing Education in Indian Universities as also a few Vice-Chancellors and some senior adult educator in Indian Universities.

At Madurai and Trivandrum, discussions were held with Principals and staff manning Departments of Adult and Continuing Education. Interaction thus took place with over 150 persons from this field.

The Committee also invited views of some experienced persons in the field of adult education, continuing education, population education, rural development, etc. including U.G.C. representatives on Advisory Committees of Universities.

The Committee took note of the report of the Government of India, Indian Universities Association for Continuing Education, Indian Association for Adult Education, Indian Society for Community Education and Population Education, etc. on adult education, population education, continuing education as also of the proceedings of a large number of seminars/workshops held in India during the past three years on the themes of Adult Education, Continuing Education. Population Education. etc.

Aspects Covered

Keeping in view of objective of the review, the Committee has focused attention in the report on the various dimensions of the following aspects:

(i) Eradication of illiteracy through the involvement of universities and colleges.
(ii) Giving extension an equal status with teaching and research.
(iii) Other extension programmes including continuing education, population education, planning forums, rural development,

science for the people, legal literacy, environmental education and national integration through colleges and universities.

(iv) Recommendations based on the discussions at various regional meetings with functionaries and available documents on the subject.

8.2 IMPORTANT OBSERVATIONS

Extension – Third Dimension

1. Adult *Education*/Continuing Education should not be an *ad hoc* programme, but should continue to be an integral part of university activity and should get institutionalised, as a permanent component of the University system.
2. Extension should be the 3rd important major activity of the universities like teaching and research as envisaged by the University Grants Commission in the policy frame. It should receive equal importance with teaching and research.
3. The University system should absorb the concept of "Extension Culture" as its integral component and beginning be made by providing at least 25% time allocation for the off-campus extension work through community education type programmes.

Seventh Plan Directions and Strategies

1. The programmes of eradication of adult illiteracy in the age group 15-35 should be planned keeping in view the national commitment of completing it by 1990.
2. A very high priority should be given during the seventh plan period, to fulfil this among the adult illiterate population of women throughout the country.
3. As the scheduled caste and scheduled tribe population together accounts for 23.6% of the total population of India, educational development of these groups needs to be specially promoted.
4. The national commitment to the eradication of illiteracy requires the involvement and active support of every educated person individually and through institutions. Each educated person, in which students are expected to play a leading role, would be expected to take some responsibility for imparting literacy.
5. In fact working with the community and serving the community

in its developmental activities are the best learning opportunities for students to develop their moral, social, ethical and vocational attitudes. Students learning through field and social service activities along with the relevant component of theoretical knowledge should be a part of the curricula with due credits as a part of requirement of degree.

6. Functional literacy and universalisation of primary education should be simultaneously undertaken and given the same importance. Primary school dropouts (6-14 age group) should also be enlisted separately as learners under the Adult Education Programme.
7. It is necessary to elaborate the aims and objectives of the UGC programme of extension in a more specific way.
8. The objectives of extension involve not only generation of more out-of-school activities but changes in the attitudes and approaches of the academic functionaries. To achieve these larger objectives, it is necessary to adopt multipronged approaches.
9. To adopt a multipronged and elastic approach, taking into account abundant diversity to suit different needs of life and culture of the mass of people, greater initiative at the base institutions of university system is necessary.
10. Universities and colleges, as autonomous institutions educating younger generation of students to prepare for future responsibilities, have greater potentialities to undertake such challenging tasks of eradication of illiteracy and containing population growth, etc.
11. Universities should adopt areas preferably of their jurisdiction of otherwise, as major projects for imparting literacy, post-literacy and continuing education concurrently. The plans for eradication of illiteracy by drawn in consultation with and involvement of colleges and officials of the state departments of Adult Education and all local agencies including Panchayat. Municipality, Co-operative Societies. Dairies, and voluntary agencies and schools, technical institutes, etc. as well as other semi-government agencies. A specific area/community-wise target plan should be formulated. The plan should cover all illiterates yearwise upto 1990. The plan should be widely publicised and disseminated to make people aware of this programme.
12. The Adult Education/Continuing Education Departments of

Universities should formulate their own programmes of awareness and functional literacy so as to secure consequential literacy and numeracy to fulfil the needs of contemporary society for development and progress.

13. Motivating all the students and teachers of colleges and universities are vitally important in ensuring wider participation and successful implementation of the programmes.
14. Literacy should be made a major activity under the National Service scheme in the universities at least up to 1990.
15. Promotion of functional literacy should be an obligatory community service activity for college students of first degree.
16. Provision of functional literacy should be treated as a curricular activity for the students through restructuring of courses at the first degree level.
17. Each first degree student in a college be allowed to offer a paper on Adult Education involving theory and field-work of 100 marks. The performance in this paper be taken into account while determining the over all merit of the student. Performance of the student should be recorded in the degree/diploma and due weightage be given in further studies/employment.
18. Students of the first degree course in all non-professional courses should be required to opt for any of the six-semesters of his/her three years course, to work for at least 90 days wholly, in specifically assigned areas for eradication illiteracy.
19. It must be made obligatory for every B.Ed/M.Ed. student to make at least 10 persons literate before conferment of his/her degree.
20. Rural colleges with smaller enrolment should be specially encouraged to transform themselves as community colleges with programmes of adult literacy and population education as major in built components of their curricular system in every subject.
21. Proportionate reduction in workload may be given to teachers engaged in the programme for ensuring increased involvement of teachers.
22. The universities and colleges through their students and teachers as also associating schools, junior colleges, other educational institutions. Mahila Mandals, Youth Clubs, etc. including educated persons from all walks of life such as house-wives, retired personnel and others will work for total eradication of illiteracy and cultivate an environment conducive to a learning society, in adopted areas during the 7th Plan Period. In doing this,

the universities should utilise fully all the infrastructural facilities available with their institutions in the areas by adopting appropriate diverse strategies and multiple approaches, ensuring the total coverage in the adopted areas by 1990.

Role of Universities, Colleges and Functionaries

1. The professional and technical services required for the implementation of the programme is abundantly available in the universities, if the potentialities of their staff and other physical infrastructure is utilised.
2. The universities and colleges should participate in the adult education programmes through their student body, teachers and the departments or centres of adult or continuing or non-formal or extension education. The colleges should organise adult education centres with the guidance of the universities.
3. There may be three options in field work for students:

    (i) conducting an Adult Education centre as an Instructor.
    (ii) Participating in "Each-One Teach-One" and "Each-one Teach-a-Family" programmes.
    (iii) Organising and conducting supporting programmes at adult education centres.

4. The Vice-Chancellor and the University Advisory Committee should provide the policy thrust and necessary support to the programme.
5. Principal should help in motivating the staff students and public so as to mobilise the maximum number to participate in the adult literacy programme.
6. The Director will be the key person to implement the programme at the university level; he/she will coordinate and oversee the entire programme undertaken by the University and College.

Institutionalisation of Extension

1. The college has to become a catalyst in the future learning society, a centre of education and development for the students and the community through both formal and non-formal means. The students would use the community as a social laboratory for

their practical, moral and attitudinal education and learn by working in and serving the community. The UGC during the Seventh Plan, therefore, should institutionalise extension so that it continues to grow along with the progressive development of higher education.

2. Institutionalisation of extension can be achieved by giving the activities their due place in teaching and research by ensuring proper manpower and resource support.
3. The extension activities be incorporated in the under-graduate courses in foundation courses, applied courses, community service, project work, and in basic or core courses.
4. Institutionalisation of extension needs academic acceptance which is automatically ensured when the activities enter at a stage of studies and research which enlarges our understanding and contributes to knowledge. Extension activities can enter into research through:

   (i) Project work or field-based dissertation at undergraduate and post-graduate levels.
   (ii) Post-graduate courses with research component related to extension activities in the form of case studies.
   (iii) M.Phil and Ph.D. as well as post-doctoral programmes.

5. It is essential to transform some selected colleges into Community Colleges. They should be given complete academic autonomy for innovation and experimentation.
6. Radio, TV, Video-Audio tapes, VCR, VCP, etc. are the modern electronic communication media that are reaching slowly every village and house. The access to these equipment should be available to the disadvantaged regions and communities through Community Education Centres with active participation of the community itself. Colleges can play a great role in organising and maintaining such centres and make them very effective centres of extensions.

University System and Adult Education Programme

1. In the Seventh Plan, the colleges and universities should be assigned the major role of providing resource and monitoring and promotional support to the total adult education

programmes in the country right up to the grass-root levels, besides the role of actually running the adult education centres. Now that the colleges are spread upto the district and block levels, the resource support given by these colleges becomes locally relevant and effective. Further, since they already have definite structures and organisations, the new role and obligation requires only marginal financial support. So it would be economical for the programme to use colleges and universities as resource centres and as monitoring and evaluation agencies for the total adult education programme in the country.

2. It is within the ability and structural conduciveness of the colleges and universities to assume effectively the role of resource centres for adult education for research, orientation, material development, and evaluation, etc. The colleges are best suited to be developed as local resource centres for adult education as they are the knowledge centres with community of scholars and students pursuing knowledge in different disciplines.
3. For post-literacy and continuing education programmes, the colleges and universities are the most appropriate agencies to be involved.
4. Colleges and universities can also be effectively used for the monitoring and evaluation support to be given to the adult education programmes.

Post-Literacy and Follow-up

1. The spread of literacy has created an urgent obligation for creating a mechanism to ensure a lifelong education process for the learners.
2. One of the major objectives of the post-literacy and follow-up programme should be a continuous reinforcement of literacy skills to prevent relapses and its further development to enable the neo-literates to put them into practice in various life situations leading to habit formation of reading and writing.
3. Post-literacy, follow-up and continuing education programmes have to be related to the social, cultural, political, economical, environmental and other needs of the neo-literates and are to be organised in a manner suited to local conditions, situations and

the interest of the neo-literates.

4. The universities/colleges should prepare materials with greater focus on awareness, scientific temper, functionality and other issues.
5. Post-literacy and continuing education activities should form part of the moral training of the adult education programme.
6. The Commission has already agreed to assist the universities/colleges for the period of 12 months for instructors, supervisors, college teachers, etc. which should not, therefore, call for any additional manpower for the implementation of the post-literacy and follow-up programme save and except the materials required for the post-literacy. The Commission may, however, provide funds for post-literacy material as per norms of the Government of India which may be suitably adapted where necessary.
7. The same student instructor or a non-student instructor identified for the purpose should be the post-literacy and follow-up programme worker. The supervisor and the college teacher in-charge will be responsible for successful implementation of the programme.

Monitoring and Evaluation

1. It is, therefore, extremely important for the universities to send their monitoring return to the State Directorate of Adult Education so as to apprise them of the innovative attempts and contributions made by the universities in this programme.
2. Monitoring is an essential requisite in any programme and it is more so in the eradication of illiteracy among adults. It is aimed at steering clear of all hazards with a view to achieve the targets. Timely feedback is needed for ensuring proper conduct of the programme and that is the major aim of monitoring.
3. The universities should periodically (twice a year) apprise the UGC of the administrative, academic and financial position of the programme.
4. The university will collect all the necessary returns from the colleges and after consolidation, they will sent to the UGC and the state Directorate of Adult Education for onwards transmission to the Directorate of Adult Education, Government of India as per schedules prescribed in this regard.

5. It is essential that an abstract information indicating the number of colleges implementing Adult Education programme, number of centres functioning and enrolment by sex and caste is sent by the university to the state Government latest by the 5th of the month succeeding each quarter. This information is required by the State Governments to send abstract information on monitoring of 20 Point Programme to the Directorate of Adult Education. Government of India, New Delhi by the 10th of succeeding of each quarter.,

Adult Education Research and Universities – Some Guidelines

1. The university in India have a major role to play, especially in the task of conducting applied research so as to improve upon the machinery and policy-planning of adult education programmes.
2. The universities should establish linkages of adult education to various development programmes through well-designed and effectively conducted research programmes. Universities should also undertake projects that display innovations for combining adult education with productive activities, and common cost benefits or cost-effectiveness.
3. The UGC should formulate guidelines and provide financial support for augmenting more qualitative research in this field.
4. The College can further undertake the task of investigation the socio-political, religious, cultural, economic, demographic and environmental needs and awareness of the illiterate adults before starting any programme of adult education. Moreover, they can locate, through village information schedules, the problems of adults, availability of reading materials, suitability of reading materials and visuals, etc. While the universities are to undertake research projects with macro perspective of fundamental or applied nature, the college should concentrate on problems of regional variations that would fall in the domain of action-research.
5. Since the non-formal adult, continuing and extension education programmes are growing very fast in all the sectors, namely, universities, voluntary organisations and government agencies, it is urgent and imperative that systematic efforts are to be initiated to develop professional manpower suitable to conceive,

plan, train and implement those programmes effectively.

6. Both of the strengthening of the short-term training programmes and also the diploma courses, it is imperative that a systematic and meaningful base of professional knowledge is developed. This means it is necessary to undertake a well directed academic activity of study, research and experimentation. To generate such an activity in a systematic manner, it requires an organisational frame-work. In the university set up, integrated M.Phil/Ph.D. programme built on the post-Master's Diploma programme, provides such a frame-work of organisation. The UGC should promote this programme of studies and research intended to break new ground in developing and consolidation appropriate body of knowledge in non-formal adult, continuing and extension education. The UGC should identify a few universities to start with on the basis of availability of senior academic persons with proven commitment, experience and academic abilities in the field of non-formal education and fully support its funding.
7. The nature of M.Phil./Ph.D. programme in non-formal adult, continuing and extension education should essentially be interdisciplinary in nature and should function as a power house to generate appropriate systematic body of basic and applied knowledge to develop professional manpower resources at various levels of functioning.
8. The course would have two terminal points, viz. M.Phil and Ph.D., though it is desired that those who enter into M.Phil. will go through Ph.D programme. No candidate should be admitted into this programme directly for Ph.D. It should essentially be an integrated M.Phil and Ph.D programme.

Special Target Groups

1. Women, scheduled caste, scheduled tribe, other backward communities, educationally backward minorities, rural population, handicapped should receive high priority in adult education activities.
2. In the total enrolment of the centres, an attempt should be made to secure at least 50% women, scheduled castes and scheduled tribe learners.

Umbrella Approach

1. There should be a single mechanism in the university system where by all activities like adult literacy, NSS, continuing and extension programmes and all other forms of non-formal learning are organised under one umbrella.
2. A faculty/school of non-formal education be created in the universities to promote and co-ordinate all such activities. While the departments of Adult Education would be responsible for programme of adult and continuing education, there may be other centres on other aspects of non-formal education such as rural development, etc.
3. *Organisation*: The departments of Adult and Continuing Education should have the same status as an academic department and universities should provide such recognition in their statures/ regulations wherever necessary.
4. Since adult education is a field activity with a multi-disciplinary thrust, traditional authority structures should not be applied to it. A separate faculty of non-formal education may, therefore, be more congenial to the aims and purposes of adult and continuing education.

Posts

1. The UGC should persuade the State Governments for giving concurrence to take over as a committed expenditure of staff at the end of 1990.
2. The posts sanctioned at present are up to 1990 which are of a temporary nature. However, all benefits as given to the permanent corresponding staff of the universities be given to such staff of the Departments of Adult and Continuing Education.
3. The State Governments may be persuaded to expedite their acceptance of the merger of these posts into the maintenance grants of the universities after 1990, when the UGC assistance ceases.
4. The colleges having adopted an area to organise about 100 centres. besides participation in other extension programmes should have a full time college programme officer as in the university.

5. The university Departments of Adult and Continuing Education should have adequate staff such as Directors, Assistant Directors, Project Officers, besides technical, administrative and statistical staff to ensure effective and target-oriented implementation of adult education programmes within the time bound frame.
6. Qualifications and Scales of Pay: Appropriate qualifications conducive to extension work should be modified on the following lines:
7. Both the new staff and the present staff be eligible in the scales of pay as recommended by the Commission lately, i.e. Rs 700 to 1,600 for project Officers Rs. 1,200 to 1,900 for Assistant Directors and Rs. 1,500 to 2,500 for Directors, subject to prescribed qualifications.
8. The revised qualifications as suggested by the Committee are to be acquired by both the new as well as the present staff as under:

   - In the case of Project Officer and Assistant Director/Coordinator, in a case a suitable candidate is not available who meets the prescribed qualifications or a qualified candidate is not found suitable by the Selection Committee, the condition of Post Master's Diploma and M.Phil/Ph.D or published learning materials or published research in the subject as stated in the qualifications be relaxed on conditions that the candidate selected fulfil the above condition within next 8 years from the date of appointment, otherwise the increment will cease at the stage where the incumbent is at that point of time.
   - As far as present incumbents holdings posts of Project Officer, Assistant Director/Coordinator, Director, appointed on permanent basis, who are appointed through properly constituted Selection Committee are concerned, they will be placed in the revised salary scales, irrespective of their present qualifications, on condition that they improve their qualifications to meet those prescribed above, within a period of their reaching the maximum of the unrevised scale (i.e. Project Officer at Rs. 1,300; Assistant Director/Coordinator at Rs. 1,600; and Directors at Rs. 2,000) failing which they will not be permitted to draw further increment in the revised grade.

Students

In order to motivate the students to take up adult education work, it should be integrated in the curriculum as a project or assignment to the considered for internal assessment. For this purpose a uniform system of credit should be devised for all the universities.

Supervisors

Appointment of full-time supervisors for centres should be encouraged rather than present part-time supervisors. This implies that every college or department should organise at least 30 centres.

Advisory Committee

1. The Advisory Committee should be at the university, college and centres levels to ensure proper implementation, Co-ordination, monitoring and achievements of targets.
2. University representatives should also be represented on the State/District level committees relating to the programmes of adult education, population education, etc.

Co-ordination and Collaboration

1. Co-ordination mechanisms must be evolved to ensure mutual help at all levels between National/State/Area Development plans and universities and colleges. through several committees suggested in this regard.
2. Effective collaborative linkages should be established and strengthened with voluntary organisations engaged in adult literacy or community development work.

Training and Manpower Development

1. Professional competence of adult education functionaries in the universities needs to be improved considerably. All functionaries of adult and continuing education be motivated to participate in series of three-week summer institutes. It should be made obligatory for all Assistant Directors and Project Officers to qualify in the post-M.A. Diploma and M.Phil course in Adult/Population Education.

2. M.Phil programmes in Adult and Continuing Education as a sequel to the post M.A. Diploma in Adult and Continuing Education or building it into an M.Phil programme to attract competent persons be instituted.
3. The training/organisation aspect needs to be seen in a more comprehensive frame than programme formulation and preparation of the manual/handbook. It needs to take into account preparation of training packages including printed materials, slide-cum-cassettes sets, transparencies, video-cassettes, etc. For the training of functionries at various levels.
4. Greater stress is needed for offering training/orientation programmes in continuing and population education.
5. Teacher fellowships on the lines of those in other disciplines should be provided by the UGC under faculty improvement programme for adult, continuing and population education.
6. 'National Lectureship' on the lines of other subjects should be created every year to sustain awareness on the entire gamut of the programme.

Teaching and Learning Materials

Materials should be made available on a large scale. Common materials related to media technology, e.g. slides, cassettes, should be prepared and replicated at Resource Centres and Media Centres and provided to all university Departments of Adult and Continuing Education.

Mass Campaign

A proper climate should be created in educational institutions and the neighbourhood community through publicity campaigns, mohalla committees, volunteer groups, mass media, placards, hoardings, banners, etc.

Local Community Involvement

Community leaders should be involved in the organisational aspects of the work by inviting them on Advisory Committees, Village community members should also be invited in identifying learners and programme planning.

Expectations from Universities

Universities have special responsibility in raising the quality of instruction at Adult Education Centres so as to enlighten the learners with latest knowledge in all relevant spheres of life in the most simplified manner.

Incentives

A system of recognition through incentives at different levels be introduced.

N.S.S

1. NSS Officers at the Centre/State/University and college levels should always be associated on the committees of adult education programme.
2. The scheme of NSS and Adult Education programme through universities and colleges in the country may be implemented by the UGC. This will also facilitate the integration of extension and community services in the curriculum.

8.3 UGC GUIDELINES ON THE SCHEME OF AUTONOMOUS COLLEGES (1987)[2]

Provision of Autonomy in National Policy on Education, 1986

"In view of mixed experiences with the system of affiliation, autonomous colleges will be helped to develop in large numbers until the affiliating system is replaced by a freer and more creative association of universities with colleges. Similarly, the creation of autonomous departments within universities on a selective basis will be encouraged. Autonomy and freedom will be accompanied by accountability." (Para 5.28).

Courses and programmes will be redesigned to meet the demand of specialisation better. Special emphasis will be laid on linguistic competence. There will be increasing flexibility in the combination of courses. (Para 5.29)

---

2. Published by University Grants Commission, New Delhi, 1987.
Note: Para numbers relate to the paras of Programme of Action.

8.4 PROGRAMME OF ACTION ON NATIONAL EDUCATION POLICY (1986)

(a) Development at Autonomous College (Para 5.28)

7. The system of affiliated colleges does not provide autonomy to deserving colleges to frame curricula, courses of studies, or their own system of evaluation. Although the UGC has been supporting this programme, only 21 colleges have been conferred autonomous status so far.
8. It is envisaged that about 500 colleges should be developed as autonomous colleges in the seventh Plan, and the existing affiliating system might be replaced in the long run. Due care will be taken to evolve a suitable framework for Autonomous Colleges.
9. In order to achieve this objective, it is proposed:

   (a) to make provision in the University Acts where necessary, to enable colleges to become autonomous;
   (b) to frame guidelines and pattern of assistance including the extent of academic, administrative and financial freedom and the corresponding responsibilities devolving on the autonomous colleges, their management structures, including provisions for safeguarding the interests of teachers, etc.;
   (c) to formulate a scheme of incentives such as special assistance to selected colleges, creation of posts of Readers and Professors, provision of a higher level of grant for development, etc. to colleges which becomes autonomous;
   (d) to provide special assistance to colleges in tribal/backward areas to enable them to develop into autonomous colleges;
   (e) to make statutory provision, if necessary, to enable autonomous colleges to award their own degrees or to confer deemed university status on them to develop other appropriate mechanisms to accelerate the process of curricular reforms, design of courses, reforms in teaching and evaluation procedures, etc.
   (f) to develop appropriate instruments for review/appraisal of the scheme of autonomous colleges at regular intervals, and to develop interaction among colleges to promote the scheme of autonomous colleges;

(g) to initiate detailed studies to develop alternate methods of university-colleges relationships that could replace the existing affiliating system in the long run.

10. The programme of autonomous colleges will be fully funded by the Central Government for a period of five years. Funds for this purpose will be made available to the UGC. However, the maintenance expenditure of those colleges will continue to be met by the resources which provide such expenditure, at present.

(b) **Design of Courses (Para 5.29)**

11. Higher Education Programme have to be redesignated to meet the growing demands of specialisation, to provide flexibility in the combination of courses, to facilitate mobility among courses, programmes and institutions, to update and modernise curricula, to integrate work/practical experience and participation in creative activities with the learning process, and to facilitate reforms in the evaluation procedure. The present rigid structures do not permit these reforms.
12. In order to achieve this objective, it is proposed:

(a) to secure full involvement of the Universities and Faculties in designing and reorienting the courses in higher education;
(b) to review comprehensively the existing guidelines on restructuring courses framed by the UGC to incorporate the new concepts in the design, content and structure envisaged in the policy;
(c) the foundation course proposed in the UGC scheme of restructuring courses will be an important element of general undergraduate programmes. A special emphasis should be laid on the study of India's Composite culture so as to foster unity and integrated of the country among students. Women's studies will be one of the components of the Foundation Course. The curricula of different disciplines will also reflect issues concerning women's status and development;
(d) to reorganise the Boards of studies in the Universities to facilitate redesigning of courses and to promote inter disciplinary programmes and inter-faces with employment;
(e) to make provision for academic reorganisation/credit for

participation in creative activities like NSS, NCC, Sports, Games, etc;

(f) to organise regional/national seminars to generate enthusiasm in an commitment to the new design of courses, flexibility in the combinations modular structure, accumulation of credits etc.; and

(g) to link development grants to universities with the willingness and interest in reorganisation of course and commitment to innovation as a continuing effort.

13. During the Seventh Plan, the UGC has set up 24 Curricular Development Centres. This number will be increased and their work will be oriented to the design visualised in the policy. The International Centres of Science & Technology Education may be utilised to coordinate and develop curricula in the field of Science & Technology. To begin with, in the next three years, model course material in 15 subjects will be developed in the form of audio/video cassettes with the help of best available teachers. The material could also be used for self-instruction and put out as radio/TV broadcasts. Eventually, such material is proposed to be made available as multi-media packages.

14. Autonomous colleges and autonomous Departments will be major instruments in promoting the redesign of courses. The College Development Councils to be set up will encourage local initiative in the design of courses especially the application oriented component and strengthening of linkages. The State Councils of Higher Education will ensure the implementation of these programmes and monitor the progress of their implementati

(c) **Teacher's Training (Para 5.31)**

15. The present system does not accord teachers a proper economic and social status, opportunities for professional and career development, initiative for innovation and creative work, proper orientation in concept, techniques and value system to fulfil their role and responsibilities. Motivation of teachers is important for implementation of the policy.

16. In order to achieve this, it is proposed:

(a) to organise specially designed orientation programmes in teaching methodologies, pedagogy, educational psychology, etc., for all new entrants at the level of lectures;

(b) to organise refresher courses for serving teachers to cover every teacher at least once in 5 years;

(c) to organise orientation programmes by using the internal resources of universities and by bringing a number of colleges together.

(d) to encourage teachers to participate in seminars, symposia etc.

17. The Indira Gandhi National Open University will run special programmes to promote self-learning among teachers. The recommendations of the Committee on revision of pay scales of teachers in universities and colleges will be examined for implementation. Teachers will be recruited on the basis of a common qualifying test the details of which will be formulated by the UGC. Methodologies will be developed for evaluation of teacher performance through self-appraisal, through peer groups, and also by students. Career advancement of teachers will be linked with professional development and performance appraisal. The Management structures of universities will be remodelled to provide opportunities for greater participation of teachers at all levels in academic administration.

UGC Guidelines

Need for Autonomy

The system of affiliating the colleges to a university was designed at a time when the number of colleges and universities was small. The universities acted as examining bodies and awarded degree on behalf of the colleges. The Colleges looked towards the universities for any changes in the educational system and curricula. The communication from universities did not always get similar interpretation and in the process of clarification a lot of time was lost. After independence, the number of educational institutions has increased manifold, and moreover, these institutions are now regarded as instruments of change in the society. Our society is however, diverse and its problems may vary from place to place. These need variation of approach and the acute problems ask for a quick response. The academic decisions also need quicker pace for making innovations and designing curricula and methods more relevant to the area in which an institution works the affiliating system does not allow the required freedom to the colleges to meet the demands cast upon them. The existence of a large number of affiliated colleges in a university has become a drag on the process of modernisation and improvement of standards. The decision for bringing about innovations can be taken speedily in a smaller body and can also be implemented more effectively if it is acted on by those who take the decision.

The Education Commission (1964-66) regarded the exercise of academic freedom on the part of teachers as crucial to the promotion and development of an intellectual climate in the country which is conducive to the pursuit of scholarship and excellence.

A meaningful system of education has to involve deeply not only the academia but also the students. The Education Commission recommended autonomy for colleges as under:

> "We should like to refer to the question of 'autonomous' colleges which has been under discussion for many years. Where there is an outstanding college or a small cluster of very good colleges within a large university which has shown the capacity to improve itself markedly, consideration should be given to granting it an autonomous status. This would involve the power to frame its own rules of admissions, to prescribe its courses of study, to conduct examinations and so on. The parent University's role will be one of general supervision and the actual conferment of the degree. The privilege cannot be conferred once for all and it will have to be continually earned and deserved and it should be open to the university, after careful scrutiny of the position, to revoke the autonomous status if the college at any stage begins to deteriorate in its standards. We recommend that provision for the recognition of such autonomous colleges be made in the constitution of the Universities".

The need for providing autonomy to such of the colleges as have *inter alia* the capacity to undertake innovations, design curricula, evolve methods of teaching and learning, frame own rules for admission, prescribe own courses of study and conduct the examinations has also been recognised in the National Policy on Education, 1986:

> "In view of mixed experiences with the system of affiliation,

> autonomous colleges will be helped to develop in large numbers until the affiliating system is replaced by a free and more creative association of Universities with colleges. Similarly, the creation of autonomous departments within universities on a selective basis will be encouraged. Autonomy and freedom will be accompanied by accountability".

In short, the autonomous status for colleges aims at giving opportunity to the teachers and students to make innovations, utilise their creative talent, improve the standards of teaching, examination and research and quickly respond to social needs. It is a vital step in the restructuring of relations between a college and a university. An autonomous college will take up the responsibility of the academic programmes, the content and quality of teaching and for the admission and assessment of students. The students would also receive greater individual attention on the basis of their needs and aptitude. It will be a joint pursuit of scholarship and excellence by teachers, students and the management.

Objectives of Autonomy

The set up of autonomous colleges represents a radical departure from the existing structure of the university system in India. An autonomous college will have the freedom to:

- determine its own courses of study and syllabi;
- prescribe rule of admission, subject of course to the reservation policy of the State Government; and
- evolve methods of evaluation and to conduct examinations.

The autonomy shall rather be a means to achieve higher standards and greater creativity in the future. For the time being the parent university of an autonomous college will continue to confer degrees upon the candidates declared eligible, on successful completion of the prescribed syllabi and valuation by the autonomous colleges. An autonomous college will be fully accountable for the content and quality of education that it imparts. It will be responsible for evaluation of the students for awards of degrees which will be accepted by the parent university.

Promotion of National Integration will be an important feature of the autonomous colleges through their academic programmes and other activities.

Relationship with Parent University and other Educational Institutions

The autonomous colleges will have autonomy to draw upon the expertise of the University departments and other institutions in framing curricula, devising the methods of evaluation, conduct of examinations and selection of teachers. The autonomous colleges will also have freedom to enter into collaborative teaching, research or extension education programmes with other colleges and institutions of higher learning with a view to strengthen their programmes and take benefit of facilities existing elsewhere.

While the parent universities of the autonomous colleges will accept the methodologies of teaching, evaluation and examination, course curriculum, etc., the universities will help the colleges to develop their academic programmes, improve the faculty and provide necessary guidance through participation in different statutory bodies recommended for autonomous colleges.

Award of Degrees

The degrees will be awarded by the parent University and the name of the College will be mentioned in the diploma. It may, however, in due course be possible to consider the cases of selected colleges to award their own degrees by considering them under the deemed university provision of the UGC Act.

Criteria for Identification of Institutions for Grant of Autonomy

While the following factors can help identify the institutions to claim autonomous status, it needs to be emphasized that autonomy should be less a reward for good performance during the past but rather a means to achieve higher standards and greater creativity in the future.

i. Academic reputation and previous performance in University examinations and their academic/co-curricular activities.
ii. Academic attainments of the faculty.
iii. The mode of selection of students and teachers viz., whether such selection is without regard to caste, creed or social class.

iv Physical facilities, e.g., library, accommodation and equipment.
v. Institutional management, viz., whether it is motivated by and responsive to academic considerations.
vi. The financial resources that the management/State Government can provide for the development of the institution(s).
vii. The responsiveness of the administrative structure to the views of staff and students.
viii. Extent of academic freedom enjoyed by the faculty for advanced scholarship, research and experimentation and involvement in educational innovation and reforms.

An autonomous college shall shed its pre-university/intermediate classes when the 10+2+3 scheme becomes operational so as to devote its efforts to the development of academic programmes at the degree and post-graduate levels.

Conferment of Autonomous Status

The autonomous status to a college will be conferred by its parent university to which it is affiliated, with the concurrence of the UGC and the concerned State Govt. The Act and Statutes of some of the Universities may not have provision for allowing autonomous status to its constituent or affiliated colleges. Necessary provision in this regard may be got made by the concerned universities. While granting autonomy, the university has to ensure that the management structure of the autonomous colleges should be such that it gives a lot of participation to academics alongwith responsibility.

The right of autonomy may not be conferred once for all. The exercise of rights on conferment of autonomous status by a college will however, have to be continuously earned and deserved. The status of autonomy may be granted initially for a period of five years but a review should be undertaken after three years by the University with the help of a Committee to be constituted for the purpose. The Committee may comprise academic experts as follows:

(a) One nominee of the parent university;
(b) One nominee of the state Government concerned;
(c) One nominee of the UGC;
(d) One Principal of an autonomous college to be nominated by the parent university; and

(e) An officer of the parent University.

In case of evidence of declining standards, it should be open to the university, after careful scrutiny to revoke the autonomous status.

In the case of Government colleges and the colleges managed by corporate management, it would be helpful if the faculty is not transferred from the college after autonomous status is conferred on it. Further, it would be advisable that appropriate statutory and advisory bodies are constituted for proper governance of the colleges, on the lines similar to those in other autonomous institutions.

Procedure for Conferment of Autonomous Status

i. With a view to effective implementation of the scheme of autonomous colleges, each university will constitute a Standing Committee including representatives of the UGC and the State Government.
ii. The University will invite proposals from colleges for conferment of autonomous status on the basis of guidelines. . . . The proposals may be placed before the Standing Committee that may be constituted by the university, according to the forgoing para (i) above. The Committee may like to visit the colleges and discuss the proposal with the management and/or faculty members to formulate its recommendations.
iii. The recommendations on approval of the Vice-Chancellor may be forwarded to the UGC and the State Government. . . . after the concurrence of the UGC and the State Government is available, the university will notify the conferment of autonomous status to the college. . . .

Mechanics for Implementation of Autonomy at College Level

Preparing a College for Autonomy: There are several areas where proper preparation is necessary if college autonomy is to be implemented successfully. These are: Staff preparation, departmental preparation, institutional preparation, preparing the students and the community and so on. They all should be completed well before autonomy is conferred to a college, so that no part of the college community is found unprepared for the new responsibility which the college is called upon to shoulder.

Staff Preparation: It is essential to get the entire staff of the college involved in the thinking and planning process for autonomy from the very beginning, so that they have a sense of participation in the decision making process at every stage of preparation. Every possible step should be taken to motivate the faculty members towards the concept of college autonomy. This can be done through seminars and workshop sessions to make them familiar with the objectives and rationale of autonomy.

Departmental Promotion: An important responsibility of the department will be to evolve suitable courses for the major and related subjects, prepare course materials, revise the courses and bring them up-to-date or modify them in the light of experience and in tune with the changing needs of society.

Institutional Preparation: Since an autonomous college will be called upon to perform many of the functions hitherto done by the University, the college will have to study the academic, administrative/management and financial implications of such a change-over and prepare itself to discharge its new functions efficiently.

Governance of an Autonomous College

The college will have the following committees to ensure proper management of academic, financial and general administrative affairs:

1. The Governing Body/Board of Management (as may be named)
2. The Academic Council
3. The Board of Studies

The college will in addition, have non-statutory advisory bodies like Finance Committee, Planning and Evaluation Committee, Grievances/Appeals Committee, Examination Committee, Admission Committee, Library Committee and a committee on students welfare and extra-curricular matters for help and advice to facilitate smooth working and development of the college.

(i) *Governing Body*: The Governing Body or Board of Management will *inter-alia*, have the representatives of State Government and University.

(ii) *Academic Council* will be solely responsible for all academic matters such as the framing of academic policies, approving courses, regulation, syllabus, etc. The council will ensure involvement of faculty at all levels and also outside experts including the representatives of University. The decision taken by the academic council will not be subject to any further ratification by the University academic council or other statutory bodies of the University.

(iii) *Boards of Studies* are basic units in the academic system. Their functions will include prescribing the regulations and syllabus for various courses, reviewing and updating the syllabus from time to time, introducing new courses, determining the details of the elements for continuous assessment, recommending panels for appointment of examiners for the end-semester examinations etc.

Monitoring, Evaluation and Accountability of Autonomy

Each autonomous college will with the approval of its Academic Council constitute appropriate mechanism to evaluate its academic performance, improvement in standards, success of the laid down regulations on different matters and how best it has used the autonomous status.

The autonomous college may in this regard profitably utilize the expertise from the University or other institutions. The parameters of monitoring to be devised could be the report of the autonomous college providing information relating to such aspects as the composition character of students, teacher recruitment and qualifications, innovative, curricular and co-curricular programme, remedial teaching for weaker students, in-service training for teachers, research output, publications, inter-collegiate, state, national and international level conferences, extension programmes, etc. Outstanding achievements of individual students and teachers, distinctive academic thrusts of the institution and development programmes and proposals too should form part of the information furnished by the autonomous college.

There will be self evaluation each year by the colleges. In addition, there will be two external evaluations, one after three years and the second after five years which will also determine continuance or otherwise of the autonomous status.

Suitable norms need to be formulated by the autonomous colleges for their accountability for personnel, financial and physical resources in relation to the specific academic objectives and overall national development.

The *external* accountability may include — Analysis of contents of courses, course options, co-curricular and extra-curricular activities, performance of students, students' employment, teachers' contribution to generation of knowledge and teachers' contribution to extension etc.

The *internal* accountability may include — Resource acquisition, efficiency index, average workload, average time distribution between lectures, tutorials/practicals, group discussions, project work, teaching aids used, programmes and activities planned and implemented, professional development of teachers, utilisation of infrastructural facilities, number of books/journals in the library.

A job analysis of faculty may also be taken up periodically.

Pattern of Financial Assistance

UGC will provide assistance to autonomous colleges to meet their additional and special needs.

The assistance to meet additional needs will be payable on yearly basis as a block grant which will be non-lapsable and will be termed as normal assistance. This assistance will enable the college to meet the expenditure involved on items such as:

i. additional faculty including visiting faculty;
ii. additional administrative/laboratory/library staff;
iii. redesigning of courses, development of teaching and learning material, organisation of workshops, seminars, orientation of teachers, faculty exchange and participation of teachers in conferences etc.;
iv. Examination reforms, development of question banks etc;
v. Provision of Audio Visual aids (TV, VCR, Video-cassettes, etc.);
vi. Development of monitoring instruments and evaluation guidelines;
vii. Improvement of laboratories;
viii. Strengthening of libraries;
ix. Cultural activities and sports; and
x. Procurement of office equipment.

The ceiling of normal assistance will be as follows:

(a) Undergraduate level only

(i) Arts/Science/Commerce	Rs. 4.00 lakhs p.a.
(ii) Arts, Science and Commerce	Rs. 7.00 lakhs p.a.

(b) Both Undergraduate and Postgraduate levels: Rs. 7.00 lakhs p.a.

The normal assistance as above will be for autonomous colleges offering not less than 6 programmes at the undergraduate level and 6 programmes at the undergraduate level and 6 programmes at the postgraduate level.

For the special needs of the autonomous colleges, assistance in respect of buildings, major equipment, laboratories etc. will be provided to them on the merit of each case.

In addition to the normal assistance and special assistance, autonomous colleges will also be eligible to receive grants for research, book writing, COSIP, COHSSIP etc.

The colleges providing professional education in the field of Education, Engineering and Technology etc. will also be eligible for financial assistance from the UGC, depending upon the size and stage of development of the colleges, on their attaining autonomous status. The colleges in the hilly/rural areas and the women's colleges will require improvements and changes in the curricula to make them more relevant to the needs of the people of these areas. They will be provided financial assistance to encourage such developments and the UGC will go out to develop the movement towards autonomous colleges in these areas.

General Matters

i. Each University will set up mechanism with the college Development Council of the University for encouraging the movement towards autonomous colleges and processing the proposals for conferment of autonomous status.

ii. (a) The employees both teaching and non-teaching; of a college on conferment of autonomous status will continue to be governed by the same terms and conditions of service as on the date of conferment of autonomous status. The benefit of revision of any terms and conditions of service will become available to the employees *mutatis mutandis* when the respective university to which the college is affiliated decides to review the service conditions of its employees.

(b) All recruitment of staff shall be directed by the Governing Council/Board of Management of the autonomous College and in accordance with the Policy recommended by the UGC namely advertisement in newspaper and selection by a Committee including two external experts approved by the University.

iii. It would be necessary to orient the Principals of the colleges and provide intensive training to teachers of autonomous colleges in areas such as:

- objectives of autonomy and accountability;
- Innovation to make teaching and learning more effective;
- Evaluation methods;
- Linking of their creative activities with Societal needs through Research and Extension;
- Planning of academic programmes;
- Financial management;
- Administrative management etc.

The orientations and re-orientation of Principals/College teachers should be done periodically on a continuing basis.
The UGC will provide financial assistance for the orientation of Principals and Heads of departments of colleges at selected places all over the country. These trained Principals/Heads of Departments would later train the other teachers of autonomous colleges.
Universities and autonomous colleges may jointly draw appropriate orientation training programmes.

iv. Universities should ensure that students of autonomous colleges are not denied or treated otherwise for admission in courses at higher levels in the Universities/Non-autonomous colleges. Some measures such as admission tests, reservation of seats for students of autonomous colleges may be considered.

v. UGC will welcome research projects which may promote and improve the functioning of autonomous system in Indian Universities. These may include studies, development of model acts, statutes, guidelines on academic, financial and academic freedom, development of monitoring instruments, instruments for review/appraisal, models on alternative University-College relationship etc.

vi. Autonomous colleges will be free to explore the possibilities of having research projects from agencies such as the ICSSR, ICAR, CSIR, DST, industry etc., etc.

vii. Organisation of special need-based short-term courses of continuing education may be an important activity of autonomous colleges.

viii. The UGC may allocate a few earmarked Junior Research fellowships exclusively for autonomous colleges under its scheme of 'Research Fellowships at any one time'.

ix. The guidelines are suggestive; universities and autonomous colleges could adopt alternative strategies with a view to achieve the objectives of autonomy. The ideals of autonomy would be better appreciated and implemented in a participatory approach between the State Government, University, UGC and Autonomous colleges.

8.5 UGC GUIDELINES ON COACHING CLASSES FOR COMPETITIVE EXAMINATIONS FOR WEAKER SECTIONS AMONGST EDUCATIONALLY BACKWARD MINORITY COMMUNITIES (1988)[3]

Introduction

The scheme of Coaching Classes for Minorities is framed in pursuance of Point No. 11 of the Prime Minister's 15-Point Programme regarding the fullest integration of minorities in all walks of national life by encouraging starting of coaching classes in educational institutions.

The *National Policy on Education (1986)* states:

> Some minority-groups are educationally deprived or backward. Greater attention will be paid to the education of these groups in the interests of equality and social justice. This will naturally include the constitutional guarantees given to them to establish and administer their own educational institutions, and protection

3. Published by the University Grants Commission, New Delhi, 1988.

Note: Para numbers relate to the paras of the document concerned.

> to their languages and culture. Simultaneously, objectivity will be reflected in the preparation of textbooks and in all school activities, and all possible measures will be taken to promote an integration based on appreciation of common national goals and ideals, in conformity with the core curriculum.
>
> (Para 4.8)

In order to implement the National Policy on Education, the Programme of Action approved by the Government of India, in this regard reads as under:

> "According to 1981 Census, the religious minorities constitute about 17.4% of the population of which Muslims are 11.4%, Christians 2.4%, Sikhs 2%, Buddhists 0.7%, and Jains 0.5%. Ministry of Home Affairs have identified Muslims and Neo-Buddhists as educationally backward at national level. It was agreed that the State Governments may also identify other groups which are educationally backward at the State level. Special efforts need to be taken to bring these educationally backward minorities on par with the rest of the society and to make them participate fully in the national development activities".
>
> (Para XIV.2)

Accordingly, this Scheme for the students belonging to weaker sections amongst educationally backward minority communities would be applicable on an all-India basis.

Aims and Objectives

The selected Universities/Colleges will organise appropriate coaching classes to prepare persons belonging to educationally backward minority communities so as to enable them to compete in various competitive examinations for (a) recruitment to services under the Central and State Governments, Public and Private Undertakings, Banks, etc.; (b) admissions to Engineering, Medical, Agricultural, Management Courses etc.; and (c) acquiring proficiency in typing, shorthand and secretarial courses etc.

Organisation

The Coaching Centres for higher competitions may normally be located in universities and those for lower services in colleges, but relaxation can be made as may be required by the local conditions. Each centre will have an appropriate catchment and service area attached to it. The universities, in addition to higher competitions, may also cater to preparation for junior competitions. This will help the university to broad-base their activities, keep coaching going on uninterruptedly throughout the year and create a general awareness.

Each institution shall constitute an Advisory Committee which will be responsible for overseeing implementation, monitoring, evaluation, followup, coordination of the Scheme in terms of its objectives for tailoring the Scheme to local requirements, creating awareness among the target groups.

The University level committee will be under the Chairmanship of the Vice-Chancellor and that at the College level under the Principal. The Advisory Committee will, *inter alia*, include representatives of the State Government, the Chairman of the State Minorities Commission or his nominee and not less than three members of the educationally backward minorities communities and will meet at least once in each quarter.

The Scheme should be run as an independent scheme and should not be merged/associated with any other scheme. This would ensure a meaningful focus on the desired target groups.

Location of Centres

It would be desirable, wherever possible, to locate the coaching centres at institutions which are managed by the educationally backward minorities, followed by institutions located in their concentration areas with a view to ensure admissions in such centres of an adequate number of students from educationally backward minority communities.

Activities

The Coaching Centres will organise instructions to provide knowledge, improve attitudes and refine techniques so as to enable candidates to compete successfully in competitive examinations for the Central/State level/ Public undertaking/Banking service and/or admission to various professional courses. The courses provided in the coaching classes may include tutorials and group discussions aimed at removing the short-comings of candidates and preparing them for success.

Training

For orientation of key-level functionaries, the UGC will encourage holding of summer institutes, seminars and workshops so that the problems faced in conducting the coaching classes can be resolved, and the functioning of the centres is improved.

The initial orientation of key-level functionaries will be organised centrally under the guidance of resource persons, whose services could be temporarily secured from appropriate institutions.

Master trainers, having undergone intensive orientation centrally, would later impart training to other faculty members/college teachers.

Teaching/Learning Material

Each centre will be adequately equipped with proper books, journals and appropriate teaching/learning and other related materials.

Coordination

The UGC Standing Committee will undertake coordination, monitoring and review of the Scheme at all-India level.

Awareness

Concerted measures be undertaken by the Centres to promote awareness about the Scheme including the dissemination of suitable material, organisation of meetings etc., in the catchment/service area.

Admissions

The competitive examinations for which the coaching classes are to be organised and the intake for each course will be decided by each institution according to its local situation under the directions of its Advisory Committee.

The notification for admission by a coaching centre may preferably be based on the guidelines given by the Advisory Committee.

A nominal tuition fee may be charged from the candidates and the funds so collected should be utilised towards helping the needy students.

Motivation

All efforts be made to motivate the desired target groups for achieving the objectives of the Scheme. This may, *inter alia*, involve the following:

i. Organisation of appropriate pre-coaching/preparatory remedial classes for the identified bright students of minority communities in schools and colleges so as to enable them to become potential candidates to be effectively benefited by the Scheme; and
ii. Financial incentives to poor students.

Funds normally up to 15% of the year's allocation may be utilised for organising pre-coaching remedial classes as also for financial incentives. This provision will not be re-appropriated for any other purpose.

Motivational efforts will be an important activity in the catchment/service area of each coaching centre.

Financial Pattern

The UGC will provide financial support to the selected institutions for organising coaching classes.

The number and nature of staff, whether full-time or part-time and visiting-faculty at different levels may be decided by each institution, keeping in view its programmes/activities, the levels and aspirations of the candidates.

Normally, assistance up to the level indicated below may be provided for each coaching centre:

Type	*Non-Recurring*	*Recurring*
A. University	Rs. 2.50 lakhs for a 5-year period	Rs. 2.00 lakh per annum
B. College	Rs. 1.50 lakhs for a 5-year period	Rs. 1.00 lakh per annum

The specific purposes for which these funds are to be utilised will be decided by each institution keeping in view the activities/programmes of the centre during the year as per directions of the Advisory Committee.

Special needs, if any, will be considered separately on merit.

An honorarium of Rs. 100 per lecture be paid to an outstation expert and Rs. 50 per lecture to a local expert, subject to a maximum of Rs. 750 per expert in a session. However, in exceptional cases, the limit of Rs. 750 may be relaxed up to Rs. 1,000 with the approval of the Vice-Chancellor.

Synopsis and lecture notes will be prepared by the Resource Persons in advance for circulation to students. These will be kept in the library of the Centre and periodically updated.

Monitoring and Evaluation

The Advisory Committee will monitor the programme continuously and in detail, once every quarter. It will send the quarterly Progress Report to the UGC, the Minority Commission of India, and Minority Cell, Ministry of Welfare in Government of India.

An annual evaluation report stating clearly the weaknesses, strengths and achievements of the programme as approved by the Advisory Committee will be sent to the UGC, as well as to the Ministry of Welfare in the Government of India by the first weak of the second month following the year under report.

The UGC will get the programmes reviewed thoroughly at least once in three years with the help of its Standing Committee and experts and make such changes as are deemed necessary.

The Standing Committee of the UGC will meet at least once in a quarter to monitor the progress of the Scheme at the all India level.

Centres for Women

Special assistance and facilities may be given for coaching of women including residential accommodation.

Regional Resource Centres (R.R.Cs.)

A few coaching centres on the recommendations of the UGC Standing Committee may be designated as Regional Resource Centres (R.R.Cs.) for effective implementation and coordination of the Scheme. The funding pattern of the RRCs will be somewhat different from other centres in the sense that supplementary funds and staff will be provided for the additional work. The staffing and financial patterns although indicated at Annexure V, may vary for each centre on recommendations of the UGC Standing Committee.

The functions of the RRCs will be:

(i) To perform a coordinating role in developing linkages with other RRCs, Minority Commission, UPSC, SPSC, Staff Training Colleges, Voluntary Organisations for the welfare of Minorities etc.
(ii) To organise orientation programmes for the functionaries of the coaching centres in the respective regions.
(iii) To prepare and exchange learning material for coaching classes including review and upgrading of available materials and preparation of new material.
(iv) To plan and conduct evaluation studies specially to identify factors connected with the extent of participation of educationally backward minorities in the coaching classes and assessing their needs and tailoring of material to their requirements and levels.
(v) To facilitate promotional and publicity work related to the Scheme.

There will be an Advisory Committee to advise the RRC, to discharge aforesaid functions effectively and such an Advisory Committee may be constituted by the Vice-Chancellor of the University where the RRC is located. The coordinators of the Coaching Centres located in the region of the RRC shall also be the members of the Advisory Committee.

Supportive and Promotive Measures

(i) The service of retired and young civil servants and teachers endowed with required motivation be liberally utilized in organization of coaching centres.
(ii) Teachers with required inclination may be chosen and properly trained for organising coaching classes.
(iii) Faculty appointed in coaching centres be treated as non-vocational. For all other purposes, it will be treated as an academic staff and given all benefits to which teachers are entitled.
(iv) Special care is to be taken in the selection of staff so as to ensure that committed and dedicated persons are appointed in the Centres.

(v) Remedial coaching in core subjects e.g. English Arithmetic, General studies etc. be always provided.

(vi) All efforts be made to identify the promising students at the school/college level and to give them remedial and supportive assistance suitably.

(vii) Necessary measures be adopted suiting to local situations for achieving the objectives of the Scheme.

(viii) Adequate publicity on a constant basis should be effected in the catchment area.

(ix) A list of core reference material, question banks and bibliography etc. would also be made available centrally to all the centres through the Regional Resource Centres.

(x) Joint meeting of Co-ordinators/Teachers incharge of centres once in three months will promote co-ordination among centres.

(xi) The core of the coaching scheme should be a year-long course in subjects common to a large number of examinations namely English, General Studies and Arithmetic. This core course would be supplemented by special preparatory efforts relating to individual examinations, such as civil services, banking services, defence services etc.

Submission of Proposals

The universities will forward all proposals received by them for starting coaching centres with their comments to the UGC. In order to avoid delay the applications may be forwarded as they are received. The colleges will invariably send a copy of their application directly to the UGC.

The UGC will have all the proposals scrutinised with the help of a Sub-committee of the Standing Committee on coaching classes. Where necessary, the good offices of the Ministry of Welfare, Govt. of India be utilised for having inquiries conducted. The recommendations made by the Sub-committee will be considered by the Standing Committee of the UGC.

Approval of Proposals

The UGC will approve proposals on the recommendation of its Standing Committee.

Each proposal will be assisted initially for a period of three years.

Further assistance will be based on review of the work of the centre.

Release of Grants

The first instalment (75%) of the grant will be released at the time of approval of the proposal and the remaining 25% will be released later. For each such instalment, the institution will submit progress report and expenditure statement etc.

MODEL ADVISORY COMMITTEE

University Level

1. Vice-Chancellor	Chairman
2. State Education Secretary or his Representative	Member
3. Chairman State Minority Commission or his Nominee (where the Commission exists)	"
4. Three Representatives of Educationally Backward Minority Communities	"
5. Two Professors of the Universities	"
6. Two principals of Colleges having coaching, classes, by rotation, if necessary	"
7. Incharge of the Scheme in the University	Member Secretary

College Level

1. Principal	Chairman
2. A representative of State Education Deptt.	Member
3. A Representative of State Minorities Commission (where the Commission exists)	"
4. Three Representatives of Educationally Backward Minority Communities	"
5. One Teacher of the College	"
6. Teacher-incharge of the Scheme in the College	Member Secretary

Functions of the Advisory Committee

1. To recommend the training programmes to be run at the coaching centre and lay down admission rules for such programmes.

2. To suggest steps for giving publicity to the training programmes.
3. To suggest fees to be charged from the candidates seeking admissions to the coaching classes.
4. To exercise a watch over expenditure at the centre and lay down appropriate regulations thereof and
5. To suggest steps for proper monitoring and evaluation of the training centre.

8.6 UGC COMMITTEE ON ACCREDITATION AND ASSESSMENT COUNCIL (1988)[4]

Background

Programme of Action of the National Policy of Education, 1986, *inter alia* recommended that:

> "Excellence of institutions of higher education is a function of many aspect: Self-evaluation and self-improvement are important among them. If a mechanism is set up which will encourage self-assessment in institutions and also assessment and accreditation by a Council of which these institutions are corporate members, the quality of process, participation, achievements, etc. will be constantly monitored and improved.
>
> It is proposed to develop a mechanism for accreditation and assessment for maintaining and raising the quality of institutions of higher education. As a part of its responsibility for the maintenance and promotion of standards of education, the UGC will, to begin with, take the initiative to establish Accreditation and Assessment Council as autonomous body".

Constitution and Terms of Reference

In pursuance of this directive, the University Grants Commission constituted a Committee under the Chairmanship of Dr. Vasant Gowariker, Secretary, Ministry of Science and Technology "to make recommendations regarding setting up of Accreditation and Assessment Council in order to develop a mechanism for maintenance and raising of quality of institutions of higher education, while keeping

4. Published by the University Grants Commission, New Delhi, 1988.

in view the objectives, uses and various methods/procedures that are currently being followed by different countries or that can be adopted".

Introduction

In brief, what is wrong with Indian universities is that they are not generative. They do not give rise to a vital and self-supporting intellectual life. Though it is true that they do not have realistic funding, their achievement is still not proportionate to the time, effort and intellectual resources expended on them. Perhaps the major cause of their failure is the manner of their governance, which does violence to the operations of mind and the growth of knowledge. Academic institutions must be built around the principle of intellectual autonomy. Most of ours are not.

Historical roots of the mediocrity of Indian higher education can be traced to the exigencies of British rule, in the need to contain the dangerous potential of self-rule in the realm of ideas. The present structures are descended practically unaltered from that time. The governance of universities is part of a larger pattern, the command-and-control style of bureaucracy, which was established in the interests of British supremacy and which still continues to dominate our public life.

Management of Higher Education

Command-and-control management entails a hierarchical notion of "accountability" and top-down initiative. Goals and values are formulated from the outside, and the various ways in which their implementation can go wrong are taken into account and sanctions are provided against these. The governing attitude is suspicion. Dignity and authority are vested largely in the supervisory levels, most of all in the remote government bureaucracy, and next to none with working academics. Intellectual and pedagogical initiative are stifled, and experimentation, innovation and the finding of appropriate responses to local circumstances become impossible. The goals of universities get pitched at a very modest level, to achievements peripheral to the real purpose of a university such as the regular holding of examinations and the announcement of results. The management of universities gets reduced to a law-and-order problem, with a limited and crude repertoires of political–bureaucratic actions to bring them to a semblance of control.

The situation of colleges is particularly bad, because of their subordination to affiliating universities. This suffocates the initiative of college faculty and denies them the necessary control over the circumstances of their work. On the other hand, factors like the recent raising of the college entrance age with the addition of two years of secondary education and the raising of lecturer qualification to the doctoral level have made the issue of academic autonomy at the college level both more urgent and more promising.

There is an alternative style of management to the command-and-control, hierarchical bureaucratic method. It is a style which has been demonstrating its superiority world-wide, not just in the academic realm but in business and government as well. It means putting people first. In the words of one of the leaders of the Japanese ascendancy, "To motivate people, you must bring them into the family and treat them like respected members of it". A system which does this is decentralized, democratic and facilitative.

In the academic sphere the first postulate of the new system is the authority and dignity of the working academic. Once this is conceded, the organizational patterns that are coherent with it follow naturally. These include collegiality in the life of the department and of the institution, and the derivation of administrative authority from departmental and faculty councils.

Though it is widely conceded that nothing worthwhile can be accomplished without academic autonomy, the tendency is to let the fear of potential abuse lead back to the bureaucratic-hierarchical system.

Accreditation

As a way to assure the effectiveness of academic institutions while maximally supporting academic self-regulation, the Programme of Action of the Nationai Policy on Education 1986 has called for the setting up of an autonomous Council on Accreditation and Assessment. The accreditation policy forms part of a reform which must be viewed as a whole and whose other important aspects include the provision for autonomy of colleges and the projected National Testing Service.

While the central motive to the accreditation system has come from the requirements of college autonomy, it also answers the need for a systematic and regular means for assuring that colleges and universities and functioning effectively.

The hierarchical-bureaucratic approach to possible academic abuses is like administering a dope-test while the race is still on. The system of institutional accreditation, on the other hand, is based on first giving an institution the maximum freedom in defining its goals and the means to achieve them, and then examining it closely, as a whole. The crucial difference from the bureaucratic system with its cumbersomeness and enforced uniformity is made possible by reliance on the of faculty judgment, in particular the judgment of responsible educators who know what academic excellence is through their own participation in it. They are able to evaluate the institution as a whole and to assess its parts in terms of their functional relation to this, and they are not constrained to see those parts only in terms of adherence to some preconceived bureaucratic prescription.

Operationalisation of an effective system of accreditation in the country will gradually lead to the establishment of norms and criteria for institutional performance assessment, and methodologies and tools for systematic institutional self-study and self-evaluation. Moreover, institutions themselves will collectively benefit through integration of this element of assessment into the institutional culture.

Important Features of an Accreditation System

Institutional accreditation originated in the United States and has existed there in close to the present form for some decades and is also to be found in Canada and Japan among others. The division of authority and responsibility between central government and states in the field of higher education is similar in North America and India. Some of the main features of an operational institutional accreditation system which commend themselves are the following:

(1) Institutional accreditation, the recognition of the performance and integrity of an educational institution, is granted by an association of institutions of higher education. Accreditation means membership in the association, and the accrediting commission of the association is elected by the institutional members.

Accreditation, which is the assurance by a non-governmental body of the quality of an educational institution, must be distinguished from the granting by the (state or federal) government of a charter or licence to an institution, legally enabling it to award degrees. An institution must have a charter before it can be accredited.

(2) Institutional accreditation is a means for the self-regulation of the academic profession, with minimal political and bureaucratic interference.

(3) Institutional accreditation does not imply that accredited institutions have a similarity of goals or uniformity of process or that they are comparable. It permits diversity and innovation.

(4) The first part of the accreditation process is a self-study by the institution, involving in this activity all of its major constituents including faculty, students and administration. Included in this process is the sharp defining by the institution of its primary mission or goals. This must be soundly conceived; it must be realistic as well as appropriate to the collegiate level.

(5) The second part of the accreditation process is an onsite evaluation by a team of professional educators (faculty and administrators). Though they have the help of published association policies, their main reliance is upon their own experienced judgement. Institutional evaluation is ultimately subjective.

(6) Institutional accreditation indicates that, in the judgement of responsible members of the academic community, an institution's own goals are soundly conceived and appropriate, that its educational programmes have been intelligently planned and are competently conducted, and that the institution is accomplishing the majority of its goals substantially and has the resources to continue to do so for the forseeable future.

(7) Institutional accreditation is a matter of "yes" or "no" to the institution as a whole. It embraces all educational endeavours conducted by a single institution regardless of its complexity. Institutional accreditation must be distinguished from specialized or professional accreditation; where the latter applies, institutional accreditation is usually a prior necessity. Institutional accreditation must also be distinguished from the nation wide comparative assessments of departments in a particular discipline. This is usually carried out by a professional association in that discipline.

(8) In order to be accredited an institution must meet the Association's qualitative criteria for the assessment of institutional effectiveness in each of the principle areas of

institutional activity and responsibility, as follows:

a. Institutional Missio ives
b. Evaluation and Plann
c. Organization and Governance
d. Programmes and Instruction
e. Special Activities
f. Faculty
g. Student Services
h. Library and Learning Resources
i. Physical Facilities
j. Financial Resources
k. Ethical Practices
l. Publications and Advertising

(9) The accreditation agency is not simply a body for the assurance of educational quality. The process of accreditation encourages institutional improvement through continual self-study and evaluation. Accreditation agencies develop criteria and guidelines for assessing institutional effectiveness. And the expert criticism and suggestions of the evaluating team are invaluable.

(10) Developing or newly applying institutions can prior to accreditation, be awarded candidate status on satisfying certain criteria. These Requirements of Candidature concern institutional characteristics largely capable of objective verification. Candidature is usually granted for a two-year term. If progress is being made, candidacy can be extended for up to six years.

(11) Accreditation must be periodically reaffirmed, within a period of five years after initial accreditation, and within ten years thereafter. Accrediting bodies reserve the right to review member institutions any time for cause. They also reserve the right to review any substantive change in the institution; such changes are reviewed within two years after the changes become effective. An accredited institution which shows serious weakness in one or more areas, but which also shows firm potential for remedying the deficiencies, may be put on probation. Accreditation continues, but generally for a sharply reduced term.

(12) The accrediting associations are institutional-membership organizations supported by annual dues, from the candidate and accredited institutions. They elect the accreditation commissions, the bodies which make the final decision on accreditation after receiving the institution's self-study report and the report of the evaluation team.

Expenses for accrediting activities are borne by the institution on a cost basis. This is kept low by the extensive use of volunteers on evaluation visits.

A typical Commission consists of sixteen members who are elected at the Annual Meeting for staggered three-year terms. Provision is made for different types of institutions and the general public to be represented on the Commission. Commissioners serve without compensation, and those who are institutional representatives are currently active on the faculties or staffs of institutions accredited through the Commission. The Commission normally meets four times a year, but various committees may meet more frequently. The day-to-day activities of the Commission are conducted by a Director of Evaluation, professional staff, and support staff.

(13) Though accreditation agencies are non-governmental their accreditation has come to be recognized as a necessary qualification for eligibility to receive federal funds. The federal government in turn recognizes, for a four-year duration, those accrediting agencies which it finds to be a reliable indicator of educational quality

(14) Despite the diversity of accredited institutions, there are some substantive curricular requirements that they must all meet, most notably a coherent and substantial programme of liberal or general studies, amounting to no less than a quarter of all course-work in a four-year undergraduate programme. This requirement is also extended to post-baccalaureate degrees, in the sense that undergraduate work with a sufficient general education component must at least be a prerequisite to those post-baccalaureate programmes.

Steps Toward an Accreditation System

1. These above features of an operational accreditation system will serve as benchmarks in establishing a system of institutional

accreditation in the Indian context as a means of reorganising the assurance of educational quality of making expert academic consultation widely available, and as a way of mobilising local initiative and energy through self-definition and continual self-appraisal.

2. The initial impetus for an accreditation system will come form the UGC, through its selection of a group of about twenty good autonomous institutions for initial candidature.

   Until such time as twenty institutions are accredited, there will be a provisional Accreditation Association made up of candidate institutions, the original twenty plus those that are later admitted into candidature. After twenty institutions are accredited they will constitute the core of the Accreditation Association or Accreditation Council and candidate institutions will thereafter have observer status. The Association will be an autonomous, self-governing body-to begin with, a registered society. It will meet once a year.

   Each institution's representative to the Annual Meeting of the Association will be appointed by the administrative head of the institution, the Vice-Chancellor or the Principal. At the Annual Meeting the representatives will elect Commissioners the members of the Accreditation Commission, the body which will make the final decision on accreditation. The Commission will comprise fifteen members, serving three-year terms. Eventually, the appointments will be staggered, with about one-third of the positions being vacated each year. Commissioners will be drawn from institutions of different types as well as from outside the academic world. From among these the Association representatives will at their first meeting elect a Chairman of the Commission and an Associate Chairman for one-year terms. Subsequently, the Associate Chairman will succeed the Chairman, and a new Associate Chairman will be elected annually. The Commission will meet about four times a year.

   The Accreditation Commission will, with the consent of the University Grants Commission, initially and then whenever necessary appoint a Director of Evaluation, who will conduct the day-to-day activities of the Commission with the help of a secretariat of professional and support staff. The Director's term will normally be five years, but can be terminated earlier for valid reasons by Accreditation Commission. His status, method of appointment and terms and conditions of service will be comparable with those of a Vice-Chancellor of a University.

The Commission will also, with the consent of the University Grants Commission, appoint an Associate Director of Evaluation, who will report to the Director. He will normally succeed the Director.

The Director will supervise the codification of the principles, guidelines, methods and observations of the accreditation agency into a Handbook, and will submit these to the Commission for its approval.

The Director will draw up a list of potential evaluators, with critical biographies, for the approval of the Commission. The accreditation agency will keep on file a list of at least a hundred approved evaluators. They will serve in an honorary capacity. The other terms of their association with the Commission, will be determined by the Commission.

The ultimate decision on accreditation will be made by the Commission after seeing the self-appraisal and evaluation reports and related material.

The Accreditation association will eventually be encouraged to function on a zonal basis, for reasons of tractability and economy.

3. The following are some of the major points on which an institution will face scrutiny in the process of accreditation, and which it will address in its self-appraisal:

(a) *Institutional Mission and Objectives*

These should be practical, appropriate to the university/collegiate level, and socially responsible.

(b) *Evaluation and Planning*

There should be sharply defined institutional goals and effective mechanisms for periodic, systematic self-evaluation, planning and review of objectives. The process should take into account state and central plans.

(c) *Organisation and Governance*

There should be published a clear statement based on the acts and statutes defining the respective powers, functions, responsibilities of each organisational component (Senate, Executive Council, Academic Council, governing board, administrative officers, faculty, departments, students and other constituencies) and their inter-relationships. Provisions for the distribution of authority and responsibility should be depicted in an organisational chart that represents the actual working of the institution. The faculty must have a major role in shaping and conducting academic policy. There should be provision for the consideration of student views in matters of direct and reasonable interest to them. The public interest should be adequately represented in the determination of the overall policies of the institutions.

(d) *Programmes and Instruction*

Every undergraduate programme whether professional, specialised or general ought to show an appropriate regard for the humanities, natural sciences and social sciences. Usually, at least a quarter of each student's programme should consist of courses in these areas, but experimentation with other ways of meeting the end of well-roundedness should be encouraged. Courses should adhere to clearly defined institutional standards of scholarship. There ought to be appropriate means for monitoring the effectiveness of the educational programmes. (The development of some of these, such as a National Testing Service, will be the job of educational bodies and authorities outside the institution). There should be some systematic procedures that tend to assure that assessments are fairly awarded while at the same time preserving the integrity of the educational process. There should be some means of assuring that the number of sessions planned for a course are actually held, and that the students and teachers are fulfilling their responsibilities in respect of the course.

(e) *Faculty*

The qualifications and numbers of the faculty should be adequate to discharge their academic responsibilities. Their recruitment, promotion, retention and security of tenure and other conditions of service, particularly the teacher's academic autonomy, in determining the content of the course, the teaching method and the method of evaluation, should be at a level consonant with the dignity of the academic profession. There ought to be formal or informal forums for open communication amongst the faculty and between faculty and administrative officers.

(f) *Student Services*

There should be an orderly and ethical admissions procedure, and compliance in spirit as well as law with special provisions for disadvantaged groups. Academic, personal and career counselling services, grievance-redressal services, health services and services for foreign students and the handicapped should be available. There should be clear published statements on student rights and responsibilities. Current information about graduates and their progress in careers should be maintained, and the interest of alumni in the development of the institution encouraged.

(g) *Library and Learning Resources*

Books and non-print materials and library services, study space and staff should be adequate to the educational programme and there should be systematic planning for future needs.

(h) *Physical Facilities*

Buildings, grounds and equipment should be adequate to meet the needs of the institution. They should be well-maintained and aesthetically pleasing. Classrooms and laboratories ought to be properly equipped and adequate in number and size.

(i) *Financial Resources*

The institution should be financially stable, with sufficient resources to carry out its objectives into the foreseeable future. It should have control of its financial resources and budgetary procedures, and be free from undue influence or pressure from external funding sources. There should be a clearly defined and consistently implemented process by which the budget is established and resources are allocated. There should be a yearly external audit, reviewed by the appropriate individuals or groups in the institution.

(j) *Ethical Practices*

In all its dealings the institution should show concern for basic values and observe the spirit as well as the letter of legal requirements.

(k) *Publications and Advertising*

The institution should publish a catalogue or handbook describing clearly and accurately its objectives, its admission policies, each academic programme or course of study, the requirements for a degree or other recognition, the members of the faculty with their academic qualifications, the fees and charges, the refund policy, the learning and physical resources, and other information the institution considers significant.

4. The Accreditation Agency should be a self-financing institution. Its recurring expenditure should be met entirely from the membership fees paid by member institutions. The fees paid by the institutions should be accepted as an admissible item of expenditure for purposes of grants-in-aid to them. The initial expenditure on setting up the Accreditation Council should be met by the UGC for a period of three years.
5. Within five years of the setting up of the Accreditation Council, only accredited institutions will be eligible for Central funding. Some painful decisions will have to be made, but if there is to be any point to an accreditation system, it must be operated with

great integrity, and therefore there must be no exceptions.

State governments will be free, as before, to found, charter or recognise, and to fund, new institutions, but those institutions will not receive any Central funds until they become accredited. Funding, development or support of as yet unaccredited. Funding, development or support of as yet unaccredited state institutions will be entirely the concern of the States.

For the founding of a new Central institution, separate funds will be allocated to sustain it until it wins accreditation, and planning for the new institution will be undertaken with the requirements of candidature in mind. If a central institution fails to win accreditation even after a reasonable period of time and investment of funds, the Accreditation Council will recommend its closure.

6. The implications of non-accreditation and loss of accreditation, including the consequences for faculty and past and present students, must be spelled out in advance and publicised.

   Denial or loss of accreditation must not come as a surprise. Consultancy services recognised by the Association should be also be available to provide an early warning of deficiencies and advice in dealing with them.

7. The right to academic self-determination of the individual academic, the department, and the college or university is fundamental. The *prima facie* satisfaction of it (as evidenced, for example, by the rule and composition of the statutory bodies of the institution) will be a requirement of candidature.

8. Autonomy is not a prize for the deserving. It is a precondition for any worthwhile work. So it cannot be made a consequent to accreditation or even to candidature, but must precede them.

   The accreditation system is designed, above all, to make college (and university) autonomy possible by shifting to a mode of accountability that is horizontally rather than vertically organised, and which therefore does not stifle local initiative.

   The current UGC guidelines on autonomy envision two degrees of autonomy for colleges. The first, more properly designated "semi-autonomy", is under the aegis of the erstwhile affiliating university, which, along with other external agencies, has its representation on all the college's statutory bodies. Semi-autonomy does not go far enough in enabling teachers to determine their work situation, alienating them from their jobs.

And it makes the statutory bodies cumbersome and open to manipulation by persons without a legitimate stake in them. Semi-autonomy, then, though it is a great improvement over affiliation should be seen as a stop-gap arrangement.

After the accreditation system is in place, colleges should be in a position to avail of the second, more complete degree of autonomy, under conferment of "deemed university" status from the UGC, a possibility envisioned by the UGC guidelines and also by the National Policy on Education, 1986.

As for affiliated colleges proper, as distinct from semi-autonomous ones, none of them can be granted candidature by the accreditation system because their set-up is by its nature too violative of individual and departmental academic autonomy. Since accreditation involves a "yes" or "no" to the institution as a whole, no matter how complex it is, affiliating universities will themselves not be eligible for candidature until they have divested themselves of these colleges at least to the extent of semi-autonomy.

Since, within five years of the setting up of the Accreditation Council, only accredited institutions will be eligible for central funds, the goal of autonomy (or semi-autonomy) is envisioned for all colleges by them.

The UGC has decided to grant autonomous status to 500 colleges by the end of the current five-year plan (1990). Special funds will have to be made available by the UGC during the intervening period to facilitate the transition of the remaining colleges, so that they may all have a fair chance to qualify for accreditation before the deadline.

Some of the conditions for the granting of autonomous status by the UGC will be similar to the conditions for the granting of candidature by the Accreditation Council. Nevertheless, these conferments by two distinct bodies should be kept distinct.

9. There are a variety of causes which will keep an institution from accreditation, and the appropriate response of the concerned authority will vary accordingly. In most cases what is called for will be a matter of reorganisation and some additional finances, but not very substantial expansion of faculty and facilities. But some present institutions are simply too small to be able to offer a satisfactory educational

programme particularly in light of the claims of general education. In such cases, consolidation with other institutions would be called for.

10. An emphasis on general education will be a primary concern of the accreditation system and will be enforced as a Requirement of Candidature. There is no other way to realize a large number of the curricular goals enunciated in the National Policy on Education, 1986. Every college must make the students aware of the range of human knowledge; it must increase the student's capacity for the organisation and expression of thought; it should provide an opportunity for the development of the basic learning skills and foundations necessary for success in mastering advanced specialised subject-matter; it should develop within students the capabilities of forming independent judgements, weighting values, and under standing fundamental theory and it should encourage the pursuit of life-long learning.

    The value of elective courses, within the field of specialisation but more especially outside of it, should be emphasized, as this is the primary foundation of interdisciplinary study, which the new education policy is committed to. It will also give new life to some of the fields of study that few would like to specialize in but many would like to study, which are presently wasting away.

    The mode of implementing general education, whether through distribution requirements, foundation courses or some other modality, will be left up to the institution.

    The system of credits and internal evaluation (not necessarily examination based), modularity of courses of study, and admission to the college as a whole rather than to a department, will be included in the Requirements of Candidature.

Linkages

(1) The Association of accredited institutions of higher education can exert a positive influence on the standards of secondary education, through recognition of the certificates of various boards. They can also recognise independent schools, and help them to establish an accrediting Associations of Secondary Schools with strong linkages to the higher education

Association.

(2) Professional institutions in field such as engineering, medicine, architecture, management and law should be brought under the scope of institutional accreditation through the aegis of the proposed National Apex Body for Higher Education. Institutional accreditation should be made a prerequisite to professional accreditation.

(3) In assessing the educational effectiveness of an institution, evaluators will want to have some concrete measures of educational outcomes. For this the development of the National Testing Services, providing objective and up-to-date certification in a wide variety of subjects, will be extremely helpful.

Financial Implications

The financial (and political) implications of bringing most of the nation's institutions of higher education upto the level necessary for accreditation must be squarely faced. Even though the implementation of accreditation is in itself bound to improve the cost benefit ratio, effective education cannot possibly come so cheaply as what is now prevalent.

Recommendations

This report should be widely circulated in the academic community for a full scale discussion on the idea of an Accreditation and Assessment Council.

8.7 WORKSHOP ON ACCREDITATION AND ASSESSMENT COUNCIL (1988)[5]

A two-day workshop on "Accreditation and Assessment Council", sponsored by the UGC was conducted at the Department of Studies in Education, University of Mysore, Manasagangothri, Mysore, on December 30-31, 1988. The participants to the workshop consisted of professors, principals and teachers from five university areas of Karnataka, representating different faculties and discipline like arts and

5. Published by the University Grants Commission, New Delhi, 1989.

humanities, social-sciences, physical and natural-sciences, commerce and management sciences, education, law, engineering and medicine.

The workshop was inaugurated by Dr. (Miss) P. Selvi Das Vice-Chancellor of the University of Mysore. She stressed the possibility and ways of a system of accreditation contributing to significant improvement in institutional and programme standards in higher education.

Of the seven business sessions, five were devoted to general presentations and discussion, and two to group work. In the first general session brief presentations were made on the concepts of accreditation and assessment, accreditation system in different countries especially USA, and the major proposals contained in the Gowariker Committee report. The next three were devoted to more detailed discussions on different aspects of the accreditation system as proposed by the Gowariker Committee and contained in different parts of its report. Five groups were formed to cristalize reaction and recommendations on the different aspects of the theme.

OBSERVATIONS/RECOMMENDATIONS

The Concept

Accreditation by an appropriate agency or authority at the national level must be seen as a matter of acceptance and declaration of the academic standing of institutions and their courses, and as a matter of prestige and reputation, rather than as an eligibility criterion for any other kind of privilege, like funds from any agency.

Accreditation vis-a-vis Affiliation

The system of affiliation and accreditation can co-exist, and the same institutions may enjoy the double status. This is necessary to bring in a larger number of good institutions into the network and produce a larger impact.

Autonomy vis-a-vis Accreditation

The Gowariker Committee has made full institutional autonomy an essential pre-requisite for even candidate status in the system of accreditation. For the fact that the policy of granting of autonomy to institutionsl may not be effectively implemented in some parts of the country and certain university areas for various reason, it is necessary to delink accreditation from autonomy and extend accreditation to fully autonomous, semi-autonomous and even affiliated institutions provided they satisfy other criteria pre-determined for the purpose of accreditation.

Institutional vis-a-vis Professional Accreditation

While the Gowariker Committee seems to think of institutional accreditation as a prior necessity for professional accreditation, the sequence could in fact be the other way, professional accreditation of most of the courses offered by an institution, or of an institution as a whole awarded by professional bodies like Indian Medical Council, being considered a pre-requisite for institutional accreditation by the common agency like Accreditation and Assessment Council.

Gradation

Since a system of accreditation with full membership or status and candidate status as suggested by the Gowariker Committee would in any case bring class distinctions there is no harm in institutionsl that satisfy all the generally accepted pre-determined criteria covering various aspects in a good way being accredited (whether they are fully autonomous, semi-autonomous or affiliated) and grading them, for example, on a three point scale A-B-C (A meaning 'excellent exemplary or outstanding', B-meaning 'very good', and C-meaning 'good') in the overall assessment. This would motivate even accredited institutions to continuously strive for improvement of quality and attainment of higher status.

Council Status and Setup

(a) While the principal of autonomous functioning of the Accreditation and Assessment Council should be upheld, there may be no harm in having it set up by and under the UGC to begin with and the proposed National Council of Higher Education which would have jurisdiction over and concern with the entire spectrum of higher education, in due course when it is set up. This would imply that a large part of the resource requirements of the Accreditation and Assessment Council are met without the Council becoming a burden on the member institutions, which may be required only to pay nominal fees for the benefits of assessment accreditation and membership.

(b) While the Accreditation and Assessment Council may be a national body it may establish regional branches or chapters, 4 or 5 to begin with, and later enlarge the number to have a chapter for each large state or group of small states depending on the number of institutions accredited or to be considered for accreditation, and the work load. The central council may have an executive director with adequate number of associate directors, and there may be regional joint directors in charge of the regional centres. They may appoint adequate number of full-time or part-time evaluation officers, and maintain panels of subject experts and other consultants.

(c) The Accreditation and Assessment Council may have a general body consisting of representatives of all the accredited institutions, and possibly candidate institutions, and nominees of bodies like National Council of Higher Education, University Grants Commission. Association of Indian Universities, and other Professional bodies mentioned earlier. It may have a governing council of limited membership with appropriate representatives of the above and any other national level apex body of relevance (like ICSSR and CSIR) to establish and maintain meaningful linkages with all such bodies. Further it may have a standing accreditation commission or committee of limited membership to be constituted through election or nomination, and recommendatory accreditation committees at the regional level. It may only be the standing committee or accreditation commission at the national level that would formally grant accreditation on the recommendations of the evaluation teams and the regional accreditation committees.

(d) Since assessment is instrumental to accreditation and is an essential part thereof, it would be meaningful to name the body 'Accreditation Council for Higher Education' (unless Accreditation and Assessment Council would also accept responsibility for having other institutions-non-members or those seeking membership assessed on its own initiative or on behalf of the UGC or the universities concerned – and graded as D & E if so desired).

Accreditation vis-a-vis Funding

The Gowariker Committee has recommended that once the accreditation system is set in motion only accredited institutions should be eligible for central funds. Even if accreditation is delinked from autonomy and such other criteria, other than quality and standards, it is desirable to delink funds from accreditation, which should be considered as a matter of academic status and prestige. Funds on different bases and in relation to developmental needs should be available in an equitable way to all types of institutions – from different agencies like the Central Government and its funding agencies, the State Government, and so on.

Assessment

The assessment for accreditation must be both internal and external, as emphasised by the Gowariker Committee, and both should be comprehensive, covering the various aspects identified by the committee and other relevant once, each assessed by well defined criteria. While the internal evaluation is to be done continuously, with built-in programme evaluation and frequent status assessment, an external evaluation team set up by the national/regional accreditation committee must make a comprehensive assessment before considering/granting accreditation, and once it is granted, after a lapse of two or three years, and thereafter at the end of every five years in the normal courses; special assessment may be arranged, for special reasons and/or purposes, as end when necessary.

Criteria for Assessment

The criteria for assessment would be essentially qualitative, but in respect of all resources and facilities, quantified standards for different levels of satisfaction must also be pre-determined, indicated, and followed. Proformas be developed for internal evaluation and external assessment, facilitating descriptive assessment and grading of different dimensions or components of the various aspects by appropriate criteria, and for summation of such assessments of each major aspect and for the performance of the institution as a whole.

The criteria developed should be applied in a relative and flexible way – with due consideration to relevant factors like the special objective of the institutions, the number and nature of courses offered, the area of operation (rural urban etc.), the nature of the clientele (highly selective or not), student strength and so on.

Role of National Testing Service

The services of the National Testing Service (when established) could be utilised for requirement of teachers, assessment of quality of staff, selection of students in some cases, and the assessment of the achievement of students in respect of basics in the respective disciplines at appropriate level.

General Education Component

The Gowariker Committee has recommended that 25% weightage to a general education component must be insisted on – in all bachelor (first degree) degree programmes and for the administration to P.G courses – as a prerequisite or condition for accreditation. As all the students for the bachelor degree programmes in general or professional areas would have had twelve years of general education and as the nature and scope of the first degree programmes would vary considerably among the general and professional degree programmes, it is neither feasible nor desirable to insist on such a component in all cases. However, if any course is designed with focus on national concerns and aspirations like national identity and integration cultural renaissance, etc., that could be made an essential component of all programmes.

Some Other Conditions

The Gowariker Committee has stressed among other things, that "the system of credits and internal evaluation (not necessarily examination-based), modularity of courses of study and, admission to the college as a whole rather than a department will be included in the requirements of candidature". While it is desirable (i) to design degree programmes with flexibility and choice, variation in assortments, and a system of cumulative credits, etc., (ii) to develop detailed curriculum plans and teaching-learning materials approximating to self-contained, self-sufficient, self-learning materials, (iii) to plan for, notify and conduct comprehensive evaluation covering different kinds of learnings, performances and development on appropriate bases and criteria employing a variety of suitable techniques and tools, and summate such assessments with balanced weightages to different performances, it may not be feasible or even desirable to insist on such things as pre-requisites or conditions for accreditation. Institutions including universities can only be encouraged and guided to move with clearly planned strides in a time-frame, if possible, in such directions. Further, where independent departments of post-graduate studies operate directly under and as part of universities, it is not necessary to insist on admission to a college as a whole. While it may not be feasible to organise them into comprehensive graduate schools on the American model, groups of related disciplines or departments that naturally go together with a lot of inter-relationship and inter-disciplinary, can possibly be organised into larger schools of natural science, social sciences, language, humanities visual and performing arts, law, education and commerce and bosons/ management sciences.

8.8 AIU COMMITTEE ON DISMISSAL AND SO-CALLED RESIGNATIONS OF VICE-CHANCELLOR IN BIHAR UNIVERSITIES AND DR. H.S. GAUR VISHWAVIDYALAYA, SAGAR, (1989)[6]

Introduction

The Report of the Committee of Elders set up by the Association of Indian Universities (AIU) on September 6, 1988, to enquire into en-masse dismissal or so-called resignations of the Vice-Chancellors in Bihar Universities and of Dr. Hari Singh Gaur Vishwavidyalaya, Sagar in 1988 and some other issues were considered by the Standing Committee of the AIU in its meeting held on February 23, 1989. After due deliberations, it was resolved by the Standing Committee that taking into account the issues vital to the survival of the higher educational system itself, referred to in the report of the committee, the report be first widely circulated in the draft from and comments and suggestions invited and considered before the report is finalised.

6. *Source*: *University News*, May 15, 1986.
   Note: Para number related the paras of the report.

Constitution

1. Prof. R.C. Paul – Chairman
2. Prof. Rais Ahmed
3. Prof. M.V. Mathur
4. Prof. M.M. Chakraborty
5. Prof. (Mrs) Vanaja Iyengar
6. Prof. S.K. Agarwala – Secretary

Terms of References

(i) to enquire into the circumstances leading to the dismissal and so-called resignations of the following Vice-Chancellors in the Universities in Bihar:
Prof. Ekbal Bahadur Singh, VC, Bhagalpur University;
Prof. Shakeelur Rehman, VC, L.N. Mithila University;
Dr. R.D. Munda, VC, Ranchi University;
Dr. S.N. Das, VC, Patna University;
Prof. (Mrs) Lalita Sinha, VC, Bihar University;
Prof. Mangal Dubey, Vc, Magadh University;
Dr. B.S. Kumar, VC, Kameshwara Singh Darbhanga Sanskrit University.

(ii) to enquire into the circumstances leading to the resignation of Dr P.D. Hajela, Vice-Chancellor Dr. Hari Singh Gaur Vishwavidyalaya, Sagar;

(iii) to suggest appropriate provision for the appointment of Vice-Chancellors;

(iv) to suggest measures to ensure that the Governor when acting as Chancellor acts independently and not on the aid and advice of the council of Ministers;

(v) to suggest legal modalities for ensuring the security of tenure of Vice-Chancellors, and in this context to examine the provisions of university enactments providing for the supersession of university bodies and authorities and/or for the removal of Vice-Chancellors, and to suggest viable alternatives;

(vi) to review the provision of the orissa Universities Act, 1989 (which replaced the Orissa Universities Ordinance of 1988) and finalise following report in the order and

The Committee of Elders met on September 21 1988, Ocober 27, 1988 and February 13, 1989 and finalised the following report in the order:

Section I : Dismissal and so-called Resignations of Vice-Chancellors in Bihar University in 1988 : (A) Background : Funding of Universities and Constituent Colleges in Bihar. (B) Dismissal and so-called Resignation of Vice-Chancellors in Bihar. *Section II* : So-called Resignation of Dr. P.D. Hajela, Vice-Chancellor, Dr H.S. Gaur University, Sagar. *Section III* : Appointment of Vice-Chancellors and some related issues : (A) Appointment of Vice-Chancellors and Pro-Vice-Chancellors; (B) Governor to act as Chancellor in his individual capacity : (C) Should Chancellor be a person other than the Governor ? *Section IV* : Security of tenure of Vice-Chancellor. *Section V* : Some Comments on the Orissa Universities Act, 1989. *Section VI* : Summary of Findings and Recommendation. *Section VII* : Concluding Remarks.

Main Findings and Recommendations

26.1 During the past two decades it is being increasingly experienced that amongst other reasons, the absence of norms of relationship between the Chancellors and the State Government regarding the Universities on the one hand and between the Chancellors/State Government and the Universities on the other, has contributed significantly to the erosion of academic atmosphere in the several universities in the country and to the progressive crippling of the university system itself. The recent happenings in Bihar, Kerala, Andhra Pradesh and Madhya Pradesh are symptomatic in this regard.

26.1 Under 6(a), the programme of Action lays down : "Certain norms of performance must be laid down for observance by the administration (Government, as well as managements of educational institutions), teachers, students and educational institutions". In 6(d) it says " One of the malaise which has eaten into the educational system is unwarranted interference by political and administrative centres of power. While it is not possible to insulate the educational system from the socio-economic and socio-political forces, it will have to be ensured that the working of the system is not undermined by the political, bureaucratic and anti-social elements-within or outside the educational system."

26.2 It cannot, of course, be expected of this Committee to spell out the details of a code of relationship and conduct for the high dignitaries themselves or for their conduct *vis-a-vis* the universities, but under the legitimate expectations that the Chancellors and Chief

Ministers shall expeditiously lay down a viable code of conduct for themselves to govern their own relationships inter as concerns the affairs of the universities and a code of conduct for the Chancellors and the State Governments *vis-a-vis* the universities under them, this Committee offers certain suggestions in this regard:

(i) It is axiomatic that the question of university finances cannot be left to the arbitrary whims of the State Governments as is happening in Bihar, for example. If a university has to serve with responsibility, the finances needed by it should come to it as a matter of courses, regularly, and in good time. The quantum of financial needs of a university could/should be determined by the State Council for Higher Education as proposed in the N.P.E.

(ii) The culture needs to be imbibed that the Chancellor and/or the state Government just has no powers *vis-a-vis* the universities beyond what has been specially provided for in the university enactment.

(iii) All provisions in university enactments which endow the chancellor/State Government with arbitrary powers (some of which have also been illustrated/referred to in section IV of this Report) should be done away with, i.e. deleted from the relevant Acts.

Other Findings and Recommendations

27. The distressing state of education in the universities in Bihar has been énquired into by the Bihar Universities Enquiry Commission under the Chairmanship of Dr. V.S. Jha in 1983 and by the Chancellor's Committee on the Problems of Universities in Bihar 1986 under the Chairmanship of Dr. Devendra Nath Sharma. Appropriate recommendations have also been made. No concerted action, however, has thus far been taken on these two important reports.

27.1 Two problems of university education in Bihar, amongst others, are most basic for the smooth governance of a Bihar university, namely inadequacy of finances and the unrestricted creation of constituent colleges under the universities.

27.2 Unless an appropriate solution is found to these problems, no Vice-Chancellor can fell secure in his tenure whatever be the protection that may be provided to him through legal provisions.

28. It is common practice in Bihar to remove the Vice-Chancellors en-masse whenever a new Chief Minister or Chancellor takes over. Such mass removal of Vice-Chancellors has been taken place four times in Bihar, in 1972, 1977, 1985 and 1988. No Vice-Chancellor, except one, has completed his full tenure in Patna University.

28.1 The rumours that circulate anticipating the removal of the Vice-Chancellors on the coming in of a new Chief MInister/ Chancellor, are extremely damaging to the positions, dignity and stability to the Vice Chancellor and the University.

Such rumours must be firmly refuted by the Government, through all media, and the Chancellor/State Government should abide by the principal that the office of the Vice-Chancellor is not something that can be doled or taken away at the sweet will of the Chief Minister, Chancellor or the Education Minister.

28.2 It appears that the en-masse removal of the Vice-Chancellors in Bihar in 1988 was contemplated and discussed by the then Chancellor with with several persons and also perhaps with then Chief Minister and the Education Minister.

28.3 The Vice-Chancellor of Bhagalpur University tendered his resignation in June 1988 which was accepted in July.

28.4 The Vice-Chancellors of L.N. Mithila University attempted to introduce various reforms in university administration; consequently, he came in conflict with the then Education Minister whose vested interests in L.N. Mithila University, Darabhanga were adversely affected. The promotion of the then Education Minister as University Professor was also cancelled.

28.4.1 His services were terminated in August 1988 on the supposed pretext that he had not attended a meeting convened by the Chancellor.

28.4.2 There is no evidence against the Vice-Chancellor either for adopting a communal attitude in university administration, or for having taken recourse to illegal or irregular practices, or for any attempt to gain cheap popularity with political ambitions in mind.

28.4.3 His removal was completely arbitrary, illegal, and vindictive. Non-attendance of a meeting called by the Chancellor cannot be a ground for the dismissal of a high dignitary like the Vice-Chancellor. He was not even given an opportunity to explain the reason for not having been able to attend the meeting.

28.4.4 The removal even under the pleasure clause was not legal because it is established law that pleasure by any functionary of the State including the President cannot be exercised arbitrarily.

28.5 The removal of the Vice-Chancellor of Ranchi University in August 1988 was also illegal, arbitrary, and politically motivated.

28.5.1 The committee found no evidence that the Vice-Chancellors was actively involved in the Jharkhand political movement during his tenure as Vice-Chancellor.

28.6 Possibly, to cover up the mounting public criticism in the press and outside as well as to placate the Central Congress leadership before whom these issues seem to have been highlighted by the dissident group in Bihar politics, the Government throught of removing the rest of the Vice-Chancellors too, under the general plea of mal-administration in universities and the incapability of the Vice-Chancellors to handle the universities.

28.6.1 In order to effect this purpose, the Chancellor called a meeting of the Vice-Chancellors on August 5, 1988, suggested them to tender their resignation letters on the false pretense that they were not to be used. These resignations were accepted on 3rd September, 1988.

28.6.2 There is nothing in record to show if there is any established procedure which is followed in case of the removal of the Vice-Chancellor, nor there was any record suggesting the charges against each individual Vice-Chancellor who was removed and that the removal of each one of them was considered separately and independently in the context of separate and specific charges against each.

28.6.3 It appears that in the initial stages when the relations between the Chief Minister and the then Chancellor were cordial, some discussions and understanding about the removal of Vice-Chancellors en masses must have been arrived at; however, when the relations between the Chancellor and the Chief Minister deteriorated, the Government disowned all responsibility for removal whereas the chancellor owned it, mostly in order to assert his independent powers regarding the removal and appointment of Vice-Chancellors. The tendency to shift responsibility and/or to disown it (or even to own it only in the game of power politics) smacks of sheer wilfulness on the part of the authorities which is completely irrational.

28.7 En-masse removal of Vice-Chancellors is patently arbitrary and illegal. It cannot stand judicial scrutiny. It should no under no circumstances be resorted to.

28.7.1 The fact that in Bihar it has been resorted to four times, in

1972, 1977, 1985 and 1988, in itself goes to establish that there is something radically wrong in the State of Bihar.

28.7.2 The practice of obtaining resignation letters from the vice-chancellors through arm twisting and similar devices, by the Chancellor or State Government is mediaeval in character and unethical in content. It is no different from dismissal.

29. Dr. P.D. Hajela, Vice-Chancellor, Dr. Hari Singh Gour Vishwavidyalaya, Sagar did not resign on his own volition. It appears that it was suggested to him by the governmental authorities. This was a most inapt handling of the situation by the State authorities. Making the Vice-Chancellor as the scapegoat for it was most unethical and extremely damaging to his status and self-respect.

Dr. Hajela resigned on 14th August, 1988; the resignation was accepted by the Chancellor on 16th August 1988.

29.1 Dr. Hajela had no direct responsibility for the so-called objectionable question that appeared in an admission test question paper of the university.

29.2 The admission test question-paper (which was an objective type) and which sought the various items of information from the candidates about the news items appearing in the media-one in favour of the Prime Minister, one against and one neutral, to judge their awareness, was well-designed.

29.3 The agitation over the issue of the so-called objectionable question in the question paper was engineered by a section of students who are said to belong to the Youth Congress(I). The matter under any stretching of interpretation, gave no justifiable cause to any section of students of indulge in the type of rowdy and humiliating behaviour with the Head of the Department and the Vice-Chancellor as also on the campus, as those students did.

29.4 The Government and the local authorities failed to take any deterrent measure against the rowdy students even though some of them had been identified and reported by the Vice-Chancellor to the Chief Minister.

The Government and local authorities thus acquiesced in this behaviour of the students.

29.5 Dr. Hajela was placed in such an unfortunate position that he was left with no alternative but to resign. With no police action coming forth against rowdy elements, he would have been the victim of violence and manhandling by them had he resisted tendering his resignation.

30. Provisions like Ss. 14 and 52 of the M.P. Vishwavidyalaya Adhiniyam, 1973 should be deleted from the statute book. During the past ten years Dr. Hari Singh Gour Vishwavidyalaya has had as many as eight Vice-Chancellors. They were replaced by invoking the said S.52(1).

31. Only such a person should be eligible for appointment as Vice-Chancellor who has status, competence, integrity, courage and commitment to the values for which a University stands.

He should also be able to command credibility in the academic community. He should be appointed solely on consideration of merit and ability to provide leadership to the University community. He must invariably be a distinguished educationist.

31.1 The Vice-Chancellor should be selected out of a panel of at least three names. This panel should be proposed by a committee consisting of (i) a nominee of the Executive Council of the University, being a person not connected with the University or its colleges; (ii) the Chairman of the UGC or his nominee and (iii) a nominee of the Chancellor in his personal capacity.

31.1.1 The U.G.C. must develop a viable mechanism so as to be able to perform this added responsibility meaningfully, effectively and expeditiously.

31.1.2 The persons to be appointed on the Search Committee itself must also be distinguished educationists.

31.1.3 The nominees of the Chancellor and the University on the Search Committee should in no capacity be associated with the University for which the panel is to be prepared.

31.1.4 The search Committee should be asked to submit its recommendations only once. No fresh recommendations should be called from the Search Committee, nor should Search Committee be reconstituted.

31.2 The power to appoint the Vice-Chancellor should rest with the Chancellor in his individual capacity. He may appoint the Vice-Chancellor out of the panel, after such consultation as he deems necessary.

The subject of the appointment of Vice-Chancellors should be completely insulated against the current politics of the State.

32. The Pro-Vice-Chancellor should be appointed only on the recommendation of the Vice-Chancellor and his term of office should be co-terminus with that of the Vice-Chancellor.

33. The term of Office of the Vice-Chancellor should be five

years and it should not be renewable.

34. The Vice-Chancellor must retire at the age of 65, under any conditions.

35. The Governor when he is called upon to act as Chancellor has to act in his individual capacity and not on the aid and advice of the Council of Ministers. The Chancellor is appointed by an Act of the legislature incorporating the University and not under the provisions of the Constitution. A person other than the Governor can also be entrusted with the responsibilities of the Chancellor by an Act of the legislature. It is only when a person is acting as Governor that he has to act on the aid and advice of the Council of Ministers under constitutional provisions.

This constitutional position has been reiterated in several court opinions, though some dicta to the contrary also exists. However, for further clarity, if considered necessary, the Central Government can request for advisory opinion of the Supreme Court on the subject.

36. No useful purpose would be served if the functions of the Chancellor were to be entrusted to a person other than the Governor. There is no method to ensure that in the appointment of a person other than the Governor as Chancellor impartiality and detachment shall, *inter alia*, be considered as the basic requirements, if they are not so considered in case of the appointment of the Governor himself.

36.1 Since the Committee has recommended that the Governor should continue to be the Chancellor of the State Universities, it is necessary that the President ensures that a person appointed as Governor has all the qualities which shall enable him to act as Chancellor.

37. For providing an atmosphere of stability in the universities under which alone could learning, teaching and research thrive, as well as to attract the best educationists as Vice-Chancellors, it is an indispensable condition that a person when appointed as Vice-Chancellor should feel completely certain in his position that he will enjoy the full tenure of his office and that it shall not be interfered with for extraneous the existing provisions in several university enactments which enable the state authorities to meddle with their tenure, must be done away him.

37.1 In the opinion of the Committee, Sections 14 and 52 of the M.P. Vishwavidyalaya Adhiniyam, 1973 (as amended): Section 11 and the amended Section 10(3) incorporating the pleasure clause and S. 14 of the Bihar State Universities Acts, S. 31 of Orissa Universities Act,

1989 or parallel provisions elsewhere should be deleted from the respective university enactments.

37.2 The 'pleasure clause' under which a Vice-Chancellor is to hold office at the pleasure of the Chancellor wherever it exists should be deleted.

37.3 In place of the above provisions, this Committee recommends the retention or introduction of a provision like Section 5 of the Banaras Hindu University Act 1915 which exists in almost all Central Universities and in some State universities acts also.

37.4 The Central Universities have no provision for the removal of Vice-Chancellors. There is no need either for such a provision, once a provision like Section 5 of the BHU Act, 1915 has been introduced.

37.4.1 However, the removal of a Vice-Chancellor should be contemplated only in case he has been charged with an offence involving moral turpitude and has been found guilty after proper enquiry by a sitting or retired judge of a High Court or Supreme Court, after having been given an opportunity of being heard in accordance with the principles of natural justice.

38. The Orissa Universities Act, 1989 brought into force retrospectively from 15th November, 1988 has been issued to consolidate and amend the laws relating to Orissa Universities. It repeals the Orissa Universities Ordinance, 1988 which was much criticised.

38.1 The power given to the Chancellor to issue directions or instructions on any matter connected with a university is highly extensive and goes against the basic tenants of the autonomy of a university [Section 5(9) of the Act].

In the past when a similar provision was introduced in the Osmania University enactment in 1966, there was a strong resentment in academic circles in the State as well as in the country as a whole and consequently the provision had soon to be dropped by the State Government the same year through another amendment.

38.2 Section 6(2) which gives the power to the Chancellor to call for a fresh panel of names or even to constitute another Search Committee preparing the panel for Vice-Chancellorship.

38.3 The Comptroller of Finance has been given extensive powers undermining the position of the Vice-Chancellors; they need to be curtailed.

38.3.1 The Finance Officer/Comptroller of Finance of the University should be a person appointed by the university itself through open advertisement as the University considers appropriate. State Finance service personnel could also apply along with others.

38.4 Section 31 of the Act providing for super-session of the Senate and other authorities including the Vice-Chancellor and handing over management to an administrator, is highly undesirable and should be deleted.

38.5 The composition of the Senate (S.9), composition of the syndicate (S.10), appointment of teachers (S.21); framing of statutes (S.24), have been changed as compared to what was contained in the Ordinance of 1988. However, the provision for appointment of teachers through a panel of experts prepared by the syndicate as now provided by the Act of 1989, is inappropriate as it would politicise such appointments and would promote inbreeding. It needs to be changed.

Action to be taken by University Grant Commission

39. The Committee understands that the University Grants Commission (UGC) does not approve the enactment of a new university if it is found wanting according to the norms that have been set up by the UGC. But the Committee is not aware of any process in the UGC to examine the amendment of the University Act (by legislation or by ordinance) which introduce provisions which would not have been approved by the UGC in the original enactment.

The Committee, therefore, recommends that the provisions introduced through amendments in the university enactments should also be periodically examined and the modifications or deletion of the same insisted upon by the UGC. It should be made obligatory on the universities to intimate the UGC about any amendment as and when it is effected. The case of Orissa Universities Act, 1989 is an illustration in point.

39.1 In case the recommendation made by this Committee is accepted that the UGC nominee should be there on the Search Committee for each university, the UGC should take immediate steps to devise a mechanism through which it could perform this function effectively and meaningfully.

It may also be noted that provisions already exist in certain university enactments to have a nominee of the UGC Chairman on the Search Committee for the appointment of a Vice-Chancellor.

Action to be taken by Association of Indian Universities

40. The AIU should advise the Vice-Chancellors not to tender their resignations if they are not inclined to do so on their own. The Vice-Chancellors be advised to bring out all facts in the open and should even challenge the illegal dismissal in the court of law.

The AIU must extend full support to him if he takes recourse to such an action.

40.1 On several occasions in the past, the AIU has examined the provisions of the university enactment when the university has sought regular admission to AIU. Since the provisions of the enactment were found to be wanting in terms of Regulation 2(c) on p.7 of the AIU Handbook, the permanent membership of the Association has either been denied to them or it has been delayed till the provisions were rectified.

40.1.1 It seems that of late the AIU has not been as vigilant in the admission of new members. It would be highly desirable that the AIU is vigilant in this regard while granting regular membership.

40.1.2 Similarly, it should be possible for the AIU to disaffiliate a member in case, at any subsequent stage, a provision is introduced in the university enactment which is inconsistent with the AIU norms, including those relating to the tenure of a Vice-Chancellor, for example, introducing a provision to the effect that the Vice-Chancellor shall hold office at the pleasure of the Chancellor.

41. *Action to be taken by Central Government*

41.1 The Centre has been entrusted with the responsibility of 'coordination and determination of standards in institutions for higher education or research and scientific and technical institutions' under Entry 66, List I of 7 Schedule of the Constitution. Education including technical education, medical education and universities has become a concurrent subject since the 42nd Constitution Amendment Act, 1976 was passed. This gives a power to the Parliament to pass a law with relation to such matters in the field of education wherein some uniformity and overriding norms are found to be absolutely necessary.

41.2 The question of appointment and removal of Vice-Chancellors has become extremely important over the years since the State Governments and its functionaries have been found treating that office with little consideration to its importance, independence and dignity. In the same genre would fall the pro-provisions in the university enactments which provide for the supersession of university bodies. Such provisions and the actions under them tend to undermine the credibility of the university system completely, besides the fact that certain high placed individuals are hurt and humiliated in the process.

41.3 The Committee, therefore, feels and suggests that a Central Legislation overriding the provisions of the enactments of all the universities in the country, in the limited areas indicated above, is absolutely necessary and should be framed, passed and implemented without any loss of time to save the universities from further deterioration.

Concluding Remarks

Many and more worthy committees and commissions have made far more comprehensive reports on the reform of university education in India. Bihar itself had two such important committees in the recent past, as referred to in this Report. Yet, by and large, these excellent reports are gathering dust with none or little implementation in sight. With this continued neglect, the disease has now become systemic. This Report deals with certain specific issues relating to Vice-Chancellors, yet the remedies on these limited issues even can have a meaning only when the system as a whole improves. Not any one particular section alone, but all sections and strata of the Indian society have contributed to this pitiable condition of higher education in the country, either actively or by acquiescence, either directly or indirectly in a small measure or in a big way, either consciously or unconsciously. Whether a teacher, a student, an assistant in a college, a guardian, a politician or a member of the general public – each one has thus far only attempted to get as much as one could from the university system, instead of contributing their mite to it.

'The system of education is an integral part of the total socio-economic system and that transformation of the system of education will have to go side by side with critical changes in the rest of the system', rightly observes the document 'Challenge of Education – a policy perspective'.

If the disease which afflicts the universities has become systemic, the universities cannot become functional again without the active and conscious effort of each constituent as well as beneficiary of the system. Even certain basic meaningful reforms e.g. for safeguarding the tenure of office of a Vice-Chancellor or for the appointment of a suitable Vice-Chancellor (as this Committee has attempted to do), will either founder on the bed-rock of opposition by vested interests, or even if they go through, they by unless the general environment in the universities and in the society is not supportive of academic freedom and values.

The Committee, therefore, fervently and most humbly appeals to all sections of the society to wake up to their responsibility to the society, to themselves and to their progeny and do some heart-searching to rescue the higher educational system from the quagmire into which it has fallen. Each one has to observe certain norms of behaviour and has to actively and effectively protest if these norms are violated by others howsoever highly placed.

Pandit Nehru had said "If the universities discharge their duty adequately, then it is well with the nation and the people". It is the sacred duty of all of us to keep the universities in good health so as to keep the nation vibrant and moving forward.

The Committee places this draft Report in the hands of all concerned, under the found hope and wish that a serious public debate ensues on the subject-matter of the Report.

LIBRARIES AND LIBRARIANS

9.1 PLANNING COMMISSION WORKING GROUP ON MODERNISATION OF LIBRARY SERVICES AND INFORMATICS FOR THE SEVENTH FIVE YEAR PLAN, 1985-90 (1983)[1]

Terms of Reference

1. To take stock of the position in respect of library services and informatics as is likely to be reached by the end of 1984-85, to identify problem areas and suggest remedial measures;
2. To suggest feasible perspective of development of library services and informatics up to 2000 A.D.; particularly with a view to equalising these facilities to all sections of the people and to enable the national library and informatics system make its maximum contribution to the development of a modern society;
3. To specify in clear terms the objectives of library services and informatics development programme in relation to national development goals; and
4. To formulate proposals for the Seventh Five Year Plan (1985-90) in the light of the above perspective indicating priorities, policies and financial costs.

Recommendations for Library Services

1. Formulation of National Policy for Library and Information Service (L & IS).

---

1. Published by the Planning Commission, Government of India, New Delhi, 1984.

2. Establishment/strengthening of separate Library Directorate/ Departments etc.
3. All India Library and Information Service.
4. Publication/Production of materials to meet and promote reading habits among the people.
5. *Public Libraries*: should be established/developed on priority basis; coordinated with other Agencies; a network to be planned, enactment of public library law in all states on top priority and existing public libraries run by private organisations to be integrated in the concerned areas.
6. *Academic Libraries*: substantial increase in their book budgets, to improve their resources and services through resource sharing, to establish library system for Universities, dormitory libraries on local and regional basis, emphasis on library services including lending facilities, active role for professional staff in providing services, larger funds for library building furniture, equipment, reprographic facilities.
7. *School Libraries*: sufficient provision for their establishment, development and expansion should be provided.
8. *Special Libraries, Information Centres and Systems*: Strong commitment of the parent institution to provide the required support and infrastructural facilities, need for larger budgets; Dormitory libraries, National Information System to be further expanded and strengthened.
9. *National Libraries*: Define the aims and activities of the four National Libraries (NL, NML, NSL, IARI) in specific terms. One copy of each of the core research journal and other research materials should be available in the concerned National Library. Under the Delivery of Books, Act (1954) copies of documents published in India are deposited in these four libraries, Central Reference Library and INB - Central Reference Library be shifted/established at Delhi and work of INB assigned to it, to established national libraries in areas such as manuscripts and social sciences during the VII Plan, to modernise existing National libraries.
10. *National Centre for Education and Research in L & IS*: to promote education and research activities of high academic standards a National Centre for Education and Research in L & IS be established on the pattern of other national level centres such as NCERT, NIEPA . . ., consolidation of existing

library schools, to revise syllabii and include areas of Information Science and Computer Applications, continuing programmes, user studies for teachers of L & IS and practising librarians, incentives in the form of research fellowships, travel grants etc. to attract good quality students.

11. *Library Associations*: To provide adequate financial support on regular basis to professional bodies at National and State level to enable them discharge their responsibilities in an active manner.

Informatics and Computer Applications

While explaining information as a resource and its role in planning, informatics is described as processes, methods and laws related to the recording, analytical/synthetic processing, storage, retrieval and dissemination of (scientific) information. Informatics relates to all problems and methods affecting Information. Various information services and information infrastructure in Indian context is further reviewed. Computer Applications in libraries have been described in details with respect to areas of application, Indian scenario, giving a chronology of the major events of computer applications in Indian libraries. Advantages of on-line bibliographic data bases have been enumerated. An on-line bibliographic database developed at National Informatics centre (NIC) in 1980 – Information System on Electronics is given with objectives, features of the system and details of the sub-systems computerised. Further, concept and organisation of the Library and Information networks in General and Objectives and development of National library and information networks in particular and discussed. It gives information sources, developmental steps, structures and implementation aspects of the network. The report describes the new information technologies now available. Details of Fascimile, Video Conferencing, Electronic Mail, Video text/Teletext, Word Processors, Intelligent Terminals/Copiers, Micrographics, COM, Video Discs have been described.

Further the proposed computer networks in India are described. The three networks are as follows:

(i) RINSCA – Regional Informatics Network for South and Central Asia;
(ii) NICNET – Computer Network for Government;
(iii) INDONET – Computer Network for Commercial use.

A proposal for computerisation of small, medium and large types of libraries is then given. The computer configuration required for the project, interlinking of the library system and investment profile is described.

Recommendations on Informatics

1. The present library community should be exposed to the concept of computers and its usage. For this awareness and specific library-oriented programmmes should be conducted.
2. The library training courses should be enlarged to include computer application aspects. Emphasis should be more on information handling, organisation and usage.
3. During the 7th Plan period the goal should be to computerise most of the major libraries. This should be carried out in a systematic manner so that information exchange is possible. Certain standards with respect to hardware and software have to be evolved.
4. A Group has to be set up at the apex level to work out the Plan for computerisation. The group should also work out standard specifications for hardware and software for implementation at various levels. This group should consist of computer specialists, library scientists and educational experts. The group should be made responsible for monitoring and evaluating the computerisation in the libraries.
5. Software development activities have to be initiated for evolving a standard software for meeting the library requirements. This should be implemented on standard indigenous systems.
6. In developing the computer applications, first importance should be given for developing a union catalogue, and a national bibliography.
7. A plan for interlinking the library systems should be worked out. It should give a detailed plan of action for developing the library network.
8. New technologies (telematics) like videotext, teletext provide ample opportunities for dissemination information at the cheapest possible manner. Such systems should be experimented with a view to study its impact on the society. It will enable to access a wide variety of data in the shortest time.

Financial Profile

The Working Group emphasises that Library and Information Services should be considered as a separate entity in itself and proposes a separate investment profile for the 7th Plan. Of the total investment of Rs. 996 crores proposed, some portion of it had to be provided in the state plans.

While arriving at the financial profile, due emphasis is given for all components of Library and Information Services. Allocations have been made in such a way that priority areas like Public Libraries, National Libraries and Systems and Informatics have been given emphasis for fast development.

9.2 COMMITTEE ON NATIONAL POLICY ON LIBRARY AND INFORMATION SYSTEM (1985-86)[2]

Introduction

1. The need for the formulation of a National Policy on library and Information Systems has been engaging the attention of the Indian library profession since the 1950s as emphasised particularly in the writings of Dr. S.R. Ranganathan and in the recommendations of the Library Advisory Committee Report, 1958. It began to receive the active attention of the Government of India in the early 1970s and it was included as one of the principal objectives of the Raja Rammohan Roy Library Foundation established in 1972.
2. The National Information System for Science and Technology (NISSAT) was established in 1977 and as library services in India began to expand rapidly, Professor R.K. Das Gupta, Director, National Library, Calcutta and Chairman, Raja Rammohan Roy Library Foundation urged upon the Government th necessity of enunciating a National Policy for Library and Information Systems.
3. The foundation took up the task in 1981 and after careful deliberations submitted a Draft National Policy on Library and Information Systems to tne Government in July 1984.

2. Published by Ministry of Human Resource Development, Department of Culture, Government of India, New Delhi, 1986.

4. Meanwhile, in 1979 the Indian Association of Special Libraries and Information Centres (IASLIC) discussed the topic at its 12th Conference held at Roorkee. The Indian Library Association considered the matter at its 30th Conference at Jaipur in 1984. On behalf of the Indian Library Association a draft policy statement was submitted to the Government of India in early 1985. The need for this policy was also emphasised by the Planning Commission Working Group in its report 'Modernisation of Library Sciences and Informatics for the 7th Five-Year Plan 1985-90'.
5. The Government of India set up a Committee under the Chairmanship of Professor D.P. Chattopadhyaya for the formulation of a National Policy on Library and Information Systems vide office order No. F. 18-14/85-libs. dated, October 7, 1985.

Terms of Reference

(a) To consider the document 'National Policy on Library and Information System' prepared by the Raja Rammohun Roy Library Foundation in the context of an expanding library movement, disseminating information of neo-literates, illiterates, children and backward communities. The Committee may also consider a document on national policy prepared by the Indian Library Association.

(b) To circulate these documents to relevant experts and institutions all over the country and determine their reaction.

(c) To arrange a public discussion on the policy statement by way of holding seminars or by conducting interviews of selected people.

(d) On the basis of its own discussions of the documents and on the basis of public reactions as determined through (b) and (c), the Committee should prepared a final document for the consideration of Government.

Composition

1. Professor D.P. Chattopadhyaya
   Chairman
   RRRLF 25, Park Mansions
   Park Street
   Calcutta 700016

2. Shri B.S. Kesavan
   39, Anand Lok
   (Opp. Kamala Nehru College)
   New Delhi

3. Professor Ashin Das Gupta
   Director
   National Library
   Calcutta
4. Shri Girja Kumar
   138, Self-Financing Scheme
   Outer-Ring Road, Kalkaji
   New Delhi 110 019
5. Shri T.S. Rajagopalan
   Scientist-in-Charge, INSDOC
   4/6, M.S. Flat, NPL Staff Qrs.
   New Delhi 110 060
6. Professor K.A. Isaac
   Visiting Professor
   Deptt. of Library and Information Science
   Calicut University P.O.
   Kerala 673 635
7. Professor B. Anderson
   2, Villa Theresa
   24th Road, T.P.S. III
   Bandara, Bombay 400 050
8. Professor P.B. Mangla
   Deptt. of Library Science
   Delhi University
   Delhi 110 007
9. Professor P.N. Kaula
   Visiting Professor
   Lucknow University
   C-239, Indira Nagar
   Lucknow 226 016
10. Dr. (Mrs.) Suseela Kumar
    5, Shiv Ganga Road
    Madras 600 034
11. Shri S.C. Biswas
    Director
    Central Secretariat Library
    Shastri Bhawan
    New Delhi 110 001
12. Professor V. Rajaraman
    Chairman
    Computer Centre
    Indian Institute of Science
    Bangalore 560 012
13. Joint Secretary to the Government of India
    Department of Culture
    Shastri Bhawan
    New Delhi 110 001
14. Dr. B.P. Barua
    Member-Secretary
    Director, RRRLF
    Calcutta 700 027

Co-opted Members

1. Dr. B.D. Nag Chowdhury
   43A, Biren Roy Road (East)
   Calcutta 700 008
2. Professor Ravinder Kumar
   Director
   Nehru Memorial Museum & Library
   Teen Murti House
   New Delhi 110 011

The Committee held its first meeting on December 9, 1985, at Calcutta and visited different parts of the country either as a whole or by members separately.

Public opinion was ascertained regarding the two documents on National Policy on Library and Information Systems prepared by the Raja Rammohun Roy Library Foundation and the Indian Library Association in the context of the new education policy then in national debate. The Chairman of the Committee sent some preliminary findings to the Government of India in a letter dated March 8, 1986.

The Committee after considering an interim report and one further draft submitted to the Government its final findings on May 30, 1986.

Objectives of National Policy

Library and information sources are vital for all sectors of national activity. The availability of information, expeditiously and pinpointedly, supports all decision-making processes at all levels. Relevant information accelerates the pace of national development. An informed citizen is an asset to a democratic system of government and the proper utilisation of information can improve the quality of life of citizens. The Government of India therefore realises the value of coordinating and upgrading the existing library and information systems and services and initiating new programmes relevant to our national needs, taking advantage of the latest advances in information technology.

The following will be the main aims of library and information policy:

(i) To foster, promote and sustain, by all appropriate means, the organisation, availability and use of information, in all sectors of national activity;

(ii) To take steps for mobilising and upgrading the existing library and information systems and services and initiating new programmes relevant to our national needs, taking advantage of the latest advances in information technology;

(iii) To encourage and initiate, with all possible speed, programmes for the training of library and information personnel, on a scale and of a calibre adequate of provide the library and information services and to recognise their work as an important component of the quality and level of such services.

(iv) To set up adequate monitoring mechanisms for ensuring a rapid development of library and information facilities and services for meeting the information needs of all sectors and levels of the national economy;

(v) To encourage individual initiative for the acquisition and dissemination of knowledge, and for the discovery of new knowledge in an atmosphere of intellectual freedom;

(vi) In general, to secure for the people of the country all the benefits that can accrue from the acquisition and application of knowledge; and

(vii) To preserve and make known the nation's heritage in its multiple forms.

The Public Library System

1. The most important task before the Government is to establish, maintain and strengthen the free public libraries in the country and enable them to work as a system.

2. The main thrust in this area should go to the rural public library. A village or a village cluster with an adequate population should have a community library which will also serve as an information centre. Resources of different agencies engaged in the work of public health, adult education, local self-government and such others may be pooled to build up this composite centre.

3. An important link should be established between the community library of the village and the village primary school. If the school does not have a library of its own, the community library should provide the children with an adequate book-corner.

4. The community library should also importantly cater for adult education and make adequate audio-visual aids available to attract the illiterate villagers.

5. The district library should serve as an apex library for each district with public libraries at city, town and village levels constituting important components in the district library system. In addition to the usual services to be rendered by it, it should also provide for learning facilities and recreation for the handicapped. Wherever possible, district libraries and comparable city public libraries should provide literature in Braille. The district library and branch libraries should also arrange mobile and circulating library services within its area wherever it is necessary and feasible. Special services should be rendered to hospitals, prisons and the infirm in their homes.

6. Libraries for special groups should be built in areas of tribal concentration or of minority communities to develop their distinctive cultures. Government will provide all encouragement for such communities to develop their own libraries through voluntary effort.

7. Each public library should have a section for children and, in addition, separate libraries for children with attractive books and audio-visual supporting material should be established wherever possible.

8. The district library will take the leadership in establishing

linkages between all other public libraries of the district and work towards resource-sharing within the area.

9. The key role of public libraries as chief sustaining agencies of distance education should be recognised and they should be adequately equipped with the relevant resources for this purpose.

10. All the libraries within a State should form part of a network extending from the community library of the village through intermediary levels to the district and to the State Central Library. This State network should eventually connect with the national level.

11. The role of the State Central Library is crucial in networking and the establishment of uniform library procedures within the State. The State Central Library/Directorate of Public Libraries has to perform as the co-ordinating agency for public libraries in the State.

12. To bring about this development of the public libraries in a State it is vital that each State enacts its own library legislation. The Central Government should revise the Model Public Library Bill, which it has already prepared, in the light of experience gained in recent years and urge upon the State the importance of enacting such legislation. Finances for library development should be found by each State either from its general revenues or from local taxation.

13. The Central Government should assist the State in the development of public libraries in a larger way than it has done so far. The Raja Rammohun Roy Library Foundation as the national agency for co-ordinating and assisting the development of public libraries be suitably strengthened enabling it to discharge its responsibilities effectively.

The Academic Library System

1. Libraries are central to education and the only way that our education system can be freed from cramming is to build teaching round the library resources of the educational institutions. Children should be introduced to the pleasure and importance of books at an early age. The librarian should be regarded as a full member of the academic community.

2. No school or college should be established without a library and a properly qualified librarian. Primary schools where such facilities cannot be provided should share the resources of the community library. In areas where the community library does not exist the primary school should be so developed as to serve as the base of the

village library. But children must know the library and they must be helped by the library even if they are no longer in the stream of formal education.

3. There should be an agency at the State level for proper development of the school libraries of the State and a national agency for co-ordination at the national level. The national agency should maintain a data-base on Indian school libraries and devise norms for them.

4. The university and college libraries must be given adequate facilities in staffing, buildings, furniture, books etc. before a university and college can function properly. The University Grants Commission should devise the impose norms for the proper functioning of college and university libraries in the country.

5. As far as possible, universities, collages and research institutions, in a particular area, should establish linkages among themselves and share their resources. In this process, it may also be possible to devise a common acquisition programme which will make books available to the Indian readers not normally imported by the book trade. Such resource-sharing may also reveal the extent of duplication and under-utilisation of resources in academic libraries. Teaching, specially at universities and colleges, should be built as far as possible round the resources of the library which should be well rounded and made known to the users as much as possible.

6. Distance education is the most dynamically growing segment of the Indian education system. There is, however, no provision for supporting resources for students enrolled in this programme. Apart from public libraries, college and university libraries will have the obligation to cater to students in the stream of distance education and should be provided with the necessary means to render this service.

7. With the increase in the number of teaching departments, faculties and also because of the possibilities to establish multi-campus universities, there is a need to develop library system on the university campuses. The departmental and faculty libraries should be closely linked with the Central Library for acquisition of documents and services.

8. In addition to the usual lending services, the university and college libraries should lay more and more emphasis on reference and bibliographical services including SDI (Selective Dissemination of Information) and CAS (Current Awareness Service).

Special Libraries and Information System

1. In the organisation of special libraries and information centres in a national network the Committee recommends that the National Information System for Science and Technology (NISSAT) scheme of providing for different levels such as national, regional, sectoral and local should be further strengthened and expended.

2. Special libraries in social sciences, humanities and in language areas should be organised in similar systems and databanks should be developed in the various subject areas.

3. A larger number of existing, planned and projected information systems such as Health Science Information System, Environmental Information System, Biotechnology Information System Agricultural System, Non-Conventional Energy Information System, etc. should receive due attention for development.

4. A special library function as an integral part of its parent institution in supporting its programmes and activities. It is, therefore, essential that the parent institution should have a strong commitment to provide it the required support and infrastructural facilities.

5. A special library must have a strong document collection at least in the core area, properly qualified staff and the required physical facilities and equipment. The need for larger investments in the development of special libraries is called for in view of the specialized nature of clientele and collection, the service being more often information contained in the documents rather than the documents themselves.

6. In collection development among the special libraries, the existing strengths and weaknesses should be identified in order to aim at improving the national collection of uniquely held titles.

7. The special libraries, in addition to conventional library services, should offer various information services such as repackaging of information, Selective Dissemination of Information (SDI), Current Awareness Service (CAS), referral and others.

8. In the matter of services relating to foreign literature/information, more particularly in acquisition of and offering current and retrospective services from commercial bibliographical databases, special libraries and information centres should share responsibilities among themselves in a cooperative manner.

The National Library System and the Bibliographical Services

1. The National Library of India should discharge the following functions:

(i) To collect and preserve and production of the nation in print and in non-print form and all that is printed about the nation,
(ii) To render to the nation and to the world bibliographical and other services to meet the requirements of different user groups,
(iii) To interface between the national systems and international systems wherever feasible, and
(iv) To play a role of leadership in the country in the task of expanding and improving the library and information services.

2. The National Library, based in Calcutta, historically Indian's pre-eminent library, needs to be strengthened and supported in a manner which will enable it to discharge, in close co-operation with other national level libraries, the fourfold functions enumerated above.

3. To meet the library needs at the national level there should be a system of National Libraries (NLS) consisting of the National Library, Calcutta, as the National Library of India, National Depository Libraries in different regions of the country, National Subject Libraries and such other libraries of national importance. These National Libraries should form parts of one integrated system so that there is no unnecessary replication of functions within the system and the different parts form a coherent and functional whole. Each constituent of the National Library System (NLS) should be so planned and developed that it can assume a truly national character. The position of National Library, Calcutta, in the fully developed form of NLS, shall be that of prime among the equals.

4. The National Depository Libraries should in the different regions concentrate intensively upon the collection and preservation of Indian culture in the languages of the region concerned, supplementing and complementing the efforts of the Indian National Library.

5. Information needs of the users in the country should be met by the establishment, maintenance and development of national subject libraries and national documentation/information centres.

6. Dormitory libraries should be established in regions having an important cluster of libraries and these dormitory libraries should take care of the less used documents of different service libraries.

7. Manuscripts are important treasures of cultural heritage and indispensable documents for Indological research. An effective programme should be adopted for the conservation, documentation and exploitation of these valuable resources. There is a strong and urgent need for building up a national data-base of manuscripts. The National Libraries should assist in this work. Efforts should be made to assure access to all significant Indian documents at home or abroad to Indian researchers.

8. Government should take steps to create a national awareness of the urgent necessity to preserve the nation's cultural heritage, National Libraries should carry the responsibility of this preservation and national preservation facilities should be created at the National Libraries as also apart from the National Libraries to undertake this national task. Linkages should be established between libraries, archives and museums for the purpose of national preservation.

9. The Indian National Bibliography should have a comprehensive coverage about the national output of documents and should be brought out in an updated form on regular basis. This responsibility should be vested in the National Library of India as one of its essential functions.

10. The Delivery of Books Act, 1954, along with the Press and Registration of Books Act, 1867, and the Copyright Act, 1957, should be reviewed and amended suitably so as to ensure effective supply of publications to the National Libraries. In view of the pressure upon the publishing industry the Government may consider reducing the number of copies to be deposited and removing postal charges. At the same time, the Government should remove any legal lacuna for penalising default in the deposit of publications by the publishers.

11. The National Library of India should establish effective linkages with all other National Libraries through a National Library Board.

12. It is also desired that the State Central Libraries of the States will preserve all publications in the local language(s).

Manpower Development and Professional Status

1. In view of the rapidly expending library and information services and the fast changing character of library and information science, the development of manpower in a planned manner becomes essential. The Indian librarian and information scientist in particular will face the difficult task of carrying the literacy drive on the one hand and dealing with the technological revolution on the other.

2. The library and information science courses run by the universities and comparable institutions at the post-graduate level should continue to maintain the high standards that have been reached and improve their quality, in particular by the incorporation of advancing information technology.

3. Para-professional training courses may be undertaken by other appropriate agencies, but care must be taken to ensure uniformity and quality of such training all over the country.

4. In view of the challenging and dynamic situation in the profession, the Indian library and information professional must be given every facility to refresh his/her expertise, so as to keep abreast of advancing knowledge by a planned development of continuing education programmes in the field.

5. Considering the fact that library and information science courses tend to proliferate, introducing on occasions a dilution of standards, there should be an accreditation agency to ensure the standard and the quality of the training imparted.

6. The national need of furthering higher education and research in library and information science may be undertaken by a National Centre to be established for the purpose.

7. Library and Information Science professionals should be given the status and pay scales as well as academic facilities commensurate with their responsibilities with due regard to the fact that every library is an academic/research centre and has to function as such.

8. The Government of India should recognise the need for the creation of an All India Library Service and implement the plan when feasible. The creation of such a service will strengthen the national network of library and information systems.

Modernisation of Library and Information Systems

1. Modernisation of library operations and services, in the context of advances in information technology, will be the country's primary concern in increasing productivity and efficiency, improving speed of delivery of service, optimum utilisation of available resources and facilities and overall cost effectiveness.

2. To keep pace with advancing electronics, computer technology, telecommunication and reprography and micrography technology, all of which is needed for future library work, new systems compatible with Indian conditions must be developed.

3. Use of main-frame, mini and micro computers with large memory capabilities, in major libraries in the country, should be encouraged and supported to improve access and availability of information. Care is to be taken to ensure compatibility in hardware and software specifications, so as to facilitate linkages, among themselves and to national computer networks.

4. Priority should be given to development of application software packages for library and information activities for use in indigenously manufactured computer systems.

5. Use of communication facilities for developing inexpensive local library and information networks has to be supported for practising resource-sharing. These local library and information networks can be utilised for evolving national library and information network. Such developments will enable library and information centres to have local, regional and national inter-library co-operation, optimum utilisation of present resources and facilities and resource-sharing. Any user should have ready access to documents/information wherever he/she is located. This will also contribute to overall cost effectiveness, as development of resources and facilities in individual libraries and information centres beyond a threshold limit will be attempted rationally.

6. Low-cost copying services through provision of reprography and micrography facilities, should be available in major libraries so that document backup could be provided.

7. Compaction of library and information material, by increasingly resorting to acquisition of microform media, magnetic tapes, video discs, etc. wherever possible, should be encouraged, in the context of saving storage space.

8. Development of application software packages for provision of information services in Indian languages should be taken up. Computer translation services in Indian languages should be attempted.

9. Provision at district level should be made for mobile audio-visual information services in Indian languages for rural areas to serve neo-literates, post-literates, students of open universities etc. as a supplement to national TV network.

10. On-line facilities, through national data communication networks should be evolved in order to provide for interactive use of locally generated databases as well as to have access to international information networks.

11. New technologies like videotext and teletext provide ample

opportunities for disseminating information quickly and effectively. Such systems should be experimented, with a view to study their impact on the society and on the mechanism of their introduction.

General Professional Issues

1. Isolation is the common and abiding factor as far as Indian libraries are concerned. To break this isolation the nation requires a national network within which will be accommodated libraries of different kinds and at different levels from the rural society to the modern city, from the schools to the research organisations.

2. The establishment of such a network is therefore the Committee's principal recommendation to the Government.

3. In order that libraries and information centres should develop in their resources in a well planned and coordinated manner, they should develop various programmes of mutual cooperation and resource-sharing. In this manner they should be in a better position not only to make the best utilisation of their finances and other resources, but would also meet the varied and complicated information needs of their users in a more effective manner. For this purpose, tools such as Union Catalogues of Materials and other bibliographical tools would have to be compiled.

4. The national should make every effort to make its people aware of the significance and importance of its libraries. Librarians, on the other hand and the educational programmes at every level should be involved in discovering the needs of the people which the libraries can satisfy. It will be the task of the librarian and the information scientist of plan for an expansion of library services taking note not only of the actual users but the potential users of the system to be expected in years to come.

5. The library should be linked with its community and this linkage can only become effective when the user is educated through regularly arranged programmes in the various kinds of services to be expected from the library. Such linkages should also assist the library in continuously increasing the utilisation of its resources.

6. The user should be allowed as free and unrestricted access to library resources as possible and in doing so losses of documents may occur. Such losses should be guarded against as best a library can. But ultimately the librarian should not be held responsible for the losses which could not be avoided.

7. Library associations at the national level and the State level play important roles in promoting and strengthening library movement in the country. They may be given necessary patronage and encouragement for their effective functioning.

8. The committee recognises the need for formulating standards for different areas such as staffing pattern, building and equipment, tools, techniques, hardware and software etc. and for that purpose recommends that necessary steps should be taken to formulate guidelines for different types of libraries and information centres.

9. Government should take steps for the removal of barriers in communication and flow of information such as high postal tariffs, delays in postal communications, telecommunication bottlenecks, foreign exchange regulations, customs restrictions etc.

10. The Committee is concerned about the production of relevant and attractive reading material as well as audio-visual packages for the different kinds of users. It recommends, in particular, that relevant agencies be selected and assigned such tasks by the Union and the relevant State Governments. Such publications should be available at reasonable prices, if necessary at subsidised rates. Particular emphasis should be placed upon the production of materials for the neo-literates, the children and the physically handicapped.

Implementing Agencies and Financial Support

1. A National Commission for Libraries and Information Systems should be constituted by the Government of India to oversee the implementation of the National Policy. The Commission will have the responsibility of monitoring the progress and the development of Indian library and information systems and report periodically to the Government of India.

2. The Union Government and State Governments should establish separate divisions in the relevant Ministries and Departments for promoting the development of library and information systems in their respective areas. In the States such divisions may function as coordinating agencies for the improvement of the State libraries.

3. The proposed National Library Broad should establish effective linkages among library and information centres at the national level.

4. The coordinating, monitoring and developing of the Indian library and information systems may be entrusted at the national level to agencies such as (a) The Raja Rammohun Roy Library Foundation for

public libraries ana (b) the University Grants Commission for university and college libraries as well as other institutions of higher education.

5. The Government of India should designate appropriate agencies for the coordinating of school libraries and special libraries respectively.

6. Adequate financial support for the development of libraries and information systems will be made available by the Government of India and the State Governments. The national as well as State governments should provide for an expenditure of 6-10% of their education budgets for the libraries. All educational institutions should similarly provide for their own libraries 6-10% of their total budget. Institutional and departmental libraries should be adequately provided for by their parent organisation. Public libraries, especially at the rural level, should draw resources from all official agencies working at the level (e.g., national adult education programme, agricultural extension programme, etc.) including those concerned with distance education. Industrial organisations should be obliged to provide finances for adequate library services to their own employees. Such organisations should also extend this service to the community concerned. Finance from private organisations and philanthropic concerns should be encouraged in the library field especially in developing libraries for the use of children, handicapped persons and backward communities.

9.3 UGC COMMITTEE ON REVISION OF PAY SCALES OF LIBRARIANS AND DIRECTORS OF PHYSICAL EDUCATION IN UNIVERSITIES AND COLLEGES (1983-86)[3]

Background

The University Grants Commission appointed a Committee on December 24, 1983 under the Chairmanship of Professor R.C. Mehrotra, Emeritus Professor, Rajasthan University to consider the revision of pay scales, career/professional development and service conditions of teachers in the universities and colleges.

In October, 1985, the Commission, in consultation with the Government of India, requested the Committee to consider the revision of Pay Scales of Librarians and Directors of Physical Education in addition to the pay scales of University and College teachers.

3. Published by the University Grants Commission, New Delhi, 1986.

The Committee decided to submit the first part of its report on the original terms of reference and to take up subsequently the second part of the report on pay scales of Librarians and Directors of Physical Education in the Universities and Colleges.

The Committee met on 11th June, 1986, 2-3rd July, 1986, 18th July, 1986, 31st July, 1986 and 9th August, 1986. The Committee also consulted some representatives of the Associations of University and College Librarians, Associations of Directors of Physical Education and also some experts in the field of library management, physical education and sports.

Recommendations

1. It is evident that in order to fulfil the important role that:

   (a) Libraries,
   (b) Games, Sports and Programmes of Physical fitness are required to play in the intellectual and physical development of the nation, the two systems will have to be over-hauled, expanded and modernised. But the revision of scales of pay need not await that; it can precede the re-organisation and be sustained by it. The core of this Committee's recommendations, therefore, relate to the revision of scales of pay. The recommendations that it makes regarding qualifications and professional development are tentative and provisional in character.

2. The Committee noted that the principle of parity has been established in the matter of scales of pay between university and college teachers and Librarians and Directors/Instructors of Physical Education in the Universities and Colleges. In the case of teachers, the Committee has recommended pay scales in the existing framework; the same may be applied to pay scales of these categories. These pay scales may, therefore, be treated as notional and would have to be converted in the light of the recommendations of the Fourth Pay Commission. The Committee recommends that while converting these scales, it should be ensured that the Librarians and Directors/Instructors of Physical Education in Universities and Colleges are not put to any financial disadvantage and envisaged parity is maintained.

3. *Librarians*

The pay scales recommended for the various categories of Librarians in Universities and Colleges are as follows:

Universities	*Pay scale in the existing framework*
i. Asstt. University Librarian/ Documentation Officer	Rs. 700-40-1100-50-1600
ii. Asstt. University Librarian (Senior Scale)/Documentation Officer (Senior Scale)	Rs. 1200-50-1300-60-1900
iii. Asstt. University Librarian (Selection Grade)/ Documentation Officer (Selection Grade)	Rs. 2000-125/2-2250
iv. Deputy University Librarian	Rs. 1500-60-1800-100-2000-125/2-2250
v. University Librarian	Rs. 1800-100-2000-125/2-2750-125-3000

Colleges

i. College Librarian	Rs. 700-40-1100-50-1600
ii. College Librarian (Senior Scale)	Rs. 1200-50-1300-60-1900
iii. College Librarian (Selection Grade)	Rs. 2000-125/2-2250

4. *Directors of Physical Instructions and Sports*

The categories of Directors of Physical Instructions and Sports in the Universities and Colleges and the pay scales recommended for them are as follows:

University/College	*Pay Scale in the Existing framework*
i. Director of Physical Instructions & Sports	Rs. 700-40-1100-50-1600

ii. D.P.I.S. (Senior Scale)	Rs. 1200-50-1300-60-1900
iii. D.P.I.S. (Selection Grade)	Rs. 2000-125/2-2250

The Committee felt that in the new set-up of Physical Instructions and Sports it might be necessary to appoint Coordinator(s) of Physical Instructions and Sports in affiliating universities. Where there is a large network of colleges having substantial sports and physical fitness activities, the post of a Chief Coordinator of Physical Instructions may also be required in the University. Details regarding these may be worked out by an Expert Committee.

5. *Qualifications and Professional Development*

1. In order that the library and physical education staff are able to discharge their responsibilities adequately, it is essential to attract talent at initial stage. This should be accompanied by the creation of infrastructural facilities on a massive scale. The continuous self-improvement and professional development of the entrants should be secured through well-organised orientation programme, distance education courses, refresher courses, training programmes for emerging specialisations. At present two deficiencies in the library system attract adverse notice. First, the library staff is not qualified or trained for running a modern library system; second, the librarians tend to ignore academic excellence and concentrate on the routine functions. It is, therefore, recommended that:

   (a) the Libraries should be liberally funded to support modernisation and computerisation; and librarians and library staff should be appropriately trained for the purpose.
   (b) Among the qualifications prescribed for librarians, academic (subject) excellence should figure prominently.

   Similarly, in respect of Directors of Physical Instructions and Sports, stress should be laid on (i) training in modern techniques and (ii) stamina and fitness.

2. The Committee, however, stops short of making detailed recommendations in this direction and would suggest the constitution by the UGC of two expert committees with suitable

academic components. The committees be required respectively to review the existing systems of the management of (a) Libraries, (b) Physical instructions and sports, and to make recommendations for their re-organisation in the context of the roles devolving on them under the Education Policy (1986). The recommendations should cover the provision of infrastructure and equipment, qualifications and training of personnel, avenues of self-improvement and career development, motivation, monitoring, modernisation, periodical appraisal, accountability and performance-based promotion. It should be the effort of the Expert Committee on Libraries to bring about through its recommendations a transformation in th status, funding and functioning of the Libraries so that they could create a climate of general awareness and intellectual clarity and objective thinking. It should be the endeavour of the Expert Committee on Physical Instructions and Sports to recommend the restructuring and broad-basing of the system in such a manner that physical fitness becomes a byeword in educational institutions, which should also make in full measure their overdue contribution to national prowess in games and sports.

The basic recommendations of the Committee relate to (a) scales of pay; (b) avenues of promotion and (c) conditions of service. The remaining recommendations may be taken as tentative in character. While making their recommendations on the restructuring of the systems, the Expert Committee may be requested to pay special attention to the following:

1. *Minimum Qualifications*

   (a) for open All India recruitment at different levels;
   (b) for promotion to higher grades within the same cadre; and
   (c) for completion of satisfactory period of probation.

2. Specific items to be included in the self-appraisal and evaluation forms.
3. Facilities for professional training and development, taking into account the expansion of activities and augmentation of refresher courses and tests.
4. Workload to be defined, specifically to meet the special nature of their duties and functions (i.e. staggering of hours, etc.)

6. *Conditions of Service*

1. *Selection Procedure*
   Selection for the post of University Librarian, Deputy University Librarian, Assistant University Librarian/College Librarian/Documentation officer, and Director of Physical Instructions and Sports should be made strictly on merit on an All India basis. The selection committee should include at least two experts not connected with the university.
   Promotion of candidates to the senior scale and selection grade should also be done on the recommendations of a Selection Committee having at least one expert not connected with the university.
2. *Probation*
   An Assistant University Librarian, Dy. University Librarian, University Librarian, College Librarian and Director of Physical Instructions and Sports may normally be put on probation for a period of two years.
3. The committee has dealt in detail with the conditions of service of teachers.
   Broadly, the same conditions should apply to the Librarians and Directors of Physical Instructions and Sports. However, the very nature of duties of Librarians and DPIS would necessitate some change in conditions of service. The Committee would recommend the following modifications:
4. The Librarians and the Directors of Physical Instructions should be treated as non-vacation staff and entitled to the leave admissible to other non-vacation staff in universities. The work-load of the Directors of Physical Instructions and Sports would be different from the class room teaching because of the nature of the job which they have to perform. Therefore, the norms of work in their case would be different. The hours of work would be staggered: early morning, late after-noon and during the working day, the total work load aggregating to 40 hours a week. The working hours of librarians will similarly conform to the library timings. During the vacations, the Librarians and Directors of Physical Instructions and Sports should participate in programmes for their professional development. The Directors of Physical Instruction (DPIS) should also organise games and camps during the vacations.

5. *Housing Facilities*
   The Committee would urge that keeping in view the special duties of the DPIS which are to be performed both in the mornings and in the evenings, they should receive priority in allotment of houses on the campus.
6. *Age of Superannuation*
   The Committee recommends that the age of superannuation of the Librarians and Directors of Physical Instructions may continue to be 60 years. No extension of re-employment be given.
7. *Code of Conduct*
   The Committee had recommended a Code of Ethics for the teachers. The recommendations regarding this may be suitably modified in the case of Directors of Physical Instructions and Librarians keeping in view the duties to be assigned to them.

9.4 UGC EXPERT COMMITTEE ON MINIMUM QUALIFICATIONS AND WORKLOAD, ETC., FOR LIBRARIANS AND DIRECTORS OF PHYSICAL EDUCATION IN UNIVERSITIES AND COLLEGES, (1986-87)

See Chapter 12.3

9.5 UGC INTER-AGENCY WORKING GROUP ON DEVELOPMENT OF AN INFORMATION AND LIBRARY NETWORK, (1988)[4]

Background

The University Grants Commission constituted a Committee on National Network System for Universities/Libraries to suggest measures to network libraries in the country, so as to share the literature resources towards optimum utilisation and to avoid duplication in holdings, to the extent possible. Professor Yash Pal, Chairman, UGC has been the Chairman of the Committee. The first meeting of the Committee was held on 22nd April, 1988. The meeting stressed upon the need to provide the academic and research communities in the country easy and timely access to literature and information resources. It also expressed that, in the context of raising

4. Published by the University Grants Commission, New Delhi, 1988.

cost of books and journals, it is imperative on the part of various libraries to share the resources by evolving an effective network system.

The Committee, in the meeting, decided on constituting a Working Group on Information and Library Network (INFLIBNET) to prepare a project report within 3 months for consideration and further action.

Terms of Reference

1. To review the present scenario of Library automation and computerised bibliographic information services in India, taking into account similar services/experiences in some of the developed countries, with a view to propose a mechanism to establish a Network of Libraries in universities, colleges, special libraries and documentation centres in the country;
2. To identify the possible areas of cooperation for resource sharing and to minimise duplication in acquisition of books, serials, etc;
3. To propose a mechanism for using such a network for scientific communication among the research community in the country and abroad;
4. To specify the objectives of the Network at National, Regional and Unit level;
5. To suggest a suitable architecture for the Network;
6. To define the areas of standardisation required in the Network and to suggest minimum level of standardisation for effective compatibility and participation in the three component areas of the Network, viz., database, data communication and computer hardware and software;
7. To suggest (a) an action plan for implementation and (b) management mechanism including financial and personnel requirements to maintain and sustain the Network in short-term and long-term;
8. To prepare within 3 months a project Report (PR) for developing a Network based on the above factors.

The members of the Working Group have been drawn from different departments to work on a full time basis to prepare a comprehensive blue-print of the INFLIBNET, along with essential details necessary for implementation. Further, experts/senior officials of some representative organisations from library/information, computer and communication fields have been associated with the Working Group.

National Information Policy

The document on "Background to Evolving a National information Policy" has recognised information as indispensable for the functioning of a true democracy where people have to be kept informed about current affairs and broad issues – political, social and economical. In this context, the document described the role of mass communication, press and parliament and stipulated specific guidelines for Akashvani, Doordarshan, Films, Press Information Bureau, Publications Division, Research and Reference Division, etc.

National Policy on Library and Information System

To formulate a National Policy on Library and Information System, the Ministry of Human Resource Development, Government of India, set up a committee in October, 1985 under the chairmanship of Prof. D.P. Chattopadhyaya. The Committee had submitted its report, "National Policy on Library and Information System: A Presentation" in May 1986.

As a follow-up action, the Department of Culture set up an *Empowered Committee in November, 1986* under the chairmanship of Prof. D.P. Chattopadhyaya. The Committee started functioning in March 1987 and completed its work in March 1988. It addressed itself to the needs of (i) Public Library System, (ii) Academic Library System, (iii) Special Library and Information System, and (iv) National library and Bibliography Services, in terms of bringing India's library movement and services closer to the needs of (a) National Policy on Education (b) Library movement, and (c) Preservation of our cultural heritage. The Committee formulated the objectives of the National Policy on Library and Information System as follows:

> Library and information services are vital for all sectors of national activity. The availability of information expeditiously and pin-pointedly supports decision-making processes at all levels. Relevant information accelerates the pace of national development. An informed citizen is an asset to a democratic system of government and proper utilization of information can improve the quality of citizens. The Government of India, therefore, realizes the value of co-ordinating and upgrading the existing library and

information systems and services and initiating of new programmes relevant to our national needs, taking advantage of the latest advances in information technology.

Main Aims of Library and Information Policy

(i) To foster, promote and sustain, by all appropriate means, the organisation, availability and use of information in all sectors of national activity;
(ii) To take steps for mobilising and upgrading the existing library and information systems and services and initiating new programmes relevant to our national needs, taking advantage of the latest advances in information technology;
(iii) To encourage and initiate, with all possible speed, programmes for the training of library and information personnel, on a scale and of a calibre adequate to provide the library and information services and to recognise their work as an important component of the quality and level of such services;
(iv) To set up adequate monitoring mechanisms for ensuring a rapid development of library and information facilities and services for meeting the information needs of all sectors and levels of the national economy;
(v) To encourage individual initiative for the acquisition and dissemination of knowledge, and for the discovery of new knowledge in an atmosphere of intellectual freedom;
(vi) In general, to secure for the people of the country all the benefits that can accrue from the acquisition and application of knowledge; and
(vii) to preserve and make known the nation's cultural heritage in its multiple forms.

Seventh Plan Initiatives

The Government of India, in its Seventh Five Year Plan, has given due recognition and emphasis on the provision of library and information services and to the introduction of information technology. The Report of the Steering Group on Science and Technology and Environment for the Seventh Five Year Plan (1985-1990) has recommended that the present library community be exposed to the concept of computers and their usage and that during the Seventh Plan, the goal should be to computerise most major library operations.

Report of the Planning Commission Working Group on Modernisation of Library Services and Informatics for the Seventh Five Year Plan (1985-90)

The Planning Commission set up a Working Group on Modernisation of Library Services and Informatics for the Seventh Five Year Plan (1985-90) under the chairmanship of Dr. N. Seshagiri, Additional Secretary, Department of Electronics. The Working Group submitted a report entitled "Report of the Planning Commission Working Group on Modernisation of Library Services and Informatics for the Seventh Five Year Plan (1985-90)". The report was an attempt to draw an integrated plan balancing the modernization and the conventional imperatives. The report recognised library as the richest and the most economical source of information required for economic and social development and felt that it is one of the least coordinated and poorly planned sectors at the national level. The report noticed that if properly used, the investment effectiveness of library services through indirect benefit can be very high and suggested that adequate, timely and efficient library services could be best provided through appropriate modernization using the sophistications of computer networking, computer output micro-filming, computer aided reprography, facsimile transmission, opto-electronic video discs and such other advancements in information technology and by balancing the modernisation and the conventional requirements of library services such as expanding and enriching the existing collections in the libraries, providing adequate documentation services and efficient management of libraries.

The report dealt with the requirement of library services in the Seventh Plan with respect of academic, public and special libraries, the manpower requirements for expansion and improved performance, the informatics developmental activities in the library systems and specific proposals for implementation in various libraries. Finally, it proposed development of a computer network interlinking all special libraries in India by 2000 AD.

INFLIBNET

1. The Project on Information and Library Networking (INFLIBNET) aims at the establishment of a national network of libraries and

information centres in universities, colleges, research and development organizations, etc., in India. The Working Group on INFLIBNET has taken due note of (a) Scientific Policy Resolution and Technology Policy Statement, (b) National Policy on Education and (c) proposed National Policy on Library and Information System. It has also recognised the various efforts already made and being planned in the country for modernization of libraries and information centres and the developmental programmes of NISSAT, NIC, DESINET, ERNET, CALNET, DELNET, and the CSIRNET.

The INFLIBNET aims at providing a framework to the existing and planned efforts in networking of libraries and lays emphasis on interconnecting university and academic libraries which have been the most neglected ones so far.

2. Objectives of INFLIBNET

INFLIBNET is to be a computer-communication network for linking libraries and information centres in universities, deemed universities, institutions of national importance, UGC information centres, R&D institutions and colleges. The main objectives of INFLIBNET are:

(a) to evolve a national network, interconnecting various libraries and information centres in the country and to improve capability in information handling and service;

(b) to provide reliable access to document collection of libraries by creating online union catalogue of monographs, serials and non-book materials (manuscripts, audio-visuals, computer media, etc.) in various libraries in India;

(c) to provide better access to worthwhile bibliographic information sources, with citations and abstracts, such as periodical articles, conference papers, preprints, technical reports, standards and specifications, patents, monographs, etc. through indigenously created databases of the Sectoral Information Centres of NISSAT and UGC Information Centres and such others and by establishing gateways for online accessing of international databases held by international information networks and centres.

9.6 EMPOWERED COMMITTEE ON NATIONAL POLICY ON LIBRARY AND INFORMATION SYSTEM, (1986-88)[5]

Background

The Ministry of Human Resource Development, Government of India had set up a Committee in October 1985 to formulate a National Policy on Library and Information System under the chairmanship of Prof. D.P. Chattopadhyaya. This Committee submitted its Report in May 1986. The Department of Culture, Government of India then appointed an Empowered Committee in November 1986 under the chairmanship of Prof D.P. Chattopadhyaya to lay down a Programme of Action for implementation of The National Policy on Library and Information System. The Empowered Committee submitted its report to the Government on II May 1988.

Highlights of Report

(1) A nominal one time membership fee of Re. 1 to Rs. 10 from all public library users;
(2) Rural library information centres should be made available under Minimum Needs Programme by 2001 AD;
(3) One Community Centre with library facilities in every Panchayat under 8th Five Year Plan;
(4) Children's section for every public library with 20% collection for children;
(5) Audio visual material and equipment in all public libraries who should play important role in Adult Education;
(6) District library as apex library for each district;
(7) Recognition of key role of public libraries as chief sustaining agencies of distant education;
(8) All public libraries within a State should form part of information database network;
(9) Development of library standards and guidelines on model library service at several levels;
(10) All the States and Union Territories to have public library Act;
(11) Every school and college must have a library and a qualified trained librarian;

5. Published by the University Grants Commission, New Delhi, 1988.
Source: *Herald of Library Science*, January-April 1989.

(12) Organising refresher/orientation courses for user/staff of school/college libraries; and university library should bė treated as academic unit;
(13) Resource sharing of universities, colleges and research organisations in one region/state through linkages and network;
(14) Short term orientation courses in modern library management ana information technology for library staff and teachers in science faculties;
(15) High powered committee to identify the institutions and disciplines for National Network;
(16) National Library, Calcutta to be recognised as the apex of the country's library network system, with suitable amendment in relevant Acts. The three Delivery of Book Act recipient libraries in Delhi, Bombay and Madras be treated as libraries of National Importance and serve as Regional Depository libraries;
(17) Devise a suitable manuscript collection and preservation programme;
(18) All India Council for Technical Education be the accreditating agency for professional teaching programmes;
(19) Department of Culture is to draft suitable bill for establishing the National Commission on Libraries for guiding and coordinating library development programme of both the centre and the states;
(20) Total gross annual allocation of funds on 'Library' may be at 6-10% of that on 'Education' head in Central and State Government budgets.

10

NATIONAL LITERACY MISSION (1988)

Objectives

The National Literacy Mission (NLM) was launched in May 1988 to impart Functional Literacy to 80 million illiterate persons in 15-35 age-group — 30 million by 1990 and additional 50 million by 1995.

Functional Literacy Components

The NLM has given the following components of functional literacy:

- Achieving self-reliance in literacy and numeracy:
  - Becoming aware of the causes of their deprivation and moving towards amelioration of their condition through organization, and participation in the process of development;
  - Acquiring skills to improve the economic status and general well-being;
  - Imbibing the values of national integration, conservation of the environment, women's equality, observance of small family norm, etc.

With a view to deriving optimum results eradication of illiteracy, a nationwide network of continuing education will be established through new institutional structures, better utilisation of the existing infrastructures, open and distance learning, etc.

Norms Prescribed for Functional Literacy

The NLM has prescribed certain levels in the three Rs to be achieved by the target groups.

Reading Norms: As far as reading is concerned, a person, to be declared a literate, must be able to read aloud a simple passage at a speed of 30 words per minute. While reading silently small paragraphs in simple language, a speed of 35 words per minute should be achieved.

The neo-literates must also be able to read and understand road sings, posters, simple instructions and newspapers specially produced for them. Ability to follow simple written messages relating to one's working and living environment is another requisite attribute.

Writing Norms: In respect of writing, the NLM has laid down that a neo-literate should be able to 'copy with understanding at a speed of seven words per minute'. He should be able to take dictation at five words per minute. He should be able to write with proper spacing and alignment. He should also be able to write independently short letters, application and forms of day-to-day use.

Arithmetic Norms: Proficiency in numerals has also been laid down. The new learner must be able to read and write 1 to 100. He should also be able to do 'simple calculations without fraction involving addition, substraction up to three digits and multiplication and divisions by two digits.'

The NLM also expects the neo-literates to have a working knowledge of metric units of weights, measures, currency, distance and area, and units of time. They should also have a broad idea of proportion and interest (without involving fractions) and their use in working and living conditions.

Strategy

Main features of the strategy are:

1. Increasing motivation of the learner by taking up learner need-based programmes.
2. Securing people's participation through media and communication, creation of local participatory structures, taking out of 'jathas', training of cadres of youth etc. These efforts are expected to create an environment conducive to learning.
3. Increasing significantly the involvement of Voluntary Agencies.
4. Improving substantially on going programmes.
5. Launching mass movement by involving educational institutions,

teachers, students, youth, military and paramilitary personnel, housewives, ex-servicemen, employers, trade unions etc.

6. Institutionalising continuing education for post-literacy, particularly through establishment of Jana Shikshan Nilayams and better use of existing institutional facilities.
7. Universalising the outreach by providing facilities for literacy learning, continuing education and vocational training.
8. Undertaking technology demonstration in 40 districts for development, transfer and application of technology pedagogic inputs and thereafter covering more districts after evaluating the results.
9. Establishing effective management system at different levels.
10. Involving suitable mechanism for staff selection and development, collection, flow and utilisation of information, systematic monitoring and evaluation.
11. Making available standard learning material on a wide scale, in print and non-print media.
12. Allocating finances.

Mission Clientele

The NLM will concentrate on the 15-35 age group which is crucial for the country's development.

Financial Estimates

Project Expenditure (1987-1990) (*Rs. in Crores*)

1. Field Programme	Rs 325
2. Voluntary Agencies	50
3. Mass Programme through Students and Volunteers	10
4. Continuing Education	110
5. Management and Media Support	25
6. Direct Costs for R & D	30

11

NAVODAYA VIDYALAYAS

Background

1. In order to provide good quality modern education to the talented children predominantly from the rural areas, Government of India have launched a scheme to establish Navodaya Vidyalayas on an average one in each district. Two hundred and fifty-six Navodaya Vidyalayas covering 22 States and 7 Union Territories have so far been established in the country.

2. Admission to Navodaya Vidyalayas is at the level of Class-VI. In view of the fact that most of the students so admitted would have been taught earlier through the medium of the mother-tongue/regional language, instruction is provided through the same medium up to Class-VI or VIII, during which time intensive teaching of Hindi/English both as a language subject and co-media is undertaken. Thereafter, the common medium would be Hindi/English. At this stage, there is a migration of 20% students from each Navodaya Vidyalaya to another Navodaya Vidyalaya, in a different linguistic region. The migration is mainly between Hindi and non-Hindi speaking districts. The first batch of students has migrated from Navodaya Vidyalaya, Jhajjar to Amravati and *vice versa*, as these two Vidyalayas have reached Class-IX stage this year. The Navodaya Vidyalayas follow the normal three language formula. At present, there are 123 Vidyalayas in Hindi Speaking States and 133 in non-Hindi Speaking States and third language has been introduced in all these Vidyalayas.

Admission

3. The basis of admission to Navodaya Vidyalayas is a test conducted by NCERT. The medium of the test is the mother-tongue or

regional language. Test is largely of non-verbal nature, class-neutral and so designed as to ensure that talented children from rural schools are able to compete without suffering a disadvantage.

4. The examination for Academic Session 1988-89 was conducted on 15-05-88 in all the districts where the Navodaya Vidyalayas are functioning. The test was conducted in 18 languages.

5. Break-up of the students selected for 256 Navodaya Vidyalayas is as follows:

Rural	10934	Boys	11298
Urban	2870	Girls	2506
	13804	SC	2360
		ST	1602
		General	9842

6. Navodaya Vidyalayas are co-educational and primarily for children from rural areas. Hence admission of children from urban areas is restricted to a maximum of one-forth. Efforts are made to ensure that atleast one-third of the students in each Navodaya Vidyalaya are girls.

7. Reservation of seats in favour of children belonging to the Scheduled Castes and Scheduled Tribes is provided in proportion to their population in the concerned district, provided that in no district such reservation is less than the national average.

Construction Programme

8. The Central Building Research Institute, Roorkee, has been designated as the nodal agency for implementing the works programme for Navodaya Vidyalaya. For implementing the programme a Construction Co-ordination Committee has been set up in the Samiti. Twenty-six Construction Agencies have been identified and Vidyalayas allotted to them. The Samiti has given clearance for construction of first phase of building (for classes VI to IX) in 100 Vidyalayas and of minimal structures with tubular trusses in 120 Vidyalayas.

Principals and Teachers

9. At the moment, 256 schools are functioning with 256 principals and 2719 teachers.

12

PHYSICAL EDUCATION AND SPORTS[1]

12.1 NATIONAL SPORTS POLICY (DRAFT) (1982)

Present Policy

1. The earliest authentic official statement of policy on games, sports and physical education in India was incorporated in the National Policy on Education announced by the Government in 1968. It reads as follows:

> "Games and Sports: Games and Sports should be developed on a large scale with the object of improving the physical fitness and sportsmanship of the average student as well as those who excel in this department. Where playing fields and other facilities for developing a nation-wide programme of physical education do not exist they should be provided on a priority basis."

Sports — A State Subject

2. Under the Constitution of India, sports is a State subject. Physical Education, which is part of education, is in the Concurrent List. To evolve a mutually agreed approach and to devise some common programmes in the field of Physical Education and Sports, it is necessary to arrive at a consensus with the State Governments and the State Sports Councils. Such a consensus was arrived at in November, 1974, and certain guidelines with regard to policy and programmes to

---

1. Published by the Ministry of Education and Culture, Government of India, New Delhi, 1982

be followed were issued in 1975.

Autonomy of Indian Olympic Association and National Sports Federations

3. Under the Charter of the International Olympic Committee the competitive aspect of amateur sports in India at national and international levels is the responsibility of the National Olympic Committee and the National Sports Federations who must function autonomously without governmental, political, religious or commercial interference.

Role of Government of India

4. In India the Central Government's role in the field of sports has hitherto been confined generally to providing coordination and consultancy services to the States and of laying down guidelines to the National Sports Federations and to use powers of persuasion for their improved functioning in the matter of competitions, coaching and selections. The Central Government has also been serving as a clearing house of information.

Existing Central Schemes and Programmes

5. Within the broad policy framework enunciated in para 1 and within its constitutional and legal limitations mentioned in paras 2 and 3 the Central Government have been taking steps within the funds available for the purpose to promote and develop Physical Education and Sports in the country. The more important of the Central Government schemes in this area are:

(a) assisting the States in spotting sports talent at a young age through its schemes of Sports Talent Search Scholarships;
(b) giving financial assistance to the States Councils for setting up rural sports centres, holding of annual coaching camps, developments of playfields, purchase of equipment of non-expendible nature, construction of stadia, swimming pools etc.;
(c) giving financial assistance through the University Grants Commission and the Association of Indian Universities for the

promotion of sports in the colleges and universities for the development of playfields, construction of gymnasia, holding of coaching-cum-competition camps and scholarships to talented sportsmen and women in colleges and universities;

(d) giving financial assistance for improving facilities in physical education teacher training institutions in the country;

(e) holding rural sports tournaments at the national level and giving assistance to State Governments for holding such tournaments at lower levels;

(f) holding national festivals for women preceded by similar festivals at lower levels;

(g) conducting the National Physical Efficiency Drive to promote the physical fitness and health of the people.

Consensus arrived at in the Meeting of the State Ministers of Sports, Presidents of State Sports Councils and President/Members of the All India Council of Sports, held in November, 1974

1. With a view to broad-basing sports and games from the grass roots level upwards, each of the state Governments/State Sports Councils should undertake to involve around 1500 youth in active sports, in each Block, thus ensuring the participation of about 80 lakhs of young men and women. This programme should be given the top-most priority in the plans of the State Governments for promotion of sports.

Games popular in the local areas and also those which do not involve much expenditure on the purchase of equipment etc. or on the creation of new physical facilities should be given preference. Proper training and coaching of young people in the various sports and games should be given the highest priority and the services of coaches provided under the National Coaching Scheme and the Nehru Yuvak Kendras should be fully utilised.

2. The State Governments would take urgent action to activize the State Sports Councils, and constitute these State Sports Councils where they do not exist, so that these Councils play a meaningful role in the development of sports and games and effective coordination of the activities in this field in collaboration with the State Sports Association.

3. It was agreed that the State Governments and State Sports

Councils would adhere to the guidelines circulated vide the Ministry's letter dated 9th April, 1974 in respect of the grant of financial and other assistance to State Sports Associations.

4. The State Governments would seriously consider the possibility of making physical education, sports and games compulsory at the school level, and making participation therein a precondition for eligibility in school examinations and for qualifying therein.

5. The State Governments and State Sports Councils would formulate programmes of sports competitions districtwise for women during 1975, as a part of the celebrations of the International Women's Year.

Emphasis will be on sports involving comparatively less expenditure, in respect of those games which are more popular amongst women.

6. The State Governments would take suitable steps including enactment of legislation as necessary, for the preservation and improvement of open spaces in urban and rural areas for play-fields.

7. The State Governments and the State Sports Councils would draw up a plan for provision of basic physical facilities like playfields, utility stadia, gymnasia, swimming pools etc. in areas where such facilities were lacking. The State Governments would ensure that these projects are carefully selected in order of local priorities, and undertake to complete them within the shortest possible time, so that public funds from the State and Central Governments are properly utilised. The State Governments and State Sports Councils agreed in this connection to maximise utilisation of the offer of central financial assistance for provision of such facilities. The Government of India would consider the suggestion for enhancement of the quantum of assistance under various categories of the scheme for financial support to State Sports Councils.

8. The State Sports Councils and the Nehru Yuvak Kendras will co-operate with each other in drawing up and implementing programmes for organising of sports events at the grass root level.

9. The State Sports Councils would avail themselves of the opportunity to organise matches in their States for visiting foreign, teams under bilateral Cultural Exchange Programmes with friendly countries.

10. State Governments will consider providing suitable incentives to all such sportsmen and women who have achieved distinction in national/international sports.

11. The meeting expressed the hope that the State Sports Councils, State Sports Associations, the All India Council of Sports and the National Sports Federations/Associations, would cooperate fully with each other in the promotion and furtherance of sports and games in the country.

12.2 UGC COMMITTEE ON REVISION OF PAY SCALES OF LIBRARIANS AND DIRECTORS OF PHYSICAL EDUCATION IN UNIVERSITIES AND COLLEGES (1983-86)

See Chapter 9 (Para 9.3)

12.3 UGC EXPERT COMMITTEE ON MINIMUM QUALIFICATIONS AND WORKLOAD, ETC., FOR LIBRARIAN AND DIRECTORS OF PHYSICAL EDUCATION IN UNIVERSITIES AND COLLEGES (1986-87)[2]

Background

1. The University Grants Commission appointed a Committee on December 24, 1983 under the Chairmanship of Professor R.C. Mehrotra, Emeritus Professor, Rajasthan University, Jaipur to consider the revision of pay scales, career/professional development and service conditions of teachers in the universities and colleges.

2. In October, 1985 the Commission in consultation with the Government of India, requested the Committee to consider the revision of pay scales of Librarians and Directors of Physical Education, in addition to the pay scales of Librarians and Directors of Physical Education, in addition to the pay scales of university and college teachers.

3. The report of the Committee on revision of pay scales of Librarians and Directors of Physical Education in universities and colleges was submitted to the Commission on 3rd September, 1986.

4. The main recommendations/observations of the Committee are as follows:

4.1 "The Committee noted that the principle of parity has been established in the matter of scales of pay between university

2. Published by the University Grants Commission, New Delhi, 1987.

and college teachers and Librarians and Directors/Instructors of Physical Education in the universities and colleges. In the case of teachers, the Committee has recommended pay scales in the existing framework; the same may be applied to pay scales of these categories. These pay scales may, therefore, be treated as notional and would have to be converted in the light of the recommendations of the Fourth Pay Commission. The Committee recommends that while converting these scales, it should be ensured that the Librarians and Directors/Instructors of Physical Education in universities and colleges are not put to any financial disadvantage and envisaged parity is maintained."

4.2 Librarians

The pay scales recommended for the various categories of Librarians in universities and colleges are as follows:

		Pay scale in the existing framework Rs.
Universities		
(i)	Asstt. University Librarian/Documentation Officer	700-40-1100-50-1600
(ii)	Asstt. University Librarian (Senior scale)/ Documentation Officer (Senior Scale)	1200-50-1300-60-1900
(iii)	Asstt. University Librarian (Selection grade)/ Documentation Officer (Selection grade)	2000-125/2-2250
(iv)	Deputy University Librarian	1500-60-1800-100-2000-125/2-2250
(v)	University Librarian	1800-100-2000-125/2-2750-125-3000
Colleges		
(i)	College Librarian	700-40-1100-50-1600
(ii)	College Librarian (Senior scale)	1200-50-1300-60-1900
(iii)	College Librarian (Selection grade)	2000-125/2-2250

4.3 Director of Physical Instructions and Sports

The categories of Directors of Physical Instructions and Sports in the universities and college and the pay scales recommended for them are as follows:

University/College		*Pay scale in the existing framework*
1.	Director of Physical Instructions & Sports	700-40-1100-50-1600
2.	D.P.I.S. (Senior scale)	1200-50-1300-60-1900
3.	D.P.I.S. (Selection grade)	2000-125/2-2250.

The Committee felt that in the new set up of Physical Instructions and Sports, it might be necessary to appoint Coordinator(s) of Physical Instructions and Sports in affiliating universities. Where there is a large network of college having substantial sports and physical fitness activities, the post of a Chief Coordinator of Physical Instructions may also be required in the university. Details regarding these may be worked out by an Expert Committee.

4.4 **Selection Procedure**

Selection for the post of University Librarian, Deputy University Librarian, Assistant University Librarian/College Librarian/ Documentation Officer and Director of Physical Instructions and Sports should be made strictly on merit on an All India basis. The selection Committee should include atleast two experts not connected with the university. Promotion of candidates to the senior scale and selection grade should also be done on the recommendations of a Selection Committee having atleast one expert not connected with the university.

4.5 **Probation**

An Assistant University Librarian, Dy. University Librarian, University Librarian, College Librarian and Director of Physical Instructions and Sports may normally be put on probation for a period of two years.

4.6 The Librarians and the Directors of Physical Instructions should be treated as non-vacation staff and entitled to the leave admissible to other non-vacation staff in universities. The work-load of the Directors of Physical Instructions and Sports would be different from the class room teaching because of the nature of the job which they have to perform. Therefore, the norms of work in their case would be different. The hours of work would be staggered: early morning, late afternoon and during the working day, the total work load aggregating to 40 hours a week. The working hours of Librarians will similarly conform to the library timings. During the vacations, the Librarians and Directors of Physical Instructions and Sports should participate in programmes for their professional development. The Directors of Physical Instructions should also organise games and camps during the vacations.

4.7 Housing Facilities

The Committee would urge that keeping in view the special duties of the Directors of Instructions which are to be performed both in the mornings and in the evenings, they should receive priority in allotment of houses on the campus.

4.8 Age of Superannuation

The Committee recommends that the age of superannuation of the Librarians and Directors of Instructions may continue to be 60 years. No extension or re-employment be given.

4.9 Code of Conduct

The Committee had recommended a Code of Ethics for the teachers. The recommendations regarding this may be suitably modified in the case of Directors of Physical Instructions and Librarians keeping in view the duties to be assigned to them.

5. The basic recommendations of the Committee relate to (a) scales of pay; (b) avenues of promotion and (c) conditions of service. The Committee suggested the constitution of two Expert Committees. The Expert Committees may be requested to pay special attention to the following:

(i) Minimum qualifications:

- (a) for open All India recruitment at different levels;
- (b) for promotion to higher grades within the same cadre; and
- (c) for completion of satisfactory period of probation.

(ii) Specific items to be included in the self-appraisal and evaluation forms;

(iii) Facilities for professional training and development, taking into account the expansion of activities and augmentation of refresher courses and tests;

(iv) Workload to be defined, specifically to meet the special nature of their duties and functions (i.e. staggering of hours etc.).

6. The Commission at its meeting held on 27th October, 1986 considered the report and generally agreed with the recommendations of the Committee relating to (a) scales of pay, (b) avenues of promotion, and (c) conditions of service. The Commission desired that an Expert Committee may be appointed to consider the minimum qualifications and workload, etc. as envisaged in para 5 above.

7. **Composition**

In view of the above decision of the Commission, an Expert Committee was constituted with the following members:

1. Professor G. Padmanabhan, Department of Bio-Chemistry, Indian Institute of Science, Bangalore. — Convener
2. Professor N.M. Swani, Director, Indian Institute of Technology, New Delhi.
3. Professor (Miss) A.K. Anand, Librarian, Panjab University, Chandigarh.
4. Dr. Ashin Das Gupta, Director, National Library, Calcutta.

5[3]. Professor N.N. Mall,
Director,
Laxmibai Nation College of Physical Education,
Shakti Nagar,
Gwalior.

6. Professor M. Robson,
Director,
Department of Physical Education and Sports Sciences.
Annamalai University,
Annamalainagar 608 002 (TN).

7. Dr. C.M. Muthiah,
Director-General,
Netaji Subhash National Institute of Sports,
Motibagh,
Patiala.

8. Shri S.K. Chaturvedi,
Joint Secretary,
Ministry of Human Resource Development,
Department of Youth Affairs and Sports,
New Delhi.

9. Shri C.R. Pillai,
Deputy Secretary,
Ministry of Human Resource Development,
Department of Education,
New Delhi.

10. Shri R.P. Gangurde, Member-Secretary
Joint Secretary,
University Grants Commission,
New Delhi.

8. **Terms of Reference**

The terms of reference of the Committee is to consider further the recommendations of the Committee on revision of pay scales of Librarians and Directors of Physical Education in universities and colleges (Mehrotra Committee report part 'B') as envisaged in para 5 above.

3. Expressed his inability to attend the meeting. Professor Karan Singh of BHU was nominated for the meetings held on 11th March, 1987 and 30 March, 1987.

(i) Minimum qualifications

(a) for open All India recruitment at different levels;
(b) for promotion to higher grades within the same cadre; and
(c) for completion of satisfactory period of probation.

(ii) Specific items to be included in the self-appraisal and evaluation forms.

(iii) Facilities for professional training and development, taking into account the expansion of activities and augmentation of refresher course and tests.

(iv) Workload to be defined, specifically to meet the special nature of their duties and functions (i.e. staggering of hours etc.)

9. **Time Schedule**

The Committee had its meetings on 6th February, 1987, 11th March, 1987, 30th March, 1987, 30th April, 1987 and 9th July, 1987. The Committee had discussions with the representatives of All India Association of Librarians and Directors of Physical Education on 30th March, 1987.

10. The Committee appointed two sub-Committees to work out the details regarding the self-appraisal and evaluation forms and various training programmes for career development of Librarians and Directors of Physical Education.

13

POPULATION EDUCATION

National Population Education Project (NPEP)

1. Realising the potential of education in tackling the problem of growing population, the Ministry of Human Resource Development, Government of India launched the National Population Education Project with effect from April 1980. The first cycle (1980-85) of the project has successfully been completed. The second cycle has been started w.e.f. 1st January, 1986. The Project being implemented in 26 States and Union Territories has completed third year of second cycle. The Project has been developed in collaboration with the United Nations Population Fund (UNFPA) and with the active involvement of Ministry of Health and Family Welfare which is the nodal Ministry for Population Education.

2. The Main objectives of the programme are:

(i) to give students an insight into inter-relationships between population growth and the process of social and economic development at the individual family society, national and international levels;
(ii) to make the children and teachers aware of the population situation in the country and targets and efforts of the Government of India in solving this problem;
(iii) to institutionalise population education in the formal education system, including universities and non-formal education programmes at the national and state levels;
(iv) to develop desirable attitudes in the teachers and students as well as the community at large towards population issues so that they

make rational decisions about their family size and the quality of life that they would like to have.

3. During the Seventh Five Year Plan, the scope of the project has been expanded to cover the students and teachers at the plus two stage (Classes XI & XII) which is considered to be a very crucial target group in view of the impending entry of the students of this stage into the reproductive age-group. The financial and other inputs required by the States for implementing the projects are provided by the Ministry of HRD through NCERT. The NCERT provides the technical assistance.

4. The project activities carried out by States and Union Territories focused on development of materials for plus two-stage, non-formal education sector and training of different target groups, orientation of teachers and instructors on non-formal education centres, evaluation of different components of the project and co-curricular activities. The efforts of Population Education Cells in respect of integration of Population education elements into textbooks being revised were circumscribed by the delay in the initiation of the revision of textbooks in majority of States.

5. By the end of 1987-88 as many as 18 States and Union Territories completed the activity of development of curriculum on population education for plus two-stage. These documents will facilitate the integration of population education elements into the syllabi and textbooks being revised in the wake of implementation of NPE 1986. Sixteen States/UTs have incorporated population education elements into the syllabi. Fifteen States and UTs have developed curriculum in population education for non-formal education sector and eight of them have been able to integrate these elements into the ongoing syllabi. Twenty States have developed curriculum for elementary teacher training and fourteen of them have incorporated population education elements into ongoing syllabi. The number of titles brought out on instructional and training materials on Population education during the current year was 435 as against last year's number of 367. States and Union Territories have published 21 titles for non-formal education sector. Fourteen States/UTs have brought out 41 supplementary reading materials for different stages and thirteen States/UTs brought out regular issues of Newsletter. A total of 403 programmes have been broadcast on AIR so far. Sixteen programmes on population education were telecast during the current year. Eighteen

States/UTs have developed non-projective aids like posters, charts, flip charts, etc. and nine States have developed audio visual material on population education. During the year, State/UTs have oriented 1,04,971 teachers, 1761 key and resource persons and 9595 instructors of non-formal education sector.

14

REGIONAL COLLEGES: NCERT Committee on Transformation of Regional Colleges of Education into Regional Institutes (1987)[1]

Introduction

In pursuance of NCERT order dated June 2, 1986 a committee was set up under the Chairmanship of Dr. R.C. Das ex-Vice-Chancellor, to recommend steps to be taken to convert the Regional Colleges of Education into Regional Centres of NCERT. The terms of reference of the Committee also stipulated that it may also take note of the National Policy on Education, 1986 and the priority attached to the pre-service training of teachers and indicate the role of the Regional Centres of Education to be played in pursuance of this policy decision. The Committee submitted its report is January 1987.

Recommendations

The recommendations of the Committee are as follows:

4.1.1 Four year integrated courses of teacher education in Science and Arts with intake of 60 students in each course may be continued at each Regional Institute.

---

1. Published by the National Council of Educational Research and Training, New Delhi, 1987

Note: Para numbers relate to para number in the document.

4.1.2 One year B.Ed. course in its present form be discontinued at each Institute. In its place a One-year B.Ed. course designed to prepare teachers both for secondary and higher secondary (+2 level) be offered to only Master's degree holders.

4.1.3 One year B.Ed. (Ely) course be discontinued and 3 to 4 months in-service training course in elementary education be offered to elementary teacher educators and supervisors.

4.1.4 B.Ed. (SSCC) Course be stopped as there is no back-log of untrained secondary teachers.

4.1.5 The M.Ed. course may be continued after restructuring it with intensive specialisations in Special Education, Educational Technology and Primary Teacher Education with total intake of 30 in each Institute.

4.1.6 The M.Sc.Ed. course may be continued to be offered until the M.Sc.Ed. course on campus-cum-distant learning pattern to trained graduate teachers of science in-service stabilized. As soon as the campus-cum-distant learning course stabilizes itself, the regular on campus course should be phased out.

4.2.1 Suitable in-service course of 6 to 8 weeks duration be offered to teachers in Work-experiences/SUPW and in vocational education in the areas of Technology, Agriculture and commerce. Alternatively the 3 year Diploma course in Industrial crafts after X class which was offered at one time may be revised with suitable modifications for the above purpose.

4.2.2 A course of 4 to 6 months duration leading to a certificate in special Education with due emphasis of integrated education of handicapped (of one category) be offered to trained graduates.

4.2.3 A certificate course of 4 to 6 months duration in Educational technology be offered to trained graduate with emphasis on script writing for radio and TV educational programmes including software development for other technologies.

4.2.4 In-service education of teachers in pre-school education may be taken up in collaboration with state Government with the Regional Institute training teach educators and resource persons and other profession learners.

4.2.5 A certificate course of 3 to 4 months duration elementary education be offered to trained graduate teachers to enable them to develop competencies required of elementary teacher educator/supervisors Alternatively such a course may be organised on a campus-cum-distant learning pattern.

4.2.6 Advanced level in-service programmes in special subjects be offered during summer vacation to secondary teacher educators for their professional growth in collaboration with University/U.G.C.

4.2.7 Orientation/training to teachers/teacher-educators in the identification and development of talent may be organised.

4.2.8 In-service training for secondary school teachers in the new core curriculum be organised in consultation with State Governments to train resource persons who in their turn, will train the teachers.

4.3 The Regional Institution should undertake in a big-way the development and dissemination of a variety of relevant and useful instructional materials and other media resources relating to different subjects to school education and teacher education.

4.4 Using the facilities of the Workshop, the Regional Institute should design the produce a variety of useful teaching aids and learning kits for children.

4.5 The Institute should undertake development of a variety of software in educational technology, such as slice film-strips, films, audio and video programmes, computer programmes.

4.6 In each institute, a comprehensive education resources centre may be developed with the following divisions:

(a) Library
(b) Instructional Materials Division
(c) Learning Kits Division
(d) Other Media Resources

Policy studies and services may be taken up by forming a separate unit consisting of a few staff members who would plan and coordinate such studies.

Field Programmes and extension services may be organised by forming another unit to plan and coordinate the programmes.

There should be collaborative planning and effective sharing of work between the NIE and the Regional Institute of Education for implementing national policies and programmes. National level modal centres in respect of some specified programmes and projects may be located at the Regional Institute.

5(a) A post of Joint Director for Regional Institutes and Field Services be created and filled to guide supervise and coordinate the work of the Regional Institutes and the Field Offices. He should be assisted by a Deputy Secretary and supporting staff.

(b) A Coordination Committee for Regional Institutes with Director as Chairman, Joint Director (RIE & FA) as Vice-Chairman, Principals as members should be formed. It should meet at least once a year, preferably twice, to consider major policies and programmes and budget provisions for the Regional Institutes.

5.2 The Regional Colleges be renamed as REGIONAL INSTITUTES OF EDUCATION instead of Regional Centres as the Institutions will be conducting various pre-service and in-service teacher education courses leading to degree/diploma of a University.

5.3 The designation of the Head of the Regional Institute may continue to be 'Principal'. but his status and powers may be raised to that of a Joint Director.

5.4 There will be a Management Committee for each Institute with Vice-Chancellor as its Chairman and Principal as Vice-Chairman, nominee of Director, NCERT, the two Deans of the Institute and representatives of the State Education Departments of the Region, as members apart from a few experts from the region.

5.5 To consider and recommend all academic activities and programmes there will be a Programme Advisory Committee with Principal as Chairman and Director of SCERT/SIEs, two academic representatives from each State of the region, Deans and professors of the Institute, and two nominees of Director NCERT, one each from NIE some professors and one from a national level organisation, such as NIEPA, KVS, CBSE, etc.

5.6 There may be two Deans in each Regional Institute, one for Instruction and the other for Development and extension, to coordinate work in these areas.

5.7 The organisational structure of the Regional Institute will consist of Five academic Departments and two Units for policy studies and extension programmes.

5.8.1 There shall be a Principal's Advisory Committee with Principal as its Chairman, both Deans, Heads of Major Departments and the Headmaster of the D.M. School as members, which shall meet frequently to monitor and evaluate the progress of programmes and make recommendations on new policies and programmes.

5.8.2 The Regional Institute should obtain the status of autonomous College in the University to which it is affiliated. This will enable it to design and run innovated courses leading to degrees/diplomas and certificates of the University. An academic Committee/ Council with subject-wise Boards of studies may be formed as per rules of the University to plan and develop the courses.

5.9.1 As per the recommendations of the Task Force, 25 per cent of available vacancies may be filled on deputation basis from personnel of State Governments for a period not exceeding 3 years at a time.

5.9.2 Some additional academic staff particularly in Social Sciences, Technology, Agriculture and Commerce will be needed in each Institute to perform the new roles and functions. As and when necessary posts of Project Assistants/Associate for approved projects may be created and assigned to each Regional Institute.

5.9.3 The provision of two Junior Fellowships already available may be continued to promote academic research of high level leading to Ph.D.

5.10 There shall be a Coordination Committee of Field Services under the Chairmanship of the Principal and Dean (Development and Extensions) as Vice-Chairman, consisting of F.A.'s in the region and two representatives from each State in the region as members to plan, guide and coordinate the programmes. A few senior faculty members could be invited to attend the meeting from NCERT and the RIE. In addition each field office will have its own Programme and Planning Committee.

5.10.1 Each Field Office may be strengthened with one more A.F.A. for every ten districts in plains and five districts in hill areas and supporting staff. It may draw upon academic resources of the RIE and the state level institutions.

5.11.1 *D.M. Schools' Programmes and Courses.*
The School will continue to run academic course from Class I to XII and in addition vocational courses at +2 stage, as approved by Central Board of Secondary Education. The school will work in close collaboration with the Regional Institute. The Institute faculty will not only guide but participate in School programmes for innovation and experimentation. The teachers of the school will be involved in in-service programmes etc. of the Regional Institute.

5.11.2 The Headmaster should be the academic leader of the School and give full attention for improvement of quality of education in the School. He may be relieved of such administrative duties as can be looked after by the Administrative Officer of the Regional Institute.

6.1 Each Regional Institute shall develop its own Institutional plan with the help of an internal Committee, consulting or associating a few experts from outside.

6.2 The courses should, as far as possible reflect integration between subject of specialisation and professional education.

6.3 In all courses leading to degree/diploma, tuition fee should be charged as prevalent in similar courses of the University. Scholarships may be given to the top 50% of the students enrolled in order of merit, maintenance stipend may be given only for the period of campus course when it is carried with distance/field learning for teachers in-service.

6.4.1 The academic staff available be reallocated among the new departments and units. Additional staff need be provided only in areas of critical shortage, such as Social sciences, Technology, Agriculture and Commerce.

6.4.2 Academic staff may be treated as Semi-Vacational; i.e., can avail one-half of the vacation period and be entitled to 15 days earned leave for working for the other half of the Vacation period. This will facilitate availability of full staff during teaching sessions and half of the staff during vacations to look after programmes being organised during vacation period.

6.4.3 Each members of academic staff should work 6-1/2 hours a day (40 hours a week) which will be suitably distributed over teaching, institutional projects including development and extension) academic and professional and personal research. While some members of staff may be allotted teaching and research work for 80% of time and development and extension work for 20% of time, some other members of staff may be allotted development and extension work for 10% of time and teaching and research for 20% of time.

6.5 Regional Institute should establish effective formal and informal linkages with State agencies of education. Directors of SCERT/SIEs should be members of their programmes Advisory Committee. Also State Governments be requested to include Principals of Regional Institutes as members of the Programme Advisory Committee of SCERT/SIEs.

6.6 After utilising the available equipment for in-service courses in SUPW/Work Experience and Vocational Education, for preparing teaching aids and learning kits, and for maintenance and repair of equipment, any equipment considered surplus may be disposed off as follows:

(a) by donating to an educational institutions of the region;
(b) if (a) is not possible, auction/tender on "as the where is" basis.

6.7 Action may be taken as per time schedule given in the report so that the Colleges might function as Regional Institutes and perform all the ten functions recommended by the Task Force from 1988-89 onwards, if not earlier.

15

SCHEDULED CASTES AND SCHEDULED TRIBES: Working Group on Development of Scheduled Tribes (1980-85)[1]

We feel that while tne core economic sectors might hold primacy in planning, education is the key to tribal development. The tribal segment of the society is placed in a position of handicap *vis-a-vis* the non-tribal sections as it has little access to education and, hence, knowledge of the modern affairs. The isolation of the tribal communities has limited their world-view severely and in dealing with the present day administrative systems like law courts, police, revenue, forest, money-lending trading etc., they find themselves incapacitous. Education is, therefore, an input not only for economic development but also for inner strength of the tribal communities so that they can meet the new challenge on terms of some degree of equality.

2. Education has to be tackled on both the non-formal and formal levels.

3. Since it is a concurrent subject, the connected problems should engage the attention of both the Central and State authorities. A substantial programme of non-formal education and citizenship training has to be mounted in order to disseminate widely among the scheduled tribe people knowledge and information which should enable them face confrontation with non-tribal forces. In the non-formal education programme organised by the Ministry of

1. Extracts from Chapter 14 (relating to Education) of the recommendations of the Working Group on Development of Scheduled Castes and Scheduled Tribes (1980-85).

Education, coverage of tribal areas and enrolment of members of scheduled tribes have been given a high priority. These need to be quantified. But, apart from mere numbers, the preparation of curricula and reading material need perceptive and sensitive handling by both the central and State agencies. The course content should include instruction as to how to deal with problems connected with land, credit, currency, weights and measures, hygiene, local geography, local administration, lower government functionaries, liquor vendors etc. Organisational effort should be looked into carefully. Periodical evaluation of the programme should enable a plateau of continued optimality.

4. On the formal educational side also, both the qualitative and quantitative aspects should engage serious attention. The current conventional syllabi might not suit children of the tribal communities. Steps should be taken to work out syllabi for education taking into account their culture, technology, ethos and assimilative power. The new syllabi should not, however, place the tribal students in any position of disadvantage with reference to entry into higher educational institutions or employment. At the national level, the Ministry of Education, the National Council of Educational Research and Training, the National Institute of Educational Planning and Administration might set up a body to evolve broad guidelines for imparting the requisite orientation to the conventional system. But since there is considerable variation in the socio-cultural backgrounds even among the various scheduled tribe communities in a State, the content and bias may have to differ from one tribe to another. The question of evolving relevant courses of study for the various tribes should receive the earnest attention of State Education Department, the Tribal Development Department, the State Institute of Education. The State Council of Educational Research and Training and the Tribal Research Institute, Expert Committees may be constituted to prepare syllabi and courses, in accordance with the guidelines to be issued by the aforesaid national body. For the purpose, it will be necessary to establish strong separate wings in bodies like NCERT, SCERT, NIEPA, SIE, TRI, etc. financed by the Education Ministry.

5. Article 350 A lays down that it shall be the endeavour of every local authority within the State to provide adequate facilities for instruction in the mother-tongue at the primary stage of education to children belonging to linguistic minorities groups. We feel that the Education Ministry might ask the States to what extent it has been

possible for them to provide instruction in the mother-tongue of tribal children and, if as appears to be the case, the provision has remained largely unoperative for want of books, teacher etc., the States might be asked to take definite steps in this direction. We recommend that the use of mother-tongue should be extended to adult education.

6. By the end of Sixth Plan period, at least 5% of schools in tribal areas in a State should run primary classes as per the revised syllabi.

7. In an adequate number of the usual educational institutions, vocational facilities should be provided, e.g. agriculture training, industrial trades, sports etc. so that services become actually available to the tribal. In the context of resources constraint, priorities will have to be worked out. The low literacy pockets and backward communities, as also areas where intensive economic programmes have been or are being taken up should be identified for special educational effort. In the periphery of growing industrial and mining complexes education is the only investment which would enable the concerned community to take advantage of new opportunities: The pattern of education in these zones should be linked with job opportunities also.

8. Inability on the part of members of scheduled tribe communities to utilise secondary and higher education facilities as well as job opportunities in full can partly be explained by defects in their education at the successive lower tiers. For example, it has been reported that the tribal boys and girls are not able to gain entry into ITIs and other technical institutes due to their weakness in science learning. In order to overcome it, science teaching should be strengthened in the middle and high schools. For science teaching and coaching in other concerned subjects, special classes outside the school hours might be held for which result-linked honorarium may be paid to teachers.

9. In the field of employment, absence of contacts, in fact, absence of nexus between tribal areas and the concerned urban centres, stands in the way of exploitation of employment potential Employment exchanges seem to have been established in certain tribal areas without much results. Vocational guidance centres should be set up in these areas so that tribal boys and girls get sound advice regarding their ability and qualification and ability *vis-a-vis* job opportunities. Such centres will promote utilisation of employment facilities.

10. Low enrolment ratio (Comparison of enrolment to corresponding schoolage population, reported to be 66.4% in 1978-79 as compared to 84.5% for all communities), spareseness of educational institutions

serving tribal habitations, high wastage rate, absentee teachers are some of the features of educational programmes in tribal areas. Some of them stem from the economic status of tribals, some from neglect in establishment of educational institutions and some others from lack of facilities for government employees obtaining in the tribal areas. We feel that all these need attention. Inducement to tribal children for better enrolment might come in the form of a more comprehensible educational system, scholarship assistance, attendance incentive, uniforms, mid-day meals etc. But, apart from these inducements, compensation need to be paid to tribal parents or opportunity costs.

11. Pre-matric and post-matric scholarships are being disbursed by the States to students belonging to scheduled tribe communities. There have been complaints of delay in disbursement as much so that on account of late availability of the first instalment some students have been unable to join the institutions as they have no funds to make advance payment of the initial fees, caution money, hostel dues etc. The scholarship amounts should be disbursed in advance in order to meet such contingencies; with appropriate safeguards. The procedure in this regard may be evolved by the State Governments.

12. Elsewhere, we are suggesting incentives to be provided to Government employees posted in tribal areas. Along therewith there would be a consistent effort to improve infrastructural facilities like communications, health institutions etc. Efforts in these two directions is likely to reduce the inhospitability of tribal areas and thereby the incidence of absentee-teacher. Further, the teachers and other serving personnel need to be given orientation courses. In fact, the teacher should become the fulcrum of developmental activities in the village.

13. The norms for establishment of educational institutions at the primary, middle and secondary level need to be scrutinised once again to ensure their relevance for tribal areas particularly on account of the facts that the density of population is low and habitants are spread far apart. The structural balance among the primary, middle and secondary institutions should be properly struck and maintained. The problem of remoteness and inaccessibility can be overcome by decentralisation of the educational institutions and hostels. Accent on building up of hostels will be necessary. Residential institutions will be of advantage, but their initial and running costs should be curtailed.

14. Multiplicity of governmental organisations running educational institutions might be rationalised. Coordination with Education Department should be ensured by the concerned organisations. Special

effort will be needed to boost education among tribal children and among tribal girls particularly. For the purpose, availability of women teachers would have to be paid special attention.

15. We feel that there can be considerable improvement in education among tribals provided teachers are located and appointed in schools. In some States, there may be paucity of educated tribal men and women, but efforts to locate them will yield dividends. There should be special drive to identify and train them in concerned teachers-training institutions.

16. One of the major constraints in the expansion of educational programme is finance. Large investment in *pucca* buildings curtail the programme. Further, limited and delayed availability of construction material like cement, iron rods etc. acts an effective brakes. At the same time, it has been found that in case of certain tribal communities, modern structures run counter to the grain of tradition and sensibility of the children of those tribes. With a view to economy in construction and harmony of environment, indigenous material and specifications, with such refinement as may be necessary, may be adopted.

17. We are aware that some progress has been made in the field of education among tribals since independence. The Ministry of Education is, however, handicapped in assessing the extent of the progress in the want of feedback from the States. We feel strongly that a sound monitoring system should be set up from the grass-root level through State to national level. There is a need, in fact, to appoint in the State Directorates of Education specific officers in the rank of Joint Director of Deputy Director to specifically attend to the problems of education among scheduled tribes and to monitor data.

16

SCHOOL MAPPING:
NIEPA Guidelines on School Mapping

Introduction

School mapping, as a technique of micro-level planning for expansion and rationalisation of educational facilities particularly at the elementary and secondary levels of education, has been stressed in the 'Programme of Action' for the implementation of the National Policy on Education,1986. In the chapter on 'Elementary Education, Non-Formal Education and Operation Blackboard' of the Programme of Action, it has been observed, "Detailed school mapping exercises will be initiated forthwith, and completed by the end of 1987-88, in order to prepare a Master Plan of Universal Provision of Facilities for Elementary Education (EE). The basis of school mapping would be to ensure that every habitation which can potentially have 50 children in the primary school should be provided one and an upper primary school opened on primary school catchment basis." Similarly, in the chapter on "Secondary Education and Navodaya Vidyalayas" it has been stated, "As a medium and long term measure a programme of school mapping in each State for locating schools to cover all areas will be taken up. The technique of school mapping will be followed both for planning and implementation for location of secondary schools on the basis of clearly defined norms and standards."

The National Institute of Educational Planning and Administration initiated some exercise in this regard and organised a National Workshop on October 28-29, 1986. The Workshop discussed the scope, coverage, contents, methodology and process of school mapping.

Organisational Requirements

School mapping as a part of micro-planning is a continuous process and needs to be built into the system of educational planning, statistics, survey and monitoring. As these all are interlinked tasks, it is essential to take a coordinated view of their infrastructural requirements. Creation of a separate machinery for these tasks would not only result in duplication and overlapping of efforts but also in under-utilisation of the staff.

As the process and system of planning, statistics and survey vary from State to State, no common pattern can be suggested for general adoption. However, the following guidelines are suggested for staffing pattern at various levels. These guidelines are based on the recommendations of the Working Group on "Monitoring and Evaluation of Educational Programmes (1984)" of the Seventh Five Year Plan and also on the report of the "Higher Level Committee on Educational Statistics" of the Ministry of Education (1982).

(a) *Block Level*

Block has to undertake the major responsibility for micro-level area planning in education particularly at the elementary stage. At this level planning would include school mapping, identification on catchment area, maintaining information system, etc. It is suggested that at least one full-time planning and monitoring assistant, preferably with the background of mathematics/statistics and education, may be provided to help the Block Education Officer in his task of planning, monitoring and statistics. For this post, a teacher having mathematical background with aptitude of field work may be given preference.

(b) *District Level*

At the district level, there should be a strong unit for planning, monitoring and statistics as it is to cater to the needs of not only elementary education but also other sectors of education. The District Education Officer need to be provided with one gazetted staff officer and a statistician for the work pertaining to statistics and monitoring. In case of large districts (having more than 10 blocks), a planning and monitoring assistant may be provided having qualifications suggested for such an assistant at the block level.

(c) *Regional Level*

In States where there are educational regions, suitable machinery for planning, monitoring and statistics may also be provided, if such functions are also undertaken at that level. There has to be one statistician to coordinate monitoring and information work of different districts covered in the region.

(d) *State Level*

At the State level a Planning, Monitoring and Statistical Unit need to be created and placed under the charge of a Deputy Director (Joint Director in case of big States). This officer may be assisted by one Assistant Director (Statistics and Survey) and in case of big States, one additional Deputy Director (Planning and Monitoring) with the necessary supporting staff.

(e) *Training*

There is also a need for training of the staff which is assigned the responsibility of planning, monitoring and statistics at various levels. Facilities for training of officers working at the State level should be provided at the National level in institutions like NIEPA. For officers working at the regional and district levels, training should be conducted at the State level.

Implementation Strategies

Adoption of school mapping techniques for expansion and rationalisation of educational facilities at primary and secondary stages of education has assumed importance in view of the "Programme of Action" approved for implementation of the National Policy on Education, 1986. It is necessary that appropriate steps are taken by the Ministry, NIEPA and State Governments on the following lines:

(a) *Ministry of Human Resource Development and NIEPA*

(i) Letter from the Ministry may go to each State/UT indicating importance, time schedule, organisational arrangements etc. for undertaking exercise on school mapping and Operation

Blackboard so that it could be completed by 1987-88 for the elementary education.

(ii) Ministry may also convene a meeting of Education Secretaries and Directors of Education of all States/UTs to discuss concept, process and techniques of school mapping and also its importance in the light of NPE.

(iii) Ministry may also ensure that there is effective coordination at the national level in different exercises being undertaken simultaneously, i.e., school mapping, Operation Blackboard and 5th All India Educational Survey.

(iv) Ministry may also entrust NIEPA with the responsibility of helping all the States/UTs in undertaking school mapping exercise by providing guidelines, manual etc. and conducting training programmes and field surveys. This Institute may also be entrusted with the task of monitoring the progress of this work in various States/UTs at various stages on behalf of the Ministry.

(v) NIEPA may organise training courses in technique of School Mapping for selected senior level officers from each State/UT — particularly those belonging to Secretariat, Directorate and Inspectorate of Education. These officers should act as Resource Persons on their return to State/UT.

(vi) NIEPA may also immediately undertake action oriented study project on School Mapping to study the existing practices followed for locational planning in various parts of the country.

(b) *State Government/Union Territory Administrations*

(i) Every State/UT may nominate a senior officer as a Liaison Officer for undertaking exercise for mapping.

(ii) On the basis of guidelines from Ministry/NIEPA, every State/UT may prepare a time-bound project.

(iii) Every State/UT may also identify senior officers for training at NIEPA in school mapping.

(iv) Every State/UT may immediately select one or two blocks for undertaking exercise on school mapping on experimental basis with the help of NIEPA.

17

TEACHERS AND TEACHER EDUCATION

17.1 NATIONAL COMMISSION ON TEACHERS: I (1983-85)[1]

In February 1983, the Government of India set up the National Commissions on School Teachers to advise the Government on various aspects relevant to the teaching community as specified in the terms of reference.

1. Prof. D.P. Chattopadhyaya, — Chairman
   25, Park Mansion, Part Street,
   Calcutta.
2. Prof. V.G. Kulkarni,
   Tata Institute of Fundamental Research
   Homi Bhabha Centre for Science Education,
   Homi Bhabha Road,
   Bombay - 400 005.
3. Prof. Satya Bhushan,
   Commissioner and Secretary to the Government,
   Higher Education Department,
   Jammu & Kashmir Government,
   Jammu/Srinagar.

---

1. Published by the Controller of Publication, Government of India, Delhi.

Note: 1. National Commission-I deals with issues relating to the teachers at the school stage.

2. After taking over as Director, NCERT, Dr. P.L. Malhotra became a member of the Commission on June 10, 1983.

4. Commodore Sat Bir,
Commissioner,
Kendriya Vidyalaya Sangathan
Nehru House
4, Bahadur Shah Zafar Marg,
New Delhi - 110 002
5. Director
National Council of Educational Research and Training
Sri Aurobindo Marg,
New Delhi - 110 016.
6. Fr. T.V. Kunnunkal,
Chairman,
Central Board of Secondary Education,
17-B, Indraprastha Estate
New Delhi - 110 002
7. Dr. K. Venkatasubramanian,
Member,
State Planning Commission,
Ezhilagam,
Madras - 600 005
8. Shri Hari Dang,
Rector,
St. Paul's School,
Darjeeling - 734 103
9. Shri Veda Prakasha,
14 DDA Flats,
Vasant Enclave,
Palam Marg
New Delhi.
10. Sr. Mary Braganza,
General Secretary,
All India Association for Christian Higher Education
C-6, Community Centre
Safdarjang Development Area,
New Delhi - 110 016
11. Dr.(Smt.) Chitra Naik,
Director
State Resource Centre for Non-Formal Education,
128/2, Karve Road
Kothrud,
Pune - 411 029.

12. Dr. Mrugavati Shah,
    Director,
    State Institute of Education,
    Gujarat State,
    Raikhad,
    Ahmedabad - 380 001.
13. Km. Ahalya Chari,
    The School - K.F.I.,
    Damodar Gardens,
    Besant Avenue,
    Adyar, Madras - 600 020.
14. Dr. M.P. Chhaya,
    Bharatiya Vidya Bhavan
    Mehta Sadan,
    Kasturba Gandhi Marg
    New Delhi - 110 001
15. Shri H. Mukherjee
    Commissioner-cum-Secretary,
    Government of Tripura,
    Education Department,
    Agartala.
16. Dr. M. Mohiuddin,
    Chairman,
    Bihar College Service Commission,
    Patna.
17. Shri David Horsburgh,
    Rayalpad, P.O.,
    Srinivaspur Tq.,
    Kolar Dt.
    Karnataka - 563 134
18. Km. Kamal Vasudeva,
    Principal,
    Teacher Training Institute,
    Daryaganj,
    New Delhi - 110 002
19. Shri Anil Sadgopal, — Member Secretary
    Kishore Bharati,
    P.O. Bankhedi,
    Distt. Hoshangabad,
    M.P. 461 990

20. Shri Kireet Joshi,
Educational Adviser
Ministry of Education and Culture
(Department of Education)
New Delhi - 110 001

Terms of Reference

(1) To lay down clear objectives for the teaching profession with reference to the search for excellence, breadth of vision and cultivation of values in keeping with the country's heritage and ideals of democracy, secularism and social justice;
(2) To identify steps to be taken to give an appropriate status to members of the Profession;
(3) To suggest measures for fostering dynamism in the profession and responsiveness to developments elsewhere in the world;
(4) To recommend measures needed for attracting and retaining talented persons in the teaching profession and widening the base for recruitment particularly, of women;
(5) To review the existing arrangements for pre-service and in-service training/orientation for teachers and to recommend improvements;
(6) To review and recommend the application of improved methods and technology for teaching;
(7) To recommend measures to enhance the role of teachers in facilitating, motivating and inspiring students in the acquisition of knowledge, skills and values, and promoting through them the spread of the scientific temper, secular outlook, environmental consciousness and civic responsibility;
(8) To identify the role of teachers in integrating education with development work in the community and home;
(9) To study the special requirements of teachers in the field of non-formal and continuing education and to suggest ways and means by which these requirements can be met;
(10) To identify the role of teachers' organisations in professional growth and professional consciousness;
(11) To look into the feasibility of evolving an acceptable and implementable code of conduct for teachers; and
(12) To assess the adequacy of arrangements for promotion of teachers' welfare with special reference to the National

foundation of Teachers' Welfare and to suggest modifications where necessary.

The Teacher and Society

The National Commission on Teachers-I entitled its report 'The Teacher and Society' as it was of the considered opinion that "the excellence or lack thereof of the teaching profession is intimately related to the attending socio-economic conditions". The Commission came to the conclusion that the "nation must unreservedly commit itself to the welfare of the teacher and also to raising of its status in society. The teacher, in turn, is expected to dedicate himself to his duties and to the improvement of his professional competence and career."

Contents

The report entitled 'The Teacher and Society' includes the following:

(i) Approach and Methodology; (ii) National Goals And the Role of the Teacher; (iii) Towards A New Design of Education; (iv) Social Justice : Universalisation of Elementary Education; (v) The Status, Working Conditions and Welfare of the Teacher; (vi) Supply And Recruitment of Teachers; (vii) Training of Teacher; (viii) The Case For In-service Education; (ix) Society's Expectations of the Teacher; (x) Translating Words Into Action : Implications for Implementation. Annexure containing Resolution No. F.23-1/81-PN.2 Government of India, Ministry of Education and Culture (Department of Education), New Delhi, the 16th February, 1983; Summary of Recommendations and Appendices.

Six Important Recommendations of the National Commission on Teachers-I.

While presenting the report of the National Commission on Teachers-I relating to teachers at the school stage, Prof. D.P. Chattopadhya, Chairman of the Commission, made the following observations:

1. Our findings have persuaded us that the nation must unreservedly commit itself to the welfare of the teacher and also to the raising of its status in society.

2. The teacher, in turn, is expected to dedicate itself to his duties and to the improvement of his professional competence and career.
3. Teachers' organisations have a very constructive role to play in determining the quality of the teaching profession.
4. In the new Educational Policy of the Government, the goal of the Universalisation of Elementary Education must not only find its due place, but also must be backed up by adequate financial resources.
5. It is very clear that unless budgetary allocations of the Union and the State Governments for education are substantially raised, the aims of teaching profession and the ideal of a new educational system will continue to elude us.
6. The educational system must be made more relevant both to our traditional roots and the present socio-economic needs.

Summary of other Recommendations

1. *National Goals*: There are four national goals having critical urgency for the well being of the Indian people. The goals are: (a) A United Secular India, (b) A Modern Nation, (c) A Productive People, and (d) A Humane and Caring Society. Education can have no greater concern today than to promote these. (2.3)[2]

2. *Towards a New Design of Education*: The existing system of education does not serve the educational needs of our people. Hence the need to search for a new design keeping in view the following criteria:

(a) It should provide education to the majority of the people;
(b) It should be truly developmental enabling the student to discover, develop and discipline his abilities;
(c) It should conform to nationally prescribed minimum standards;
(d) It should have planned linkages with real job opportunities;
(e) It should function as a full articulated system permitting vertical and lateral mobility for purposes of further education or training; and
(f) It should effectively contribute to national development. (3.02)

2. (a) The number in bracket at the end of the para, indicates the number of relevant paragraph in the concerned Chapter.
(b) Adopted from the Report and Sub-titles inserted at various places.

3. *10+2+3 to Continue*: The existing system of 10+2+3 has provided a uniform national structure and should continue. (3.03)

4. *National Core Curriculum*:

(a) *Core Curriculum at the Primary Stage:* We must recognise the urgent need for a national core curriculum. At the primary state, there should not be more than two text books for classes I & II, one for language and the other for mathematics. Formal teaching should not start before the age of 5. No home work should be assigned at the primary stage. (3.06)
(b) *Core Curriculum at the Secondary Stage:* At the secondary stage, national core curriculum should form 70% of the total syllabus leaving 30% for local and regional needs. Curricular objectives should be translated and concretised into measurable and specific learning outcomes in terms of knowledge, understanding, skills, attitudes and values. (3.07)
(c) *Core-Curriculum at the Middle Stage:* At the middle stage, children should be helped to develop study skills, thinking skills, intellectual curiosity, culture of the mind and discipline of the intellect. Further mastery of at least one language is absolutely essential for the quality of education and quality of life. Social Science, General Science, Arithmetic and elementary craftsmanship are equally important. (3.10)
(d) *SUPW at The Secondary Stage:* At the secondary stage, SUPW should add a third dimension to education giving it greater context, meaning, depth and reality. (3.13)

5. *Vocationalisation*: Millions of educated unemployed youths is a pointer that vocationalisation of secondary education must receive priority. The objective of vocationalisation is to provide adequate training, orientation and cultivation of appropriate attitudes in students so as to generate a sufficient number of middle level skilled manpower, for the organised as well as the unorganised sectors and, to the extent possible, also for self employment. (3.14)

It is also necessary that the graduates of the vocational courses should have the facility of upward and lateral movement in the professional courses. (3.15)

6. *Open and Flexible System*: The present educational system must give way to a more open and flexible system. This means that we move definitely toward a credit system. (3.16)

7. *Fostering National Values*: The new system must be 'sold' to all sections of the society through a wide and systematic campaign using mass media imaginatively, and a new climate created to foster national values. (3.18)

8. *A National Testing Service*: A National Testing Service should be established and one of its priorities should be to develop suitable competency-based and standardised test. (3.18)

9. *Bridge Courses*: Suitable bridge courses should be provided to make up the partial deficiency when passing from one stage to another. (3.18)

10. *The Teacher as a Facilitator*: In the new system the teacher has to assume his role as a facilitator and guide. The inspiration, motivation and support provided by him will result in improving the quality of education. (3.18)

11. *Strategies for UEE* (Universalisation of Elementary Education):

(a) *Macro-Planning*: Macro-Planning in UEE must give way to micro-planning and top-to-bottom planning model must be replaced by planning from the local grass roots level. (4.12)
(b) *School Complexes*: The basic instrument for reaching the UEE target should be the school complex or better still the educational complex. (4.17)

A complex should consist of all the primary schools in the area, which in turn would be supported by all the middle schools of the area, both of which will have the support and supervision of the secondary and senior secondary schools, and all three assisted and aided by a college or institution of higher learning, if it exists, as well as by other institutions which can provide educational support to the complex. When forming a school/educational complex, care must be taken that it is neither too small, nor too big or unwieldy. The other necessary steps in this direction are:

(a) suitable person of proven competence and commitment should be appointed as head of the complex.
(b) The first task for a school complex will be to conduct a local survey to collect information such as the following:

(i) Children attending school;
(ii) Drop-outs;

(iii) Children of school-going age who have never been to school;
(iv) Socio-economic difficulties of the non-enrolled and drop-outs;
(v) Particulars of teachers and other staff working in the schools of the complex.

(c) *Institutional Plans*: Preparation of individual institutional plans by the schools giving targets and strategies for carrying them out in a time bound manner.
(d) *Women Teachers*: Recruitment of women teachers in largest possible numbers.
(e) *Use of Modern Media*: Use of folk and modern media to stimulate community motivation and participation.
(f) *Systematic Monitoring*: Systematic monitoring to identify bottlenecks and programme deficiencies and to take remedial measures.
(g) *Local Advisory Committee*: Appointment of a local Advisory Committee to further the UEE programme. (4.17)
(h) *Role of the Teacher in the Universalisation of Elementary Education*: The teacher can play a direct and active role in the universalisation of elementary education by establishing a paternal relation between the student and himself, by establishing communication with parents and helping them to see the value of education, by providing remedial help and above all by making his own teaching interesting, relevant and effective. Similar help can be rendered by him in the programme of non-formal education. (4.25)
(i) *Meeting of the Central Advisory Board*: A meeting of the Central Advisory Board of Education be convened to consider the school complex-based strategy. (4.31)

The kind of academic support and other assistance required by the State should be provided by the Centre in accordance with the development plans approved by the Central Advisory Board of Education. (4.30)

(j) *Early Childhood Education*: Early childhood education can play a supporting role to UEE. Norms should be prescribed for minimum space and accommodation as also the kind of equipment needed for a Nursery school. (4.35)
(k) *Role of Nursery School Teacher*: The nursery school teacher

should be brought into the main stream of education and their emoluments, service conditions, etc. should be at par with primary school teacher in the state. (4.37)

12. *Special Education Programmes*

(i) *Expansion of Facilities.* At present Special education facilities exist only for 5% of the blind and deaf and 0.5% of the mentally retarded children. These must be expanded. (4.38)

(ii) *Special Education to form an Integral Part.* We recommend that all education programmes for the handicapped and the disabled form an integral part of the educational system and be dealt with by the Department of Education. Education of disabled children should no longer be treated as a welfare measure. (4.42)

It should be possible to complete such a study and to prepare a suitable plan of follow-up action with in 4-6 months. (6.41)

(a) *Maximum Use of Qualified Man Power*: The school authorities should explore every possibility of utilising to the maximum extent the existing qualified man power for the teaching of science and mathematics on a part time or overtime basis. (6.44)

(b) *Suitable Programmes for Meeting Shortages*: The Central Ministry of Education in collaboration with NCERT should arrange a detailed survey to determine the nature and extent of teacher shortages in the rural and backward areas and develop suitable programmes of remedial action. (6.46)

(c) *Recruitment of Teachers to precede Training*: The idea that a teacher should first be recruited and then trained, should be of particular interest to states where unemployment among trained teachers is considerable. It has the added advantage that with an assured career, the quality of the average recruit to the profession will in all likelihood improve. (6.48)

(d) *Monetary Incentives to Women*: State governments should institute scholarships for women who have had seven or eight years of schooling and are willing to teach in the rural schools. We feel that the provision of a monetary incentive will assist materially in attracting rural women to teach in rural elementary schools. (6.55)

(e) *Construction of Quarters for Women Teachers*: We further recommend that in the Seventh Plan there should be a provision for the construction of one lakh quarters for women teachers in the rural areas. In our opinion it should be possible to construct a modest residential unit at a cost of Rs. 25,000. (6.56)

18. *School Complexes*: As a first step towards improving the quality of school education, we suggest the creation of school complexes already mentioned. A reasonably compact school complex will cover all schools within a radius of 5 to 10 miles and will ordinarily include one or two high/higher secondary schools, six to seven middle schools and 30 to 35 primary schools. The human and material resources of the school forming a complex should be shared freely by all the schools for developing their formal, non-formal and in-service education programmes. (6.60)

19. *Credibility and Objectivity of Public Examinations*: It is of the highest importance that immediate practical steps be taken to restore and maintain the credibility and objectivity of the public examinations. (6.61)

20. *Quality Textbooks*: In line with the good work done by the NCERT in this area, states must give much greater attention to the improvement of the quality of textbooks in their schools. (6.64)

21. *Research on Teacher Training*: The curriculum and training procedures for teacher education are based on tradition rather than study and research. As a subject for research, teacher training deserves a much higher priority. Training should be evaluated in terms of teacher competencies and pupil learning gains. (6.66)

22. *Learning Materials For Non-Formal Education*: The learning materials for non-formal education should be prepared according to the following criteria:

(a) The materials should be related to the life style and life experiences of the Community;
(b) they should be based on the local needs and problems of the people;
(c) the materials should be supported by supplementary materials to develop interest in extra reading;
(d) the materials should be of help in preparing children for the formal school examination. (6.70)

23. *Non-Formal Education Resource Centres*: We welcome the idea of non-formal education resource centres at Block and village levels. The schools complex would be a good agency to promote these. (6.71)

24. *Non-Formal Education and Formal Stream*: Non-formal education should help children in joining the formal stream as this is very much part of the popular aspiration. (6.72)

25. *Non-Formal Teacher*: We recommend that a teacher at a NFE Centre should as far as possible be a local person who has done matriculation and is between 20-30 years of age. The minimum training period for such a teacher should be a months orientation to be followed by a six day refresher programme every six months. The content of such programme should be properly field-validated to ensure relevance to the non-formal system. (6.74)

26. *Recruitment of Teachers*

(a) *Practical Research in Recruitment*: To recruit teachers more scientifically, the desirable competencies of a teacher should be listed on the basis of practical and applied research. The experts should then prepare a set of guidelines to help the selection committees. We feel that high proficiency in the teaching subject, good linguistic ability, efficiency in communication skills and love for children are some of the desirable qualities of a good teacher. (6.78)

(b) *Practical Guidelines for Selection Committees*: To overcome the problems arising from a lack of basic tools of general ability and aptitude for teaching in Hindi, English and the regional languages, we recommend a series of conferences of psychologists, mental measurement specialists and educationists to work out a set of practical guidelines to help the Teacher Selection Committees to do their selection jobs more objectively and scientifically. In the meantime research organisations and institutions should consider pooling their resources and cooperatively developing within a period of 5 years or so, at least the basic tools needed to assess scientifically the aptitude and general suitability of intending teachers. (6.79)

27. *Decentralised Control and Management of Schools*

If excellence and quality are not to remain mere words or pious expressions, we suggest that the government involvement in the management of the nation's schools should be minimal. In our humble judgement, it should be the endeavour of the government from now onwards to shift as much as possible the control and management of government schools to their heads and local communities. (6.85)

28. *Crucial Role of the Headmaster*

As a corollary, there should be a planned effort at decentralisation of recruitment of teachers, the ultimate goal being making the headmaster fully responsible for the appointment of his staff. (6.84)

29. *The Training of Teachers*

(i) *Four-Year Training Course:* The present arrangements for training of secondary school teachers are either under one year B.Ed. course or the four year integrated course. A four-year training course after senior secondary, or preferably a 5-year course leading to graduation and training is recommended. Each state may make a beginning during the 7th Plan period by starting atleast one four-year integrated college of education. Also the first degree in teaching, B.A./B.Sc. B.Ed., should be considered adequate to pursue post-graduate courses. To ensure this planning of the contents of the four-year integrated course should be done in consultation with university authorities. (7.05)

A four-year integrated college will need a capital grant of Rs.20 lakhs to enlarge and improve its physical facilities. Its recurring support will imply an expenditure of Rs. 2400 per annum for every additional member of the faculty during the Seventh Plan Period. (7.07 & 7.08)

(ii) *Extension of One Year B.Ed. Course by two summer months*: The duration of one year B.Ed. course should be extended by two summer months ensuring an academic session of 220 days with longer working hours. (7.09)

(iii) *Two-year Training Course for Elementary Teachers*: For elementary teachers it is desirable to have a two year training course after class XII. Efforts may be made to have this pattern established as the normal pattern of training for elementary teachers as early as possible. The possibility of developing a four-year integrated programme after class X with a built in provision for upward mobility should also be explored. (7.11 to 7.13)

(iv) *Selection of Teachers for Training*: While selecting a teacher for training, the following factors may be taken into consideration:

(a) Good physique;
(b) Linguistic ability and communication skills;
(c) A fair degree of general mental ability;
(d) General awareness of the world;
(e) A positive outlook on life; and
(f) Capacity of good human relations.

Selection of trainees should be made through a combination of objective tests, rating scales, group-discussion and personnel interviews. (7.14)

The approach to recruit a untrained first class graduate/post-graduate and then give him on-the-job training to be followed by full training through correspondence and contact programme, could also be tried out. (7.16)

(v) *Two Elements in the Integrated Four-year Curricular*: The integrated four-year curriculum for a degree in education should consist of two elements, namely, general education and professional preparation. General education will include:

(1) Study of a language.
(2) Three or four disciplines from among the subjects taught at school.
(3) Seminars, Projects and study visits. (7.19)

(vi) *Contents of Professional Preparation*: The professional preparation part should consist of:

(a) study of education as a discipline including educational psychology, sociology of education and educational philosophy;
(b) practice of teaching and its content-cum-methodology; and
(c) learning a variety of skills related to the role of a teacher, including educational technology and preparation of software. (7.27)

(vii) *Cadre of Teacher Educators*: A cadre of teacher educators in educational technology may be formed. One such educator may be appointed in each college of education. (7.32)

(viii) *College of Education and Practice Teaching School*: The preparation of a teacher must be regarded as a joint responsibility of the College of Education and the practice teaching school. (7.34)

(ix) *Internship in Place of Practice Teaching*: Apart from teaching methods, the pupil teachers should also gain experience of his other roles such as organisation of co-curricular activities and working with the community. The words practice teaching should be replaced by the word Internship as it suggests a much more comprehensive concept of teacher training. (7.35)

(x) *Contents of the Internship*: The duration of the Internship should not be less than four weeks in the third year and 3 weeks in the fourth year of study. During this period, stress should be laid, among other things, on black-board writing, drawing skills, making and improvising aids to learning, and using technological equipment. Participation in co-curricular activities like games, sports, music, dance, drama should be obligatory. (7.36 and 7.37)

(xi) *Right Tools for Evaluation of Pupil Teacher Performance*: The faculty must evolve the right tools for evaluation of pupil-teacher performance in the class and also take into account such factors as attitude to work, love for children, scientific outlook etc. Self assessment and pre-lesson and post-lesson discussion should be encouraged. (7.39)

(xii) *Introduction to the Life and Work at School during Internship*: In the case of the one year B.Ed. a minimum of six weeks preceded by a general introduction to the life and work at school for one week should be the minimum. (7.40)

(xiii) *Modification in the Teacher Education Curricular*: The teacher education curriculum prepared by the National Council for Teacher Education (1978) should be reviewed by Boards of Studies in Education of various universities, and suitably modified. (7.45)

(xiv) *Qualification of Teacher Educators*: The teacher educators in Colleges of Edûcation should be drawn both from disciplines of various school subjects and educational disciplines such as psychology, sociology, philosophy etc. The minimum qualification for a teacher educator should be a post-graduate degree in the subject and a B.Ed., preferably an M.Ed. degree. The need for their continual in-service education must also be recognised so that Colleges of Education can form part of the main stream of academic life of their respective universities. (7.47)

(xv) *Adequate Staff in Teacher Training Colleges*: Some lecturers in the teachers' training colleges are not qualified to teach the subjects entrusted to them. To obviate this difficulty in future, it is desirable that colleges of education should offer only such subjects for specialisation for which they have the qualified staff. Also steps should be taken by the universities to ensure full staff strength keeping in view the needs of the trainees. (7.42)

(xvi) *Teacher Educators to be Well-versed with Educational Technology*: The teacher trainers themselves should be proficient in the use of skills they seek to develop among their trainees. In particular they should be proficient in the service and maintenance of hardware of educational technology and must be knowledgeable about the available sources for software (educational technology). (7.32)

(xvii) *Training in Co-Curricular Activities*: Colleges should depute their teacher trainers to participate in specially conducted workshops to develop planning and organisational skills in co-curricular activities, for which help of institutions like Bal Bhavan, National School of Drama and National Film Institute could be taken. (7.44)

(xviii) *Training Curriculum for Elementary Teachers*: The training curriculum for elementary teachers will also consist of general education and professional preparation. Sufficient emphasis needs to be given to the mastering of language and communication skills and to the trainee's value orientation. (7.49 and 7.50)

As for professional preparation, pedagogy, practice teaching, development of skills such as story telling, recitation, writing on the black-board, use of new technology etc. are important. A greater emphasis on art, music, craft and dance is essential. (7.51)

(xix) *Practice Teaching*: Not less than six to eight weeks in the Ist year and twelve weeks in the IInd year should be allotted to practice teaching. The trainees may start with one or two lessons a day but should gradually be accepted to stay for the whole day and take on full responsibilities of a regular teacher. This alone will develop in them needed professioned competence and personal confidence. (7.52)

(xx) *Qualification for Teacher Educators*: The teacher educators for the elementary training institute should be drawn primarily from the cadre of practising primary schools. The minimum qualification of the other staff should be a post-graduate degree with B.Ed. training. Their continued in-service education is equally important. (7.54)

(xxi) *Separate Cadres for Teacher Educators*: The Commission noted that sometimes the least effective district Inspectors of Schools are transferred to the Teacher Training Institutes. This practice must stop forthwith. If necessary, a separate cadre for those in teacher training, in-service education and research should be formed to ensure qualitative improvement in elementary teacher preparation. (7.55)

(xxii) *Correspondence-cum-Contact Courses*: There may be no objection to correspondence-cum-contact courses for B.Ed. training but this should be allowed only if satisfactory arrangements exist for practice and proper supervision. (7.59 and 7.60)

30. *M.Ed. Courses of Studies*

The existing M.Ed. courses should be thoroughly revamped to provide for greater specialisation and must be specifically geared to the preparation of:

(a) teacher educators
(b) curriculum consultants for the SCERTs, Science Institutes and State Boards of Education and
(c) School inspectors, supervisors and educational administrators. (7.64)

31. *Review of Norms for the Teacher Training Institutes*

Norms developed by the NCTE for the physical and staff resources of elementary and secondary teacher training institutes will have to be reviewed particularly in view of our recommendations in favour of a four-year integrated course and greater stress on acquisition of practical skills. (7.67)

32. *Grants to Training Colleges*

It is recommended that each of the better and viable 300 training colleges should be given a non-recurring grant of Rs. 3 lakhs during the 7th Plan to improve its infrastructure; and each of the 500 elementary training schools to be selected for the purpose of a grant of Rs. 1 lakh for a similar purpose. (7.69)

33. *The Case for In-Service Education*

The present facilities for in-service education for both elementary and secondary teachers are woefully inadequate quantitatively, and very poor from the point of relevance and effectiveness. Measures essential for their enlargement and upgrading will include, among others, the following:

(a) The class-room and other practical needs of teachers should be identified through field surveys and studies. (8.11)
(b) Systematic feed back from schools is necessary for further improvement of the in-service programmes (8.11)
(c) Forthcoming programmes should be announced well in advance and suggestions invited from the field to make them more popular, need based and effective. (8.12)
(d) The resource persons should not come exclusively from the ranks of educators; they could also be drawn from other fields such as industry and agriculture including specialists from the university and practising teachers and supervisors. (8.14)
(e) Every course should normally be in the nature of a workshop, offering opportunities for real practical work including the preparation of instructional materials which the participating teachers could take back with them for use in their schools. (8.16)
(f) Extensive use should be made in in-service programmes, of radio, television, audio and video cassettes, overhead projector, film projector and the computer. (8.16)
(g) Priority must be given to training in the production of indigenous software by the participants. (8.17)

(h) Evaluation of the programmes must be done towards the end of the course in a frank and free atmosphere without fear or favour. (8.19)

34. *Areas of In-Service Education*

Some of the key areas where in-service education can make a real contribution to the qualitative improvement of education are:

(a) Development of reference and study skills. (8.40)
(b) Production of textual and related materials such as curriculum guide, graded work sheet, unit test etc. (8.41)
(c) Enrichment of co-curricular activities through training in crafts, dramatisation, group singing, folk dance etc. (8.42)
(d) Identification of talented teachers doing good work in a limited specialised field and encouraging them through award of visiting fellowships, study leave and deputation to work at centres of advanced learning. (8.44)
(e) Certification on the basis of a credit system for attending in-service education programmes. (8.46)

35. *Attendance at In-Service Education Courses*

It is recommended that attendance at the in-service education courses should be made mandatory for every teacher at least once in five year. Assuming that the average length of an in-service programme is two weeks, a provision of Rs. 500 per trainee is suggested, of which Rs. 300 will go towards his daily allowance and Rs. 200 towards meeting the cost of his travel and pocket expenses. (8.20)

36. *School Complexes and In-Service Education*

As an organisational device the school complex has tremendous potential for developing inexpensive need-based programmes of in-service education. (8.22)

37. *Agencies doing In-Service Education*

Among the agencies doing commendable work in in-service education that need to be supported liberally with funds are the State Institutes of

Education (SIEs) and State Council of Educational Research and Training (SCERTs). Equally important is the role of the Regional Colleges of Education, particularly in the in-service orientation of teacher educators at elementary and secondary levels and for the training personnel of the SCERTs and SIEs. (8.48)

38. *Society's Expectations of the Teacher*

(a) *Academic Freedom and Job Security*: A teacher must have job security and adequate academic freedom to perform his professional duties, which means he must have, among other things, a say in the choice and use of teaching materials, teaching methods and evaluation techniques. (9.6 and 9.7)

(b) *Professional Obligations of a Teacher: At the same time a teacher* has to fulfil his professional obligations such as punctuality and regularity in the performance of his duties, honesty and being above board in the matter of admissions, class room teaching and testing of students. He must not engage himself in any remunerative activity without the prior permission of the authorities. His attitude towards students is expected to be one of affection and understanding and yet firm and consistent. (9.8)

(c) *Removal of 'Over-Security'*: The first step towards improving teacher performance is to remove the existing "over security" of service in government and government aided institutions and restore the mutuality and reciprocity of security and performance. (9.15)

(d) *Recognition of the Meritorious and Disciplining of the Non-Performing*: Another important step will be the easy natural recognition of the meritorious and disciplining of the non-performing and the inefficient. The conduct of disciplinary proceedings has to be made quicker and more efficient. (9.16)

(e) *Institution-based Teachers*: We should move in the direction of decentralisation of recruitment of teachers by making it institution-based. The concept of teacher transfer as it operates at present needs to be banished from the system. (9.17-9.18)

39. *Code of Conduct for Teachers*

A code of conduct for teachers should be formulated at the national level in consultation with teachers organisation. (9.23)

The responsibility for the enforcement of the code has to remain essentially with the head and the local management committee of the school. A parent organisation, if one exists, or can be established could also play an important role in stimulating teachers to perform better. (9.24)

40. *Proper Roles of Teachers' Organisations*

The main pre-occupation of teacher' organisations has been with the improvement of the salary scales and service conditions of teachers. Some of their other roles which need strengthening are:

(a) Research, publication and in-service education,
(b) Establishment of subject teacher associations,
(c) Building a favourable atmosphere to achieve a higher status and recognition for the teaching profession.
(d) Clearing house role for new ideas and information, and
(e) Building high grade expertise and specialisation among some of their staff members. (9.33)

41. *Effective Machinery for Attending to Demands of Teachers*

There is need in the States for an effective machinery to attend to the demands and grievances of teachers on the lines indicated by the Kothari Commission. (9.35 to 9.38)

42. *Election of a Teacher for a Teachers' Constituency*

It is recommended that once a teacher is elected to a teachers' constituency, he should be treated as on leave from his institution and he should not be entitled to any salary during this period. (9.39)

43. *Number of Teachers' Organisations*

The mushrooming of teachers' organisations during the past two decades has sometimes been seen as a threat to the unity of the teaching profession. In the Commission's judgement, the question of how many teachers' organisations to have, is entirely a matter for the teachers to decide. (9.40 to 9.42)

44. *Teachers' Representation in Various Bodies*

Insofar as the problem of providing representation to teachers' organisations in official or semi-official bodies is concerned, the advice is that before making the nomination or inviting nominations, the concerned authority should make it a rule to lay down clearly a set of criteria reflecting the basic objectives of the concerned body, to guide the selection or identification of representatives. (9.43)

45. *Teachers Participation in Policy Formulation*

Regarding the participation of teachers and teachers' organisations in policy formulation and related matters, it has been suggested that if these organisations strove to build among their staff members a high level expertise and specialisation in different fields of education, such participation would become easier and more effective. (9.48 and 9.49)

Translating Words into Action : Implications for Implementation

46. *Time-bound Institutional Plans*

A greater stress is indicated on the preparation and implementation of time-bound institutional plans by the individual institutions of a school complex. (10.3 to 10.6)

47. *Institution of a School Fund*

A School Fund may be instituted in each school wherein donations, voluntary contributions from local community, development fees, etc. could be deposited. The Fund should be available for direct use by the school authorities. (10.7 and 10.8)

48. *Preference to Local Persons in the Recruitment of Teachers*

In the recruitment of teachers in the rural and tribal areas, preference should be given to local persons. If necessary, the recruitment qualifications should be relaxed to facilitate this. Such teachers should be encouraged to join correspondence courses and other programmes to acquire in due course the minimum qualifications. (10.09)

49. *Leave Reserve Teachers for School Complexes*

One or two leave reserve teachers should be posted in the central school of the school complex to overcome the problem of teacher absenteeism and leave in single teacher schools in the area (10.09)

50. *Functions of the Supervisors for Non-formal Education*

The supervisors of the non-formal educational system should, as far as possible, be recruited locally. Their functions will include:

(a) Guidance to teachers and children;
(b) contact with local leaders;
(c) liaison with the departments; and
(d) monitoring of NFE programme in their area and collection of related statistical and other information. (10.13-10.14)

51. *Merit-cum Seniority Basis*

In view of the critical importance of the role of the headmaster in the work of a school, his selection must always be on the basis of merit-cum-seniority and not on seniority-cum-fitness. (10.15)

52. *Financial Powers for the Headmasters*: A headmaster should enjoy the following financial powers

(a) Routine repairs etc. to the school plant and school furniture for which an imprest of Rs. 1,500 should be provided;
(b) sanction of loans out of Provident Fund;
(c) writing off of unserviceable and lost articles upto a value of Rs. 1000 at a time; and
(d) purchase of books, periodicals and other equipment within the budget provision. (10.16 & 10.17)

53. *Administrative Powers for the Headmasters*: A head master should have the following administrative powers

(i) Sanction of admissible leave to teachers and other staff;
(ii) appointment of teachers against leave vacancies on a temporary basis;

(iii) A say in the posting of the staff to his school;
(iv) rustication of a student;
(v) deputation of teachers for in-service training;
(vi) permission to teachers for further education;
(vii) engaging local workers and skilled artisans for SUPW on a temporary basis. (10.19-10.20)

54. *Special Student Fee for Remedial Teaching*

To discourage private tuitions, it is suggested that a system of remedial teaching in the school be introduced, and the concerned teachers remunerated suitably out of the special student fee to be levied for the purpose. (10.22)

55. *Transfer of Control of Government Schools to Local Managing Committees*

Steps must be initiated for eventual transfer of control of government schools to local managing committees to be constituted for the purpose and having adequate administrative and financial powers. (10.23)

56. *Autonomous Schools*

Deserving schools, selected in accordance with published criteria, may be given autonomy with regard to curriculum, methodology and evaluation to encourage innovation and experimentation. (10.23)

57. *More Authority to District Education Officer*

The District Education Officer should be given more authority to function effectively, and he must be encouraged and supported to use his authority. Performance must be assessed more rigorously. (10.25 to 10.28)

58. *Greater Emphasis on Educational Research*

Greater emphasis should be laid on educational research and the overall effort should be to move in the direction of at least 1% of the educational budget going into research. (10.29 & 10.30)

59. *Grant for Action-oriented Research*

UGC may consider providing at the rate of Rs. 20,000 per institution for 100 selected training colleges/university departments of education to promote indigenous action-oriented research. This support should be in addition to what the states and the universities are providing for research already. (10.31)

60. *Grant for Elementary Training School*

It is further suggested that each elementary training school should receive an annual grant of Rs. 10,000 for research and study. This modest amount should be utilised primarily for examining some of the more common educational problems from the field. (10.32)

61. *Guidelines for Research Workers*

It is recommended that a representative group of some 25 persons consisting of educationists, administrators, and enthusiastic young researchers below the age of 40, should be set up by the UGC/of the NCERT to sponsor a workshop to prepare guidelines for research workers and to determine overall research priorities in education. The recommendations of the group should become available within a period of 3 months. (10.33)

62. *Task Force for National Educational Statistics*

The present state of educational statistics is very unsatisfactory. The Ministry of Education should immediately set up a task force to look into the present practices of data collection, and make practical recommendations to stream line the system of National Educational Statistics. (10.29)

63. *National Organisation for Improvement of Standards in School Education*

A National Organisation for improvement of standards in school education should be established forthwith, among others, with the following functions:

(a) to set goals and standards for school education;
(b) to lay down norms for minimum facilities in elementary and secondary schools;
(c) to undertake periodically, assessment of students' attainments as well as of the state school systems to identify deficiencies and suggest remedies;
(d) to organise a National Testing Service;
(e) to appoint and maintain a national panel of academic supervisors;
(f) to conduct sample inspections of schools to provide guidance to state governments and individual institutions; and
(g) to perform all other functions incidental to the maintenance and coordination of standards in school education. (10.37 to 10.39)

A meeting of the Union and State Education Ministers should be held to consider the proposal for the National Organisation for Standards in School Education, and to decide on important detail such as name of the organisation, location, objectives and functions, cost details, and networking among others with the NCERT, SIEs and the SCERTs. A token provision of one lakh may be made in the Ministry's budget for the current year (1985-86) for this purpose. (10.46)

64. *Statutory Powers for National Council for Teacher Education*

The National Council of Teacher Education should be vested with following statutory powers:

(a) accreditation of teacher training institution;
(b) disaffiliation of recommendation to that effect of an institution on violation of rules;
(c) inspection of training institutions; and
(d) prescription of standards and norms for teacher education institutions. (10.47)

65.. *Revival of Indian Education Service*

The revival of Indian Education Service to enhance the status of the teaching profession, to promote national integration and to accelerate the pace of educational development in the country is strongly recommended. (10.51 to 10.54)

66. *Financial Estimates*

Of the several recommendations that we have made in the foregoing pages of this document the ones with large financial implications are the following:

(1) Universalisation of Elementary Education;
(2) Improvement of salary scales of teachers;
(3) Construction of residential quarters for women teachers in rural areas;
(4) Improving infrastructure and other facilities of teacher training institutions;
(5) In-service education of teachers;
(6) National Organisation for Standards in School Education; and
(7) Research and Statistics.

I. *Universalisation of Elementray Education (UEE)*

The estimates of additional enrolments to be reached by 1990 through formal and non-formal channels of elementary education have already been provided in para 6.16 of Chapter VI of the report. To recall the data:

	Enrolment through Formal channels (in lakhs)	Enrolment through Non-formal channels (in lakhs)	Total
Primary	233.00	78.00	311.00
Middle	288.00	32.00	320.00
	521.00	110.00	631.00

We suggest that the cost estimates of the programme be worked out for four levels of projections, namely,

(a) Hundred per cent level
(b) High level (aimed at achieving 75% of the target)
(c) Medium Level (50% of the target)
(d) Low Level (25%)

The projections for the high, medium and low levels are given below:

	Formal Channel	Non-Formal Channel	Total
	High Level Projections (75%)		
Primary	174.35	58.50	233.25
Middle	216.00	24.00	240.00
	390.75	82.50	473.25
	Medium Level Projections (50%)		
Primary	118.50	39.00	155.50
Middle	144.00	16.00	160.00
	260.50	55.00	315.50
	Low Level Projections (25%)		
Primary	58.25	19.50	77.75
Middle	72.00	8.00	80.00
	130.25	27.50	157.75

We have to make another assumption regarding the distribution of the projected enrolments over the 5 years of the Seventh Five Year Plan Period. A simple assumption often made in such exercises nationally and internationally is to provide for 20% of the total additional enrolment every year. By this assumption the proportions of the total enrolment to be reached in the different years of the plan work out as follows:

1985-86	20%	=	20%
1986-87	20%+20%	=	40%
1987-88	20%+20%+20%	=	60%
1988-89	20%+20%+20%+20%	=	80%
1989-90	20%+20%+20%+20%+20%	=	100%

Choice of per pupil cost

The All India per primary pupil cost in 1970-71 was Rs. 57.00. By

1977-78 this had risen to Rs. 127.1 indicating a net increase of 122.98 per cent. We do not have any statistics available for a very recent year but if the assumption can be made a similar increase in the per pupil cost has occurred during 1977-78 to 1984-85, the present figures should be Rs. 283.41. We suggest this per pupil cost be rounded off to Rs. 300.

The per pupil cost in a middle school in 1970-71 stood at Rs. 84.9. By 1977-78 the figure had risen to Rs. 164.8. Assuming a similar rise (arithmetically) by 1984-85 we get a figure of Rs. 319.89. We suggest that this figure also be rounded off to Rs. 300 per pupil. It is interesting that both our rounded figures come to Rs. 300. This is for the formal channel.

For the per pupil cost in the non-formal channel, it is suggested that it may be taken at 50% of the cost in the formal channel, that is Rs. 150 per pupil. Except for this we do not propose to make any further differentiation in the calculation of the estimates for the two channels.

The cost estimates for total plan period for the four levels of projections are now worked out below:

	1st Year of the Plan (1985-86)	Last Year of the Plan (1989-90) = 5(1)	Total Plan Period (1985-90) = 3× (2)
	(1)	(2)	(3)
100% Enrolment[1]	37860	189300	567900
High Level (75%)	28395	141975	425925
Medium Level (50%)	18930	94650	283950
Low Level (25%)	9465	47325	141975

Notes: 1. These estimates have been presented simply to indicate the cost implications of UEE under 4 different assumptions. The necessary allocations for the purpose will continue to be made in the plan Budgets of the State Governments as heretofore.

2. See Table II of Chapter VI of the report.

II. *Improvement of Salary Scales*

Our expectation regarding the recommendations made in Chapter V is that each State Government will determine its own running scale keeping in view the general principles enunciated at pages 101-104. It was mentioned there that as a result of the new pay fixation approach we have suggested we would like to see the secondary teachers of the country have on an average a benefit not less than Rs. 100 per month and the primary teacher not less than Rs. 150 per month.

We don't know the exact number of teachers in the country but the figures for the year 1982-83 for which statistics are available are 138956[2] primary teachers, 856389 middle school teachers, and 993115 secondary teachers. The three figures add upto a total of 3238860 teachers. For the present estimates it is suggested that we n ˙ ˜ht use constantly a figure of 25 lakhs for primary and middle schoo! achers and 10 lakhs for secondary teachers.

Assuming further the rate of increments for these two cat ɔries of teachers to be Rs. 20-30-30-30 and Rs. 30-30-40-40 for pr ary and secondary teachers for the 2nd, 3rd, 4th and 5th years o! ıe Plan rᵉspectively, the estimates work out as follows:

	1985-86	1986-87	1987-88	1988-89	1989-90
	1	2	3	4	5
Average benefit for a primary and middle school teacher	150	170	200	230	260
Number of teachers (in lakhs)	25	25	25	25	25
Total benefit (in lakhs) for primary and middle school teachers	3750	4250	5000	5750	6500
Average benefit for a secondary teacher	100	130	160	200	240
Number of secondary teachers (in lakhs)	10	10	10	10	10
Total benefit for secondary teachers (in lakhs)	1000	1300	1600	2000	2400
Total benefit for school teachers (in lakhs)	4750	5550	6600	7750	8900

Note: The total financial implication for the plan period comes to Rs. 33550 lakhs.

III. *Construction of Residential Quarters for Women Teachers in the Rural Areas*

We have suggested the construction of one lakh residential units @ 25,000 each during the Seventh Plan period. The total cost of the proposal comes to Rs. 25,000 lakhs.

IV. *Implication of Improved Teacher Training Facilities*

(a) Existing training college/university departments of education elementary training schools

Two of our important recommendations (Chapter VIII) concern the improvement of infrastructure of the existing training colleges, and the establishment of four year integrated colleges. We have suggested that each of the 300 training colleges to be selected for the purpose be given a capital grant of Rs. 3.00 lakhs. For 300 institutions, this implies an outlay of Rs. 900 lakhs.

We have also recommended a non-recurring grant of Rs. 1 lakh each for 500 elementary Training schools to improve their physical facilities. The total cost of this programme comes to Rs. 500 lakhs.

(b) Establishment of four year integrated colleges

We have recommended the establishment of an integrated college for each State. For the country as a whole, it is suggested that this be taken to mean the establishment of 25 four-year institutions. We have further suggested that to meet the need for additional physical facilities, nothing less than Rs. 20 lakh per institution will be needed. In fact, if the project is not executed expeditiously and suffers from procrastination, a familiar weakness in Indian planning, our fear is that this provision may have to be increased by at least 5 per cent for each year of the postponement.

For working out the estimates of the recurring costs, we had assumed an enrolment of 100 trainees in the first year and suggested that from the second year[3] on there should be on an average an addition of 7 staff members every year for three years. This will give us a teacher ratio of 100/7 (14.3). As regards emoluments, we have suggested an average salary of Rs. 2,000 per month for the teacher educator.

On these two assumptions, the recurring costs for a four-year

3. We assume that these 25 four-year Integrated Colleges will for the most part be established by converting existing institutions.

institution for the Plan period work out as follows:

(Per Institution)

	Additional enrolment	Total enrolment	Addl. Faculty	Cost	Total Cost for 25 institutions (in lakhs)
1985-86	0	100	0	0	0
1986-87	100	200	7	1.05	26.25
1987-88	200	300	14	2.10	52.50
1988-89	300	400	21	3.15	78.75
1989-90	300	400	21	3.15	78.75
			Total	9.45	236.25
			or say	9.5	240.00

The total cost - recurring and capital - for 25 integrated colleges for Seventh Plan period thus comes to Rs. 1,140 lakhs (900+240).

V. *In-service Training*

Our main recommendation on the need for every primary and secondary teacher to be given an opportunity for in-service training at least once every 5 years was elaborated in Chapter VIII. We have suggested a provision of Rs. 50 per teacher for this purpose. Though modest, the estimate may serve as a basis for determining the cost implications of this programme. We have nearly 3.5 million primary and secondary teachers in the country. If 1/5th of this are to covered every year, the cost will come to Rs. 3,500 lakhs. For 5 years this bill comes to Rs. 17,500 lakhs.

VI. *A National Organisation for Standards in School Education*

We have suggested a capital grant of Rs. 50 lakhs for its accommodation, equipment and related facilities, and a recurring provision of Rs. 20 lakhs for the first year of the Plan period which may be progressively raised to stabilise at Rs. 50 lakhs in the penultimate year of the Plan. The recurring provision for 5 years comes to Rs. 20, 30, 40, 50 and 60 lakhs respectively.

The proposed National Testing Service, when developed fully, could be a source of income, but it is not possible to make any estimates at this stage. Depending upon the income, the Government liability could be suitably adjusted.

The total cost of the proposal comes to Rs. 50 lakhs capital and 190 lakhs recurring.

VII. *Research and Statistical Information*

We have suggested that UGC may consider providing annually at the rate of Rs. 20,000 for 100 selected colleges/university departments of education to promote indigenous action-oriented research. The cost of this programme works out at Rs. 20 lakhs annually, or Rs. 100 lakhs for the Plan period.

At the elementary level we have recommended an annual provision of Rs. 10,000 for each of the 1,000 training schools in the country. This means an annual expenditure of Rs. 100 lakhs, or Rs. 500 lakhs for the plan period.

Summary of Financial Estimates

(Rupees in lakhs)

		Capital Expenditure	Recurring for one year (average)	Expenditure for the 7th Plan period
I.	UEE			
(i)	100% Enrolment		113580	567900
(ii)	75% Enrolment		85185	425925
(iii)	50% Enrolment		56790	283950
(iv)	25% Enrolment		28395	141975
II.	Improvement of Salary Scales		6710	33550
III.	Construction of Residential Quarters	25,000	—	—
IV.	Training Colleges			
(i)	Upgrading of 300 colleges	900	—	—
(ii)	Upgrading of 500 elementary schools	500	—	—
(iii)	Establishment of 25 four-year integrated colleges	500	48	240
V.	In-service Training	–	3500	17500
VI.	National Organisation for Standards in School Education	50	38	190
VII.	Research and Statistics			
(i)	Elementary level	—	100	500
(ii)	Secondary level	—	20	100
	Total (excluding I)	26950	10416	52080
	Grand Total for 5 years of the 7th Plan (Capital + Recurring)			79030

(10.55 to 10.77)

Composite Running Pay Scale (Excluding All Allowances) for School Teachers, Heads of Institutions, School Inspectors, Administrators and other Education Officers — Illustrative Model

National Pay Scales*

500-20-600-20-700-30-850-30-1000-40-1200-40-1400-40-1600-50-1850-50-2100-50-2350-50-2600-60-2900-60-3200-75-3575-75-3950

		1	2	3	4	5	6	7	8	9	10	11	12	13	14	15	16
A. Stage No.		500	600	700	850	1000	1200	1400	1600	1850	2100	2350	2600	2900	3200	3575	3950
B. No. of Years of Service Completed of the Stage		0	5	10	15	20	25	30	35	40	45	50	55	60	65	70	75
C. Rate of Increament		20	20	30	30	40	40	40	50	50	50	50	60	60	75	75	—
D. Salary of Entry Point for Posts shown in E Below		500	—	700	—	1000	1200	—	1600	1850	—	2350	2600	—	3200	—	—
E. Illustrative Appointments and Relevant Entry Points	a) Teachers	Primary Stage	—	Trained Graduate Teacher	—	Post Graduate Teacher	—	—	—	—	—	—	—	—	—	—	—
	b) Head of Institutes	—	—	Head (Primary)	—	Head (Middle)	Head (Secondary)	—	Head Senior (Secondary)	—	—	—	—	—	—	—	—
	c) School Inspectors	—	—	—	—	Sub Deputy Inspector	Deputy Inspector	—	—	Inspector School District	—	—	—	—	—	—	—
	d) Administrators	—	—	—	—	—	—	—	—	—	—	Deputy Director	Joint Director	—	Director	—	—
F. Posts	a) Teachers →	PST - - - →		TGT - - →		PGT	—	—	—	—	—	—	—	—	—	—	—
	b) Heads	—	— - →	Head (P) - - -		Head(M) - -		Head(Sec) - - - →		Head(S.S.)		—	—	—	—	—	—
	c) Inspectors	—	—	—	→	Sub Dy. Insp. —		Dy. Insp.	—	Inspector of Schools	—	—	—	—	—	—	—
	d) Administrators	—	—	—	—	—	—	—	—	—	—	Deputy Director →	Joint Director - - - →		Director	—	—

⟶ Direct Recruitment
- - → Promotion Channel
⟷ Inter Changeability Lines

G. Maximum Pay with Age of Entry of

	Post	Pay at the Entry Point	Presumed Age of Entry	Retirement Age	Expected Years of Service	Expected Maximum
i.	Primary School Teacher	500	25	60	35	1600
ii.	TGT/Hm. (Primary)	700	25	60	35	2100
iii.	PGT/Hm. (Middle) SubDy. Insp.	1000	25	60	35	2600
iv.	Hm. (Secondary)	1200	30	60	30	2600
v.	Dy. Inspector of Schools	1200	30	60	30	2600
vi.	Head (Senior Secondary)	1600	35	60	25	2900
vii.	Inspector of Schools	1850	40	60	20	2900
viii.	Deputy Director of Education	2350	40	60	20	3575
ix.	Joint Director of Education	2600	45	60	15	3575
x.	Director of Education	3200	50	60	10	3950

* *Efficiency Bar* — At the end of five years from on entry point and every ten years thereafter.

17.2 NATIONAL COMMISSION ON TEACHERS-II (1983-85)[4]

Introduction

The National Commission on Teachers for Higher Education was set up by the Government of India vide Notification No. F. 23-1/81/P.N. 2 dated 16-2-83. The Commission submitted its report in March 1985 but was released in 1987.

Contents of the Report

The report includes the following:

(i) Approach and Methodology;
(ii) Higher Education and National Development;
(iii) Erosion of the Social Status of Teachers;
(iv) Standard of Material Life;
(v) Work Environment;
(vi) Professional Excellence – Recruitment and Career Development;
(vii) Professional Ethics and Values;
(viii) Main Recommendations and Appendices.

Terms of Reference

(1) To lay down clear objectives for the teaching profession with reference to the search for excellence, breadth of vision and cultivation of values in keeping with the country's heritage and ideals of democracy, secularism and social justice;

4. Published by the controller of Publications, Government of India, Delhi.

Note:

1. National Commission-II deals with issues relating to the teachers at the higher education level (including technical education).
2. The number in bracket at the end of the para indicates the number of relevant para in the concerned chapter.

(2) To identify steps to be taken to give an appropriate status to members of the profession;
(3) To suggest measures for fostering dynamism in the profession and responsiveness to developments elsewhere in the world;
(4) To recommend measures needed for attracting and retaining talented persons in the teaching profession and widening the base for recruitment particularly, of women;
(5) To review the existing arrangements for pre-service and in-service training/orientation for teachers and to recommend improvements;
(6) To review and recommend the application of improved methods and technology for teaching;
(7) To recommend measures to enhance the role of teachers in facilitating, motivating and inspiring students in the acquisition of knowledge, skills and values, and promoting through them the spread of the scientific temper, secular outlook, environmental consciousness and civic responsibility;
(8) To identify the role of teachers in integrating education with development work in the community and home;
(9) To study the special requirements of teachers in the field of non-formal and continuing education and to suggest ways and means by which these requirements can be met;
(10) To identify the role of teachers' organisations in professional growth and professional consciousness;
(11) To look into the feasibility of evolving an acceptable and implementable code of conduct for teachers; and
(12) To assess the adequacy of arrangements for promotion of teachers' welfare with special reference to the National Foundations of Teachers' Welfare and to suggest modifications where necessary.

Composition

1. Prof. Rais Ahmed,
   Vice-Chairman,
   University Grants
   Commission
   Bahadur Shah Zafar Marg,
   New Delhi-110002,
   – Chairman
2. Prof. N.C. Parashar,
   Member of Parliament,
   9, Mahadev Road,
   New Delhi-110001

3. Prof. Iqbal Narain,
Vice-Chancellor
Banaras Hindu University,
Varanasi-221005
4. Prof. S.V. Chittibabu,
Vice-Chancellor,
Annamalai University,
Annamalainagar
5. Dr. B.C. Parekh,
Vice-Chancellor,
The Maharaja Sayajirao
University of Baroda,
Baroda-2
6. Shri Anand Sarup,
Adviser (Evaluation)
Planning Commission,
Yojana Bhawan,
New Delhi-110001
7. Prof. S.S. Bal,
Department of History,
Punjabi University,
Patiala-147012
8. Prof. S. Rameseshan,
Indian Institute of
Science,
Bangalore-560012
9. Dr. Hem Lata Swarup,
Vice-Chancellor, Kanpur
University, Kalyanpur,
Kanpur-208024
10. Dr. M.S. Valiathan,
Sree Chitra Tirunal Institute
Medical Sciences and
Technology
Trivandrum-695011
11. Dr. B.K. Anand,
Director, Sher-I-Kashmir
Institute of Medical
Sciences,
Sri Nagar-190011
12. Prof. Moonis Raja,
Director, National Institute
of Educational Planning and
Administration, 17-B, Sri
Aurobindo Marg,
New Delhi-110016
13. Dr. A.R. Verma,
Director, National Physical
Laboratory, Hill Side Road,
New Delhi-110012
14. Prof. Durganand Sinha,
Director, A.N.S. Institute
of Social Studies,
Patna-800001
15. Prof. R.C. Mehrotra,
Professor-Emeritus,
Department of Chemistry,
University of Rajasthan,
Jaipur-302004
16. Dr. (Smt.) Anita Banerji,
Professor of Economics,
Jadavpur University,
Calcutta-32
17. Prof. S. Izhar Hussain,
Head of the Department of
Mathematics,
Aligarh Muslim University,
Aligarh (U.P.)
18. Prof. R.P. Bambah,
Deptt. of Mathematics,
University of Punjab,
Chandigarh-160014
19. Prof. S. Krishnaswamy,
Head, School of Biological
Sciences, Madurai Kamaraj
University, Palkalai Nagar,
Madurai-625021

20. Dr. (Km.) S.M. Luthra,
Principal, Lady Shri Ram
College for Women, Lajpat
Nagar, New Delhi-110024

21. Shri Kireet Joshi,
Educational Adviser,
Ministry of Education
and Culture
(Department of Education)
New Delhi
– Member-Secretary

Major Recommendations and Extracts

Higher Education and National Development

1. *General Role of Teachers.* The significance and the role of the teaching profession in any society flows out of what society expects from education at a human level, what role it assigns to education in national development and what goals of development are pursued by the nation. These three levels and considerations are interrelated and they flow from the historic and socio-cultural situation as much as from the economic policy of the country. (2.01)

2. *Education and Self Reliance.* The goals of national development translated in human terms imply the cultivation of a personality with knowledge and awareness not only in the special fields but also of culture, tradition and the needs of our peoples; a personality endowed with values which would promote socialism, national integration, secularism and scientific temper together with enthusiasm to change society through personal commitment and involvement. (2.05)

3. *Education as Investment in Development.* These goals of economic, social and cultural development at once require provision of education with special characteristics at all levels. (2.06)

4. *Higher Education as Cornerstone of Self-reliance.* Higher education has special importance because it provides ideas and men to sustain all other facets and levels of education. Higher education supplies the wide variety of increasingly sophisticated and ever-changing manpower needed by industry, agriculture, administration and services. (2.07)

5. *Need to enhance Support for Education...* We have to go a long way in providing adequate funds for higher education. (2.08)

6. *Excellence in Higher Education.* To achieve education of high quality is a complex task, involving, selection of teachers and students based on merit. . . . It also involves the strengthening of the infrastructure of institutions, modernisation and changes in curriculum,

including the raising of the quality and performance of the teachers. (2.09)

7. *Breadth in Higher Education*. Most importantly, higher education in our context must ensure wider awareness and breadth of vision on the part of the student, as also the cultivation of a sense of values and purpose conducive to national integration and effective citizenship in our Republic. (2.10)

8. *From Teaching to Facilitation of Learning*. All this requires a transformation of the interaction between students and teachers. Students would learn on their own through resources and situations provided for the purpose. They would develop an enquiring mind discover knowledge and arrive at attitudes and outlooks according to their own light. . . . (2.11)

9. *Relevance in Higher Education*. Relevance too requires a study of the social circumstances, employment potentialities and the possibilities of growth and development in the region. (2.12)

10. *Research and Higher Education*. The research activities could be linked once again to the social, cultural, economic and natural environment so as to focus attention on problems of local and regional development in the country. (2.13)

11. *Linkages of Resources*. The concept of relevance requires both linkages of education with socio-economic activities and enhanced resources for the implementation of the new form and content of education. (2.14)

Role and Responsibility of Teachers (2.15)

1. *Teachers as an Agent of Change*. It is he who interacts with students of different ages and frames of thought to ensure that wide-ranging educational objectives are achieved without reducing education to either brain-washing or propaganda. . . As an agent of change, he has himself to be flexible and ready to change. (2.15.01)

2. *In the Context of Explosion of Knowledge*. . . . Consequently, in order to remain up-to-date, teachers have to be on their toes; they have themselves to learn continuously. (2.15.02)

3. *The Need for a New Methodology*. New visual aids, more versatile and effective. . . . are available. . . . . Teachers have, therefore. to equip themselves with new tools of their trade, to utilize interactive methods of instruction. (2.15.03)

4. *Creative Opportunities*. Since radio and television are already

taking up the broadcast of such educational programmes, this also requires an opportunity to teachers to use their creative ability. (2.15.04)

5. *Teacher as a Procurer of Knowledge.* Teachers have, therefore, to enlarge the sphere of their knowledge, they have to learn how to obtain expert advice from others, and how to implement such programmes on a cooperative basis. (2.15.05)

6. *Teacher as Agent of Cooperation with Community.* In fact when teachers will take the initiative in establishing educational programmes with the involvement particularly of government agencies and departments, public sector industry, and voluntary organisations, only then will highly relevant programmes be evolved and put on the ground, improving employability of the students graduating in the system. (2.15.06)

7. *Teachers and Problem Solving Research.* Linkage with socio-economic activity is also necessary for conducting studies and research in highly pertinent subjects. . . (2.15.07)

8. *Teachers to Initiate Management Change.* A "system approach' will replace the ivory tower approach. (2.15.08)

9. *Government and Teachers to Share Responsibility.* If the teacher is not inspired, but is frustrated, if he is not given the encouragement to perform his role and is in fact, neglected or deprived even of the basic necessities, then we cannot expect from him a human or a professional role which is appropriate to current needs. The National Commission on Teachers in Higher Education would therefore make a fervent plea on the one hand to the Government to appreciate how patent the teacher is in engineering social change and hence to provide him status, encouragement and resources for the purpose, and on the other, to teachers to open their minds and hearts to the new possibilities, and to discharge their responsibilities with an urgent sense of social purpose. (2.15.09)

Social Status of Teachers

1.*Present Position regarding Social Status of Teachers.* There is a widespread feeling that no profession has suffered such downgrading as the teaching profession. . .the present state of affairs is highly unsatisfactory and calls for speedy remedial action. (3.02)

2. *Factors Perceived as Responsible for Deterioration of Status.* Salary and service conditions. . .lack of recognition by the

government. . .lack of devotion to the work, integrity and sense of pride. (3.06)

3. *Qualities Considered Essential for Good Teachers' Status.* 'Devotion to duty'. . . . 'good academic record' and 'quest for knowledge and excellence'—'inspiring/motivating students towards learning and creative activities'. (3.07)

4. *Factors Viewed as Necessary to Improve Teachers' Status.* Professional competency, its recognition and increase in emoluments . . . status is achieved rather than ascribed, teachers have to prove by their professional excellence and character that they deserve the trust placed on them. . . . While the importance of the economic factor is in no way to be underplayed, it is felt that no amount of improvement in salary and other benefits would raise his status if the teacher is negligent in his work and is not involved fully in his profession. (3.08.01)

Standard of Material Life of Teachers

1. *Living and Working Conditions.* In order to attract talent to the teaching profession and to provide it an opportunity to give of its best to our students and scholars, we have to greatly improve the living and working conditions throughout the country. . . . (8.09)

. . . . We recommend that the salary scales, dearness allowance, promotional opportunities, working conditions as well as service conditions, particularly, such as, study leave and sabbatical leave must be uniform for the whole country except for hardship allowances in difficult areas, such as, Ladakh, Lahual Spiti, north-eastern region, etc. (8.09)

2. *Other Benefits and Facilities in Cash or Kind.* (other than salary)

(a) *Housing.* It is necessary that housing facilities are made available, as far as possible, on the campus, or near it. (4.08.01)

. . . To encourage teachers to have their own house,, schemes of investment on housing have to be reformulated. (4.08.03)

We suggest that a revolving loan fund for each institution should also be provided; at the same time 20 to 30 per cent of the money provided by financial institutions may be earmarked for teachers.

Loans should also be earmarked by State Governments for construction of private houses by teachers, as has been done for other employees. (8.09)

A fund of Rs. 250 crores may be created for giving loans to institutions at a nominal rate of interest, say 4%. (8.09)

(b) *Medical Care*. Wherever free facilities are not available in colleges and Universities, a medical allowance of Rs. 50 per month may be given to the teachers for spending on minor ailments. For major diseases like cancer or TB, heart ailment, accidents etc. where hospitalization is required, the full cost must be met by the institutions and leave on full pay should also be given for such period.

(c) *Education of Children*. Such schools (Central) should give high priority to the admission of teachers' children. (8.09)

(d) *Conveyance Facilities*. We also recommended there should be a loan facility for teachers to buy a conveyance.

(e) *Lockers and Cubicles*. Lockers should be provided for all teachers to keep their records and student assignments and cubicles should be provided for at least 25 per cent undergraduate college teachers who can share them in each college or department,. All post-graduate teachers should have a cubicle each. In our view 8 or 9 sq. metres would be sufficient for such a purpose. This requires about 1.5 lakh cubicles and about 150 crores rupees should be provided for this purpose, this requirement being the most urgent. (8.09)

(f) *Retirement and Accident Benefits*. The provision of retirement benefits like a contributory provident fund, gratuity, pension and group insurance etc., as also of compensation for accidents and work hazards does not seem to be adequate.

Work Environment

Work Environment and Efficiency of Teachers. An environment which will maximise the efficiency and well-being of teachers should, therefore, be looked upon as a 'sin qua non' of a healthy and developing society. (5.01)

1. *Academic Freedom*. The obvious solution to the problem is really to modify the whole system of affiliation in the direction of greater freedom to the colleges.... (5.04.01)

Linkages with research agencies must also be developed. (5.04.01)

. . . We therefore recommend a system of rotation. Faculty or the Academic Council. . . . (5.04.01)

2. *Representation on Governing Bodies* . . . Almost half the membership of the Executive Council and at least 30 per cent of the

Senate should certainly go to teachers . . .

. . . . We recommend that a small advisory body of teachers should be constituted which could be consulted by the Finance and the Establishment Departments of a College or University, (5.04.02)

3. *Role of Teachers' Organisations in Decision Making.* We urge the associations to broaden their concerns, to help improve the image of the teacher; this will be an asset for demanding the long overdue benefits. (5.04.03)

4. *Mechanism for Removal of Grievances.* But it will probably be desirable to have an Ombudsman directly under the Executive Council of the affiliating University. . . .

On the whole, the Tribunal is the simplest method of dealing with grievances. (5.05.02)

5. *Grades of Punishment.* A system should be evolved by which punishments are possible. (5.05.04)

6. *Work Ethos and Work Environment.* If the teacher is to have professional pride and a feeling of devotion of his work it is essential that his working environment should be one of intellectual challenge, that he should be involved in the making of decisions that are important to academic activities and that such grievances as he may have from time to time should be expeditiously redressed. (5.06)

Professional Excellence

Standard of material life is the necessary condition for status; professional excellence is the sufficient condition. (6.01)

Factors Comprising Professional Excellence. First, the quality of human material inducted in the profession. . . .

Second, pre and post-induction training in professional skills and deepening of understanding and appreciation of values. . .

Third, . . . professional competence should be viewed in a dynamic frame – as a continum of rising levels of competence in the performance of defined functions in a rapidly changing society.

Fourth, greater mobility of teachers both within the teaching profession and between the teaching and other professions. (6.01.01)

Recruitment of Teachers

A candidate's academic performance should be give much greater weightage than any other factor at the time of his first appointment.

1. *The National Yardstick – An All India Merit Test.* An All India Merit Test may be held in each subject under the auspices of a technically competent national body with level of credibility, and only candidates securing grades above a given cut-off point in this test may be considered to be eligible for being appointed as lecturers in any college or university in the country. (6.02.03)

2. *Enlargement of Catchment, Area and Minimisation of Inbreeding.* We, therefore, suggest that at least 25 per cent of teachers recruited at the initial level should be from outside the State in which they are recruited. (6.20.04)

3. *Advertisement.* All India advertisement may be considered to be a crucial step towards improving recruitment procedures.

4. *Selection of Experts.* But since the UGC as well as the AIU have compiled a list of the staff of all Universities, this should serve as a master panel. (6.02.09)

We are not in favour of the Vice-Chancellor doing it . . . (6.02.09)

Training of Teachers

It is necessary that a person entering the teaching profession is adequately trained so that he is able to competently perform the various functions expected of him. (6.03)

(a) Teachers can be given some training at the pre-induction stage itself . . . [6.03(a)]

(b) Facilities should be provided for retraining of teachers periodically throughout their career. [6.03(b)]

Career Development

It is equally important to provide adequate and suitable opportunities for vertical mobility to teachers at multiple stages in their career. (6.04)

Principles of Career Development

(a) The highest salary of a professor should be the same as that of the Vice-Chancellor. (6.04.06)

(b) . . ., Upward movement should not be automatic (Proforma) has been suggested by the Commission. (2.04.06)

Professional Ethics and Values

As a man devoted to learning, to the pursuit of truth in his creative endeavours, and hence being in a position to see faster than many others–as a social critic, the teacher has to struggle for the propagation of values. Therefore, we believe that teachers should be the first to introspect, and scrutinise their own value system so as to raise it to the highest moral standard. (7.07)

We would like to say unambiguously that no professional and no service can survive without its do's and dont's.

We would urge the teaching community to apply worthy criteria of performance to itself so that it earns the most honourable place in the society. (7.07)

17.3 UGC COMMITTEE ON REVISION OF PAY SCALES OF TEACHERS IN UNIVERSITIES AND COLLEGES (1983-86)[5]

The University Grants Commission constituted a Committee on December 24, 1983 under the chairmanship of Professor R.C. Mehrotra, Professor Emritus, Rajasthan University, terms of reference:

(i) To examine the present structure of emoluments and conditions of service of university and college teachers, taking into account the total packet of benefits (such as superannuation/medical/housing etc.).

(ii) To make recommendations on the above having regard to the necessity of attracting and retaining talented persons in the teaching profession and providing professional advancement opportunities to teachers of universities and colleges.

The Committee while formulating its recommendations may keep in view the relevant recommendations of the National Commission on teachers. (1.1)

Subsequently, the following items were referred to the Committee:

(i) In August 1985, the Commission referred the question of creation of Super Time Senior Scale (Professor's Grade) in the colleges affiiiated to Delhi University.

5. Published by the University Grants Commission, New Delhi, 1987

Note: The member in bracket at the end of the para indicates the number of relevant para in the concerned chapter.

(ii) In October 1985, the Commission informed the Committee that the revision of pay scales of Librarians and Directors of Physical Education in universities and college be also considered along with the pay scales of teachers. (1.2)

Composition

The Committee consisted of 18 members including the Chairman.

Extracts from the Report and Major Recommendations

Rationale of the Present Proposals

The basic philosophy behind this revision of scenes of pay of teachers was to give them an appropriate status in society and to attract better qualified persons to the profession and to raise the standards of education. (6.2.1)

Considerations in Making Recommendations. In making its recommendations, the Committee has been guided by the following considerations:

(a) Teaching as a profession should promise career prospects commensurate with its importance in human recourse development.
(b) Once talent is recruited, it should not be left in wilderness. It should be cared for, nurtured and trained.
(c) An environment should be provided to the teachers where free inquiry should prevail. The autonomy of academic institutions should be guaranteed.
(d) Talent should be nourished and sustained by accountability.
(c) Merit and achievements should be adequately recognised. (6.2.15)

Pay Scales

The categories of teachers in the universities and colleges and the pay scales recommended for them are given as follows:

	University	*Pay scales in the existing framework*
(i)	Lecturer	Rs. 700-40-1100-50-1600
(ii)	Lecturer (Senior Scale)	Rs. 1200-50-1300-60-1900

(iii)	Lecturer (Selection Grade)		Rs. 2000-125/2-2250
(iv)	Reader		Rs. 1500-60-1800-100-2000-125/2-2250
(v)	Professor		Rs. 1800/-100-2000-125/2-2750-125-3000

College (Post-graduate and Undergraduate)			*Pay scales in the existing framework*
(i)	Lecturer		Rs. 700-40-1100-50-1600
(ii)	Lecturer (Senior Scale)		Rs. 1200-50-1300-60-1900
(iii)	Lecturer (Selection Grade)		Rs. 2000-125/2-2250
(iv)	Reader		Rs. 1500-60-1800-100-2000-125/2-2250
(v)	Professor		Rs. 1800-100-2000-125/2-2750-125-3000
(vi)	Principal	(i)	Rs. 1500-60-1800-100-2000-125/2-2250
		(ii)	Rs. 1800-100-2000-125/2-2-2750-125-3000

Posts of Readers and Professors already exist in most professional colleges. These may be created also in other selected colleges according to the criteria to be laid down by the UGC. However, the appointment to these posts must be made on an All India basis in the same manner as in the universities for corresponding posts. (6.4.1)

Pay Scale of Principal. The Principal should be placed either in the grade of a Reader or in the grade of a Professor. The criteria in this regard should be decided by the respective State Governments. (6.4.2)

Professor (UGC). A provision should be made to award UGC professorships on the lines of the Indian National Science Academy Award to some Professors who have shown outstanding merit in their field of work. They should be given the pay of Rs. 3500 (in the existing framework) and the usual allowances available to the university teachers. The selection for such awards should be done at the national level. The UGC may evolve a suitable mechanism for such awards. (6.4.3)

Award for Meritorious Work to Lecturers and Readers. The Committee further recommends that the UGC may evolve a scheme to award on an All India basis, additional increments as special pay to Lecturers and Readers for Exceptional performance in teaching or research and these should be treated as special pay. (6.4.4)

Qualifications for Lecturer. The Committee recommends the following minimum qualification for the post of lecturer:

(i) Qualifying at the National Test conducted for the purpose by the UGC or any other agency approved by the UGC.

(ii) Master's degree with at least 55 per cent marks or its equivalent grade and good academic record.

The minimum qualifications mentioned above should not be relaxed even for candidates possessing M. Phil./Ph.D. qualification at the time of recruitment. (6.45)

Selection on All India Basis. The Committee reiterates that a lecturer should be selected strictly on merit and on an All India basis with the help of a Selection Committee. The Selection Committee should include at least two outside experts not connected with the university.

Other Benefits

Dearness Allowance. The Committee is of the view that the rate of Dearness Allowance payable to all teachers in the universities, and colleges should be on par with Central universities. (6.12.1)

Provident Fund. The University Grants Commission had introduced a scheme of Pension-cum-Gratuity-General Provident Fund and Contributory Provident Fund-cum-Gratuity in the Central Universities. These schemes should be extended to teachers of other Universities and colleges. In view of he liberalization of pension scheme, the employer's contribution towards Contributory Provident Fund-cum-Gratuity be raised to 10 per cent.

Leave Travel Concession. The facility of Leave Travel Concession to visit home town and any place in the country, as available to Central Government Employees, and Central University teachers, should be made available to all university/college teachers. (6.12.4)

Insurance Scheme. The Committee has recommended that medical insurance scheme be introduced for teachers.

Group Insurance Scheme is available to the employees of Central Government, autonomous organisations, Government Undertakings and Central Universities. This facility should be made available to university/college teachers. (6.12.5)

House Building Advance and House Rent Allowance. The Committee recommends that house building advance should be made available to all university/college teachers.

The Committee has recommended an enhancement in the house rent allowance to teachers. (6.12.6)

Conveyance Advance. Travel to the place of work is time

consuming, arduous and costly. The Committee is of the view that suitable conveyance advance may be given to teachers, depending upon the type of vehicle. Provision of a suitable conveyance allowance for teachers living outside the campus may be given due consideration. (6.12.7)

Revision of Pay Scales of Teachers in Universities and Colleges (1987)

Preamble

It has been the endeavour of the University Grants Commission to improve the scales of pay of teachers and bring about uniformity in the pay structure of teachers in all the universities and colleges as a step towards achieving its objective of maintenance of standards. The UGC and the Central Government have been making persistent efforts in this direction.

The pay scales of teachers were last revised in 1973. With the institutionalisation of the Fourth Pay commission of the employees of the Central Government, the Commission in consultation with the Government of India, appointed a Committee under the Chairmanship of Professor R.C. Mehrotra, Emeritus Professor, Rajasthan University, Jaipur, to consider the revision of pay scales, career/professional development and service conditions of teachers. The scheme of revision on pay scales is based on the recommendations of the Mehrotra Committee. The Mehrotra Committee, had in it mainly academics.

Multiplicity of Grades

The new pay structure visualises, three categories of teachers, Lecturer, Reader and Professor, although there are seven scales. The purpose of introducing multiple scales is to provide promotional avenues to teachers of each category and to avoid stagnation at any level.

The Mehrotra Committee had recommended that selection of Readers and Professors must be made on All India basis. Accordingly, while appointment to position of Readers and Professor will be made on the basis of open selection the need to provide opportunities for vertical mobility for both Lecturers and Readers has been recognised.

The provision of two promotions for every Lecturer and one for Reader has been built into the scheme. While outstanding teachers will have opportunities for rapid promotion to the rank of Readers and Professors, the provision for career advancement in the scheme assures that almost every teacher will have reasonable opportunities of career advancement.

Qualifying Test

Qualifying test for the recruitment of Lecturer has been recommended in Order to ensure the quality of new entrants to the profession and removing disparities in standards of examination at Master's level between different universities. It is also hoped that with this mechanism, local influences will be minimised and the eligibility zone for recruitment to the teaching posts would become wider. All that is specified is that the qualifying test should be comprehensive and the UGC has only been assigned the responsibility of preparing a detailed scheme for this purpose. In principle, the test could be conducted through multiple agencies and recognised by all universities. There is no intention whatsoever of interfering with the powers of State Governments or other recruiting agencies.

Career Advancement of Teachers

In the teaching profession, posts are not normally filled on the basis of promotion. New positions are created mainly in response to the demands of the curriculum load and the area of specialisations and not on the basis of the organisational requirements of a. functional hierarchy. A Reader is not subordinate to a Professor nor is a Lecturer to a Reader. These differences do get reflected in the organisation of the Government services and the teaching profession. The pay scales and conditions of service cannot, therefore, be exactly similar. It does not, however, follow that the teaching profession does not offer promotional opportunities. In fact, almost all positions of Readers are normally filled by Lecturers and almost all positions of Professors by Readers. The minimum requirement for appointment as a Reader is five years' experience as Lecturer; and ten years' teaching experience for appointment as a Professor. As positions of Readers and Professors are filled through open advertisement and selection, good teacher in any college of university has a good chance of successfully competing for these higher positions in other colleges or universities throughout the country. He/she does not have to wait till a position becomes available in his/her own college or university.

The scheme provides avenues to bright teachers to reach about the same level as any officer in I.A.S. cadre, after a service of 15-20 years with outstanding performance. The best of teachers will be as well off as I.A.S. officers.

Creation of Posts of Readers and Professors in Colleges

The scheme envi ges institution of the posts of Readers and Professors in suitable and deserving colleges. It is being argued that this proposal is a part of the design to create two kinds of colleges, a few elite privileged ones and many neglected ones. The positions of Readers and Professors are to be created in individual colleges based on the type and nature of programmes offered by them and especially the quality and standards of their teaching programmes and research. Surely, these positions are not being created for the teachers working in those institutions. All deserving teachers would compete for them.

Running Grade

Academics know that we cannot have a situation where you put a person on one side of a tube and he just sails across right to the top of the Professor's grade. This is not going to work in this Profession and in no country, it is so. In this profession, one has to show excellence and ability and teachers recognise this. What has been done however is, that an incumbent entering as a Lecturer can compete for a Readers' position after five years and thereafter for a Professorship. Even if a teacher fails to avail this Promotional opportunity, he/she will still not stagnate. Even with moderate performance, he/she will eventually reach a fairly decent level of emoluments. Such opportunities were not available earlier.

Refresher Courses

Knowledge in present days, changes so fast that in about seven years, total amount of information doubles. Teachers have to keep their knowledge updated to be able to impact the excitement of the changing field to their students. Additional opportunities for refreshing oneself have to be provided. Introduction of refresher courses will provide such opportunities to the teachers to cooperatively teach each other, exchange ideas and explore new lines of teaching and research. Indeed most teachers want to do this, but cannot, because of the inadequate facilities. It is the responsibility of the universities and UGC to provide such facilities and teachers to avail them.

Evaluation/Professional Ethics

The system of continuous evaluation will have several advantages, e.g., since teachers themselves would be involved in the process of evaluation, it will have a pronounced self-regulatory effect. Further, the total system will thus, be protected from acquiring a bad reputation for fault of a few. The system of evaluation will help the career-development of teachers by securing feed-back for self-improvement as well as help to create a spirit of healthy competition and emulation. Moreover, in the process of selection and a appointments at various levels, it will acquire greater objectivity and credibility.

There is no evidence to suggest that even a substantial minority of teachers behave in an undesirable manner. Such behaviour is exceptional and it is not the intention to stress either misconduct or penalties. It is a matter of satisfaction that Teacher's Associations have themselves shown concern in this regard. It has been agreed that a code of conduct and ethics and a scheme of open, participatory and data based evaluation will be evolved through discussions with teachers' organisations.

The whole scheme is aimed to give better working conditions, scales of pay and status to the teaching community.

Union Enforcement of the Scheme

The States which do not implement this scheme will perhaps not be able to attract the best of teachers and that is in nobody's interest. However the revision of pay scales ought to be implemented immediately in all the States, and indeed the Central Advisory Board on Education which consists of Education Ministers of all States endorsed the scheme in its meeting of June 25-26, 1987.

Revised Pay Scales for College Teachers (1987)

The Government of India, Ministry of Human Resource Development announced the revised pay scales in June, 1987 with retrospective effect from January, 1986, for teachers working in Indian universities and colleges. The decisions announced by the Government are based on the recommendations of the Mehrotra Committee appointed by the U.G.C. The Committee had submitted its report in 1986.

	Designation	Existing Scale of pay	Revised Scale of pay
A.	*Universities*		
	Lecturer	700-1600	2200-75-2800-100-4000
	Lecturer (Sr. Scale)	Not existing	3000-100-3500-125-5000
	Lecturer (Selection Grade)	1200-1900	3700-125-4700-159-5300
	Reader	1200-1900	3700-125-4700-150-5300
	Reader (Sr. Scale Professor)	Not existing	4500-150-5700
	Professor	1500-2500	4500-150-5700-200-7300
	Professor of Eminence	3000 (fixed)	8000 (fixed)
	Vice-Chancellor	3000 (fixed)	7300-100-7600
B.	*Colleges*		
	Lecturer	700-1600	2200-75-2800-100-4000
	Lecturer (Sr. Scale)	Not existing	3000-100-3500-125-5000
	Lecturer (Selection Grade)	1200-1900	3700-125-4700-150-5300
	Principal	(i) 1200-1900 (ii) 1500-2500	Revised Scale of Reader or Professor
	Tutor/Demonstrators in Universities and Colleges (existing incumbents only)	500-900	1740-3000

The total pay under revised scale is inclusive of CCA and the HRA as per recommendations of the Fourth Pay Commission.

The following table published in the *Indian Express* (daily) dated June 21, 1987, shows the implication of latest pay scale revision:

Basic Pay under present scale	Total Pay under present scale	Basic Pay under revised scale	Total Pay under revised scale	Total gain
700	2060	2200	2750	690
940	2700	2725	3275	575
1200	3095	3100	3800	705
1600	3655	3700	4800	1145
		Reader's Grade		
1200	3095	3100	3800	705
1600	3655	3700	4800	1145
1900	4297	4325	5425	1128
		Professor's Grade		
1500	3570	4500	5600	2130
2000	4515	4650	5750	1235
2500	5625	5700	6800	1175

Under the new scheme, the post of 'professor of eminence' has been created which carries as salary of Rs. 8000 p.m. even higher than that of a Vice-Chancellor.

A suggestion contained in the Mehrotra Committee report regarding a code of conduct for teachers has been left it to be teachers to evolve their own code. No deadline has been set for this.

A teacher may participate in politics. If elected to an elective body, he will have to take leave but he will not suffer the loss of any benefits such as promotions or increments.

Those, who would not like this scheme of pay scales, will have the option of the existing benefits. For them the scales of pay will be Rs. 2200-4000 for lecturers, Rs. 3000-5000 for readers, and Rs. 4500-5300 for professors. No teacher will be denied benefits already accruing to them.

Under the evaluation system, a lecturer will be required to possess a Ph.D. or M.Phil for his entitlement to selection grade although at his initial appointment the requisite qualification will be M.A. with 55% marks.

Teachers in Central Universities would be entitled for allowances sanctioned by the Central Government, and teachers in universities and colleges will get allowances fixed by the State Governments.

Recruitment at the level of lecturer, reader and professor will be through all India advertisement and selection. A National Testing Service is being set up and this may also offer a specially designed test to test eligibility for appointment as a lecturer.

The Government also intends to work out schemes for providing housing and medicare facilities to teachers.

17.4 UGC GUIDELINES FOR TEACHING AND RELATED MATTERS (1984-88)

The University Grants Commission had circulated in January 1984 certain guidelines regarding minimum number of actual teaching days in an academic year in Universities/Colleges, minimum programme of Examination Reform in Universities and workload of teachers in universities and colleges. These guidelines also form part of regulations since November 1985. At a meeting of the UGC, in 1988, these guidelines were again considered and it was decided to bring the same to the notice of the universities again. The guidelines circulated to universities are as follows.

(A) *Working Days*

The number of actual teaching days in an academic year in a university/deemed to be university/constituent/affiliated colleges of the university should not go below 180 days excluding the preparation days and examination days. These are days on which classes such as lectures, tutorials, seminars, laboratories are/or may be conducted. Holidays cannot be counted although students may be studying in their homes or hostels or may even be informally consulting teachers. The time taken up for admissions i.e. when the classes are not formed, to start work, time meant for examinations or for preparing for examinations cannot be counted. It would be desirable for universities to make an effort to raise the number to 200 or more. The Universities should budget their time in regard to work, and holidays. For example, admissions should be completed by the last day of the long vacation. Examination results should also be compiled and announced during the vacations to enable admissions to take place. In a semester pattern, examinations should not be so prolonged as to take away more working days – there could be more reliance on internal assessment, examiners of first semester could be internal, so that the short vacation can be utilised for evaluation. The universities should also see that a working day in a department or faculty does not become just a few hours of the forenoon. The time table should be spread to accommodate the various academic activities over at least on 8 hours working day.

The University should also insist that the manner of conducting a course is also spelled out. The number of lectures, tutorials, seminars, lab-sessions, etc. normally adequate for each course should be worked out and preferably made known in a handbook of courses. If students cut classes, or if working days are otherwise disrupted, it should be made clear that only when the norm is reached will there be examinations. This also involves disciplined regular work on part of the teachers – which should be ensured. Every item in a given syllabus may not have to be taught in the class as a pre-requisite for the examination, but on the other hand it would be counter productive to hold examinations on reduced courses because the number of working days has been curtailed in a particular situation. If this happens, examinations will loose their credibility, students will perform poorly in competitions and inter-views, and if they are admitted to the next class its standards will also suffer.

(B) *Minimum Programme of Examination Reform*

Every university/deemed to be university shall have to adopt the following minimum examination reform.

Syllabus/Question Paper

(a) The syllabus in each paper should be demarcated into well defined units/areas of content alongwith a topicswise breakdown. The units may be numbered.
(b) Examiners should be free to repeat questions set in a previous examination. This is necessary in order to ensure that students do not leave out important portions of the syllabus. Instructions to paper setters should be amended accordingly.
(c) There is often a very wide choice given to students for answering questions, say 5 out of 10. Such overall choice restrict the area of knowledge with which a student can pass an examination and is therefore undesirable. If there is choice, it may be provided by alternate questions in each unit of the syllabus.
(d) No examination should be held without fulfilling the requirement

of a minimum number of lectures/tutorials/laboratory sessions, etc. which should be clearly laid down by the university.

(e) Examinations should be conducted in fair and impartial manner. Cheating in examinations is a cognizable offence. Universities must take all steps for the proper conduct of examinations such as effective security measures, proper supervision and invigilation, cordoning off the examination centres from the range of loudspeakers and other interference, flying squads and stern action in all cases involving copying and use of unfair means.

(C) *Work Load of Teachers*

The work-load of various activities should be not less than 40 hours a week for a teacher who is in full time employment. (Any good teacher, particularly one who is involved in creative activity and who has a spirit of challenge towards giving his best to the students, would certainly spend much more than 40 hours a week in academic pursuits).

The breakup of work load shown below is for the sake of example. It is not a rigid breakup. But, every teacher could be given duties according to some such general pattern and no one should have a significantly reduced load:

1. *Undergraduate College*

(a) Lecturers in Non-laboratory/Field work subjects

	Activity	Average No. of hours per week
i.	Teaching	16
ii.	Testing/Exams	2
iii.	Tutorials	4
iv.	Preparation of Teaching	10
v.	Supervision of Extra-curricular Work	4
vi.	Administrative Work	4
	Total	40

Where extra-curricular work or administrative work is not assigned or unfortunately tutorials do not take place, teaching work may be slightly increased, but as far as possible a teacher should not have to teach or lecture more than three hours per day.

(b) Lecturers in Science Subjects or where field work is necessary

	Activity	Average No. of hours per week
i.	Teaching	16
ii.	Lab. work	4
iii.	Testing/Examinations	2
iv.	Teaching preparation and lab-setting	12
v.	Administrative activities	4
vi.	Extra-curricular activities	2
	Total	40

2. *Lecturers in PG Colleges/Universities.*

(a) Lecturers in non-laboratory/Field work subjects.

	Activity	Average No. of hours per week
i.	Teaching	10
ii.	Testing/exams	1
iii.	Tutorials	4
iv.	Preparation for Teaching	10
v.	Research	10
vi.	Own Reading/Studies	5
	Total	40

(b) Lecturers in Science Subjects or where field work in involved:

	Activity	Average No. of hours per week
i.	Teaching	10
ii	Testing	1
iii.	Laboratory work	4
iv.	Teaching preparation and lab-setting	10
v.	Research	10
vi.	Own Reading/Administrative work	5
	Total	40

Teaching combining Undergraduate and Postgraduate teaching will have a position in between (1) and (2) above.

(c) Senior teachers like Readers and Professor, in addition to their own research work guide and supervise a fairly large number of students for M.Phil/Ph.D. Degrees. They have also to attend consultative meeting of various organisations, sometimes related to teaching and sometimes to research. Therefore, it is felt that their direct teaching responsibilities may be slightly curtailed allowing them a greater portion of time for guiding and supervising research work. However, to the 10 hours of research per week on the average, it should be possible to add not more than 4 hours, bringing the total of research to 14 hours per week. This again implies that the number of students to be supervised should be limited to perhaps 4 to 6, and that senior teachers should be able to assign specific time to each scholar whose work they are supervising.

It is also felt that with 14 hours for research and 5 or 6 hours for reading and study and perhaps another 5 hours for extra-curricular or administrative work, senior teachers should be able to put in about 8 hours of teaching and laboratory work including testing and about 8 hours for preparation of teaching work. Teachers not having such extensive research responsibilities should put in more teaching work. Ordinarily a teacher may not have more than two postgraduate theory courses to teach with some laboratory or tutorial responsibility.

It is further observed:

(i) That young people are given enough time to help in their professional growth and achievement of academic excellence particularly in the initial years of their service;

(ii) that teachers guiding research students have adequate time to look after them; and

(iii) that 'pleasant' as well as 'unpleasant' work is shared by all teachers.

In case a certain teacher likes to have an extra load at a particular time in the years, and comparatively less teaching work at some other time during the total academic year, this should be accommodated, if it does not cause any serious difficulty in the teaching programme of the department. Where teaching is organised in semesters and terms such adjustment could be made in the corresponding period, provided the teacher has given adequate notice to the university.

The underlying principle being that the maximum workload should be the same in all departments and for all teachers. In postgraduate centres where considerable research activity is envisaged it is obvious that the direct teaching of the staff will be reduced and the staff will accordingly devote the remaining time for active research.

Teachers should spend a certain amount of time every day in the department/college whether or not they have direct teaching duties on certain days. If facilities are provided, preparation for teaching can mostly be done in the department/college. This is so as to ensure that a teacher is available for his students if they need his help, and that a teacher is also available when he is needed for consultation or discussion on various matters that come up in institutions.

17.5 NATIONAL EXPERT COMMITTEE ON GRADES FOR TECHNICAL TEACHERS AND ACTION THEREON (1988)[6]

Background

The Government of India set up a National Expert Committee under the Chairmanship of Prof. R.N. Dogra to recommend grades for the Technical Teachers. These recommendations were first considered by the All India Council for Technical education at its meeting held on January 8, 1988. Thereafter, the Ministry of Human Resource Development announced new pay scales for teachers of engineering colleges and other technical education institutions of comparable status. The revised scales will benefit about 15,000 teachers and will come into effec om January 1, 1986.

The scher of revised scales shall be applicable to teachers, librarians anc hysical education instructors in engineering colleges, engineering ...d technological faculties, departments of universities and other comparable institutions of technical education, including architectural, town planning, management, pharmacy, applied arts and crafts, etc., at the degree or equivalent level.

6. Published by the University Grants Commission, New Delhi, 1987

Note: The member in bracket at the end of the para indicates the number of relevant para in the concerned chapter.

The scheme does not apply to Indian Institutes of Technology for which the matter is being examined separately.

The revised pay scales will be implemented in all technical education institutions fully financed by the Central Government and covered under the scheme. The State Governments which wish to adopt and implement the scheme of these revised pay scales would get financial assistance from the Central Government to the extent of 80 per cent of the additional expenditure for the period from January 1, 1986, to March 31, 1990. The remaining 20 per cent of the expenditure would be met by the State Governments from their own resources.

The existing teachers in technical education institutions, where the merit promotion scheme is in operation, will have an option to continue to be governed by the provisions of the scheme, provided they exercise their option in writing prior to their pay fixation under this scheme.

They will also be entitled to the designations envisaged for various categories of teachers in that scheme.

The revised Pay Scales would be asunder: Lecturer: Rs. 2200-4000; Lecturer (Senior Scale): Rs. 3000-5000; Lecturer (Selection Grade): Rs. 3700-5700; Associate Professors: Rs. 3700-5700; Professor: Rs. 4500-7300; Principal (Engg. Colleges.TTT's/degree level technical institution: Rs. 6300-7300; Director (IIMS): Rs. 7300-7600.

The age of superannuation of all teachers in technical institutions shall be 60 years with a provision for re-employment up to 65 years in deserving cases.

18

TECHNICAL EDUCATION[1]

Introduction

Technical education is one of the most significant components of human resource development spectrum with great potential for adding value to products and services, for contributing to the national economy, and for improving the quality of life of the people. In recognition of the importance of this sector, the successive Five Year Plans laid great emphasis on the development of technical education.

During the past four decades, there has been a phenomenal expansion of technical education facilities in the country. But, a lot more remains to be accomplished in the field of technical education in respect of increasing its coverage and enhancing its accessibility to various categories of people, and in improving its productivity. Moreover, the changing scenario by the turn of the century in socio-economic, industrial and technological areas needs to be considered to enable the system to play its role with greater relevance and objectivity. Based on these considerations, the National Policy on Education (NPE) as well as the Programme of Action (POA) have rightly pointed to several new initiatives to further revamp the technical education system. They include: modernisation and removal of obsolescence, promoting institution-industry interaction, restructuring of courses/programmes, entrepreneurship development, promoting technical education of women, linking technical education with development sectors and application of science and technology for rural development.

---

1. *Source*: ***Annual Report***, Ministry of Human Resource Development, Government of India, New Delhi, 1989.

The year under report witnessed some significant developments in the field of technical education. Considerable progress was made in implementing the various programmes and schemes based on the National Policy on Education vested with statutory authority, the All India Council for Technical Education (AICTE) swung into action to fulfil the tasks assigned to it. The first meeting of the statutory AICTE was held on July 6, 1988. Regulations, norms and standards for courses and institutions, fee and admission guidelines, details of accreditation for performance evaluation of courses and institution, models for State Directorates, and perspective plans and Programmes of Action (POAs) of Central institutions and States were got formulated. Several proposals for starting new institutions/courses were examined and seventy of them were approved.

The various programmes/schemes under technical education and their progress during the year are briefly summarised below:

Indian Institutes of Technology

The five Indian Institutes of Technology (IITs) at Kharagpur, Bombay, Madras, Kanpur and Delhi were established as premier centres of education and training in engineering and applied science at the under-graduate level and to provide adequate facilities for post-graduate studies and research. These are Institutes of National Importance.

The IITs conduct four-year undergraduate programmes leading to Bachelor's Degree in Technology (B.Tech.)/in various fields of engineering and technology. They also offer integrated Master's Degree courses of five-year duration in physics, chemistry, and mathematics, one-and-a half year M.Tech Degree courses in various specialisation, and one-year post-graduate Diploma courses in selected areas. In addition, the Institutes offer Ph.D. programmes in different branches of engineering, sciences, humanities and social sciences. T re are also advanced centres of training and research in each I itute in identified areas of specialisation.

19

VOCATIONAL EDUCATION: National Working Group on Vocational Education (1985)[1]

Introduction

It was stipulated by the Education Commission, 1964-66 that over a period of 20 years, about 50 per cent of the students in the +2 stage would be covered by vocational education programmes. Attempts were made by 9 States and 4 Union Territories to implement the recommendations of the Kothari Commission on vocationalisation of 10+with diffing emphases on vocational content and with varying degrees of success. The coverage in the vocational stream in +2 in 1983-84, accounted for about 2.5 per cent of the total enrolment at +2. It, therefore, became necessary to review the position, suggest methods and initiate suitable measures to accelerate the pace of implementation of the vocational programme during the Seventh Five Year Plan. In view of the explicit objective of linking education with development it was necessary to consider the whole spectrum of education and its organisation to productive processes rather than concentrating on +2 level along with this end in view the Union Minister for Education, in his capacity as the Chairman, All India Council for Technical Education (AICTE) appointed in February 1985, the National Working Group on Vocational Education. The group submitted its report in August 1985.

1. Published by the Ministry of Human Resource Development Government of India New Delhi, 1985.

Terms of Reference

The following constituted the terms of reference for the Working Group:

(i) To formulate the concept of vocationalisation at different levels at which vocational education and training should be provided to meet the massive challenge of unemployment on the one hand and to reduce the overcrowding in higher education on the other.

(ii) To consider and recommend the nature of courses to be taken up in the vocational system under different sectors such as agriculture, health, pharmacy, technical education, commerce, business and industry. To consider and recommend the distribution of time between vocational training, vocational education and general education.

(iii) To consider and recommend the linkages required among various agencies running vocational programmes in order to give coordinated thrust to vocationalisation and to ensure employment of those completing the same.

(iv) To consider ways and means, including provision of avenues for higher education, to the students of vocational stream to make the vocational courses more attractive.

(v) To consider the need for covering vocational courses under the Apprenticeship Act and make necessary recommendations on the same.

(vi) To prepare an action plan about the selection of institutions, the selection of various courses, organisation of various courses, prescription of norms for instructional facilities, training of teachers, preparation for producing necessary instructional material and other related aspects to make necessary headway in promoting vocationalisation in the country.

Composition and Meetings

The Working Group consisted of 16 Members with Dr. V. C. Kualndaiswamy, Vice-Chancellor, Annamalai University Madras, as its Chairman. The Working Group had three sittings, the first on the 28th February and 1st March, 1985 at Delhi, the second on the 18th, 19th and 20th May, 1985 at Madras and the last on the 14th August

1985 at New Delhi, and finalised the reports. Special invitees also attended the meetings.

1. *Meaning of Vocational Education.* The term 'vocational education' may be used in a broad sense to cover all educational programmes that aim at job orientation and develop in the individuals knowledge and skill. It is not restricted in this report to programmes of skill development at secondary and higher secondary levels only. It is in this context that we talk of vocational subjects and vocational education even at the degree level.

Organised sector employs only around 10 per cent of the labour force; the dominant section of the labour force in the unorganised sector must be helped to significantly improve its performance and increase its productivity. Programmes of vocational education and training must contribute to this development.

2. *Classification of Vocational Areas.* The Working Group recommends that a uniform classification of vocational areas as given below may be adopted and used in the school system:

(i) Agriculture,
(ii) Business and Commerce,
(iii) Engineering and Technology,
(iv) Health and Para-medical Services.
(v) Home Science,
(vi) Humanities,
(vii) Others.

3. *Dimension of Vocational Education.* Vocational Education and Training programmes for the following four distinct target groups are outlined in the report; they may be adopted throughout the country.

(i) School population in Classes I-X,
(ii) School population at the Higher Secondary Stage,
(iii) Out-of-school population including those in institutes and schools of vocational education,
(iv) Tertiary level population.

4. *Common Structure for the Country.* A common structure of education for the country (i.e., 10+2+3) which is agreed as necessary, is yet to be achieved. The process of change may be accelerated in the Seventh Plan period.

5. *Work Experience/SUPW for School Population from Classes I-X*

(1) The SUPW/WE programmes must be so conceived and formulated that the monetary input should be modest and the non-monetary motivational components should be the driving force behind their successful implementation, especially at the primary stage. All the teachers must be involved in the implementation of the programme and the training must be assigned the priority it deserves.
(2) The SUPW/WE may be allotted 20 per cent of the total time. At the middle and secondary school level, the programme may be given pre-vocational orientation. 'Earn while you learn' opportunities should be provided on optional basis to the middle school and secondary school students.
(3) The pre-vocational programmes of the secondary stage should as far as possible be linked to the vocational programmes of the higher secondary stage, offered in the same school or in neighbouring schools. The performance should be properly evaluated and credit given in admission into technical/vocational courses at the next higher level.

6. *Flexible Programme of Vocationalisation Higher Secondary.* The vocationalisation of higher secondary education aims at an educational transformation involving large numbers. The reform contemplated has to take note of such unfavourable factors as social prejudices, resistance to change and vaguely defined job requirements in many cases. The programme therefore must be flexible and be based on a process of iteration.

7. *Curriculum for Vocational Education Programme.* The components of the curriculum for the vocational education programme are:

(i) language(s),
(ii) related subjects and foundation courses, and
(iii) vocational theory and practice.

8. *Targets.* Nearly 2.4 lakhs of students in the higher secondary stream for 10 per cent diversion and 6.9 lakhs of students for 25 per cent diversion by the year 1990, should be covered by the proposed

vocationalization programme during the Seventh Plan period. This is in addition to the existing intake of 0.6 lakhs. It is imperative that vocationalization should cover a much larger population, for the reform that is being undertaken in the school system to make an impact.

9. *Vocational Survey*. The vocational courses chosen should have relevance to the economic life in the region and should be identified on the basis of properly conducted vocational surveys.

10. *Special Areas of Vocational Education*. Duplication of efforts made in certificate level courses such as those offered in ITI's, and diploma level courses such as those offered in polytechnics shall be avoided. There are many areas in agriculture, health, and para-medical services, home science, humanities, service-areas in engineering and technology, and business and commerce in which ITI and polytechnic-level institutions are not involved and these gaps shall be filled by the higher secondary vocationalization.

11. *Optimum Use of Resources*. Laboratory facilities available in schools or those that can be procured with marginal financial inputs should be taken into account while deciding on the vocational subjects. The vocationalization programme should aim at making optimum use of the institutional, industrial and organisational facilities available in the neighbourhood for instruction and training.

12. *Involvement of the Community*. The relevant sections of the community in general must be intimately involved in the formulation and implementation of the vocational courses.

13. *Formal and Non-formal Vocational Education Programmes*. (a) Since our constitutional requirement provides for universalization of education up to Class VIII, the non-formal courses for drop-outs should aim at bringing their general education up to the level of Class VIII, by the middle schools themselves. For those still remaining outside, some skill training must be given so that they can join the world of work as semi-skilled workers. The number involved will be of the order of 120 lakhs per year.

(b) About 20 lakhs of students who cross Class VIII but do not go for Class XI or certificate and diploma level courses join the labour force. They need some skill for development and suitable programmes will have to be designed, agencies identified and finances provided. The existing 5098 institutions offering various certificate and diploma level courses may be made use of for this task, namely, to provide short courses and intensive training programmes. The numbers involved may be of the order of 20 lakhs per year. It is suggested that as a pilot project, 10 per cent of this number may be covered every year in the Seventh Plan, starting from 1986. During the Seventh Plan period, 1000 ITI-level institutions, 400 polytechnics and 500 higher secondary schools will have to be converted into community service oriented institutions with emphasis on extension activities.

(c) The agencies of education and training under the various ministries and departments of the government should establish extension centres particularly in the rural areas.

(d) It is necessary to plan the expansion of the existing 5098 certificate and diploma level institutions, with appropriate geographical distribution, to cover much larger numbers of candidates. They should also start extension centres in rural areas for girls and weaker sections in particular. 500 new institutions may be started during the Seventh Plan period, to cover an additional intake of 62.500 candidates per year on a full-time basis.

(e) Open schools and part-time educational facilities shall be provided for offering general education to the labour force. Part-time vocational courses should also be available for semi-skilled workers to become skilled. The unemployed or the partially employed labour force should be given skill training to increase employability in the local context, by vocational and technical training institutions-schools, polytechnics, community schools, community colleges through their extension centres, voluntary agencies and service departments of the government. Skilled workmen shall be trained to become Master Craftsmen by the industries themselves. Nearly 10 lakhs of people per year will have to be covered by the above three programmes.

14. *Vocational Education and Opportunities for Further Education.* For nearly 10 to 15 per cent of vocational stream products, opportunities for further education in chosen areas of vocational specialization or in other courses of study should be available on the basis of demonstrated merit and motivation.

15. *New Diploma Courses for the Products of Higher Secondary Vocational Courses.* For the products of the higher secondary vocational stream, new diploma level courses may be instituted or the existing facilities may be extended.

16. *Vocational Electives at Degree Level Courses.* The introduction of one vocational elective in the degree level courses under the guidelines given by UGC is a welcome step. A larger number of such electives should be offered for the students to choose from. Further,

full degree courses in vocational subjects with employment orientation may be given fair trial in the system of tertiary education.

17. *Non-formal Further Education.* (a) The students receiving vocational education and training through non-formal courses and specialized institutions should also be provided opportunities through non-formal means for further education and training.

(b) Non-formal further education should be oriented towards the improvement of existing competencies to enable the out-of-school population rejoin the general education system at an appropriate level. For both groups facilities must have special relevance to 'working–learners.'

(c) The establishment of special institutes of rural development mentioned for the promotion of vocational education and training on a mass scale may be given high priority in the Seventh Plan.

18. *Reorganisation of the Management System.* The management of education especially at the state level needs reorganisation, decentralisation, strengthening in numbers and improvement in competence to meet the challenges of educational reform which in future will be a continuous activity.

19. *National/Joint Council of Vocational Education.* The activities in vocational education and training at present remain somewhat isolated and un-coordinated. As a first step to remedy this situation, a National/Joint Council of Vocational Education at the Centre may be set up.

20. *Activising All India Board of Vocational Education.* The All India Board of Vocational Education (AIBVE) that has already been established must be activised. It may mainly concern itself with the vocational education programme at the higher secondary stage and offer guidance and counsel to the state boards of higher secondary education in the formulation of curriculum and syllabi, testing and evaluation and organising training programmes besides performing other functions which it may be assigned.

21. *Setting up a Bureau of Vocational Education.* A separate Department or Bureau of Vocational Education (BVE) may be set up in the Ministry of Education, Government of India, to co-ordinate, oversee and monitor the whole spectrum of vocational education within and outside the school system and it should act as the secretariat of the National/Joint Council of Vocational Education.

22. *State Council of Vocational Education.* Each state should have a coordinating body for vocational education designated as 'State

Council for Vocational Education' (SCVE). As effective coordination among several departments and non-governmental agencies is required, it is essential that the council be constituted with necessary status and authority.

23. *Department of Vocational Education.* A separate Department of Vocational Education should be set up to work as secretariat for the State Council for Vocational Education.

24. *Five Levels of Hierarchy.* The structure of the management system may have five levels of hierarchy and four components on the basis of functions. The five levels are:

(a) National, (b) regional, (c) State, (d) district, and (e) institutional.

The four components on the basis of functions are:

(a) the policy making and coordinating bodies,
(b) research, development and teacher-training institutions,
(c) the ministries and directorates for overall administration, and
(d) the examination boards (secondary and higher secondary),

25. *Strengthening of Organisations at Various Levels.* The NCERT at the national level, the Regional Colleges of Education, the ITIs and also the Boards of Apprenticeship Training at regional level and SCERT at the state level, must be strengthened and a framework for coordinating among these organisations must be formulated.

26. *District Level Committees.* There shall be district level coordination/advisory committees for vocational education and training.

27. *Preparation of Text-books.* The development of text-books and other instructional materials should be attempted on a large scale to meet the diverse needs of a variety of vocational programmes. All material should be properly reviewed before being prescribed.

28. *Teachers for Vocational Course.* The teachers of vocational courses should possess not only adequate educational qualification but also desired job experiences. This will require employment of both full-time and part-time teachers. The part-time faculty should be drawn from industries, employment sector, expert institutions and retired personnel. To start with, one full-time teacher for the first year and another for the second year of higher secondary vocational stream for each vocational course being offered by a school should be provided

and similarly another part-time teacher and an assistant may be utilised.

29. *Use of Community Resources.* Community resources, both in terms of part-time expert teachers and by way of training facilities of industries, farms etc., should be utilised for the purpose of quality instruction at modest cost. This will necessitate creation of only the minimum of new payment facilities within the school.

30. *Training of Teachers.* A systematic staff-training and development programme should be introduced for which NCVE/JVCE and SCVE should provide necessary policies and NCERT/SCERT the necessary guidelines and details.

31. *Apprenticeship Act.* The Apprenticeship Act should be amended expediously to cover about 70 per cent of the products of the higher secondary vocational courses and its Apprenticeship Training.

32. *The Role of the Government of India.* It should provide:

(i) Policy guidelines,
(ii) Coordination and standardization,
(iii) Research and development,
(iv) Full financial assistance for some schemes and partial assistance for achieving targets prescribed, and,
(v) Regulation by enacting suitable legislation where needed.

33. *Role of State Governments.* The State Governments should establish the policy making and coordinating bodies and research institutions along with the administrative set-up as recommended, for the effective implementation of vocational education and training for the four target groups identified in this report.

34. *Changes in Recruitment Rules.* Immediate steps should be taken to incorporate necessary provision in the recruitment rules to enable the candidates from the vocational stream to compete for posts in the departments of State Governments and Central Government and private and public sector organisations. For posts requiring vocational education and training, preference should be given to candidates from vocational stream.

35. *Provision of Finance.* The overall cost of vocationalisation of education works out to Rs. 2902 crores for 25 per cent diversion of higher secondary students and Rs. 2207 crores for 10 per cent diversion.

Illustrative List of Subject Fields

1. Agriculture
   1. Agricultural Chemicals
   2. Agro-economics and Farm Management
   3. Agro-based Industries
   4. Dairying
   5. Farm Mechanics and Post-Harvest Technology
   6. Fisheries
   7. Forestry
   8. Horticulture
   9. Poultry
   10. Sericulture

II. Business and Commerce
   1. Accountancy
   2. Banking
   3. Co-operative Management
   4. Import-Export Procedures
   5. Insurance
   6. Marketing and Salesmanship
   7. Materials Management
   8. Office Management
   9. Public Relations
   10. Purchasing and Store-keeping

III. Engineering and Technology
   1. Air-conditioning & Refrigeration
   2. Automobile Servicing and Maintenance
   3. Building Maintenance
   4. Computer Maintenance
   5. Electrical Maintenance
   6. Foundry Technology
   7. Leather Technology
   8. Radio and Television Servicing
   9. Surveying and Estimating

IV. Health and Paramedical Services
   1. Dental Hygiene
   2. Health Service
   3. Hospital House-keeping

		4. Medical Record-keeping
		5. Nursing
		6. Ophthalmic Services
		7. Orthoptic Services
		8. Pharmacy
		9. Physiotherapy
		10. Radiological Services
V.	Home Science	1. Bakery and Confectionery
		2. Canning
		3. Canteen Management
		4. Catering
		5. Child Care and Nutrition
		6. Cookery
		7. Costume Design
		8. Dietetics
		9. Food Preservation
		10. Interior Decoration
VI.	Humanities	1. Drawing
		2. Journalism
		3. Library Science
		4. Local Body and Other Services
		5. Museum-keeping
		6. Music and Dance
		7. Painting and Commercial Art
		8. Photography
		9. Printing and Book-making
		10. Tourism
VII.	Others	1. Audio-Visual Assistantship
		2. Beauty Culture
		3. Law Assistantship
		4. Primary Education
		5. Pre-school Education

Targets of Vocationalisation for 1985-86 to 1989-90

(i) 7.5 lakhs of students for 25 per cent diversion in +2 stage or 3.0 lakhs of students for 10 per cent diversion.
(ii) 1260 lakhs of school students for SUPW/WE.

(iii) 0.625 lakhs of new ITI level students.
(iv) 132 lakhs out of school population.
(v) 0.975 lakh of students for further education.
(vi) 2.0 lakhs of labour force and drop outs for further education.

Overall Plan Estimate for Vocationalisation of Education at 10 per cent Diversion of +2 Students (1985-86 to 1989-90)

	Item	*Cost in Rs. lakhs*	*Percentage of Cost*
1.	SUPW/WE for School Students classes I-XII	46092	20.89
2.	Higher Secondary Vocationalisation 10 per cent Diversion	53417	24.21
3.	Vocational Education and Training for out of School Education		
	(a) School-age	92235	41.79
	(b) Work Force	4000	1.82
4.	Further Education for School and ITI Students	24924	11.29
	Total	Rs 220668 lakhs (Rs 2206.68 crore)	100.00

Overall Plan Estimate for Vocationalisation of Education at 25 per cent Diversion of +2 Students (1985-86 to 1989-90)

	Item	*Cost in Rs. lakhs*	*Percentage of Cost*
1.	SUPW/WE for School Students classes I-XII	46092	15.88
2.	Higher Secondary Vocationalisation 25 per cent Diversion	122912	42.36
3.	Vocational Education and Training for out of School Education		
	(a) School-age	92235	31.79
	(b) Work Force	4000	1.38
4.	Further Education for School and ITI Students	24924	8.59
	Total	Rs 290163 lakhs (Rs 2901.63 crore)	100.00

Items of Cost for Vocational Education

1. Cost of contingencies for providing Socially Useful Productive Work (SUPW) and Work Experience (WE).
2. Cost in Vocational courses of +2 Stage.
3. Cost of District Vocational Surveys.
4. Cost of Apprenticeship Training (Stipend).
5. Cost Curriculum Development/Resources materials Preparation.
6. Teacher Training Cost.
7. Policy-making and Coordination.
8. Expenditure on R and D Evaluation and Monitoring Bodies.
9. Expenditure on Administration and Implementation.
10. Contingencies.
11. Cost on Education and Training for V+Drop outs, VIII+Drop outs.
12. Cost of Establishment of New Vocational Education Schools.
13. Cost of Vocational Training for the Labour Force.
14. Cost of Diploma Education of Vocational Students.
15. Cost of Advanced Diploma Programme for ITI students.
16. Cost of New Vocational Degree Programmes in Colleges.
17. Establishment of the New Community Colleges.

20

WOMEN'S EDUCATION

20.1 NATIONAL COMMISSION ON SELF EMPLOYED WOMEN AND WOMEN IN THE INFORMAL SECTOR (1987-88)[1]

Appointment of the Commission

The National Commission on Self-Employed Women and Women in the Informal Sector, constituted by the Government of India vide its notification No. 9-11/85 WW dated 5 January, 1987, to make a comprehensive study of the working and living conditions of poor women in poverty, submitted its report in June, 1988. Smt. Ela Bhatt (M.P.) was the Chairperson of the Commission.

Recommendations

I. Education is both an important instrument for increasing and bettering the chances of women's employability and for empowering women as they learn to think of themselves, become confident and also develop the capability of recognising more acutely the areas of exploitation. This fact has also been recognised and accepted in the National Policy on Education, 1986 by the Government, wherein it has been mentioned that:

> Education will be used as an agent of basic change in the status of women. In order to neutralise the accumulated distortions of the past, there will be a well-conceived edge in favour of women. The

1. Published by department of Women and Child Development, Ministry of Human Resources Development, Government of India, New Delhi.

National Education System will play a positive, interventionist role in the employment of women, it will foster the development of new values through redesigned curricula, textbooks, the training and orientation of teachers, decision-makers and administrators, and the active involvement of education institutions.

II. However, although in principle the fact of empowering women through education has been recognised in the National Policy on Education and Programme of Action, the Commission suggests the following steps be taken by which the working women themselves and their children, specially the girl child, may benefit.

1. Since one of the reasons for poor enrolment of a girl child and even poorer retention of their enrolment is their contribution in helping the working mothers in domestic work and looking after younger children, and also contributing to the family economy as child labour, it is necessary that there should be shifts for girls at suitable times so that they can assist their mothers in work and go to school. It should be possible for all the school going children in a family to attend the same shift, or else, the girl will be required to remain home to mind the younger children.

2. To encourage parents to send their girls to afternoon shifts, it should be desirable that a women helper is provided on an honorarium basis for accompanying the children from the house and back to ensure their enrolment and safety.

3. The same helper as mentioned at (2) above or another helper's services could be utilised for looking after the siblings below school age of the girls going to the school in the premises of the school staff. It may be a room, a verandah or a temporary shed constructed for the purpose.

4. It would be preferable to have a regular creche attached to the primary school where the younger children could be taken care of so that the older child can attend the school.

5. Incentives for sending the girls to school will have to be given to promote their education. In many states like Haryana, cash per month and free uniform is given to scheduled caste girls. Similar facilities including midday meals, free textbooks and exercise books, could be extended to all girls students at least up to the primary school level. If the girls are attracted to education, they are likely to move away eventually from the back breaking traditional occupation of their mothers to better employment.

6. The syllabi need to be more relevant for the children of rural areas. Practical subjects like animal husbandry, cattle care, soil conservation, agriculture, social forestry may be added and such options offered along with subjects like history, geography, modern science and physics.

7. Under the Government Scheme of Condensed Courses being implemented by the Central Social Welfare Board, the adolescent girls and above, who acquire education in a non-formal manner, have to appear in the same examination for which children from public schools from metropolitan cities also appear. This needs to be changed. In certain situations, a good grounding in languages, mathematics, general knowledge and some subjects relevant to their life situation, should suffice to get them a school certificate for the purpose of getting jobs at certain levels.

8. It has been mentioned in the Programme of Action, issued by the Ministry of Human Resource Development, that women teachers should be preferably recruited at the school level to give greater confidence to the parents to send their girl children to the school. The Commission would like to add that it is possible to have more women teachers only if they are posted in their home villages, or nearly villages to which they belong or into which they marry. Certain States have a policy not to post anyone within 20 km of their home town. Such a policy should be totally discouraged. Women employees, like teachers or extension workers need the security of the home and they cannot stay, away from their families because of the basic responsibility of looking after the children. And if married, the husband and wife should be posted in the same area or as close geographically possible.

9. The Commission recognises the fact that in the rural areas there are not enough trained women who can be appointed as teachers. Urban based teachers posted in rural areas do not tend to stay in the village to which they are posted, resulting in loss of school hours for the children. The Commission, therefore, recommends an innovation in the basic requirements of school teachers. For primary schools, girls who have completed secondary school or have achieved even middle school level, may be given an intensive training for a period of one year or nine months in certain training colleges of the State Government. Their training, boarding and lodging should be free. After the training, they should be posted in their home villages, or in the vicinity of their villages. Only in this manner, will it be possible for the

schools to have women teachers who will stay there and not absent themselves from schools. We wish to reiterate again, that increasing women teachers would have a direct bearing on the recruitment of girls which would, eventually, improve their chances of employment or self-employment in the non-traditional sector.

10. The primers under the adult education programme do not have sufficient material related to women workers which will be of interest to the labouring workers. There are certain exceptions. For example, the Commission's studies reveal that the primers in Tamil Nadu were of a high quality in this respect.

11. The textbooks both in the formal and informal educational systems perpetuate labouring women's invisibility and stereotyped sex biased concept of women. The revision of the textbooks and primers need to be carried out keeping the objective of bringing of women into greater focus.

12. Greater emphasis has to be given on the vocational aspect of education. More experiments need to be undertaken to combine general and vocational education, specially for the rural areas. For a country as large as ours and to cater to the needs of the vast majority of labouring women in poverty, there cannot be a single model of education. Various alternatives of education need to be developed. These alternatives may be developed in a decentralised manner, preferably with an area specific approach.

13. The vocational training, which is being imparted at present is also stereotyped and sex biased. Trades which are more remunerative, and involving modern technology, are by and large beyond the reach of girls thereby restricting their options for employment. This needs serious attention.

14. For the vocational training of girls, there should be a revolving fund from which they may be given scholarships to bear the cost of training and hostel facilities and they should reimburse the amount after they get suitable jobs. This amount can be recycled again to help their equally deprived sisters. Experience of a private trust in this regard has been successful. After the girls get vocational training, they must be helped in job placement.

15. It is necessary to convince the parents of poor girls regarding the relevance of education to the lives of their daughters. This is possible if education and vocational training have a direct relation to their chances of employability and leading to enhancement in their remuneration. further if the parents can be convinced that by providing

education, the girls would also have the option of alternative methods of employment, they may send their daughters for education more readily. One of the important reasons for women's submitting to exploitation is that that they do not have a viable economic alternative.

16. The Commission does realise that literacy in itself is not a solution to the basic problems of poor women, viz. exploitation and hunger; and therefore, literacy has to be understood in the wider context of the social structure. Therefore, the Commission recommends that any attempt to eradicate poverty should lead the women to deal with the question of equality, social justice and development.

20.2 NATIONAL PERSPECTIVE PLAN FOR WOMEN 1988 TO 2000 AD (1988)[2]

Introduction

Pandit Jawaharlal Nehru once said, "to awaken the people, it is the women who must be awakened once she is on the move, the family moves, the village moves and the nation moves".

Soviet President Mikhail Gorbachev, in his welcome address to the World Congress of Women at Moscow in June, 1987 said "The status of women is a barometer of the democratisation of any state an indicator of law human rights are respected in it".

The National Policy on Education 1986 in its section titled 'Education for Women's Equality' stated, "Education will be used as an agent of basic change in the status of women. In order to neutralize the accumulated distortion of the paste there will be a well-conceived edge in favour of women. The National Education System will play a positive interventionist role in the empowerment of women. It will foster the development of the new values through redesigned curricula, textbooks, training and orientation of teachers, decision-makers and administration."

It gives over-riding priority to the removal of women's illiteracy and obstacles inhibiting their access to and retention in elementary education. Emphasis has been said on women's participation in vocational technical and professional education at different levels as also to promote women's participation in non-traditional occupations

2. *Source*: *University News*, June 5, 1989.

and existing and emergent technologies.

The programme of Action for implementation of NPE (POA) spells out the meaning of women's empowerment:

> "Women become empowered through collective reflection and decision making. The parametres of empowerment are:
>
> – Building a positive self-image and self-confidence
> – Development ability to think critically
> – Building up group cohesion and fostering decision making and action
> – Ensuring equal participation in the process of bringing about social change
> – Encouraging group action in order to bring about change in the society
> – Providing the wherewithal for economic independence."

The programmes entails the following:

(i) A phased time bound programme of elementary education for girls. Particularly upto primary stage by 1990 and upto the elementary stage by 1995.

(ii) A phased time bound programme of adult education for women in the age-group 15-35 by 1995.

(iii) Increased women's access to vocational, technical, professional education and existing and emergent technologies, and

(iv) Review and re-organization of educational activities to ensure that they make a substantial contribution towards women's equality and creation of appropriate cells/units therefor.

National Literacy Mission (NLM) which aims at eradication of illiteracy in 15-35 age-group by 1995 concretises what is envisaged in NPE as regard illiteracy and adult education. The Mission document emphasis the importance of imbibing the values of national integration, conservation of environment, women's equality, observance of small family norm. etc. and goes on to say that "the focus of NLM would be on the rural areas, particularly women and persons belonging to the Scheduled Castes and Scheduled Tribes."

Perspective Plans for Women's Education up to 2000 A.D.

The programmes for women's education will have to be implemented as a priority so that women attain a comparable level of education by 2000 A.D. The strategy to be adopted for raising literacy levels and education among women has to keep in view the vast cultural, geographical and ecological variations as also the problems relating to poverty and ignorance. The cultural and geographical variations call for decentralization of educational planning. Within the national perspective, planning, implementation and monitoring of educational programmes has to be done at district and block levels, keeping in view the socio-economic and geographic parameters of the area. The vocational and occupational components have to be designed in accordance with the availability of resources and job opportunities in the regions. Voluntary organisations and women's group active in the area should be involved in the task.

In view of the social and cultural handicaps that have operated against women's education and taking account of the multiples roles that women are required to play, the need for adopting a set of objective specific to women's education is imperative. The objectives to be achieved by 2000 A.D. in regard to women's education are:

(i) Elimination of illiteracy, universalisation of elementary education and minimization of the elementary education and minimization of the dropout rate in the age group 6-14 years and stagnation to negligible proportions.

(ii) Ensuring opportunities to all women for access to appropriate level, nature and quality of education and also the wherewithal for, success comparable with men.

(iii) Substantial vocationalisation and diversification of secondary education so as to provide a wide scope for employment and economic independence of women.

(iv) Making education an effective means for women's equality by (a) Addressing ourselves to the constraints that prevent women from participating in the educational process; (b) Eliminating the existing sexist bias in the system; (c) Making necessary intervention in the content and processes of education to inclcate positive and egalitarian attributes; and (d) Ensuring that teacher's perceive this as one of their essential roles.

(v) Providing non-formal and part-time courses to women to enable them to acquire knowledge and skills for their social, cultural and economic advancement.

(vi) Impetus to enrol in various professional degree courses so as to increase their number in medicine, teaching, engineering and other fields substantially.

(viii) Creating a new system of accountability, particularly in respect of the basic educational services, to the local community, inter alia, by active involvement of women.

In brief, it is reiterated that the goals and strategies spelt out in the National Policy on Education, POA and the National Literacy Mission will ensure a much larger access for women to education.

High priority has to be accorded to creating awareness, through the various communication media, of the need for women's education and their active participation in economic and political development of the nation.

The curricula for school as well as university education have to be reviewed and revised so as to remove sex bias, inculcate among the masses a recognition of equality between men and women, and make women aware of their own potential as well as provide them necessary opportunities to develop their capabilities in every field. Greater accessibility of educational facilities to girls is to be achieved by reducing the distance of schools from village habitations, and expanding non-formal elementary education, adult education, and the open school system. Appointment of lady teachers in school would help draw more girls to schools and instil confidence among their parents. Towards this end, provision of quarters for lady teachers would be essential. Efforts should be directed at training local women as teachers. Provision of creche facilities and balwadis near the elementary and secondary schools for girls would enable the girls to attend schools and ensure care of younger siblings. Incentives like mid-day meals; better rates of scholarships, freeships, etc. would go a long way in preventing dropout.

Above all, better health facilities, smaller families, and relief from drudgery through improved technology for household chores, are essential pre-requisites for better enrolment of girls at schools and higher educational institutions. Inputs from other sectors are, therefore, important. Greater coordination of health, employment, welfare and education interventions will have an effect on the status of women and girls.

Accordingly to Educational Statistics for 1984-85 published by the Ministry of Human Resource Development, the enrolment of girls at primary level, which covers the age groups 6-11 years, is 331.9 lakhs. Surveys and field research have pointed out that there is 25 per cent inflation in the enrolment figures, and 22 per cent enrolment is outside the age group. Thus the effective enrolment gets reduced by about 47 per cent. Accordingly, the coverage for 1984-85 for the 6-11 years age group may be estimated as 176 lakhs. The population projected for the age group is 422.7 lakhs. This means that only 40.7 per cent of the girls in the age group 6-11 are enrolled in schools. On a similar basis, the enrolment of 11-14 years age group gets reduced to 48.1 lakhs (from 90.7 lakhs) which is only 19.2 per cent of the population of 249.9 lakhs estimated for the age groups. The population projections for the girls in the age group 6-11 years and 11-14 years for 1989-90 are 462 lakhs and 267 lakhs respectively. In order to have full coverage, the additional enrolment required would be 286 lakhs for 6-11 age group and 219 lakhs for 11-14 years age group, the total being nearly 5 crores. The task appears to be stupendous. Alongwith enrolment, there is the problem of very high dropout rates. Stemming from highly inflated enrolment rates and subsequent dropouts in the 6-11 years age group, enrolment of 11-14 years age group girls, even at primary level, may not be possible even by 1995.

In view of the social and cultural handicaps that have operated against women's education, the need for adopting a set of objectives specific to women's education is imperative. These would need to encompass the elimination of illiteracy and measures for retention of girls in schools,substantial vocationalisation and diversification to enhance economic opportunities for women improvement in the quality of education in terms of the values it promotes and inculcates, and finally the provision of access to professional courses for women. Such measures would be necessary as also efforts to remove the inherent prejudices working against women's education.

Recommendations

1. Awareness needs to be generated among the masses regarding the necessity of educating girls so as to prepare them to effectively contribute to the socio-economic development of the country, to strengthen their role in society and to realize their own capacities. The media and various forms of communication have to be geared to be this end.

2. A fruitful rapport has to be established between the community at large and the teachers and others education personnel. As per the Programme of Action under National Policy on Education -1986, every educational institution should actively participate in bringing about such awareness.
3. Involvement of local leaders. Voluntary agencies and women's groups is also necessary. Mahila mandals need to be *revitalized* and reoriented to provide and effective forum for the purpose. One measure to achieve this could be to assign the responsibility to mahila mandals for ensuring that all children in a community attend school. An incentive scheme should be introduced to motivate panchayats to ensure 100 per cent enrolment of girls in their respective villages.
4. Early childhood care and education introduces children into the school system gradually and smoothly. When children get used to attending schools, it ensures in some measuress retention of children, including girls, at elementary stages also. Hence there is need to have a comprehensive and effective programme of early childhood care and education linked to an integrated package of learning for women. The most comprehensive example of this is the Integrated Child Development Services Programme which needs to be universalized.
5. For improving enrolment and minimising drop-outs and wastages in case of girls students, it would be helpful if learning is made more attracted by providing adequate teaching materials in schools.
6. The number of teachers should also be increased so that the interaction between the teacher and the taught, which is so essential for good education, also increases. This would help in the retention of girls in schools and would be more effective if teachers from the area are employed. In single teacher schools, the teacher must be a women. In the case of two-teachers schools, at least one teacher must be a women. In the case of two-teachers schools, at least one teacher must be a women. In Orissa all jobs of primary teachers have been reserved for women.
7. School curricula should be imaginatively developed to stimulate creativity largely through play rather than overburdening children with formal or rote learning. Regional language should normally be the medium of instruction.
8. School timings should be flexible and fixed to suit local

conditions and the needs of the working girl and must be available within the walking distance of the child. A substantial increase is required in the number of schools for girls.

9. In addition to incentives like free textbooks, free supply of uniforms, award of attendance scholarships and mid-day meals, facilities such as proper school building safe drinking water, and toilets, etc. need to be provided to encourage school enrolment and retention of girls especially girls from educationally deprived social groups and from hilly, tribal, desert and remote rural areas and urban slums.
10. Local talent must be developed in order to meet the need for recruiting women teachers at the primary and elementary levels especially in rural and tribal areas. In this endeavour national agencies like CAPART and CSWB, voluntary agencies, mahila mandals and local self-government agencies can make a significant contribution. They can also play a useful watchdog function to ensure that educational and other programmes are run efficiently and effectively.
11. There should be a reservation of 50 per cent posts for women teachers in elementary schools. Women teachers working in the rural areas should be provided suitable accommodation.
12. Multi-entry system for girls who cannot attend schools continuously should be adopted.
13. Wherever necessary, schools meant exclusively for girls may be set up. The recommended distance of 3 kilometre for locating a middle school is a handicap for many girls. To ensure participation of girls in middle schools it is necessary to provide hostel facilities.
14. The Savitribai Phule Foster Parent Scheme of Maharashtra could be adopted in other States/Union Territories to help girls to poorer families to at least complete primary school. Under the Scheme, well to do persons and organizations are persuaded to adopt one or more out of school girls and contribute in cash or kind of both @ Rs. 25 per month for her education. The money can be spent on uniforms, stationery or anything else, needed by the girl or also partly used to alleviate the economic distress of the parents. The Zilla Parishad, Block Education Officer and head-master play a pivotal role in implementing the scheme, which is purely voluntary and if district level officers for coordination of programmes for women are appointed they could also actively take it up.

15. Condensed courses of education at elementary and middle school levels for girl must be started in all the rural areas and for weaker sections of the urban community.
16. Many girls in the 11-14 years age group would first have to be brought into the primary stage through non-formal education. By devising alternative education approaches non-formal Schooling and through like intelligent use of technology, the pace of middle school education can be accelerated. If retention up to 75 per cent is achieved upto class V, universal elementary education may be possible in some parts of the country by 2000 A.D. Other backward areas would have to be given much more attention in professional as well as financial terms to enable them even to universalize primary education for girls by 1995. The National Literacy Mission will used to address these issues on a priority basis.
17. Special efforts are necessary for bringing tribal children particularly girls into the schools system. Tribal dialects, extreme poverty, problems of commuting, rigidity of formal education and its irrelevance to the tribal culture and the tribals distrust of the ways of the mainstream society, must be borne in mind in formulating strategies.
18. The educational forecasts, may look more achievable if the system is opened up for flexible non-formal education which 'the below average states' should be persuaded to adopt in a large measure. The existing educational infrastructure particularly, in tribal and rural areas should be made effectively and responsible.
19. Non-formal education is an alternative to the formal system which has the potentiality of becoming the major programme of education for girls who cannot attained during normal school hours due to various reasons. The Central Government is already implementing a centrally sponsored scheme under which grants to the extent of 90 per cent are provided towards maintenance of non-formal education centres exclusively for girls in nine educationally backward States. This programme should be strengthened further and extended to other states where education of girls is lagging behind. It should at least cover all the pockets of low enrolment of girls and areas of high dropout rate. besides literacy, it must also provide relevant information on skill development and inculcation of positive self-image among girls.
20. Secondary education for girls should entail:

(i) A ten year course in general education learning an diversified higher secondary education which may be either terminal or lead to further professional preparation; and

(ii) Diversified courses after Grade VIII in technical subjects viz., agricultural technology, health services, food production activities such as, dairy and poultry and non-traditional areas need to be untroubled. A legal literacy component is also recommended at this stage.

21. Diversified courses leading to occupational preparation should be of parallel duration to the general secondary courses. In addition, there should be a variety of short and long term, whole time, part-time and apprentice courses. The trend of thinking is now to place emphasis on the last. Keeping in view the rapid modernization and advancement in technology for agriculture, there is an urgent need for skilled artisanship for promoting productive activities on the one hand, and a variety of learning programmes for adjustment of the rural society to social-economic change, on the other. Efforts should be made to ensure that girls have very opportunity to enter into apprenticeship in areas that are non-conventional and incentives be provided for the same. Further, at least 30 per cent seats should be reserved for girls in apprenticeship training courses on a non-transferable basis.
22. General and vocational training courses should be combined so that prospects of a career immediately on completion of schooling may attract girls from weaker sections. While designing the vocational courses, available occupational opportunities as well as the need to overcome market stereotypes should be kept in view.
23. Since secondary education has remained almost beyond the reach of weaker sections, liberal incentives and other facilities to release the girls from household chores appear to be essential. It would also help to locate the institutions in the areas of their habitation.
24. Multiple entry system should be introduced in the secondary classes. Part-time education facilities should also be made available.
25. Condensed courses should be organised in cooperation with local vocational training institutions to cover all rural area and areas inhabited by weaker sections in urban areas. Such courses may be

organized for small groups of girls, and combined with job training. Efforts should be made to cover at least 215 lakhs women in the age group 15-30 years under the condensed courses programme wherever possible the condensed courses of the CSWB should be expanded and strengthened. New programmes that are to be initiated must avoid duplication in the areas where the CSWB's programmes exist.

26. Correspondence courses and self study programme can be especially useful for girls desirous of continuing education but are unable to do so because of circumstances. Apart from imparting elementary education and knowledge about farming techniques, the curriculum of non student girls should include courses of training in occupational skills. Similar programmes should also be designed for girls in the urban areas.
27. The open school system should be expanded extending the facility to all the girls in rural and backward areas.
28. Science education for girls has been neglected so far. Secondary schools for girls must be helped to build good science programmes over the Eighth Five Year Plan. Special scholarships for girls opting for science courses need to be instituted at the secondary and higher education levels.
29. Special scholarships may also be offered to rural women, who opt for teachers' training, especially those who complete the condensed courses at the secondary stage.
30. There is a need to open more colleges and polytechnics for girls, especially in rural areas.
31. Incentives like scholarships, freeships, etc., should be provided to enable girls from rural areas to pursue higher education for girls belonging to weaker sections. In addition to freeships and scholarships, bursaries should also be provided to meet their requirements for food and lodging.
32. Girls should be encouraged to enter professional courses. Reservation of seats for girls in such courses may be considered to level out the existing bias in access to certain professional streams.
33. Vocational counselling and guidance service should be organized exclusively in a more meaningful way to help girls in colleges and universities opt for suitable courses relevant to their talents and interests, and free of traditional bias.
34. Vocational and technical education for women, both formal and

non-formal, should be a major feature of the programmes of rural universities. The women's wings of the universities could undertake large scale extension programmes in order to activate girls and women in the surrounding areas to take advantage of educational and occupational facilities of various types, particularly those leading to meaningful employment, essential for reducing women's marginalization.

35. In order to increase the representation of rural girls in higher education courses, 30 per cent seats, may be reserved for girls to begin with.
36. All agencies involved with preparation of curricula prescription of textbooks and organization of educational processes will have to evince awareness towards women's issues. University/College Departments of Women's Studies appropriate voluntary agencies; women's groups, etc. should be involved in giving a new perspective to the various issues of content and processes of education. Women's universities and women's centres in colleges need to take an active role in women's development and in influencing the attitudes of future generations.
37. Facilities for part-time self study and correspondence courses should be provided on a large scale to enable girls who are not in a position to join higher educational institutions on a regular basis, to continue their studies.
38. In addition to courses leading to degree/diploma, short courses in specific subjects through summer school sessions, and ad hoc programmes like seminars, workshops, etc., should be organized for working women with a view to upgrading their knowledge and skills, not necessarily leading to degrees.
39. Integrated learning programmes for women are recommended which will not only lay emphasis on literacy but on empowering women through awareness building on social issues, bringing about attitudinal change, promoting skill training for employment, providing information on health care, nutrition and hygiene as well as on legal rights. Such programmes are beginning and must continue to be designed and structured so as to be relevant for the vast majority of rural women. The revised scheme linked to ICDS known as the 'Women's Integrated Learning for Life', should be introduced as an integral part of the non-formal education system.
40. Entrepreneurship development programmes should be organized

separately for education of women in the age group 18-30 years, with a minimum of matriculation level of education. The objective of such training should be to (i) Make them aware of the various opportunities for self-employment; (ii) Motivate them to take up self-employment; (iii) Impart needed skills and training; (iv) Promote motivation for achievement among them; and (v) Create access to resources such as capital credit, etc.

41. A large number of girls cannot participate in whole-day education programmes. Provision of non-formal and part-time programmes, with flexible school hours and sensitivity to the agricultural cycle are, of particular importance. In addition to the primary and upper primary stage, distance learning opportunities need to be provided at secondary and higher secondary level.

42. Adult education will have to be composed of three inter-related stands aimed at:

    (i) Continuous flow of new information especially to rural and tribal areas, particularly to inculcate positive attitudes towards women;
    (ii) Continuous training of the people in the use of modern tools and methods of production; and
    (iii) Acquisition of permanent reading and computation skills.

    Following from the above, three types of programmes may be offered to the learner:

    (i) Information and literacy
    (ii) Information and training in new technology and literary
    (iii) Information and training in new technology with or without literacy. Continuous information flows relating to human affairs, gender relations and the use of science and technology for betterment of life would be the common factor in all the three programmes.

43. The growing availability of communication media should be directed towards keeping up information flows and portraying positive images of women in non-conventional roles. Audio-visual materials, combined with non-formal training arrangements, could impart to various population groups the kind of instruction, they need in the use of new technologies.

Involvement of mass media in motivating women to attend literacy classes is most essential.

44. Rapid strides in the development of technologies and tools for the reduction in women's drudgery and easy access to work places, water and fuel supply, child care, health services and population control can contribute significantly to the success of learning programmes for women. Women's literacy programmes would succeed better if they centre around women's concerns and also provide opportunities of recreation and sharing of experiences.
45. District plans should be prepared keeping in view literacy requirements of the learners, identifying agencies which can take up such programmes in districts.
46. All women working in industries or employed elsewhere should be made literate by the employers by allotting time from the working hours for their education. Place of teaching, teachers and teaching material should be arranged by them. Necessary legislation to this effect may be enacted.
47. At least 50 per cent seats in pre-service courses in all teachers training institutions should be reserved for women. Spatial planning to ensure that women from rural areas are selected as teachers is essential.
48. Provision of composite teacher training courses for women who have had insufficient education to improve their educational qualifications along with their training, should be made.
49. The existing Integrated Rural Development Programme. National Rural Employment Programme, Development of Women and Children in Rural Areas, Training of Youth in Self-Employment Programme, Integrated Child Development Programme, etc. should have a component of literacy for their women beneficiaries. Training should be provided to the functionaries of various development departments by the Directorate of Education in the States.
50. The State Resources Centres should produce suitable learning material for women on a priority basis. Literature for neoliterates should be suitably devised by experts, keeping in view the needs of different groups of learners.
51. Decentralisation is the key to the successful application of the strategies outlined above. In this decentralised approach, the village cluster or the block level is seen as most appropriate for the delivery of programmes. It is, therefore, necessary that the

block is allocated a flexible budget so as to make funds available to village clusters/villages for innovative educational activities and for equalisation of educational opportunity.

52. An overall coordination of health, welfare and educational inputs would be most desirable. This would entail (a) Convergent policies in these sectors; (b) Coordination of delivery mechanisms, and (c) Pooling of allocations.
53. The strategies spelt out in the National Policy of Education 1986, the Programme of Action for its implementation and the National Literacy Mission and the successful achievement of the goals, imposed in these documents would be important for improvement in the status of women.

21

RESOLUTION ON NATIONAL YOUTH POLICY[1]

Introduction

Youth, in all ages, has been in the vanguard of progress and social change. Thirst for freedom, impatience for quicker pace of progress and a passion for innovation, coupled with idealism and creative fervour, saw the youth in the forefront of the freedom struggle in our own land. If our youth was inspired by the call of the Father of the Nation in first half of this century, the youth of today face the challenge of economic development and technological progress with social justice.

2. The youth of India, representing a third of our population, constitute a vital and vibrant human resource. They have a right, as well as an obligation, to participate actively in national development and in shaping the DESTINY OF THE NATION which is, in point of fact, their own destiny. Their problems are many and varied and their aspirations naturally high, in a country with a great Past and greater promise for the future. The need, therefore, is to create increasing opportunities for them to develop their personality and their functional capability and thus make them economically productive and socially useful.

3. Such opportunities have to be created on a large scale, to cover a wide spectrum of areas of human endeavour; and they have to be made available to youth of all strata.

---

1. Issued by the Ministry of Human Resource Development, Department of Youth Affairs and Sports, Government of India, New Delhi on 15 May, 1989.

4. Special efforts will be made to foster and develop contacts between youth from different parts of the country, with a view to inspire them to combat regionalism, communalism, linguistic chauvinism and other divisive and fissiparous tendencies, through participation in the programme of *ANTAR BHARATI*.

5. Meaningful programmes of mass education, formal and non-formal, will be undertaken, so that the benefits of education reach all young men and women, including non-student rural youth, with particular emphasis on the disadvantaged sections of our society.

6. Training programmes will be organised, aimed at imparting requisite skills to youth for self-employment improving their employability and enhancing their productivity, while making them appreciate the dignity of labour.

7. Programmes will be undertaken to offer opportunities to the youth for leadership training through personality development and character building, and for motivating them to voluntary social and community service.

8. Promotion of physical fitness through mass participation in *yoga*, indigenous games and modern sports will be made an integral part of all youth programmes, together with adventure activities calculated to develop the spirit at risk-taking, team work and endurance.

9. Young parents will be particularly sensitized to their responsibilities and their own role as catalyst of social change, by being involved in movements against various social ills and harmful practices.

ALTERNATIVE EDUCATION POLICY (1989)

An alternative education policy was formulated by the All-India 'Save Education Committee'. It seeks replacement of the National Policy on Education (1986).

Explaining the key features of the final document entitled "Towards a people's policy on education: an alternative to NPE 1986", prepared by the committee, its president, Mr. Justice V.R. Krishna lyer, former Supreme Court judge, said at a meeting, organised that the alternative policy aimed at providing education for all to promote scientific temper, a democratic and secular approach to life and social awareness. It sought to protect institutional autonomy, the rights of the academic community and democratic process of decision-making. The Central and the State Governments should bear the entire expenditure for education and ban capitation fees, donations, etc. which had assumed menacing proportion, it said.

Vocationalisation

The document lays less stress on cultivation of theoretical and fundamental knowledge together with their practical application it favour vocationalisation after the plus 2 level so that the humanitarian aspects of education are not denied to students in their formative years.

The disadvantaged sections of the community would need special and additional facilities. The policy would cover a detailed programme of education, starting from pre-school to post-graduate research and medical, engineering and law studies and suggest measures for launching a nation-wide adult education and non-formal education programmes as an "additional facility".

Ethical Norms

The paper called for cultivating and upholding ethical norms by all concerned with education. Mr. Krishna lyer hoped it would act as a catalyst to promote a national debate to compel the Centre to withdraw its non-egalatirian policy announced in 1986.

Criticising the Centre's New Education Policy, he said it only sought to perpetuate the elitist interests of the ruling class. The one-school for each district programme with barely 100 students, envisaged under the Navodaya Schools meant that a vast majority of the population would be denied the benefits of education while the privileged few would continue to have their stranglehold on the socio-economic system. The educationally rich would grow richer and the poor poorer under the NPE 1986, he said.

Explaining the far-reaching implications of the NPE, 1986, which sought to consolidate 'Doonocracy', instead of democracy in the country, Mr. Krishna Iyer called upon the people to join the campaign for a nation-wide movement for withdrawal of the Centre's ill-designed policy. "India became free in the first half of this century. Let us free Indians in the second half" he said.

Brazen Onslaught

The presidium of the committee has condemned the trend towards privatisation and commercialisation of education. The proposal to disaffiliate colleges from universities could turn the latter into mere administrative offices instead of "models" of academic institutions. Secular and scientific principles of education had been replaced by obscurantist and divisive elements.

APPENDIX II

COMMITTEE TO REVIEW NATIONAL POLICY ON EDUCATION, 1986 (1990)

Seventeen-member committee to review the 1986 national education policy and recommend the measures for taking the country towards a "genuinely egalitarian and secular social order was announced in the Lok Sabha on May 7, 1990.

The committee is required to submit its report within six months.

Composition

1. Acharya Ramamurti Eminent Educationist – Chairman
2. The members of the committee are: Prof. CNR Rao, Director, Indian Institute of Science, Bangalore, Dr Sukhdev Singh, Former Vice-Chancellor of the Punjab and MP Agricultural Universities, Dr. M.Santappa, former Vice-Chancellor of Madras University, Dr Obaid Siddiqui, FRS, Tata Institute of Fundamental Research, Bombay, Dr Bhaskar Roy Chaudhary, Vice-Chancellor , Calcutta University, Calcutta, Mr M. G. Bhativadekar, former principal of Maharaja College, Jaipur, Prof. Usha Mehta, political scientist and teacher, Bombay.

   Prof. Sachchidanand Murthy, head of the department of Asian Philosophies and Cultures and principal, University Post-graduate Centre, Guntur, A.P., Dr. Anil Sadgopal, Kishore Bharati, Hoshangabad, Father TV Kunnunkal, Chairman, National Open School, New Delhi, Prof. Mrinal Miri, Professor of Philosophy, North Eastern Hill University, Shillong, Dr Vidy Niwas Mishra, Vice-Chancellor, Kashi Vidyapeeth, Varanasi, Dr S.Z. Qasim, Vice-Chancellor, Jamia Millia Islamia, New Delhi, Mr Veda Vyasa, Chairman, DAV College Management Committee, New Delhi, Mr Manubhai Pancholi, Lok Bharati, Sanosara, district Bhavnagar, Mr S. Gopalan, Additional Secretary, Ministry of Human Resources Development, Department of Education.

APPENDIX III

THE HOSPITALS AND OTHER INSTITUTIONS (REDRESSAL OF GRIEVANCES OF EMPLOYEES) BILL (1987)[1]

A
BILL

to provide for the redressal of grievances of employees in hospitals and certain other institutions and for matters connected therewith or incidental thereto.

BE it enacted by Parliament in the Thirty-eighth Year of the Republic of India as follows:

CHAPTER I

PRELIMINARY

Short title, extent, commencement and application

1. (1) This Act may be called the Hospitals and Other Institutions (Redressal of Grievances of Employees) Act, 1987.
   (2) It extends to the whole of India.
   (3) It shall come into force on such date as,–

      (a) the Central Government may, in relation to any establishment under the control of the Central Government or any establishment wholly or substantially financed by the Central Government, by notification in the Official Gazette, appoint; and
      (b) the State Government may, in relation to any other establishment in a State, by notification in the Official

1. Bill No L II of 1987, Introduced in Rajya Sabha, by the then Union Minister of State for Labour, Shri P.A. Sangma.

Gazette,

appoint, and different dates may be appointed for different provisions of this Act, and any reference in any such provision to the commencement of this Act shall be constructed as a reference to the coming into force of that provision.

(4) Subject to the provisions contained in section 19, it applies–

(a) to every hospital, educational scientific, research or training institution;

(b) to every institution owned or managed by an organisation wholly or substantially engaged in any charitable, social or philanthropic service;

(c) to every institution engaged in khadi and village industries wherein ten or more persons are employed or were employed, on any day of the preceding twelve months.

Definitions

2. In this Act, unless the context otherwise requires–

(a) "appropriate Government" means–

(i) in relation to any establishment under the control of the Central Government or any establishment wholly or substantially financed by the Central Government the Central Government; and
(ii) in relation to any other establishment, the State Government;

(b) "award" means an interim or final determination of any collective grievance by an arbitrator or Board of arbitrators;
(c) "educational institution" includes–

(i) any University;
(ii) any college, whether or not affiliated to a University;
(iii) any school, whether or not recognised or aided by Government;
(iv) any scientific institution;

(v) any institution being an institution or a part of any other institution, which is not established with the imparting of education as one of its primary objects and in which–

(1) research in respect of any matter is carried on;
(2) the activity of imparting knowledge or training is systematically carried on;

(d) "employee" means any person (including an apprentice) employed in any establishment for hire or reward whether the terms of employment be express or implied, and for the purposes of 40 any application under this Act in relation to any grievance, includes any such person who has been dismissed, discharged or retrenched in connection with or as a consequence of that grievance or whose dismissal, discharge or retrenchment has led to that grievance, but does not include any such person–

(i) who is subject to any law for the time being in force relating to any Armed Forces of the Union;
(ii) who is employed mainly in a managerial or administrative capacity or who, being employed in a supervisory capacity, draws wages exceeding one thousand and six hundred rupees per mensem;

(e) "employer",–

(i) in relation to an establishment under the control of any department of the Central Government or a State Government, means the authority notified by the Head of the department in this behalf, or where no such authority is notified, the head of the department;
(ii) in relation to an establishment under the control of a local authority, means the chief executive officer of that authority;
(iii) in relation to any other establishment, means any person responsible for the supervision and control of the establishment;

(f) "establishment" means any hospital or other institution to which this Act applies;

(g) "hospital" includes a nursing home, a dispensary or other institution, for the treatment, or for the reception and treatment, of persons requiring medical attention or rehabilitation;

(h) "Khadi" has the meaning assigned to it in clause (d) of section 2 of the Khadiland Village Industries Commission Act, 1956 (61 of 1956)

(i) "lock-out" means the temporary closing of an establishment or the suspension of work or the refusal by an employer to continue to employ any number of persons employed by him;

(j) "registered union or association" means a trade union registered under the Trade Unions Act, 1926 (15 of 1926), or an association registered under the societies Registration, Act, 1860 (21 of 1860) or under any corresponding law for the time being in force in a State;

(k) "regulations" means the regulations made by the employer in relation to an establishment or as the case may be the model regulations set out in the Schedule;

(l) "strike" means a cessation of work by a body of persons employed in an establishment acting in combination or a concerted refusal or a refusal under a common understanding of any number of persons who are or have been so employed to continue to work or to accept employment;

(m) "University means a University as defined in clause (f) of section 2 of the University Grants Commission Act, 1956 (3 of 1956) and includes–

(i) any institution of higher education, other than a University, declared by the central Government under section 3 of the University Grants Commission Act, 1956 (3 of 1956), as an institution deemed to be a University for the purposes of that Act; and

(ii) any other institution which, under a Central Act, a Provincial Act or a State Acct, is empowered to hold examinations and grant degrees, diplomas or certificates;

(n) "village industries" has the meaning assigned to it in clause (h) of section 2 of the Khadi and Village Industries Commission Act, 1956 (61 of 1956).

(o) "Wages" means all remuneration capable of being expressed in terms of money, which would, if the terms of employment, express or implied, were fulfilled, be payable to an employee in respect of his employment or of work done in such employment, and includes–

(i) such allowances (including dearness allowance) as the employee is for the time being entitled to;
(ii) the value of any house accommodation, or of supply of light, water, medical attendance or other amenity or of any service or of any concessional supply of foodgrains or other articles;
(iii) any travelling concession,

but does not include–

(a) any bonus;
(b) any contribution paid or payable by the employer to any pension fund or provident fund or for the benefit of the employee under any law for the time being in force;
(c) any gratuity payable on the termination of his service.

CHAPTER II

AUTHORITIES UNDER THE ACT

Grievance Redressal Authority and Appellate Authority

3.(1) Every employer in relation to any establishment shall, within a period of sixty days from the date of commencement of this Act or from the date on which such establishment comes into being, whichever is later, appoint–

(a) a person eligible under the regulations to be appointed as the grievance redressal authority, as the Grievance Redressal Authority in relation to such establishment; and
(b) a person eligible under the regulations to be appointed as an appellate authority, as the Appellate Authority in relation to such establishment,

who shall discharge their assigned functions in respect of grievances in relation to any of the conditions of service of any employee (here in after referred to as individual grievance).

(2) Every appointment made under sub-section (1) shall, within a period of fifteen days from such appointment, be communicated to such officer as the appropriate Government may, be notification in the Official Gazette, specify in this behalf (hereinafter referred to as the specified officer) and copies thereof shall also be forwarded to the registered union or association, if any, functioning in the establishment concerned.

(3) Where an employer fails to appoint a Grievance Redressal Authority or an Appellate Authority under sub-section (1), the appropriate Government or the specified officer may, be notice in writing, require the employer to make such appointment within seven days of the receipt of such notice.

(4) Where an employer fails to comply with a notice under sub-section (3), the appropriate Government or the specified officer may itself make such an appointment.

(5) Subject to the regulations, the Grievance Redressal Authority or the Appellate Authority appointed under this section shall have power to regulate its own procedure.

CHAPTER III

REDRESSAL OF GRIEVANCES

Employee to make regulation in regard to certain matters

4. (1) Every employer in relation to an establishment shall make regulations to provide for the following matters, namely:–

(a) eligibility of persons to be appointed as the Grievance Redressal Authority or the Appellate Authority;
(b) the procedure to be followed by the Grievance Redressal Authority or the Appellate Authority, as the case may be.

(2) Every regulation made under sub-section (1) (including any modification there to) shall be–

(a) forwarded by registered post to the specified officer and to the registered union or association, if any, functioning in the establishment concerned; and

(b) notified on the notice board of the establishment.

(3) Every regulation referred to in sub-section (1) shall be forwarded to the persons referred to in clause (a) of sub-section (2) by the employer in relation to an establishment within a period of sixty days from the date of commencement of this Act or from the date on which such establishment comes into being, whichever is later, and every modification to such regulation shall be forwarded by the employer to the said persons within a period of sixty days from the date on which such modification is made.

(4) The employer shall supply to every employee, on a request made therefore, a copy of the regulations (including any modification there to) forwarded to the specified officer and the registered union or 'association, if any, under sub-section (2).

(5) Until regulations are made by an employer in relation to an establishment with respect to the matters mentioned in sub-section (1), the model regulations with respect to those matters as specified in the Schedule shall be deemed to be the regulations with respect to those matters in relation to such establishment.

Redressal of individual grievance

(5) (1) Any employee who has an individual grievance may apply to the Grievance Redressal Authority, established for the establishment in which he is employed, for the redressal of the grievance.

(2) The Grievance Redressal Authority shall, after giving such employee and his employer (hereafter in this section referred to as parties to the grievance) a reasonable opportunity of being heard and after making such inquiry as it deems fit, pass such order in respect of such grievance as it deems to be just and appropriate, and such order shall, subject to the other provisions of this section, be final.

(3) The Grievance Redressal Authority shall endeavour to pass a final order on an application made to it under sub-section (1) within a period of sixty days from the date on which such application is made.

(4)Where–

(a) the Grievance Redressal Authority fails to pass the final order in respect of any individual grievance within the period specified therefore under sub-section (3), any party to the grievance; or

(b) any party to the grievance is aggrieved by the final order of the Grievance Redressal Authority, such aggrieved party,

may, within a period of forty-five days from the date on which the Grievance Redressal Authority should have passed its final order on the grievance under this section or, as the case may be, from the date of such final order, prefer an appeal to the Appellate Authority referred to in clause (b) of sub-section (1) of section 3:

Provided that the Appellate Authority may, if it is satisfied that the appellant was prevented by sufficient cause from preferring the appeal within the period hereinbefore specified, allow it to be presented within a further period not exceeding thirty days.

(5) The Appellate Authority shall, after giving the parties to the appeal a reasonable opportunity of being heard and after making such inquiry as it deems fit, pass such order in respect of the grievance as it deems to be just and appropriate and such order shall, subject to the provisions of sub-section (7), be final.

(6) The Appellate Authority shall endeavour to pass a final order on an appeal made to it under sub-section (4) within a period of ninety days from the date on which such appeal is made.

(7) Where–

(a) the Appellate Authority fails to pass the final order in respect of any individual grievance within the period specified there for under sub-section (6), any party to the grievance; or

(b) any party to the grievance is aggrieved by the final order of the Appellate Authority, such aggrieved party,

may, within a period of forty-five days from the date on which the Appellate Authority should have passed its final order on the grievance under this section, or as the case may be, from the date of such final order, prefer an appeal to the Tribunal constituted by the appropriate Government by notification in the Official Gazette consisting of only one person who has, at least five years, held a civil judicial post in the State:

Provided that the Tribunal may, if it is satisfied that the appellant was prevented by sufficient cause from preferring the appeal within the period hereinbefore specified, allow it to be presented within a further period not exceeding thirty days:

Provided further that a Tribunal appointed by a State Government and specified in this behalf by the Central Government, shall be competent to entertain an appeal in relatio to any grievance in an establishment for which the Central Government is the appropriate Government.

(8) The shall endeavour to pass a final order on an appeal made to it under sub-section (7) within a period of ninety days from the date on which such appeal a preferred.

Provided that where the parties to the grievance jointly apply for the extension of such period for any reason and the Tribunal considers it necessary or expedient to extend such period it may, for reasons to be recorded in writing, extend such period by such further period as it may deem fit.

(9) The Tribunal shall, after giving the parties a reasonable opportunity of being heard and after making such inquiry as it deems fit, pass such order in respect of the grievance as it deems to be just and appropriate and such order shall be final.

Enforceability of orders

6. Every order of the Grievance Redressal Authority or the Appellate Authority or the Tribunal under this Act shall come into operation on and from such date (including a date preceding the date of the order) as may be specified therein, but where no such date is specified, it shall come into operation on the date of the order.

Persons on whom orders are binding

7. The order of the Grievance Redressal Authority or of the Appellate Authority, or of the Tribunal in an individual grievance shall be binding on–

(a) the parties to the individual grievance; and
(b) where a party referred to in clause (a) is an employer, his heirs, successors or assigns in respect of the establishment to which the grievance relates.

Prohibition of strikes or lockouts

8. (1) During the period of pendency of any proceeding in

connection with any grievance before any authority under this Act:–

(a) no employee shall go on strike or indulge in any other form of cessation or retardation of work, such as, work to rule, go slow, *gherao* or the like in breach of contract;

(b) no employer shall lock-out his employees.

Explanation – In this section "period of pendency" includes a period not exceeding fifteen days during which the matter is pending with the appropriate Government for reference of the grievance to a Board of arbitrators referred to in section 10.

(2) No person shall instigate or incite any other person to take part in or otherwise act in furtherance of a matter referred to in sub-section (1).

CHAPTER IV

COLLECTIVE GRIEVANCES

Management Council

9. (1) Every employer in relation to any establishment shall, within such time as may be specified by the appropriate Government in this behalf, appoint a Management Council consisting of members not less than two and not more than ten representing both the employer and the employees which shall discharge its assigned functions in respect of any grievance specified in sub-section (9) (hereinafter referred to as the collective grievance).

(2) Subject to the rules made by the appropriate Government, the term of office of the members of the Management Council appointed under sub-section (1) shall be three years.

(3) The number of members representing the employees in the Management Council shall be equal to the number of members representing the employer.

(4) The members of the Management Council representing the employer shall be nominated by the employer and the members of the Management Council representing the employees shall be chosen by registered unions or associations on the basis of their proportionate membership of employees in the establishment and only such unions or associations which have not less than ten per cent of the membership

of employees of such establishment shall be eligible for nominating a member:

Provided that where there is no registered union or association representing the employees in such establishment or such union or association has not the required membership of employees of such establishment, the representation of the employees in the Management Council shall be made in such manner as may be prescribed.

(5) The meetings of the Management Council shall be presided over alternatively be a member representing the employer and a member representing the employees.

(6) Subject to the rules made by the appropriate Government the Management Council shall have power to regulate its own procedure.

(7) The Management Council shall promote harmonious relations between the employer and his employees and shall advise the employer to frame bye-laws regarding conditions of service of and conduct and discipline in relation to the employees of the establishment.

(8) Where any Management Council has been established for any establishment any collective grievance shall at the instance of the employees representing not less than ten per cent of the employees in the establishment, or registered unions or associations representing the employees in the Management Council be referred to the Management Council for settlement.

(9) The grievance which can be referred to the Management Council under sub-section (8) shall be the grievance relating to–

(a) wages including period and mode of payment;
(b) compensatory and other allowances;
(c) hours of work and rest intervals;
(d) leave with wages and holidays;
(e) retirement benefits.

(10) Where any collective grievance is referred to the Management Council it shall make all efforts to promote a fair and amicable settlement of such grievance.

(11) The settlement, referred to in sub-section (10) and arrived at between the parties to a collective grievance, shall be recorded in the form of a memorandum and signed by the parties to the grievance or their authorised representatives.

(12) The members of the Management Council shall be paid by the employer such travelling and other compensatory allowances as the

appropriate Government may specify by rules.

Arbitration

10. (1) Where the Management Council fails to settle any collective grievance referred to it under section 9 within a period of ninety days from the date on which such reference is made, it shall, at the instance of either party, refer the grievance for arbitration to an arbitrator, agreed to by the parties to the grievance or, where the parties to such grievance fail to agree on the arbitrator, such grievance shall be referred by the appropriate Government to a Board of arbitrators constituted by it on a request made in that behalf by either party:

Provided that a reference for arbitration to an arbitrator or a Board of arbitrators shall specify the period within which such arbitrator or the Board of arbitrators shall submit its award on such grievance:

Provided further that where the parties to the grievance jointly apply for the extension of such period for any reason, and the arbitrator or the Board of arbitrators considers it necessary or expedient to extend such period, he or it may, for reasons to be recorded in writing, extend such period by such further period as he or it may deem fit.

(2) The Board of arbitrators referred to in sub-section (1) shall consist of an independent person having judicial experience who shall be the Chairman thereof and two other members, one on behalf of the employer in relation to the establishment to which the collective grievance relates and the other on behalf of the employees of such establishment.

(3) Where the members of a Board of arbitrators are divided in their opinion, the decision of the majority shall be deemed to be the award for the purpose of this Act.

(4) the Appropriate Government may make rules for the functioning of the arbitrators and the Board of arbitrators and the qualifications required by a person to be appointed as an arbitrator and a member of the Board of arbitrators.

(5) For the purpose of choosing arbitrators by the employer and employees, the appropriate Government shall maintain a panel of persons eligible for appointment as arbitrators.

(6) The arbitrator or the Board of arbitrators shall after giving the parties to the application and the financial institutions which are likely to have substantial financial or other interests in the settlement of the collective grievance a reasonable opportunity of being heard and after

making such inquiries as it, deems fit, pass such award in respect of the said grievance as it deems to be just and appropriate, and such award shall be final.

(7) Notwithstanding anything contained in this Act, the appropriate Government may, if it is of opinion that a collective grievance, in relation to a class or category of establishments, involves issues which may affect the national economy or social justice or the interest of the general public, refer that grievance to a Board of arbitrators for its award and the award given by such Board of arbitrators shall apply to such class or category of establishments.

(8) The remuneration payable to an arbitrator or a member of a Board of arbitrators for arbitrating any collective grievance referred to them for arbitration shall be such as may be specified by rules made by the appropriate Government and shall be paid by such of the parties to the said grievance and in such proportion as the arbitrator or a Board of arbitrators may determine.

(9) Every arbitrator or Board of arbitrators shall have the same powers as are vested in a civil court under the Code of Civil Procedure 1908 (5 of 1908) when trying a suit in respect of the following matters namely:–

(a) summoning and enforcing the attendance of any person and examining him on oath;
(b) compelling the production of documents and material objects;
(c) issuing commissions for examination of witnesses; and
(d) such other matters as may be specified by rules made by the appropriate Government.

(10) Nothing in the Arbitration Act 1940 (10 of 1940) shall apply to any arbitration under this Act.

Award

11. (1) The arbitrator or the Board of arbitrators shall give notice in writing to the parties to the collective grievance regarding the date on which the award shall be announced.

(2) An award shall, as far as practicable, be announced in the presence of parties to the grievance.

(3) The award of the arbitrator or the Board of arbitrators shall be

final and binding on both the employer and employees and shall be enforceable on the expiry of thirty days from the date of the award.

(4) Where the appropriate Government is of the opinion that it will not be expedient, on public grounds affecting national economy or social justice to give effect to the whole or any part of the award, that Government may, by notification in the Official Gazette, declare that such award shall not become enforceable on the expiry of the period referred to in sub-section (3).

(5) Where a declaration has been made under sub-section (4), the appropriate Government may, within ninety days from the date of the award by notification in the Official Gazette, make an order rejecting or modifying the award and shall on the first available opportunity lay the award together with a copy of the order before the Legislature of the State, if the order has been made by the State Government or before the Parliament, if the order has been made by the Central Government.

(6) Where an award, as rejected or modified by the appropriate Government, is laid before the Legislature of the State or as the case may be, before Parliament, such award shall become enforceable on the expiry of fifteen days from the date on which it is so laid and where no order as contemplated in sub-section (5) is made in pursuance of a declaration under sub-section (4), the award shall become enforceable on the expiry of ninety days referred to in sub-section (5).

(7) Subject to the provisions contained in sub-sections (3) and (6) the award shall come into force with effect from such date as may be specified therein but where no date is specified it shall come into force on the date on which the award becomes enforceable under sub-section (3) or sub-section (6), as the case may be.

Conditions of service, etc. to remain unchanged under certain circumstances during pendency of proceedings

12. During the pendency of any proceeding in connection with any grievance before any authority under this Act, no employer shall alter to the prejudice of the employee the conditions of service applicable to him immediately before the commencement of such proceeding or shall discharge or punish by way of dismissal or otherwise any such employee except with the prior permission in writing of the said authority.

Employer to codify terms and conditions of service of his employees

13. Notwithstanding anything contained in the Industrial Employment (Standing Orders) Act, 1946, (20 of 1946) every employer shall in consultation with the Management Council referred to in section 9, make bye-laws for codifying the conditions of service, conduct, discipline and other matters in respect of his employees within a period of six months from the date of appointment of such Management Council and every employer shall lay before the Management Council the bye-laws, by whatever name called as in force on the date of commencement of this Act concerning the conditions of service, conduct, discipline and other matters in respect of his employees.

CHAPTER V

PENALTIES

Penalties

14. (1) Any employer who–

(a) refuses or fails to appoint a Grievance Redressal Authority or an Appellate Authority as required under this Act or fails to communicate any such appointment; or
(b) fails to constitute a Management Council within the time specified under sub-section (1) of section 9; or
(c) refuses or fails to comply with any order of a Grievance Redressal Authority which has become final or any order of an Appellate Authority; or
(d) fails to codify the terms and conditions of service of his employees within the period specified under section 13; or
(e) fails to carry out such directions as may be given to him by the appropriate Government or the specified officer under section 17; or
(f) acts in contravention of the rules or regulations made under this Act.

shall be punishable with imprisonment for a term which may extend to six months or with fine which may extended to ten thousand rupees or with both and if any such contravention is continued after conviction, with a further fine which may extend to two thousand rupees for each day on which the contravention is so continued.

(2) An employee who resorts to strike or indulges in other form of cessation or retardation of work in any establishment, such as, work to rule, go slow, *gherao* or the like in violation of the provisions of this Act shall be punishable with imprisonment of not less than one month but which may extend to three months and with fine which may extend to one thousand rupees.

(3) Any person who instigates or incites others to take part in or otherwise acts in furtherance of an offence referred to in sub-section (2) shall be punishable with imprisonment of not less than two months but which may extend to six months and with fine which may extend to ten thousand rupees.

(4) any employer who resorts to lock-out in violation of the provisions of this Act shall be punishable with imprisonment of not less than one month but which may extend to six months and with fine which may extend to fifty thousand rupees.

(5) Any employer who changes the conditions of service of his employees in contravention of the provisions of this Act shall be punishable with imprisonment of not less than one month but which may extend to six months and with fine which may extend to fifty thousand rupees.

(6) Any person who commits breach of any term of settlement arrived at in the Management Council or of any order or award which is binding on him shall be punishable with imprisonment for a term of not less than one month but which may extend to six months and with fine which may extend to twenty thousand rupees.

Offences by companies

15. (1) Where an offence under this Act has been committed by a company, every person who at the time the offence was committed was in charge of, and was responsible to, the company for the conduct of the business of the company, as well as the company, shall be deemed to be guilty of the offence and shall be liable to be proceeded against and punished accordingly:

Provided that nothing contained in this sub-section shall render any person liable to any punishment if he proves that the offence was committed without his knowledge or that he had exercised all due diligence to prevent the commission of such offence.

(2) Notwithstanding anything contained in sub-section (1) where an offence under this Act has been committed by a company and it is proved that the offence has been committed with the consent or connivance of, or is attributable to any neglect on the part of, any director, manager, secretary or other officer of the company, such director, manager, secretary or other officer shall also be deemed to be guilty of that offence and shall be liable to be proceeded against and punished accordingly.

Explanation – For the purposes of this section–

(a) "company" means any body corporate and includes a firm or other association of individuals;
(b) "director", in relation to a firm, means a partner in the firm.

CHAPTER VI

Miscellaneous

Recovery of Money due from employer

16. Where any money is due to any employee under any order of any authority under this Act, the employee himself or any other person authorised by him in writing in this behalf, or, in the case of the death of the employee, his heirs or assignee may, without prejudice to any other mode of recovery, make an application to the appropriate Government for the recovery of the money due to him, and if the appropriate Government is satisfied that the money is so due, it shall issue a certificate for that amount to the Collector who shall proceed to recover the same in the same manner as an arrear of land revenue:

Provided that every such application shall be made within one year from the date of which the money became due to the employee from the employer:

Provided further that the appropriate Government may, if it is satisfied that the applicant was prevented by sufficient cause from preferring the application within the period hereinbefore specified, allow it to be presented within a further period not exceeding two years.

Power to give directions

17. Every establishment to which this Act applies shall carry out such directions as may be issued to it from time to time by the appropriate Government or the specified officer for the efficient administration of the provisions of this Act in such establishment.

Cognizance of offences

18. (1) No court shall take cognizance of any offence punishable under this Act save on a complaint made by or under the authority of the appropriate Government.

(2) No court inferior to that of a Metropolitan Magistrate or a Magistrate of the first class shall try any offence punishable under this Act.

Act not to apply to certain establishments

19. (1) This Act shall not apply to-

(a) an establishment owned or controlled by Government;

(b) a society registered under the Societies Registration Act, 1860, or under any other corresponding law for the time being in force in the State which the appropriate Government may, by notification in the Official Gazette, specify having regard to the matters, such as-

(i) whether the society is financed entirely by the Government;

(ii) whether the society has provided adequate provision for joint consultative machinery or similar machinery consisting of representatives of employees and employer for the purpose of settling collective grievance;

(iii) whether the society is within the purview of the Administrative Tribunals Act, 1985 or some other Tribunal by whatever name called in the State; and

(iv) whether employees of the society are governed by rules and regulations that are analogous or similar to rules and regulations governing the Government servants.

(2) Where an establishment referred to in sub-section (4) of section 1 is an educational institution, the provisions of this Act shall cease to apply to such institution as and when the appropriate Government makes a law for the redressal of grievances of employees of such institution.

Power to exempt

20. Where in any establishment, any joint consultative machinery consisting of representatives of employees and employers or any other body consisting of one or more persons (by whatever name called) has been set up for the purpose of redressing any individual or collective grievance therein and the appropriate Government is satisfied that the functioning of such joint consultative machinery or other body is on the whole not less favourable to employees in such establishment than the machinery provided under this Act, the appropriate Government may, by notification in the Official Gazette, and subject to such conditions as may be specified in the notification, exempt such establishment from the operation of all or any of the provisions of this Act for such period as may be specified in the notification.

Protection of Action taken Under this Act

21. No suit, prosecution or other legal proceedings shall lie against any person for anything which is in good faith done or intended to be done in pursuance of this Act or any rule or regulation made thereunder.

Effect of Contract or Laws Inconsistent with the Act

22. The provisions of this Act shall, save as otherwise provided in this Act, have effect notwithstanding anything inconsistent therewith contained in any contract of service or any other law.

Delegation of Powers

23. The appropriate Government may, by notification in the Official Gazette, direct that any power, except the power under this section and section 24, exercisable by it under this Act or the rules made thereunder shall, in relation to such matters and subject to such

conditions, if any, as may be specified in the direction, be exercisable also,–

(a) where the appropriate Government is the Central Government, by such officer or authority subordinate to the Central Government or by the State Government, or by such officer or authority subordinate to the State Government, as may be specified in the direction; and
(b) where the appropriate Government is a State Government, by such officer or authority subordinate to the State Government as may be specified in that direction.

Power to Make Rules

24. (1) The appropriate Government may, by notification in the Official Gazette, and subject to the condition of previous publication, make rules for the purpose of giving effect to the provisions of this Act.

(2) In particular and without prejudice to the generality of the foregoing power, such rules may provide for all or any of the following matters, namely:-

(a) the term of office of members of the Management Council under sub-section (2) of section 9;
(b) the procedure of the Management Council under sub-section (6) of section 9;
(c) the travelling and other compensatory allowances payable to members of the Management Council under sub-section (12) of section 9;
(d) the functions of arbitrators and the Board of arbitrators and the qualifications required by a person to be appointed as an arbitrator or a member of the Board of arbitrators under sub-section (4) of section 10;
(e) the remuneration payable to any arbitrator or member of the Board of arbitrators under sub-section (8) of section 10;
(f) the matters to be specified under clause (d) of sub-section (9) of section 10;
(g) any other matter which has to be or may be specified by rules.

(3) Every rule made by the State Government under this Act shall be laid as soon as may be after it is made before the State Legislature.

(4) Every rule made by the Central Government under this Act shall be laid, as soon as may be after it is made, before each House of Parliament, while it is in session. For a total period of thirty days which may be comprised in one session or in two or more successive sessions, and if, before the expiry of the session immediately following the session or the successive session aforesaid, both Houses agree in making any modification in the rule or both Houses agree that the rule should not be made, the rule shall thereafter have effect only in such modified form or be of no effect, as the case may be; so, however, that any such modification or annulment shall be without prejudice to the validity of anything previously done under that rule.

THE SCHEDULE

[See section 2(k) and section 4(5)]

MODEL REGULATIONS

CHAPTER I

Qualifications for Appointment of Grievance Redressal Authority and Appellate Authority

Persons Eligible for Appointment as Grievance Redressal Authority

1. The Grievance Redressal Authority shall, in relation to an establishment, be a person who is employed in a managerial capacity in such establishment.

Persons Eligible for Appointment as Appellate Authority

2. The Appellate authority shall, in relation to an establishment, be a person who is employed in such establishment and holding a post higher than the post held by the person appointed as Grievance Redressal Authority under regulation 1:

Provided that where there is no such person in any establishment, the Appellate Authority shall, in relation to such establishment, be a person who, on an application made by the employer of such establishment in this behalf, is appointed by the appropriate Government.

CHAPTER II

Procedure to be Followed by the Grievance Redressal Authority and the Appellate Authority

Procedure to be Followed by the Grievance Redressal Authority

3. Where an application has been received by a Grievance Redressal Authority under sub-section (1) of section 5, it shall give a specific number to the application and shall communicate the receipt of the application to the employee, together with the number of the application and the date of its receipt:

Provided that no such application shall be entertained by the Grievance Redrssal Authority unless it is made within a period of sixty days from the date on which the cause of grievance has arisen:

Provided further that the Grievance Redressal Authority may, if it is satisfied that the applicant was prevented by sufficient cause from making an application within the period hereinbefore specified, allow it to be made within a further period not exceeding thirty days.

Written Statement by the Employer

4. (1) The Grievance Redressal Authority shall, as soon as may be, after the receipt of an application referred to in regulation 3, forward a copy thereof to the employer and request him to furnish his statement in writing within seven days and also request him to send a copy of the statement furnished by him to the applicant or applicants, as the case may be.

(2) The statement to be furnished by the employer under sub-regulation (1) may include detailed replies to each item of grievance contained in the application, the documents on which the employer relies, the person who will represent him before the Grievance Redressal Authority (who will not be a legal practitioner) and the names of witnesses he would like to examine at the time of the hearing.

Issue of Summons

5. The Grievance Redressal Authority may, after the receipt of the written statement by the employer under regulation 4, cause a written summons to be served on the applicant or applicants and the employer requiring them to appear before him on a date and time to be specified in the summons.

Inquiry by the Grievance Redressal Authority

6. The Grievance Redressal Authority may, during the course of an inquiry, examine witnesses, if any, and scrutinise also any documentary evidence relied on by the applicant and the employer and the applicant would be entitled to seek the assistance of a past or present employee in the establishment to present his case.

Power to Summon Witnesses, etc.

7. (1) At the hearing of any application, parties shall produce their own witnesses, but for the proper disposal thereof, a Grievance Redressal Authority shall have power to issue summons, to require the attendance of any person either to give evidence or to produce a document or to do such other acts as it may consider necessary.

(2) Any person receiving summons or other process shall be bound to comply with the same.

Evidence to be on Oath and a Brief Memorandum to be Kept

8. Evidence given orally before the Grievance Redressal Authority shall be on oath and a brief memorandum of the substance of what each person deposes shall be written and kept as part of the record.

Final Order of the Grievance Redressal Authority

9. The final order of the Grievance Redressal Authority shall be in writing and shall be communicated to the parties to the application within one week of the date of the order.

Form of Appeal

10. (1) Every appeal preferred under sub-section (4) of section 5

shall be presented to the Appellate Authority to whom the appeal lies and a copy of the same shall be forwarded by the appellant to the Grievance Redressal Authority against whose order the appeal is preferred.

(2) The appeal shall contain all material statements and arguments on which the appellant relies and shall be complete in itself.

(3) The Grievance Redressal Authority which made the order appealed against shall, on receipt of a copy of the appeal under sub-regulation (1), forward the same with its comments thereon together with the relevant records to the Appellate Authority within a period of fifteen days and without waiting for any direction from the Appellate Authority.

Notice for Hearing

11. The Appellate Authority shall give notice to the parties to the appeal regarding the date and time of the hearing and shall request them to be present before it on such data and time of the hearing.

Procedure to be followed by the Appellate Authority

12. (1) On the date and time fixed for the hearing of the appeal, the Appellate Authority shall, after following the procedure specified in sub-section (5) of section 5, consider whether the procedure laid down in these regulations has been complied with by the Grievance Redressal Authority and whether the findings of the Grievance Redressal Authority are warranted by the evidence on record and pass final orders confirming, modifying or setting aside the final order of the Grievance Redressal Authority or may remit the application to the Grievance Redressal Authority with such direction as it may deem fit in the circumstances of the case.

(2) Notwithstanding anything contained in sub-regulation (1), if the Appellate Authority considers it necessary to do so in the interests of justice, it shall itself hold an inquiry which shall, as far as may be, held an accordance with the provisions of regulation 6.

STATEMENT OF OBJECTS AND REASONS

The Supreme Court, in the *Bangalore Water and Sewerage Board* Vs. *A. Rajappa and Others* (AIR 1978 SC 548), held, *inter alia*, that educational institutions and research institutes, which satisfied the tests laid down by it, would come within the definition of the term 'industry' as contained in the Industrial Disputes Act, 1947. The Supreme Court also over-ruled its earlier judgment in *the Management of Safdarjung Hospital* Vs. *Kuldip Singhi Sethi* (AIR 1970 SC 1407) and held that all hospitals would come within the purview of that Act.

2. Since hospitals, educational, scientific, research and training institutions have special and distinct characteristics of their own and an atmosphere that eschews strife and conflict has to be maintained therein, it was decided to exclude these institutions from the definition of the term 'industry' as contained in the Industrial Disputes Act, 1947. The term 'industry' was accordingly re-defined by the Industrial Disputes (Amendment) Act, 1982 so as to exclude, among others, hospitals, dispensaries, educational, scientific, research or training institutions. However, keeping in view the special characteristics of the activities of these institutions and the fact that their workmen also need protection, it was decided to have a separate law for the settlement of individual disputes as well as collective disputes in respect of workmen of these institutions and, for this purpose, the Hospitals and Other Institutions (Settlement of Disputes) Bill, 1982 was introduced in the Rajya Sabha on the 6th May, 1982.

3. This Bill elicited considerable opposition. Subsequently, during the course of the debate in the Rajya Sabha on 1st August, 1984, the Labour Minister had informed the House that as the Hospitals and Other Institutions (Settlement of Disputes) Bill, 1982 had become controversial, he would discuss the matter further with the trade unions and would not do anything without taking them into confidence. In pursuance of this assurance, meetings were held with the representatives of the Central Workers' Organisations in July/August, 1985. In the light of the discussions held with them and also with the voluntary organisations held earlier in January 1983 a Grievance Redressal Mechanism has been evolved in respect of employees of institutions and establishments to be excluded from the purview of the Industrial Disputes Act, 1947.

4. The Bill among other things provides for the following matters, namely:

(i) It shall apply to every hospital and other institution other than those owned or managed by the Government, every institution owned or managed by an organisation wholly or substantially engaged in any charitable, social or philanthropic service and every institution engaged in khadi and village industries where ten or more persons are employed.

(ii) The Grievance Redressal Mechanism under the Bill provides for a Grievance Redressal Authority and an Appellate Authority for the settlement of individual grievances and a Management Council for the settlement of collective grievances. When the individual employee has exhausted his remedies with the Grievance Redressal Authority and Appellate Authority, he will have the right to approach directly an independent Tribunal. Similarly, where the Management Council is unable to resolve a grievance within a specified period, either party will be free to refer the matter for arbitration to an agreed arbitrator failing which the matter will be referred to a Board of arbitrators which will give its award within a specified period.

(iii) Where major issues involving the national economy or social justice or the interest of the general public arise from the grievances presented for redressal, Government would have the power on its own to refer the matter to a Board of arbitrators.

(iv) In order to ensure immediate enforcement of the proposed legislation, model regulations have been included in the legislation. These indicate, *inter alia*, the qualifications for appointment of Grievance Redressal Authority and Appellate Authority and procedure to be followed by them for the settlement of grievances.

(v) The appropriate Government will be empowered to exempt any establishment from the operation of all or any of the provisions of this Mechanism subject to a condition among other things that an alternative joint consultative machinery for redressal of grievances exists therein.

(vi) Appropriate penal provisions are also provided in the Bill for ensuring strict compliance of the law.

5. The Bill seeks to achieve the above objectives.

NEW DELHI P.A. SANGMA

The 30th November, 1987.

MEMORANDUM REGARDING DELEGATED LEGISLATION

Clause 19(1)(b) of the Bill empowers the appropriate Government not to apply the legislation to societies registered under the Societies Registration Act, 1860, or under any other corresponding law in force in the State having regard to the matters specified in that clause.

2. Clause 20 of the Bill empowers the appropriate Government to exempt any establishment from the operation of all or any of the provisions of the Bill where in such establishment any joint consultative machinery consisting of representatives of employees and employer or any other body consisting of one or more persons has been set up for the purpose of redressing any individual or collective grievance therein and the appropriate Government is satisfied that the functioning of such joint consultative machinery or other body is on the whole not less favourable to employees in such establishment than the machinery provided under the Bill.

3. Clause 24 of the Bill seeks to empower the appropriate Government to make rules for the purpose of giving effect to the provisions of the proposed legislation. The matters with respect to which rules may be made, inter alia, relate to the term of office of members of the Management Council, the procedure of the Management Council, travelling and other compensatory allowances payable to the members of the Management Council, the functions of arbitrator and the Board of arbitrators and the qualifications required by a person to be appointed as an arbitrator or a member of the Board of arbitrators and the remuneration payable to an arbitrator or a member of the Board or arbitrators.

4. Every rule made by the State Government under clause 24 is required to be laid before the State Legislature and every rule made by the Central Government under that clause is required to be laid before Parliament.

5. The delegates of legislative power under the above-mentioned provisions relates to the matters of procedure or administrative detail or to matters in respect of which it is not practicable to make detailed provisions. Hence, the delegation of legislative power is of a normal character.

APPENDIX IV

SIGNIFICANT OTHER DOCUMENTS NOT INCLUDED IN MAIN TEXTS

1. ALL INDIA COUNCIL FOR TECHNICAL EDUCATION, TWENTY SECOND MEETING, NEW DELHI, MAY 17, 1974

1. While noting the decision taken by the Central Government on the revised pay scales of teachers in universities and colleges, the council recommended that these revised scales be made applicable to teachers in engineering colleges and polytechnics. The Council, however, felt that before implementing the decision on the revised pay scales of teachers in engineering colleges and polytechnics, the details of qualifications, experience and other requirements prescribed for various categories of teaching posts in technical institutions should be examined, *vis-a-vis*, those recommended by the University Grants Commission for teachers in universities and colleges for whom the revised pay scales are applicable. The Council authorised its Chairman to obtain the views of the State Governments and appoint a Committee to examine all these questions and take a decision on the revised scales of all teachers in engineering colleges and polytechnics, on the recommendations of this committee. (6)

2. The Council recommended that the State Governments be requested not to insist on the execution of bond by teachers who are sponsored for participation in various short-term training programmes with a duration of three months or less, organised by various centres under the central programme or Quality Improvement. (11-B. X)

3. The Council recommended that the existing norms for calculating recurring expenditure in engineering colleges and polytechnics may be revised as under:

Items	*Engineering Colleges*	*Polytechnics*
Staff Salary	Actual as per sanctioned posts.	Actual as per sanctioned posts.

Library (Recurring)	Rs. 50,000 for an intake of 180 and Rs. 75,00 for higher intakes.	Rs. 15,000 for an intake of upto 120 and Rs. 30,000 for higher intakes.
All other expenditure	Rs. 550 per student per year for an intake of up to 180 and Rs. 500 for higher intakes.	Rs. 350 per student per year for an intake of up to 120 and Rs. 300 for higher intakes.

The Council further recommended that the State-Governments may be requested to sanction suitable grants-in-aid to meet the recurring expenditure, on a net deficit basis, under provisions of their grant-in-code, on the basis of the revised norms mentioned above. (11-B. XII)

4. The Council recommended that the principles for revision of staff structure already recommended by the Council under which provision has been made for appointment of training reserves should be made applicable to Art Institutions also. (12-B. 2)

5. The Council recommended that the development of traditional arts and crafts shall appropriately find a place in the proposed programme of vocationalisation of courses, and the scholarship scheme for students in vocational stream should also be extended to students of Arts Schools. (12.B. 5)

6. The Council recommended that the State Governments be requested to formulate a comprehensive development programme or art education. For this purpose, each State Directorate of Technical Education/Art Education should undertake a survey of facilities and potential for development and prepare the necessary educational materials including text-books etc. The Council also recommended that the establishment of Art Museums, wherever possible, may be considered. (12-B. 6)

7. The Council emphasised that the vast technological potential available in the technical education system should be suitably harnessed for industrial development of the country. The Council noted that the establishment of an adequate institutional machinery for coordinating the activities in research, development, consultancy etc. among technical institutions, industries, research laboratories, and other organisations in already under the consideration of the Department of Science and Technology.

The Council also recommended that the Secretariat should take steps for early compilation of a basic directory setting out, institution-wise, the expertise and capabilities which the different Institutes of Technology, the Engineering Colleges and Polytechnics have so far provided, and what each can provide hereafter, in terms of consultancy functions for and liaison with industry. Likewise industry should compile another documentation on its own part setting out the problems and purposes for which different undertakings may need consultancy and liaison with the institutions of Technology and technical institutions. Based on these individual compilations, both from the side of industrial undertakings and the institutions, the Secretariat should compile, as early as possible, a comprehensive compendium of the information so collected. Copies of the documentation should be made available for bringing about better linkages between industry and the institutions of technology and technical education to Members of the Council, the State Governments and Central Ministries, the various educational and technological institutions and industrial undertakings as well as others interested in the subject. The compendium can be refined and brought up to date as time goes on, but the initial compilation should be brought out without delay.

The Council also recommended that the technical institutions should accept the responsibility within the limitations of the resources and the range of expertise and experience available with them to initiate concerted efforts by organising co-operative programmes like apprenticeship training sandwich courses and practice schools, reviewing the course-content from time to time to meet the operational and design requirements of industry, organising short-term programmes including non-formal education for serving personnel from industry, assigning specific projects on 'live problems' of industry to students and organising special seminars/symposia etc. with participants drawn from institutions and industry.

The Council further recommended that State Governments and other agencies may be requested to permit teachers in technical institutions to undertake consultancy practice etc. in accordance with the normal rules accepted by the Government. (15)

8. The Council recommended that there should be better and more effective coordination of the activities between the University Grants Commission and the Council in the programmes of engineering education. The Council also recommended that the procedure for

processing development programmes should be streamlined and that there should be an integral assessment of the needs of engineering and technological departments in the universities along with that of the other departments. The Council authorised its Chairman to forward a panel of names of experts in engineering and technology to the University Grants Commission, from which the Commission could draw the personnel for its Visiting Committees.

The Council also recommended that a Joint Committee of the Council and University Grants Commission, consisting of 15 members may be appointed to suggest suitable guidelines for assessing the requirements for engineering and technological departments and authorised its Chairman to nominate the members to represent the Council on this Committee. (16)

2. CONFERENCE OF EDUCATION SECRETARIES OF ALL STATES AND UNION TERRITORIES NEW DELHI, JANUARY 5-6, 1983

Implementation of Point 16 of the New 20-Point Programme

1. *Universalisation of Elementary Education*

1.1 Since the 1990 date line has to be adhered to, the pace of progress has to be more than doubled in the remaining years. It has also to be recognised in this context that the coverage henceforth will be of difficult target groups who have for various reasons not been able to avail of the facilities in the formal system. There is, therefore, no room for complacency. (2)

1.2 With reference to the special attention for education of girls/women, the conference recommended appropriate inter-sectoral linkages between such programmes (ICDS, Applies Nutrition, health care facilities for children) so as to make optimal use of available services. The Conference recommended in particular that health care of children in schools should get increasing attention and that more schools should be covered under schools health programmes. (10)

1.3 For strengthening the base, State/UTs will have to take various quantitative and qualitative steps. These will include in particular the following:

a) universal provision of schooling facilities giving preferential coverage to about 40500 habitations which do not have a primacy within 1 km distance.

b) conversion of all single teacher schools into two-teacher schools.

c) appointment of additional teachers to cope with additional enrolments.

d) provision of adequate administrative staff support. (12)

2. *Adult Education*

2.1 The need for providing adequate academic support to such activities through production of appropriate literature was stressed. For doing all this, apart from stepping up of the activities of the Government side, involvement of students, youth and, voluntary organisations including Panchayati Raj institutions in the implementation of the programme has also to be accentuated. The improvement of intersectoral linkages was stressed in the context of this programme also. (1)

2.3 The Conference identified payment of low remuneration to the Instructors and inadequacy of the supervisory machinery under the State Adult Education Programme (SAEP) in some States as weaknesses in the system and called for necessary remedial measures. (3)

3. *Monitoring and Evaluation*

3.1 The Conference observed that the arrangement for monitoring and evaluation of the two programmes — Universalisation of Elementary Education and Adult Education — was both inadequate and unsatisfactory. Accordingly, it stressed the need for establishment of a suitable mechanism for the purpose at the block, district and State levels. These mechanisms should provide for a regular and timely flow of information and suitable remedial/corrective measures to be initiated on a continuing basis. (1)

4. *Interlinking of Elementary (Both Formal and Non-Formal) and Adult Education with Rural Development, Social Forestry, Handicrafts and Handlooms.*

4.1 The Conference took note of the fact that educational development could not be achieved in isolation without taking into cognizance of the factors determining the life of the child, comprising his first primary physical needs of nutrition immunisation and mother's care as also the sustenance he draws from the natural environment comprising flora, fauna, agricultural crops, animal life and the socio-cultural life-style of the community including varied traditional skills, festivals etc. Educational strategy should be evolved in conjunction with other development sectors which are focusing attention on child and family welfare, environment, social-forestry, agriculture, handicrafts, small-scale industry. It was, therefore, essential for the Departments of Education in the States to keep in touch with the structurally inter-link their programmes with other agencies and programmes such as the ICDS, the RIDP etc. This would ensure an integration so necessary for ensuring organic growth of the student.

An important concern of the Conference related to mutual disassociation of the school system and the creative and productive activities of the community specially at the rural level. The Conference strongly supported the idea of drawing upon the rich manpower resources, rich and varied skills available in the community for supporting the educational system. With this in view it was recommended that educational institutions should draw upon and associate local craftsmen, artists, weavers, potters, blacksmiths and others for training children. There should be no insistence on such skilled workers to be literate. The teachers particularly of one-teacher schools should evolve curricula which would be built on local or regional arts or crafts and technologies.

The Conference was of the view that such an integrated view would help in promoting cohesiveness in society rather than alienating the educated from the community. Also an added advantage would be the availability of additional resources for elementary and adult education from the developmental sector such as National Rural Employment Programme, Social Forestry Programme and others.

5. *Promotion of Population Education*

Concern was also expressed over the need of urgently introducing population education for out-of-school children and in the Adult Education Programme.

This expression of concern by the Conference, it was felt, should result in speedy production of teaching/learning materials for 'classroom' use and immediate re-orientation of teachers/instructors for the purpose.

6. *Introduction of Ideas of 'Values' of Students*

It stressed that equal attention should be given to value orientation in education of out-of-school children also.

As in the case of population education, here again, it was urged, this expression of concern by the Conference should result in speedy production of teaching/learning materials for 'classroom' use and immediate reorientation of teachers/instructors for the purpose.

7. *Review of Text-books from the Point of View of National Integration.*

The States/UTs concerned were urged to so order the arrangements for review as to be able to revise their textbooks before the commencement of the 1983-84 academic session.

8. *10+2 Pattern of School Education with Special Emphasis on Vocationalisation.*

8.1 It was recognised in this context that introduction of mere structural changes would not be enough. The switchover had to be accompanied by appropriate changes in the curriculum also.

8.2 The Conference considered it necessary to reiterate the point that vocationalisation of the +2 stage was an integral part of the 10+2 system of education. All the other States/UT were urged to take immediate steps to make secondary school education more employment-oriented.

It was decided that the NCERT will, in collaboration with the Government of Tamil Nadu, initiate an evaluative study with the purpose of determining the experiences of the State Government in implementing the programme which would help other State Governments to plan and implement their programme of vocationalisation.

8.3 Arising from the experience of the students passing out of the CBSE system, the Conference recognised the seriousness of the problems arising from the laci of uniformity between standards in different examinations in different States. Taking an overall national view, it was considered necessary to introduce a mechanism for equalisation of different standards. In this connection the Conference noted a recommendation that it would be desirable to set-up a national testing service commonly for all States/Union Territories.

9. *Exercise of Control Over Setting up of New Universities and Other Problems of University Education.*

The Conference stressed that new universities should be established only after detailed surveys of educational needs of communities. It also stressed the need for development of non-institutional mechanisms like correspondence courses, evening classes, etc. in order to meet the growing educational expectations of students without necessarily having to open new formal institutions. (1)

Reforms in the prevailing examination system were also considered necessary to make evaluation of pupil attainments more objective and meaningful. (3)

3. MEETING OF STATE SECRETARIES DEALING WITH DEPARTMENTS OF TECHNICAL EDUCATION, NEW DELHI, MARCH 7, 1983

1. All possible steps should be taken to put an end to the unhealthy practice of charging capitation fee for admission, wherever it existed. (1)

2. The infrastructure already created at the different technical institutions and the physical facilities available should be properly surveyed by the concerned State Governments in order to assess the gaps with reference to the original schemes of development and also the present requirements to meet the curricular changes and advances in technology so as to formulate proper plans for consolidation and modernisation. (2)

3. The norms for maintenance/expenditure prescribed the All India Council for Technical Education at its meeting held in May, 1974 have already become outdated. Due to constant upward rise in prices over the years, these norms are no longer valid and required immediate updating. (3)

4. National Manpower Information System would be useful in Planning of manpower development and consequently that of technical education. The scheme, as soon as finalised, be circulated to all the States. (13)

5. Education and training has to be looked as a whole and no sector can stand on its own. The objectives of the different sectors of education can be realised effectively through an integrated approach.

In pursuance of the present policy vocational education has to be a major thrust and for the proper growth and development of vocational education, a close linkage between vocational education and higher technical education as well as nécessary help and assistance from the technical institutions at the diploma and degree level to the vocational schools is of great significance and importance. The enormous competence built in the Technical Teachers' Training Institutes for formulating curricula, development of course material and media packages and training of polytechnic teachers can be utilised for giving a thrust to vocationalisation of education at the higher secondary level not only in the engineering vocations but also in non-engineering ones. Similarly, a close link between the academic stream of higher secondary and university courses of higher learning is of great importance. The quality of the students to be trained by the universities and and institutions of higher learning is dependent on the quality of students that school will produce.

A close interaction between the schools and the institutions of higher learning at different levels was very essential for the overall development of education and all the States should take necessary action to achieve this much-needed linkage. (23)

Note: Number in brackets after the para indicated agenda item number.

4. CENTRAL ADVISORY BOARD OF EDUCATION MEETING (1989)

Central Advisory Board of Education in its meeting held on July 6-7, 1989 at Vigyan Bhawan, New Delhi, reviewed the implementation of the National Policy on Education with special reference to:

i) Status of elementary education as well as its perspective in VIII Five-Year Plan;
ii) National Literacy Mission, and perspective for the VIII Plan.
iii) Teacher Education, including NCTE.
iv) Recommendations of CABE Committee on housing facilities for women teachers;
v) Secondary Education; including;
   — Vocationalisation
   — Science Education
   — Education Technology
vi) Higher Education, including restoration of academic calendar, number of teaching days, autonomous colleges, etc.
vii) Technical Education, covering AICTE, perspective for Technical Education during VIII Plan, Community Polytechnics and thrust areas;
viii) Education for SCs/STs/minorities and disadvantaged sections; and
ix) Resources for Education including external funding. (3)

LIST OF UNIVERSITIES (as on 17 July, 1989)

1. Agra University,
Agra-282 004.
2. Alagappa University,
Karaikudi-623 004
3. Aligarh Muslim University,
Aligarh-202 001.
4. Allahabad University,
Allahabad-211 002.
5. Amravati University,
Amravati-444 604.
6. Andhra Pradesh Agricultural University
Rajendranagar,
Hyderabad-500 030.
7. Andhra Pradesh University of Health Sciences,
Vijayawada-520 005.
(as on July 17, 1989)
8. Andhra University,
Waltair,
Visakhapatnam-530 003.
9. Andhra Pradesh Open University,
Hyderabad-500 482.
10. Annamalai University,
Annamalainagar-608 002.
11. Anna University,
Sardar Patel Road,
Madras-600 025.
12. Arunachal University,
Itanagar-791 111.
13. Assam Agricultural University,
Jorhat-785 013.
14. Avadh University,
Faizabad-224 001.
15. Awadesh Pratap Singh University,
Rewa-486 003.
16. Banaras Hindu University,
Varanasi-221 005.
17. Bangalore University,
Bangalore-560 056.
18. Barkatullah Vishwavidyalaya,
Bhopal-462 026.
19. Berhampur University,
Berhampur-760 007.
20. Bhagalpur University,
Bhagalpur-812 007.
21. Bharathiar University,
Coimbatore-641 046.
22. Bharathidasan University,
Tiruchirapalli-620 024.
23. Bidhanchandra Krishi Vishwavidyalaya,
Mohanpur, Distt., Nadia,
West Bengal-741 252.
24. Bihar University,
Muzaffarpur-812 001.
25. Bhavnagar University,
Bhavnagar-304 002.
26. Birsa Agricultural University,
Kanke, Ranchi-834 006.
27. Bombay University,
Bombay-400 032.
28. Bundelkhand University,
Jhansi-284 001.
29. Burdwan University,
Burdwan-713 104.
30. Calcutta University,
Calcutta-700 073.
31. Calicut University,
Calicut-673 635.
32. Chandrasekhar Azad Univ. of Agriculture & Technology,
Kanpur-208 002.

33. Cochin University of Science and Technology, Cochin-682 002.
34. Delhi University, Delhi-110 007.
35. Devi Ahilya Vishwavidyalaya, Indore-452 001.
36. Dibrugarh University, Dibrugarh-786 004.
37. Dr.Hari Singh Gaur Vishwavidyalaya, Sagar-470 003.
38. Dr. M.G.R. Medical University, Madras.
39. Dr. Yashwant Singh Parmar University of Horticulture and Forestry, Solan-173 230.
40. Hemavati Nandan Bahuguna Vishwavidyalaya, Srinagar (Garhwal) Pin-246 174.
41. Gauhati University, Gauhati-781 014.
42. G.B. Pant University of Agriculture and Technology, Pantnagar-263 145.
43. Goa University, Bambolim P.O. Santacruz, Goa-403 005.
44. Gorakhpur University, Gorakhpur-273 009.
45. Gujarat Agricultural University, Sardar Krushinagar, Pin-385 506.
46. Gujarat Ayurveda University, Jamnagar-361 008.
47. Gujarat University, Ahmedabad-380 009.
48. Gulbarga University, Gulbarga-585 106.
49. Guru Ghasidas University, Bilaspur-495 009.
50. Guru Nanak Dev University, Amritsar-143 005.
51. Haryana Agricultural University, Hissar-125 004.
52. Himachal Pradesh University, Shimla-171 005.
53. Himachal Pradesh Krishi Vishwavidyalaya, Palampur-176 062.
54. Hyderabad University, Hyderabad-500 134.
55. Indira Gandhi National Open University, New Delhi-110 001.
56. Indira Gandhi Krishi Vishwavidyalaya, Raipur-492 001.
57. Indira Kala Sangeet Vishwavidyalaya, Khairagarh, Rajasthan-481 881.
58. Jadavpur University, Calcutta-700 032.
59. Jammu University, Jammu-180 001.
60. Jawaharlal Nehru Krishi Vishwavidyalaya, Jabalpur-482 004.
61. Jawaharlal Nehru Technological University, Humayun Nagar, Hyderabad-500 028.
62. Jawaharlal Nehru University, New Mehrauli Road, New Delhi-110 067.
63. Jiwaji University, Gwalior-474 011.
64. Jodhpur University, Jodhpur-342 001.
65. Kakatiya University, Warangal-506 009.
66. Kalyani University, Kalyani-741 235. (W.B.)
67. Kameshwar Singh Darbhanga Sanskrit University, Darbhanga-846 008.

68. Kanpur University,
Kanpur-208 024.
69. Karnatak University,
Dharwad- 580 003.
70. Kashmir University,
Srinagar-190 006.
71. Kashi Vidyapith,
Varanasi-221 002.
72. Kerala Agricultural
University,
Trichur-680 654.
73. Jamia Millia Islamia,
New Delhi-110 025.
74. Kerala University,
Trivandrum-695 034.
75. Konkan Krishi Vidyapeeth,
Dapoli-415 712.
(Ratnagiri).
76. Kota Open University,
Kota-324 002.
77. Kumaun University,
Nainital-263 001.
78. Kuvempu University,
B.R. Project,
Shimoga District,
Karnataka-577 115.
79. Kurukshetra University,
Kurukshetra-132 119.
80. L.N. Mithila University,
Darbhanga-846 004.
81. Lucknow University,
Lucknow-226 007.
82. Madras University,
Madras-600 005.
83. Madurai Kamraj University,
Palkalai Nagar,
Madurai-625 021.
84. Magadh University,
Bodhgaya-824 234.
85. Mahatma Gandhiji
University,
Kottayam-686 002.
86. Mahatma Phule Agricultural
University,
Dist. Ahmednagar,
Rahuri-413 722.
87. Maharshi Dayanand University,
Rohtak-124 001.
88. Mangalore University.
Light House Hills,
Mangalore-575 003.
89. Manipur University,
Imphal-795 003.
90. Marathwada University,
Aurangabad-431 004.
91. Marathwada Agricultural Univ.,
Parbhani-431 402.
92. M.S. University of Baroda,
Baroda-390 002.
93. Meerut University,
Meerut-250 005.
94. Mother Teresa Women's
University,
Kodaikanal-624 102.
95. Mysore University,
Mysore-570 005.
96. Nagarjuna University,
Nagarjuna Nagar,
Guntur-522 510 (A.P.)
97. Nagpur University,
Nagpur-440 001.
98. Narendra Deva University
of Agriculture & Technology,
Narendra Nagar, Kumarganj,
Faizabad-224 229.
99. North Bengal University,
PO: North Bengal University
Raja Rammohanpur,
Darjeeling-734 430.
100. North Eastern Hill University,
Shillong-793 001.
101. North Gujarat University,
Patan-384 365 (N.G.)
102. Orissa University of
Agriculture & Tech.
Bhubaneswar-751 003.
103. Osmania University,
Hyderabad-500 007.
104. Panjab University,
Chandigarh-160 014.
105. Patna University,
Patna-800 005.
106. Pondicherry University,
Pondicherry-605 001.
107. Poona University,
Pune-411 007.

108. Punjab Agricultural University, Ludhiana-141 004.
109. Panjabrao Krishi Vidyapeeth, Akola-444 104.
110. Punjabi University, Patiala-147 002.
111. Purvanchal University, Jaunpur-222 002 (U.P.)
112. Rabindra Bharati University, Calcutta-700 050.
113. Rajasthan University, Jaipur-302 004.
114. Rajasthan Agriculture University, Bikaner (Rajasthan)
115. Rajendra Agricultural University, Pusa (Samastipur) Bihar-848 125.
116. Ranchi University, Ranchi-834 001.
117. Rani Durgavati Vishwavidyalaya Jabalpur-482 001.
118. Ravi Shankar University, Raipur-492 010.
119. Rohilkhand University, Bareilly-243 001.
120. Roorkee University, Roorkee-247 667.
121. Sambalpur University, Sambalpur-768 019.
122 Sampurnanand Sanskrit Vishwavidyalaya, Varanasi-221 002.
123. Saurashtra University, Rajkot-360 005.
124. Sardar Patel University, Vallabh Vidyanagar, Pin-388 120.
125. Shere-e-Kashmir University of Agricultural Sciences and Technology, PB No. 262, Srinagar-190 001. (May to October) 45-B, Gandhinagar, PB No. 87, Jammu Tawi-180 001. (November to April)
126. Shivaji University, Kolhapur-416 004.
127. Sh. Jagannath Sanskrit Vishwavidyalaya, Puri-752 002.
128. South Gujarat University, Surat-395 007.
129. S.N.D.T. Women's University, Bombay-400 020.
130. Sri Krishnadevaraya University, Anantpur-515 003.
131. Sri Padmavati Mahila Vishwavidyalaya, Tirupati-517 502.
132. Sri Venkateswara University, Tirupati-517 502.
133. Sukhadia University, Udaipur-313 001.
134. Tamilnadu Agricultural University, Coimbatore-641 003.
135. Tamil University, Thanjavur-613 001.
136. Telugu University, Kelabhavan, Hyderabad-500 004.
137. Tripura University, Agartala-799 004. Tripura.
138. Andhra Pradesh University of Health Sciences, Vijayawada-520 005.
139. University of Agricultural Sciences, Bangalore-560 065.
140. University of Agricultural Sciences, Krishinagar, Dharwad-580 005.
141. University of Ajmer, Ajmer-305 001.
142. Utkal University, Vani Vihar, Bhubaneswar-751 004.
143. Vidya Sagar University, Midnapore-721 001.
144. Vikram University, Ujjain-456 010.
145. Visva Bharati, Shantiniketan-731 235.

INSTITUTION DEEMED TO BE UNIVERSITIES

1. Banasthali Vidyapeeth,
   P.O. Banasthali
   Vidyapeeth-304 022.
   Rajasthan.
2. Birla Institute of Technology,
   Mesra- 835 215 (Ranchi)
3. Birla Instt. of
   Technology & Science,
   Pilani-333 031.
4. Central Instt. of English
   & Foreign Languages,
   Hyderabad-500 007.
5. Central Institute of
   Higher Tibetan Studies,
   Sarnath, Varanasi-221 007.
6. Central Institute of
   Fisheries Education,
   Versova, Bombay.
7. Dayalbagh Educational Institute,
   Dayalbagh,
   Agra-282 005.
8. Gandhigram Rural Instt.
   Gandhigram-624 302
   District: Anna.
9. Gujarat Vidyapith,
   Ahmedabad-380 014.
10. Gurukula Kangri
    Vishwavidyalaya,
    Hardwar-249 404.
11. Indian Agricultural Research
    Institute,
    New Delhi-110 012.

11(a). Jamia Hamdard,
Hamdard Nagar,
New Delhi-110 062.

12. Indian Instt. of Science,
    Bangalore-560 012.
13. Indian School of Mines,
    Dhanbad-826 004.
14. International Institute of
    Population Sciences,
    Bombay-400 088.
15. Indian Veterinary
    Research Institute,
    Izatnagar-243 122.
16. National Dairy Research
    Institute,
    Karnal (Haryana)
17. Rajasthan Vidyapeeth,
    Udaipur-313 001.
18. Rashtriya Sanskrit Vidyapeeth,
    Tirupati.
19. School of Planning &
    Architecture,
    No. 4, Block B,
    I.P. Estate,
    New Delhi-110 002.
20. Shri Lal Bahadur Shastri
    Rashtriya Sanskrit Vidyapeeth,
    New Delhi.
21. Sri Sathya Sai Institute
    of Higher Learning,
    Prasanthirilayam,
    Dt. Anantapur-515 134 (AP)
22. Sri Avinashilingam Instt.
    for Home Science & Higher
    Education for Women,
    Coimbatore-641 043.
23. Tata Institute of Social Sciences,
    Deonar,
    PB No. 8313,
    Bombay-400 088.
24. Tilak Maharashtra Vidyapeeth,
    Pune-411 037.
25. National Museum Institute
    of the History of Art,
    Conservation and Museology,
    Delhi.
26. Thapar Instt. of Engg. and
    Technology,
    Patiala-147 001.

INSTITUTE OF NATIONAL IMPORTANCE

1. All India Instt. of Medical Sciences,
   Ansari Nagar,
   New Delhi-110 029.
2. Dakshina Bharati Hindi Prachar Sabha,
   PB No. 68,
   Hyderabad-500 004.
3. Indian Instt. of Tech.,
   Powai,
   Bombay-400 076.
4. Indian Institute of Technology,
   Hauz Khas,
   New Delhi-110 016.
5. Indian Institute of Technology,
   Kanpur-208 016.
6. Indian Institute of Technology,
   Kharagpur-721 302.
7. Indian Institute of Technology,
   Madras-600 036.
8. Indian Statistical Institute,
   Calcutta-700 035.
9. Postgraduate Institute of Medical Education and Research,
   Chandigarh-160 012.
10. Sree Chitra Tirunal Institute for Medical Sciences & Technology,
    Trivandrum-695 011.

INSTITUTE ESTABLISHED UNDER STATE LEGISLATURE ACT

11. Sanjay Gandhi Post-Graduate Institute of Medical Sciences,
    Lucknow-226 001.

CICIL LIST

CONCEPTS IN COMMUNICATION, INFORMATICS & LIBRARIANSHIP

(CICIL)

General Editor: **S.P. AGRAWAL**

CICIL-1 Development of Library Services in India: Social Science Information
S.P. Agrawal Rs. 150

CICIL-2 Development of Documentation in India: Social Science Information
S.P. Agrawal Rs. 250

CICIL-3 UNESCO and Social Sciences: Retrospect and Prospect
S.P. Agrawal and **J.C. Aggarwal** Rs. 250

CICIL-4 INDIANA : A Bibliography of Bibliographical Sources
M.K. Jain Rs. 200

CICIL-5 Dimensions of Library and Information Science: Kaula Festschrift
V. Venkatappaiah (Eds.) Rs. 600

CICIL-6 Book Numbers: Some Indian Methods
M.P. Satija and **S.P. Agrawal** Rs. 100

CICIL-7 National Policy for University Libraries in India: Problems and Perspectives
N.B. Inamdar and **L.S. Ramaiah** (Ed.) Rs. 250

CICIL-8 Media Utilisation for the Development of Women and Children
B.S. Thakur and **Binod C. Agrawal** Rs. 150

CICIL-9 Terrorism: An Annotated Bibliography
Susheela Bhan (Ed.) Rs. 275

CICIL-10 Transnational Library Relations: The Indo-American Experience
M.B. Konnur Rs. 175

CICIL-11 Geography of Marketing and Commercial Activities in India (Documentation on Research Information)
R.S. Dixit Rs. 130

CICIL-12 Information India 1988: Global View
S.P. Agrawal and **J.C. Aggarwal** Rs. 200

CICIL-13 Women's Education in India: Historical Review, Present Status and Perspective Plan
S.P. Agrawal and **J.C. Aggarwal** (in press)

CICIL-14 Cultural Communication in India: Role and Impact of Phonograms
J.M. Ojha (in press)

CICIL-15 Second Historical Survey of Educational Development in India: Select Documents 1985-1989
S.P. Agrawal and **J.C. Aggarwal** (in press)

CICIL-16 Documentation Encyclopaedia of UNESCO and Education
J.C. Aggarwal and **S.P. Agrawal** Rs. 800 (set of 2 parts)

CICIL-17 Attitude Towards Information: A Study of Post-Graduate Teachers and Researchers in Social Sciences
N.G. Satish (in press)

CICIL-18 Librarianship and Bureaucratic Organisation: A Study in the Sociology of Library Profession in India
P.K. Jayaswal Rs. 175

CICIL-19 Literature Search
K.A. Isaac Rs. 150

CICIL-20 Child Education in India: Index to Scholarly Writings in Indian Educational Journals and Newspapers since independence
S.P. Agrawal and **Naresh Kanta** Rs. 100

CICIL-21 Lok Sabha and Vidhan Sabha Elections in India 1989 & 1990: Process and Results with Comparative Study of Manifestos
S.P. Agrawal and **J.C. Aggarwal** Rs. 250

CICIL-22 Islamic Studies in India: A Survey of Human, Institutional and Documentary Sources
Mohamed Taher Rs. 180

CICIL-23 Panchayati Raj: An Annotated Bibliography
N.B. Inamdar, N.G. Satish and **Anil Takalkar** (in press)

CICIL-24 Information India 1989-90: Global View
S.P. Agrawal and **J.C. Aggarwal** Rs. 500

CICIL-25 First Handbook of Psychological and Social Instruments
Udal Pareek and **T. Venkateswara Rao** (in press)

CICIL-26 Educational and Social Uplift of Backward Classes: At What Cost and How? Mandal Commission and After
S.P. Agrawal and **J.C. Aggarwal** Rs. 275

CICIL-27 Mass Media and New Horizons: Impact of TV & Video an Urban Milieu **H.R. Trivedi** Rs. 180

CICIL-28 Definitional Dictionary of Agriculture
I.C. Gupta and **S.K. Gupta** (in press)

CICIL-29 Nation in Crisis
S.P. Agrawal and **J.C. Aggarwal** Rs. 200